UNDERSTANDING
STATISTICAL ANALYSIS

Cryford Mumba

ISBN: 978-1-4269-8832-5 (sc)
ISBN: 978-1-4269-8833-2 (e)

Trafford rev. 08/04/2011

 www.trafford.com

North America & international
toll-free: 1 888 232 4444 (USA & Canada)
phone: 250 383 6864 ♦ fax: 812 355 4082

C O N T E N T S

ABOUT THE AUTHOR

Dr. Cryford Mumba read Economics at The University of Zambia and graduated with a Bachelor of Arts Degree. He complemented his Economics degree with the Advanced Diploma in Project Management(Institute of Commercial Management, UK), Diploma in Banking and Financial Services(Zambia Institute of Banking and Financial services, Zambia), Diploma in Marketing(ICM, UK). He then expanded his knowledge of business through the accountancy program (ACCA, UK) for which he is a finalist. He holds an MBA(MANCOSA, South Africa) with a thesis "Limited Access to Credit Among Women Market Traders". Finally, he holds a PhD in Economics (Cambell State University, USA) with a thesis "Understanding Money Intelligence".

Dr. Mumba is the Proprietor and Chief Executive Officer of Premier college of Banking and Finance, a firm specializing in financial training and consulting. His specialist teaching areas include Financial Mathematics, Statistical Analysis, Corporate Finance, Financial Reporting and Economics. He has written extensively on banking and financial services course. He is the author of Understanding Money Intelligence, Understanding Statistical Analysis and a host of other Banking and Financial Services training manuals. He is also the Editor of The Student Banker Magazine and a columnist on financial matters for Business analysis Newspaper.

He resides in Lusaka, married and is a supporter of Arsenal Football Club. His hobbies include reading and writing.

PREFACE

If you have bought or are thinking of buying this book you will want to know what you can expect it to do for you and how you ought best to use it. The book has been developed from practical teaching of Statistical Analysis. It covers all the statistical analysis required for Statistical Analysis examination and other courses requiring Quantitative Methods.

The guiding principles for this book are that it is "user-friendly" with numerous worked examples and related to the current Statistical Analysis Practice. To this end a variety of real life examples from economics and business have been used. One difficulty encountered in the production of this book is that some students have little or no practical experience of the subject. Therefore, a step-by-step explanation has been adopted which has made me guilty of one offence: "over simplification". The book can be used with confidence because it is designed to be user-friendly, interesting to read and to stimulate learning by the use of clear examples with detailed solutions. The book seeks to set the subject of Statistical Analysis as enjoyable as any other subject.

At this juncture I should sound some caution. The book provides you with the knowledge and the skills in applying it which you need to pass. However, if you aspire to excel, perhaps even to win a place or a prize, you cannot expect to rely on one book alone! The highest marks are given to those candidates who display evidence of the widest reading absorbed by critical mind, a combination, that is, of extensive information and of a highly intellectual appraisal of it. No single book can provide either of these things. What it can do, however, is to provide an adequate amount of information and acceptable competence in handling it. No doubt the statistical analysis course will include matters which I have omitted, and some lecturers may not consider all the items I have covered as appropriate. I do hope, however, that a large proportion of the text will be helpful to students of statistical analysis.

It should be stressed that this book is written to teach you and not merely to tell you. The more work and effort you put into all your studies, the greater the chance of success. Be determined, have a positive attitude and all the very best in your future courses and exams.

Cryford Mumba

20th July 2011

ACKNOWLEDGEMENTS

I am emotionally attuned and profoundly indebted to our Great Company- PREMIER COLLEGE, for the opportunity of exposure and experience enabling me to venture into this humble project. This text grew out of the Statistical Analysis subject I have been teaching at Premier College of Banking and Finance during the past few semesters. I was very fortunate to have had many excellent and dull students, who with their questions and comments contributed much to the clarity of exposition of this text.

I owe a great intellectual debt to my brilliant former teachers at all levels in my educational radar. Quite extra-ordinary for an educational book, no one reviewed the manuscript. It is fresh from the farm.

Finally, I would like to express my gratitude to Chileshe Chanda for her efficiency and cheerful disposition in typing the manuscript.

I shall greatly appreciate guidance/suggestions for further enrichment of the compendium in course of time, both from the teachers and students of the subject.

DEDICATION

This book is dedicated to:

- My mother Janet Mumba and my late father Nelson Mumba for double gifts- life and life support (education) though themselves did not reach higher levels in education radar.

- My wife Nivea Mumba for ensuring that no paper is thrown away no matter how tattered it looks and providing an environment conducive to the writing of this book.

- Students and lecturers who will use it for it is theirs.

QUOTATIONS

"I am a beau in nothing but my books".   **Adam Smith (1723- 1790)**

"A man who kills another man destroys a living creature, but a man who kills a good book kills reason itself". **unknown**.

"If people do not believe that Mathematics is simple, it is only because they do not realize how complicated life is." **John Louis von Neumann   (1903-1957)**

Chapter One

THE NATURE OF STATISTICS

WHAT IS STATISTICS?

The word **statistics** means different things to different people. To a football fan, statistics are the information about shorts on target, fouls committed, yellow cards and red cards given and so on, at half-time. To the college principal, statistics are information on absenteeism, test scores, and teacher salaries. To a medical researcher investigating the effects of a new drug, statistics are evidence of the success of research efforts. To a college student, statistics are the grades made on all tests in a course this semester. To a credit officer, statistics are the number of non-performing loans.

Each of these people is using the word **statistics** correctly yet each uses it in a slightly different way and for somewhat different purpose.

What does statistics mean to you? Does it bring to mind summary results at halftime of soccer match, unemployment rates, accident victims admitted at hospital, numerical distortions of facts (lying with statistics) or simply a college requirement you have to complete? I hope to convince you that statistics is a meaningful, useful science with broad and almost limitless scores of application to business and economic problems. I also want to show that statistics lie only when they are misapplied. Finally, my objective is to paint a unified picture of statistics to leave you with the impression that your time was well spent studying the subject that will prove useful to you in many ways.

Statistics means "numerical descriptions" to most people. Most often, the purpose of calculating these numbers goes beyond the description of that data. Frequently, the data are regarded as a sample selected from some larger set of data. For example, a sampling of unpaid accounts for a larger merchandiser would allow you to calculate an estimate of the average value of unpaid accounts. This estimate could be used as an audit check on the total value of all unpaid accounts held by the merchandiser. So the application of statistics in a world in which so much reliance is placed on the work of statisticians, where government policy often depends on their findings and where industrial decisions involving billions of Kwacha are taken on the basis of statistical analysis cannot be overemphasized.

SUBDIVISIONS WITHIN STATISTICS

Managers apply some statistical technique to virtually every branch of public and private enterprise. These applications can be divided into two broad areas: describing masses of data (descriptive statistics) and making inferences (estimates, decisions, predictions, etc.) about some data set based on sampling (inferential statistical).

- **Descriptive statistics** describes the data set. This is achieved by using graphical descriptive measures (graphs, tables and charts that display data so that they are easier to understand), and numerical descriptive measures (measures of location, dispersion and relative standing which summarize data set).

- A **statistical inference** is a decision, estimate, prediction or generalization about the population based on information contained in a sample. It is concerned with drawing conclusions of the population based on sample results.

- The methods and techniques of statistical inference can also be used in a branch of statistics called **decision theory**. Knowledge of decision theory is very helpful for managers because it is used to make decisions under conditions of uncertainty – i.e. where there is limited information.

- From the foregoing it can be safely said that statistics may refer to quantitative data or to a field of study. In any case, statistics is a process concerned with the collection, simplification, presentation and analysis of information which can be expressed quantitatively. This definition of statistics brings to the fore the four elements of every statistical enquiry:

- The population of interest, with a procedure for sampling the population.

- The sample and analysis of information in a sample.

- The inferences about the population, based on information contained in a sample

- A measure of reliability of the inference.

TYPES OF DATA

Data are the collections of any number of related observations or facts. We can collect the number of current accounts of several bank customers, and we call this our data. A collection of data is called a **data set** while a single observation is called a **data point**.

Data are the raw material for the statistician and is distinguished from information as the later refers to analyzed data. Data may take different forms including the following:

1 **Quantitative data**. This is data that can be expressed on a numerical scale i.e. can be expressed quantitatively. Examples of quantitative data include number of people, number of cars, number of books, number of children, etc. The key to identifying quantitative data is the word "number of" which normally is aroused by the question "How many". It is about the "countable".

2 **Qualitative data**. This is data that cannot be expressed on a numerical scale. It is about the quality of something, about people's opinion, behaviour, lifestyle, preferences, etc. Examples of qualitative data include sex (one is either male or

female, and not both), taste, etc. Qualitative data is normally aroused by questions involving "yes or no". It is categorical in nature.

3 **Discrete data.** This is data which can only be expressed as a whole number. Examples include the number of people, say, 100 and never 101.5; number of cars, number of accounts, etc. Discrete data cannot be expressed as a decimal or fraction.

4 **Continuous data.** This is data which takes on decimals as well as fractions. Examples include height (e.g. 163.8cm), weight (e.g. 58.8kg), distance (e.g. 15.2km), income (e.g. K225.50). All these are capable of taking decimals hence continuous.

5 **Primary data.** This is data which is collected by the researcher for a specific purpose at hand. It involves field work hence very expensive in terms of cost and time and also very prone to error. An example would include data collected by the IT manager of a bank soliciting responses from the customers regarding the withdrawal of ATM facilities. It is data collected first hand.

6 **Secondary data.** This is data which was collected by someone else for a different or general purpose but which the researcher can still make good use of. It involves collecting published data hence the name "desk research" as one can collect all data while seated in a desk in a good library. Examples include data collected by the Central Statistical Office such as the census of population. It is cheap in terms of time and cost but must be interpreted carefully.

7 **Raw data.** This is data which is not arranged into any meaningful order. It is data recorded as it is collected. For example the raw data on the ages of 10 Bank tellers may be as follows:

36   21   26   57   41

48   32   19   38   29

Above data is not arranged into any array or order

8. **Ungrouped data.** This is data which is not grouped into classes. It is more less like raw data except that ungrouped data can be arranged into an array or some order. For example the ungrouped but arrayed data on the ages of bank tellers would be:

19,   21,   26,   29,   32,   36,   38,   41,   48,   57

9. **Grouped data**. This is data which has been grouped into classes. For example, the grouped data on the ages of bank tellers would be:

Class	Number of tellers
10 but less than 20	1
20 but less than 30	3
30 but less than 40	3
40 but less than 50	2
50 but less than 60	1
	10

It is always cardinal as a first step to be clear as to what type of data you are working with. This is so because when calculating numerical descriptive measures, one needs to understand whether data given is continuous or discrete because finding the midpoint differs in the two types of data. The same thing applies when working with probability distributions.

A STATISTICAL SURVEY

A statistical survey process involves various steps or activities that are undertaken in carrying out the survey. These activities are as follows:

1. **Problem formulation /specification of survey objectives**. This is the first step and unless the problem is understood, it will be difficult to attempt to solve it. A problem can be defined in a question form e.g. What will be the effect of withdrawing ATM facilities from the designed area? Once the problem is understood and defined, the researcher must specify what the survey is intended to achieve. Some of the survey objectives may be:

   - To determine the performance level of ATM facilities by location.
   - To identify factors which affect success or failure of ATM facilities.
   - To assess the impact of withdrawal of the ATM facilities.

2. **Develop a survey design**. This step involves developing the plan for the collection of information in order to achieve efficiency and economy in time and cost. A number of issues must be addressed and the starting point is to be clear about a type of design. Is it exploratory, descriptive or caused design? Next is the determination of sources and types of data. The choices here are between availing oneself of information which already exists (Secondary data sources) or generating new information (primary data sources).

Next is to determine what tools to be used in collecting data. The choices here are between the question method and the observational approach.

Finally, under this step would be to deal with the issue of who is to be sampled? What is the appropriate sample size and how would respondents be chosen (sampling).

3. **Collection of data**. This step involves the field work of collecting data. This phase is generally the most expensive and most prone to error for example, interviewers have to be recruited, trained, supervised and rewarded adequately. In the case of survey four major problems arise. Some respondents will not be at home and must be re-contacted or replaced. Other respondents will refuse to cooperate. Still others will give biased or dishonest information. Finally, some interviewers will be biased or dishonest.

4. **Analysis of information.** This step involves drawing meaning from the new data that has been collected. In other words, this step is about finding answers to the issues or questions raised by the survey. What are the implications of these findings in the context of survey objectives? Measures of location and dispersion are key at this stage.

5. **Presentation of findings**. This last step involves the researcher presenting the findings to the relevant parties. Management that has to make the decisions is the more appropriate authority to receive the report.

Take note that the above five steps represent one of the most commonly used ones. However, there are variations and some of the above steps could be split so that we have more than five steps in total.

SAMPLING

Statistical sampling is a systematic approach to selecting a few elements (a sample) from an entire collection of data (a population) in order to make some inferences about the total collection. In most practical situations, a population would be too large to carry out a complete survey and only a sample will be examined. You for a large bank and you need to write a report describing all the employees who have voluntarily left the bank in the last 10 years. You have a difficult task locating all these thousands group – many have died, moved from the community, left the country, or acquired a new name by marriage. How do you write the report? The best idea is to locate a representative sample and interview them, in order to generalize about entire group. The same is done when conducting a poll to try and predict the results of an election. It is not possible to ask everyone of a voting age to state how they are going to vote. Only a sample of voters is taken and the results from the sample used to estimate the voting intentions of the population.

Sometimes it is possible and practical to examine every person or item in the population we wish to describe. We call this complete enumeration or **census** e.g. the census of population conducted in Zambia every after ten years.

Generally, the advantages of sampling over complete enumeration are:

- Sampling saves money
- Sampling saves labor
- Sampling saves time

Statisticians use the word **population** to refer not only to people but also to all items that have been chosen for study. Thus, population could be employees of a bank in treasury department, white cars in Lusaka, houses in Kamwala, students studying statistical analysis, and so on.

Statisticians use the word **sample** to describe a portion chosen from the population. This could be five employees of a bank from treasury department which has twenty five, 100 white cars in Lusaka out of 10 000 white cars, 10 students taking statistical analysis out of 80, and so on.

STATISTICS AND PARAMETERS

Mathematically, we can describe samples and populations by using measures such as the mean, median, mode and standard deviation. When these terms describer the characteristics of a sample, they are called **statistics**, and when they describe the characteristics of a population, they are called **parameters**. Thus, a statistics is a characteristic of a population.

To be consistent, statisticians use the lower case Roman letters to denote sample statistics and Greek or capital letters for population parameters as follows:

Parameters	Statistics
• Population size = N	Sample size = n
• Population mean = μ	Sample mean = $\bar{x}$
• Population standard deviation= σ	Sample standard deviation = s

TYPES OF SAMPLING

Important issues that must be understood when choosing a sample, among other things, is that the sample must be representative. In other words, it should not be a biased sample. For example, there is a course in Humanities at UNZA where second year students are required to conduct some research within the institution in a group. Now, in my group there was a confirmed "monk" who resided in 'Ruins' and was given questionnaires generated through randomly selected computer student numbers to interview some "mommas" in New Res". It was quite a task for him. Given the opportunity this "monk" could have easily "cooked up" data to avoid interviewing "mommas". The survey would have been biased and as computer geniuses say "garbage in, garbage out" – GIGO.

The following are the common types of biases:

- **Inadequacy of sampling frame** – The sampling frame chosen may not cover the whole population so that some items will not be represented at all in the sample and some will be over-represented or duplicated. This bias can be avoided by a careful statement of the aim of the survey and a check that none of the sampling units is ignored.

- **Items selected in the sample not available** – It is possible that when a sample has been selected, some of the items chosen cannot be located e.g. some people may have relocated. If the missing items are not replaced or are incorrectly replaced, a bias will be introduced. This can be reduced to a minimum by returning to the sampling frame and using the same method. To select the replacement as was used to select the original sample.

- **Interviewer or observer bias** – This is often the common of all types of bias. All interviewers and observers are given a list of their sampling units. Sometimes to save time and effort they may substitute missing units on the spot without considering how the other units have been chosen. Other sources of bias arise when the interviewers do not follow the questionnaires exactly, allow their own ideas to become evident, or are careless in recording responses; observers may measure or record their results inaccurately. This type of bias can be reduced by careful choice and training of the team, and by close supervision when the survey is taking place.

Note that bias can rarely be eliminated completely, but the results of the survey may still be useful provided that the final report states the assumptions made, even if they are not fully justified, e.g. if the sampling frame is not complete.

Further, in sampling, it is always necessary to distinguish between a **sampling unit** – an item from which information is obtained e.g. a person, and a **sampling frame** – a list of all items in a population.

METHOD OF TAKING THE SAMPLE

The method to use to select a sample largely depends on the aim of the survey, the type of population involved, and the time and funds at your disposal. The methods from which the choice is usually made are:

(a) simple random sampling
(b) systematic sampling
(c) stratified sampling
(d) multi-stage sampling
(e) cluster sampling
(f) quota sampling

SIMPLE RANDOM SAMPLING

Simple random sampling selects samples by methods that allow each possible sample to have an equal probability of being picked and each item in the entire population to have an equal chance of being included in the sample.

The easiest way to select a sample randomly is to use random numbers. These numbers can be generated by a computer programmed to scramble numbers or by a table of random numbers. Alternatively, we can assign numbers, say, 00 to 99 to represent people so that when we need a sample of 10 then we can randomly select 10 numbers to represent 10 people. This is the method used by State Lotteries Board for Pick-A-Lot, as well as many mobile phone service providers during competitions where they make use of the cell phone numbers used to enter the draw.

ADVANTAGE OF SIMPLE RANDOM SAMPLING

1. It always produces an unbiased sample.

DISADVANTAGES OF SIMPLE RANDOM SAMPLING

1. Its major disadvantage is that the sampling units may be difficult or expensive to contact, e.g. in a survey sampling

SYSTEMATIC SAMPLING

In a systematic sampling elements are selected from the population at a uniform interval that is measured in time, order or space. If we wanted to interview every tenth student on a university campus, we would choose a random starting point in the first ten names in the tenth name thereafter. Systematic sampling differs from simple random sampling in that each element has an equal chance of being selected but each sample does not have an equal chance of being selected. This could be seen in a case if we had assigned numbers between 00 and 99 to the employees and then had begun to pick a sample of 10 by picking every tenth number beginning 1, 11, 21, 31, and so forth

Employees numbered 2, 3, 4, and 5 would have had no chance of being selected. Thus, the method is not purely random since once the starting point has been determined then the items selected for the sample have also been set.

ADVANTAGES OF SYSTEMATIC SAMPLING

1. The main advantage of this method is the speed with which it can be selected

2. It is sufficiently close to simple random sampling in most cases, to justify its widespread use.

DISADVANTAGES OF SYSTEMATIC SAMPLING

1. There is the problem of introducing an error into the sample process. This mainly occurs where the sampling frame is arranged so that sampling units with a particular characteristic occur at regular intervals, causing over-or-under representation of this characteristic in the sample. For example, if you are choosing every tenth house in a street and the first randomly chosen number is 8, the sample consists of numbers 8, 18, 28, 38 and so on. These are all even numbers and therefore are more likely to be on the same side of the street. It is possible that the houses on this side may be better more expensive houses than those on the other side. This would probably mean the sample was biased towards those households with a high income. The sample must be checked.

STRATIFIED SAMPLING

To use stratified sampling, we divide the population into relative homogenous groups, called strata. Then we use one of the approaches. Either we select at random from each stratum a specified number of elements corresponding to the proportion of that stratum in the population as a whole, or we draw an equal number of elements from each stratum and give weight to the results according to the stratum's proportion of total population. With this approach, stratified sampling guarantees that every element in the population has a chance of being selected. Stratified sampling is appropriate when the population is already divided into groups of different sizes and we wish to acknowledge this fact.

ADVANTAGES OF STRATIFIED SAMPLING

1. The advantage of stratified samples is that when they are properly designed, they more accurately reflect the characteristics of the population from which they were chosen than do other kinds of sampling.

DISADVANTAGES OF STRATIFIED SAMPLING

1. The main disadvantage is the difficulty of defining the strata
2. This method can also be time consuming, expensive and complicated to analyze

CLUSTER SAMPLING

In cluster sampling, we divide the population into groups or clusters, and then select a random sample of these clusters. We assume that these individual clusters are representative of the population as a whole. It is a useful means of sampling when there is an inadequate sampling frame or when it is too expensive to construct the frame. If a market research team is attempting to determine by sampling the average number of television sets per household in Lusaka, they would use a city map to divide the territory into blocks and then choose a certain number of blocks (clusters) for interviewing. Every household in each of these blocks would be interviewed. A well designed cluster sampling procedure can produce a more precise sample at considerably less cost than that of simple random sampling.

The difference between stratified and cluster sampling should be noted. With both stratified and cluster sampling, the population is divided into well-defined groups. We use stratified sampling when each group has a small variation within itself but there is a wide variation between the groups. We use cluster sampling in the opposite case – when there is considerable variation within each group but the groups are essentially similar to each other.

ADVANTAGES OF CLUSTER SAMPLING

The major advantages of this method are the reduction in cost and increase of speed in carrying out the survey. The method is especially useful where the size or constitution of the sampling frame is known. Nothing needs to be known in advance about the area selected for sampling, as all the units about it are sampled. This is mainly used in countries where electoral registers or similar lists do not exist.

DISADVANTAGES OF CLUSTER SAMPLING

One disadvantage of cluster sampling is that the units within the sample are not homogeneous, i.e. clusters tend to consist of people with the same characteristics for example, a branch of a bank chosen in a wealthy suburb of Lusaka is likely to consist of customers with high incomes. If all bank branches chosen were in similar suburbs, then the sample would consist of people from one social group and thus the sample results would be biased.

Another disadvantage of taking units such as a bank branch for a cluster is that the variation in size of the cluster may be very large, i.e. a very busy branch may distort the results of the survey.

MULTI-STAGE SAMPLING

This method consists of a number of steps and is designed to retain the advantage of simple random sampling and at the same time cut down the cost of the sample. The method is best explained by taking an example involving a bank survey.

Suppose we have decided that we need a sample of 5000 adults selected from all the adults in Zambia but that the expense of running the survey with a simple random sample is too high, then we could proceed as follows:

Stage 1:   Use all the 9 provinces in Zambia as the sampling units and select a simple random sample of size 5 from this sampling frame.

Stage 2:   Each province will be divided into districts so we use these as the sampling units for this stage and select a simple random sample of size 10 from each of the 5 provinces chosen in stage 1. We now have total 50 districts areas.

Stage 3:   Divided each of these selected districts areas into residential areas and select one of these residential areas randomly. So now we have 50 randomly selected small regions scattered throughout the country.

Stage 4:   Use the electoral rolls or any other appropriate list of all the adults in these areas as the sampling frame and select a simple random sample of 100 adults from each residential area. Note that the subdivisions at each stage can be chosen to fit in conveniently with the particular surveys that are running. For example, a survey on the health of school children could begin with local education authorities in the first stage and finish with individual schools.

ADVANTAGES OF MULTI-STAGE SAMPLING

The advantages of this method are that at each stage the samples selected are small and that interviews are carried out in 50 small areas instead of in 5000 scattered locations, thus economizing on time and cost. There is no need to have a sampling effectively a simple random sample.

DISADVANTAGES OF MULTI-STAGE SAMPLING

The main disadvantages are the danger of introducing interviewer bias and of obtaining different levels of accuracy from different areas. The interviewers must be well chosen and thoroughly trained if these dangers are to be avoided.

QUOTA SAMPLING

In all the above methods, the result of the sampling process is a list of all those to be interviewed. The interviewers must then contact the sampling units, and this may take a considerable amount of time. It is possible that, in spite of every effort, they have to record "no contact" on their questionnaire. This may to a low response rate and hence the survey result would be biased and a great deal of effort, time and money would have been wasted.

To overcome these problems, the method of quota sampling has been developed, in which a sampling frame and a list of sampling units is not necessary; it is sometimes called a **non-probability sampling method**. The major difference between quota sampling and other method is that the final choice of the sampling units is left to the sampler (interviewer).

The quota sampling works as follows: the organizers of the survey supply the sampler, usually an interviewer, with the area allocated to him and the number and type of sampling units needed. This number, called a **quota**, is usually broken down by social class, age or sex. The interviewers then take to the street and select the units necessary to make up their quota. This sounds simple but in reality selecting the quota can be difficult. It requires experience and well-trained interviewers who can establish a good relationship quickly with those people being interviewed.

ADVANTAGES OF QUOTA SAMPLING

The advantages of this method are that it is probably the cheapest way of collecting data, there is no need for the interviewers to call back on certain respondents; they just replace any respondent with another more convenient to locate; it has been found to be very successful in skilled hands.

DISADVANTAGES OF QUOTA SAMPLING

The disadvantages are that as the sample is not random, statistically speaking, it is difficult to assess the degree of confidence in the deductions; there is too much reliance on the judgement and integrity of the interviewers and too little control by the organizers.

CHOICE OF SAMPLING METHOD

The sampling method is probably the factor which has most effect on the quality of the survey results so it needs very careful thought. You have to balance the advantages and disadvantages of each method for each survey. When you have defined the aim of the survey, you have to consider the type of population involved, the sampling frame available and the area covered by the population.

If you are to avoid bias, there should be some element of randomness in the method you choose. All methods are developed for their precision, economy or physical ease. Even so, assume for the rest of the example and problems in this book that we obtain our data using simple random sampling. This is necessary because the principles of simple random sampling are the foundation for statistical inference, the process of making inferences about population from information contained in samples. If you understand the basic ideas involved in simple random sampling, you will have a good grasp of what is going on in the other cases, even if you must leave the technical details to the professional statistician.

PROGRESS CLINIC ONE

1. a) Distinguish between quantitative and qualitative data.

   b) A bank is considering offering a new product to see how consumers react to the product; the Bank conducted a preference test using 100 randomly selected bank customers in Lusaka Central Business. The customers were asked to test the product and then fill out a short questionnaire that requested the following information:

      i)   What is your age?
      ii)   How long have you been with bank?
      iii)   Are you married?
      iv)   How many people are in your family?
      v)   Are you happy with the bank's new product?
      vi)   Would you purchase this product if it were available on the market?
      vii)   If you answered yes to question (vii), how often would you purchase it?

   Each of these questions generates data set of interest to the bank. Classify the data in each data set as either qualitative or quantitative. Justify your classification.

   c) Distinguish between discrete and continuous data providing three examples of each. Also explain the importance of distinguishing discrete from continuous data in statistical analysis.

2. Most statistical surveys are conducted using a sample whose findings are generalized to the population as a whole. When selecting the sample it is always necessary to ensure that the sample is "representative" of the population.

   (a) Distinguish between a statistic and a parameter providing two examples of each.
   (b) What are the three advantages of sampling over complete enumeration (census)?
   (c) Discuss the common types of bias in sampling and suggest how they can be reduced or overcome?

3. (a) Discuss the main methods of sampling.

   (b) In each of the following situations state and briefly explain the appropriate sampling method to be used.

   i)   The bank wants to determine the effect of withdrawal of ATM facilities at a certain branch. About 100 people should be interviewed.
   ii)   You want to determine on the views of motorists in Lusaka on the issue of traffic jam. 100 motorists should be interviewed.

iii)   You want to determine the views of women on the 'diva' account. 50 women should be interviewed.

iv)   You want to know how people will vote during the General Election. Every one above 16 years must be interviewed.

4. (a) Distinguish between primary data and secondary data giving three examples of each and the possible sources.

    (b) Discuss the three commonly used methods of colleting primary data.
    (c) Refer to (b). which method would be appropriate in each of the following Situations:

i)   You wish to collect primary data on customers' view about the bank's customer service. A bank has 500 personal and corporate customers.

ii)   You wish to determine the views of the Chief Executives of the 13 commercial banks on the validity of the Banking and Finance training to the industry.

iii)   You wish to know how many minutes people take when withdrawing cash using the ATM.

iv)   You wish to determine the level of morale by bank tellers. The bank has 15 bank tellers and only one branch.

Chapter Two

GRAPHICAL DESCRIPTIONS OF DATA

Before we can use the information in a sample to make inferences about a population (which is the goal of statistical analysis), we must be able to extract the relevant information from the sample. That is, we need methods to summarize and describe the sample measurements. For example, if we look at last year's sales for 100 randomly selected companies, we are unlikely to extract much information by looking at a set of 100 sales figures. We would get a clear picture of the data by calculating the average sales for all 100 companies, by determining the highest and lowest company sales, by drawing a graph showing the average monthly-sales over the 12-month period, or in general by using some technique that will extract and summarize relevant information from the data and, at the same time, allow us to obtain a clear understanding of the sample.

In this chapter, various graphical methods for describing data are presented. You will see that graphical methods for describing data are intuitively appealing descriptive techniques that can be used to describe either a sample or a population. However, numerical methods (covered in the next chapter), for describing data are the keys that unlock the door to inferential statistics.

THE FREQUENCY DISTRIBUTION

A frequency distribution is a table that is used to summarize raw sample data in a tabular format. Few people would prefer to be faced with a table thousands of items long when they can have instead a manageable frequency distribution. Yet, something is lost, most distributions are constructed using groups or classes which may in some cases be very wide indeed. We have sacrificed detail for the sake of presenting a picture which can be absorbed fairly simply. It might seem, of course, that the use of classes will prevent our using the frequency distribution as the basis for further work. Naturally, it does create a problem and to overcome it we have to make an assumption: WE use midpoints of a class to enable further work to be carried out. Since you will be using this midpoint of a class many times, its importance of accuracy must be stressed here. You must firstly consider whether the distribution is continuous or discrete. For discrete distribution the mid point can only take whole numbers while for continuous distribution the mid point can take decimals. This is key when working on numerical methods for describing data.

Note: Mid point = $\dfrac{\text{Lowest class value + largest class value}}{2}$

Summarizing data using frequency distributions requires that you first group the data into classes. Judgement is required concerning the number and the size of the classes to be used. The important point to be borne in mind when making this judgement is that the presentation of the grouped data should enable the user to quickly grasp the general shape of the distribution of the data. Although this choice is arbitrary and no hard and fast rules can be given, the following guidelines are very useful:

- The classes must be non-overlapping, so that each measurement falls into exactly one class. Therefore choose the classes so that no measurement falls on a class boundary. The use of phrases such, "5 but less than 10" or "5 and under 10" clearly emphasizes the fact that 5 is included in that class but 10 is not.

- Choose the number to be used as a number between 5 and 20, with the smallest number of classes being chosen for smaller data sets.

- The approximate width of each class is given by the following:

Approximate class width = $\dfrac{\text{largest value} - \text{smallest value}}{\text{Number of classes}}$

Choose the actual class width to be a value close to the approximate width that is convenient to work with. Avoid awkward fractional values by rounding up.

Example 1

The following is a record of the percentage marks gained by candidates in BF 260 final examination:

65	57	57	55	20	54	52	49	58	52
86	39	50	48	83	71	66	54	51	27
30	44	34	78	36	63	67	55	40	56
63	75	55	15	96	51	54	52	53	42
50	25	85	27	75	40	37	46	42	86
16	45	12	79	50	46	40	38	57	31
35	93	54	68	67	62	51	52	54	61
93	84	28	26	62	57	45	43	47	33
45	25	77	80	91	67	53	55	51	36
56	74	50	66	52	61	46	59	57	50

Tabulate the marks in the form of a frequency distribution, grouping by suitable intervals. Also add a column for relative frequencies.

Solution

Looking at these figures we find that there are 100 marks given ranging from 12 to 96. Aiming for a reasonable number of classes, 10 classes is a natural choice for this data set, hence the class width (approximate) = $\dfrac{100}{10 \text{ classes}} = 10$

Next, we have to find how many of these marks fall within each class, and it is recommended that you should do this in this way. Firstly,. List every class vertically; now take each candidate's marks in turn, and place a dash or some other suitable mark against the class into which it falls. Having done this for every mark we can now take each class in turn and add up how many candidates fall into each class. Your rough working should appear like this. You will notice that for ease of counting we have divided our dashes into groups of five.

Class	Tally marks	Number
10 and under 20	III	3
20 and under 30	IIII II	7
30 and under 40	IIII IIII	10
40 and under 50	IIII IIII IIII I	16
50 and under 60	IIII IIII IIII IIII IIII IIII IIII	34
60 and under 70	IIII IIII III	13
70 and under 80	IIII II	7
80 and under 90	IIII I	6
90 and under 100	IIII	4
		100

Before you do anything else now, check that the total frequency (that is, the number of dashes) in your rough working is the same as the number of items given in the question. Having done this you are now ready to construct a frequency distribution. Your final frequency distribution accompanied by the relative frequency column will appear like this:

Marks awarded	Number of candidates	Relative frequency
10 and under 20	3	$\frac{3}{100} = 0.03$
20 and under 30	7	0.07
30 and under 40	10	0.10
40 and under 50	16	0.16
50 and under 60	34	0.34
60 and under 70	13	0.13
70 and under 80	7	0.07
80 and under 90	6	0.06
90 and under 100	4	0.04
	100	1.00

Note: Relative Frequency = $\frac{\text{Class Frequency}}{\text{Total Frequency}}$ and should always be equal to 1.00.

- From the frequency table we can clearly see that majority of the candidates (34) got between 50 and 60 marks and the lowest number of candidates (3) got between 10 and 20 marks. This was a fair examination as the results are normally distributed.

- Earlier we mentioned that, when data is grouped into classes though it makes it easier to grasp the distribution of the marks, something is clearly lost: We will no longer know who scored 12 marks not until we make reference to the actual results!

Example 2

Using the details of example 1, construct a cumulative frequency distribution accompanied by a relative cumulative frequency column.

Solution

Class	Frequency	Cumulative frequency	Relative cumulative frequency
10 and under 20	3	3 + 0 = 3	0.03 + 0 = 0.03
20 and under 30	7	3 + 7 = 10	0.03 + 0.07 = 0.10
30 and under 40	10	10 + 10 = 20	0.10 + 0.10 = 0.20
40 and under 50	16	20 + 16 = 36	0.20 + 0.16 = 0.36
50 and under 60	34	36 + 34 = 70	0.36 + 0.34 = 0.70
60 and under 70	13	70 + 13 = 83	0.70 + 0.13 = 0.83
70 and under 80	7	83 + 7 = 90	0.83 + 0.07 = 0.90
80 and under 90	6	90 + 6 = 96	0.90 + 0.06 = 0.96
90 and under 100	4	96 + 4 = 100	0.96 + 0.04 = 1.00
	100		

Note: cumulative relative frequency is calculated using the relative frequency by summing up. The last figure must always equal to 1.00. Similarly, the last figure for cumulative frequency column must always equal to the total frequency (100 in the above case).

GRAPHICAL METHOD FOR DESCRIBING QUALITATIVE DATA: THE BAR CHARTS

The natural and useful technique for summarizing qualitative data is to tabulate the frequency or relative frequency for each category. The frequency for the category is the total number of observations that fall in the category. The relative frequency for a category is the frequency of that category divided by the total number of observations; that is relative frequency = $\dfrac{\text{frequency of the category}}{\text{Total number of observations}} = \dfrac{f}{n}$

A common method of graphically presenting the frequencies or relative frequencies for qualitative data is the bar chart. For this type of chart the frequencies or relative frequencies are represented by bars of equal width- one bar for each category. The height of the bar for a given category is proportional to the category frequency or relative frequency. Usually bars are placed in a vertical position with the base of the bar on the horizontal axis. The area of the bar is unimportant. What is key is the height of the bars. Generally, the higher the bar, the more important it is. Thus, a bar chart is very suitable for a manager who uses "**management by exception**" principles as it is very easy to spot 'exceptions' using a bar chart.

When drawing up bar charts take care to:

- Make the bars reasonably wide so that they can clearly be seen.
- Draw them neatly and professionally
- Ensure that the bars all have the same width
- Ensure that the gaps between the bars have the same width
- Time should always be on the horizontal axis.

TYPES OF BAR CHARTS

A variety of bar charts can be drawn up to provide an overview of the data. There are many types which include:

(a) **Simple bar chart** – This is a bar chart where simple bars representing each variable are drawn either vertically or horizontally.

(b) **Component or stacked bar chart** - Here a single bar is drawn for each variable, with the height of the bar representing the total categories. Each bar is then subdivided to show the components that make up the total bar. These components may be identified by colouring or shading, accompanied by an explanatory key to show what each component represents.

(c) **Percentage component bar chart** – Here the components are converted into percentages of the total, and the bars are divided in proportion to these percentages. The scale is a percentage scale and the height of each bar is 100%

(d) **Multiple bar charts** – Here two or more bars are grouped together in each category. The use of a key helps to distinguish between the categories.

- Note: Which one of the above bar charts to be used largely depends on the arrangement of data!

Example 3

The average annual inflation rate for country Z over the past five years is summarized below:

Year	Inflation rate (%)
2003	24
2004	18
2005	15
2006	11
2007	9

Draw up a bar chart to depict these data.

Solution

Data given lends itself to simple bar chart presentation

Frequency (%)

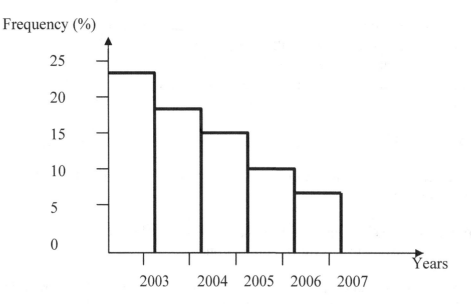

Note: It is also permissible to leave gaps in between bars

Example 4

The table below summarizes the number of people opening personal accounts in different branches of the bank in Lusaka.

Branch	Quarter 1	Quarter 2	Quarter 3	Quarter 4
Matero	10	25	5	15
Cairo	15	10	50	30
Mandahill	20	35	25	15
Total	45	70	80	60

Use a component bar chart and percentage component bar chart to depict the above data.

Solution

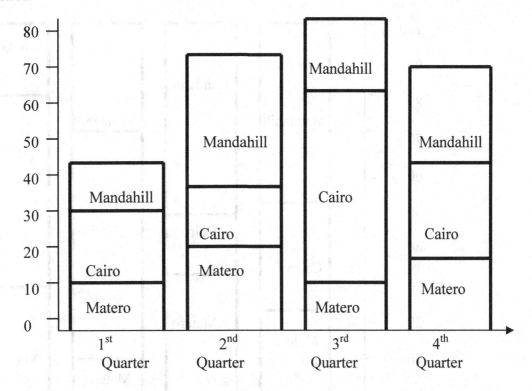

- Component bar chart

Note: For the 1st quarter Matero has 10 as its height. This is added to 15 for Cairo to give us the height of 25 to which we add 20 to give us 45 as the overall height. The same is done for the rest of the quarters.

- For the percentage component bar chart, we need to change the absolute figures into percentages.

Branch	1st Quarter	2nd Quarter	3rd Quarter	4th Quarter
Matero	22.22	35.71	6.25	25.00
Cairo	33.33	14.28	62.50	50.00
Mandahill	44.44	50.00	31.25	25.00
Total	100%	100%	100%	100%

Percentage

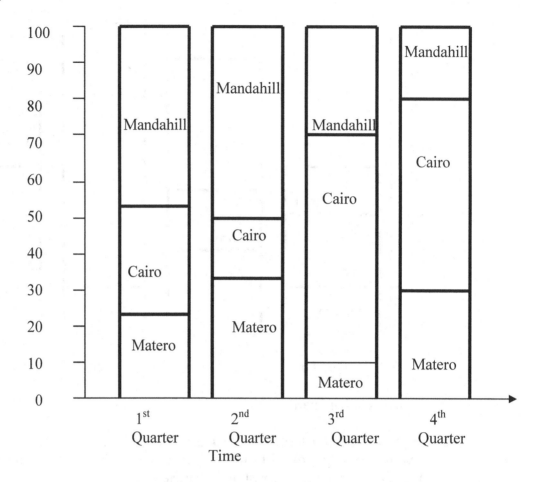

Note that the total for each quarter equals 100%. A wealthy of information can be extracted from the above component bar charts. Notably, it can be seen that the lowest number was recorded for Matero during the third quarter while the largest number was recorded for Cairo during the same quarter. The possible reasons could then be looked for.

Example 5

The sales for the bank's traditional services A and B over a period of four years have been recorded and summarized below.

	2003 (K'000	2004 (K'000)	2005 (K'000)	2006 (K'000)
Service A	1000	2500	4000	5000
Service B	4000	2500	3500	4500

Using a multiple bar chart depict these data.

Solution

K'000

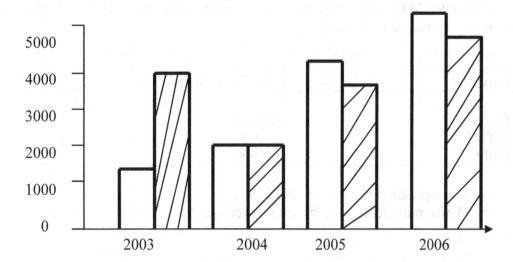

- From the chart, it can be seen that service A has been doing very fine, ever increasing in sales. B has its sales volume fall by almost 37.5% between 2003 and 2004, though it picked up slowly thereafter year by year.

GRAPHICAL METHOD OF DESCRIBING QUALITATIVE DATA: THE PIE CHARTS

A pie chart is a useful method for displaying the percentage of observations that fall into each category of qualitative data. A pie chart shows the component parts that make up the total. Generally, the larger the slice, the more important the component part is. A complete circle (the pie) represents the total number of measurements. This is partitioned into a number of slices, with one slice for each category. The size of a slice is proportional to the relative frequency of a particular category.

The following steps must be followed when drawing up a pie chart.

- Draw a circle which is 360^0 of good size

- Calculate the degrees using the given data i.e. $\dfrac{\text{given observation}}{\text{Total observation}} \times 360^0$

- Use the calculated degrees to partition the circle into slices

- Calculate the percentages for each category using: $\dfrac{\text{given observation}}{\text{Total observation}} \times 100$

  Or $\dfrac{\text{Calculated degree}}{360^0} \times 100$

- Insert the percentages into the slices.

- 23 -

Example 6

The cell phone industry in Zambia is currently being dominated by three providers namely Celtel, MTN and CellZ. Suppose a survey conducted to determine the number of subscribers revealed the following:

Provider	Number of subscribers
Celtel	70 000
MTN	20 000
CellZ	10 000

(a) Use a pie chart to represent these data.
(b) Which provider has the largest market share?

Solution

(a) We first calculate the degrees and percentages for each provider as follows:

Degrees

- Celtel: $\dfrac{70\ 000}{100\ 000}$ X $360^0 = 252^0$

- MTN: $\dfrac{20\ 000}{100\ 000}$ X $360^0 = 72^0$

- CellZ: $\dfrac{10\ 000}{100\ 000}$ X $360^0 = 36^0$

Percentages

Celtel: $\dfrac{252^0}{360^0}$ X $100 = 70\%$

MTN: $\dfrac{72^0}{360^0}$ X $100 = 20\%$

CellZ $= \dfrac{36^0}{360^0}$ X $100 = 10\%$

Now a pie chart can be drawn as follows:

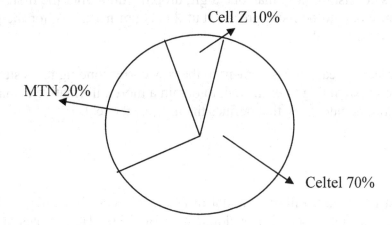

Note: we only use the calculated degrees to help us partition the pie into slices. A compass and a calculator are needed if the pie chart is to be precisely drawn, which makes it somewhat inconvenient to construct. However, even if we only approximate the size of the wedges, the pie chart provides useful picture of a qualitative data set.

(b) Celtel has the largest market share as shown by the largest slice of the pie.

GRAPHICAL METHOD FOR DESCRIBING QUANTITATIVE DATA: STEM AND LEAF DISPLAYS

Quantitative data sets are those that consist of numerical measurement. Thus, a quantitative sample is simply a list of numerical values that result from observations taken on some variable x. Most business data are quantitative, so methods for summarizing quantitative data are essentially important.

A useful graphical description of quantitative data is the **stem and leaf display**.

CONSTRUCTING A STEM AND LEAF DISPLAY

To construct a stem and leaf display, it is necessary to partition each measurement into two components: a **stem** and a **leaf**. Usually, a stem is the part of each measurement to the left of the decimal place-the units and measurement to the right of the decimal place-the tenths digit.
The following steps must be followed:

- Define the stem and leaf that you will use. Choose the units for the stem so that the number of stems in the display is between 5 and 20.

- Write the stems in a column arranged with the smallest stem at the top with the largest stem at the bottom. Include all stems in the range of the data, even if there are some stems with no corresponding leaves.

- If the leaves consist of more than one digit; drop the digit after the first. You may round the numbers to be more precise, but this is not necessary for the graphical description to be useful.

- Record the leaf for each measurement in the row corresponding to its stem. Order the leaves corresponding to each stem to obtain a more informative display. Omit decimals, and include a key that defines the units of the leaf.

Example 7

A financial analyst is interested in the amount of resources spent by computer hardware and software companies on Research Development (R and D). He samples 50 of these high technology firms, and calculates the amount each spent last year on R and D as a percentage of their total revenues. The results are tabulated below.

Company	%	Company	%	Company	%	Company	%	Company	%
1	13.5	11	8.0	21	8.2	31	9.6	41	7.1
2	8.4	12	7.9	22	8.0	32	7.2	42	13.2
3	10.5	13	6.8	23	7.7	33	8.8	43	7.7
4	9.0	14	9.5	24	7.4	34	11.3	44	5.9
5	9.2	15	8.1	25	6.5	35	8.5	45	5.2
6	9.7	16	13.5	26	9.5	36	9.4	46	5.6
7	6.6	17	9.9	27	8.2	37	10.5	47	11.7
8	10.6	18	6.9	28	6.9	38	6.9	48	6.0
9	10.1	19	7.5	29	7.2	39	6.5	49	7.8
10	7.1	20	11.1	30	8.2	40	7.5	50	6.5

Use a stem and display to depict these data.

Solution

As numerical measurements, these percentages represent quantitative data. The analysis's initial objective is to describe these data.

The stem and leaf display is constructed below:

Stem		Leaf									
5	2	6	9								
6	0	5	5	6	8	9	9	9			
7	1	1	2	2	4	5	5	7	7	8	9
8	0	0	1	2	2	2	4	5	8		
9	0	2	4	5	5	6	7	9			
10	1	5	5	6							
11	1	3	7								
12											
13	2	5	5								

Key: Leaf units are tenths.

Notes: Although the stem 12 has no leaves (meaning that none of the 50 observations fell in the range 12.0 to 12.9), we include the 12 stem in the display so that this fact is visually obvious. Note also that the decimal point is not included in the display. When there is no confusion caused by its omission, we can usually obtain a less cluttered graphical description without it.

Several description facts about these data are easily seen in the stem and leaf display. Most of the sampled computer companies (37 of 50) spent between 6.0% and 9.9% of their revenues on R and D, and 11 of them spent between7.0% and 7.9%. Relative to the rest of the sampled companies, 3 spent a high percentage of revenues on R and D-in excess of 13%.

The selection of the stem and leaf that best display a set of data is not always clear-cut, and you may have to try several to obtain the best graphical description. The lowest in the above stem and leaf display is 5 because the lowest spent on R and D was 5.2% by company 45.

Example 8

The weights in kilograms of a group of bank tellers at a named bank are as follows:

173	165	171	175	188
183	177	160	151	169
162	179	145	171	175

168	158	186	182	162
154	180	164	166	157

Construct a stem and leaf display for these data.

Solution

The first step in constructing a stem and leaf display is to decide how to split each observation (weight) into two parts: a stem and a leaf. For this example, we will define the first two digits of an observation to be its stem and the third digit to be its leaf. Thus, the first two weights are spit into a stem and leaf as follows:

Weight	Stem	leaf
173	17	3
183	18	3

Scanning the remaining weights, we find that there are five possible stems (14, 15, 16, 17 and 18) which we list in a column from the smallest to largest, as shown below. Next we consider each observation in turn and place its leaf in the same row as its stem, to the right of the vertical line. The resulting stem and leaf display shown below has grouped the 25 weights into 5 categories. The second row of the display corresponding to the stem 15 has four leaves: 4, 8, 1 and 7. The four weights represented in the second row are therefore 154, 158, 151 and 157.

Stem		Leaf						
14		5						
15		1	4	7	8			
16		0	2	2	5	6	8	9
17		1	1	3	5	5	7	9
18		0	2	6	8			

Note that a frequency distribution can be constructed, from a stem and leaf display with the stem representing chosen classes (140 but less than 150, etc) and the leaf representing the frequencies (140 but less than 150, f = 1).

GRAPHICAL METHODS FOR DESCRIBING QUANTITATIVE DATA: HISTOGRAMS

The information provided by the relative frequency histogram is similar to that conveyed by the stem and leaf display. Although the values of the individual measurements cannot be seen in a histogram (as data is summarized into classes), we are able to see the proportion of measurements in a particular class by reading the height of its rectangle on the vertical axis. Also we can more easily control the number of classes in the histogram, which gives us more control over the quality of the graphical description.

CONSTRUCTING A HISTOGRAM

To construct a histogram, the following points must be borne in mind:

- Arrange the data in increasing order, from the smallest to the largest measurement.
- Divide the interval from the smallest to the largest measurement into between 5 and 20 equal subintervals, making sure that:

(a) Each measurement falls into one and only one measurement class.
(b) No measurement falls on the measurement class boundary.
(c) Use a small number of measurement classes if you have a small amount of data, other wise use a larger one.

- Compute the frequency or relative frequency of measurements in each measurement class as follows:

$$\text{Relative frequency for class i} = \frac{f_i}{n}$$

- Using a vertical axis of about three-fourth the length of the horizontal axis, plot each frequency or relative frequency as a rectangle over the corresponding measurement class.

Example 9

Refer to the example 5, on the resources spent by computer hardware and software companies on Research and Development. Construct the frequency histogram and relative frequency histogram for these data.

Solution

To construct the histogram, we first choose the class interval width and then define the measurement classes. Classes must range between 5 and 20 measurement classes with the class width being calculated using:

Class width = largest measurement – smallest measurement
                                    Number of intervals

- If we select 8 measurement classes with the largest measurement being 13.5% and the smallest 5.2% the class width = 13.5 – 5.2 = 1.04
                                                                                                              8

- 1.04 must be rounded upward to be certain of including all observations. Therefore class width = 1.1

- Next, we determine the lower boundary of the first class by selecting the value 5.15, just 0.05 below the smallest measurement, 5.2. We use one additional decimal place for the boundaries so that no measurement falls on a class boundary. We then add the class width of 1.1 to this boundary to find the upper boundary of the first class, and lower boundary of the second and third classes is obtained by adding 1.1 again , with the result 7.35. This process is repeated a total of eight times, to generate eight intervals, with the last boundary at 13.95.

- The final step in the construction of a histogram is to plot the measurement classes on a horizontal axis and the frequency or relative frequency of each class on a vertical axis. The frequency with a base width equal to that of the measurement class and a height equal to the frequency or relative frequency.

Class	Measurement class	Class frequency	Class relative frequency
1	5.15 – 6.25	4	$\frac{4}{50} = 0.08$
2	6.25 – 7.35	12	$\frac{12}{50} = 0.24$
3	7.35 – 8.45	14	0.28
4	8.45 – 9.55	7	0.14
5	9.55 – 10.65	7	0.14
6	10.65 – 11.75	3	0.06
7	11.75 – 12.85	0	0.00
8	12.85 – 13.95	3	0.06
			1.00

- The frequency histogram is as follows:

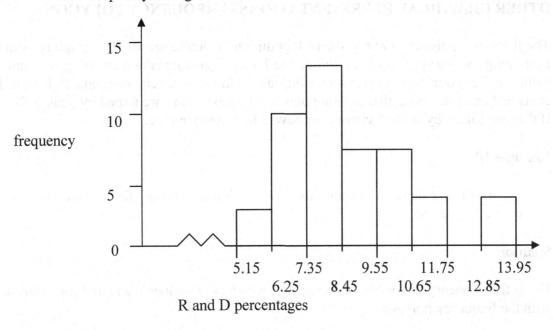

- The relative frequency histogram is as follows:

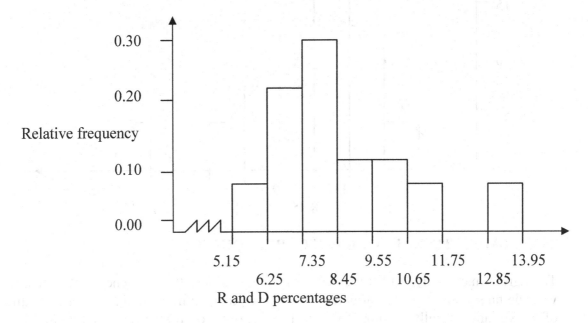

It can be seen that the histogram makes it clear that all measurements fall between 5.15% and 13.95, and that the bulk of the companies spent between 6.25%and 9.55% of their revenue on R and D.

Note: Generally, even if the frequency distribution is given in the question, you still need to re-write it by adding $\pm$ 0.05 to each lower and upper boundary. Further, if the classes are the equal take care for this when drawing the width (base) of the rectangle. Remember, unlike the bar chart, what is important for a histogram is the **area** of the rectangle.

OTHER GRAPHICAL REPRESENTATIONS - FREQUENCY POLYGON

The frequency polygon converts the histogram into a simple graph. The graph is formed by joining the mid-points of the top of the bars. This convention of using the central value of the group to represent the group as a whole is a very common technique in statistical analysis. Note that the midpoints of the top of bars are joined by straight-lines. If they are joined by smooth curves, we have a **frequency curve**.

Example 10

Refer to example 7 depicting expenditures of 50 high technology firms on R and D, and construct a frequency polygon.

Solution

Using the frequency histogram of example 7, which is reproduced here and superimposed with the frequency polygon?

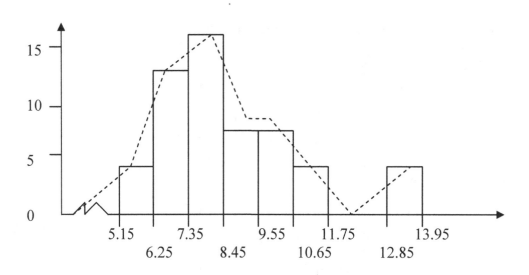

THE CUMULATIVE FREQUENCY CURVE (OGIVE)

The ogive which is also called the "less than" curve shows the frequency with which the variable falls below a particular value. The ogive plots, on horizontal axis, certain values of the variable, usually the upper value of each group, on the vertical axis it shows the frequency of the items with a value less than this. Usually a smooth curve is used to join the points.

Example 11

Refer to example 7, and construct an ogive.

Solution

Class	Measurement class	Frequency	Cumulative frequency
1	5.15 – 6.25	4	4
2	6.25 – 7.35	12	16
3	7.35 – 8.45	14	30
4	8.45 – 9.55	7	37
5	9.55 – 10.65	7	44
6	10.65 – 11.75	3	47
7	11.75 – 12.85	0	47
8	12.85 – 13.95	3	50

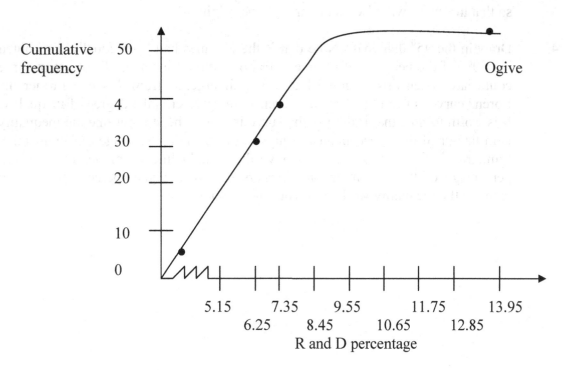

THE LORENZ CURVE

If you look at statistics of income, one of the first things that strikes you is the inequality in the distribution of incomes in most countries. Not only is the range of incomes wide, but we also find that a very small percentage of the income recipients at the top of the scale receive a disproportionately large share of total income. Equally, the very large percentage of low income earners receive very small percentage of the total income. For example, 80% of income recipients receive 10% of total income in Zambia.

Statisticians have derived a diagram, the Lorenz curve, which enables us to show graphically the extent of inequality, not only of incomes, but also of many other things.

CONSTRUCTING A LORENZ CURVE

The following are the steps:

1.   Draw up a table showing:

- The cumulative frequency
- The percentage cumulative frequency
- The cumulative variable (e.g. incomes) total
- The percentage cumulative (e.g. incomes) total

2.   On the graph paper draw scales of 0 – 100% on both the horizontal and vertical axes. The scales should be the same length on both axes.

3.   Plot the cumulative frequency against the cumulative percentage (e.g. income) total and join up that 0% of the income recipients receive 0% of the total income, so that the curve will always go through the origin.

4.   Draw in the 45^0 diagonal. Note that if the incomes had been equally distributed i.e. 50% of the people had received 50% of the total income. The Lorenz curve could have been this diagonal line. Any divergence from this line further the Lorenz curve is from this line of reference, the greater is the degree of inequality. It is worth to note that if the Lorenz curve is below the straight line the inequality is in favour of the upper income groups in that a high percentage of low income. Similarly, if the Lorenz curve is above the straight line, it implies that a given percentage of the bottom income earners receive a higher percentage of total income; the inequality works in favour of the poor.

Example 12

Assume that a weekly wage bill at a bank is K49750 000 for 500 workers with 120 highly skilled experts and 380 unskilled workers. The table below summarizes the results:

Wage group	Number of people	Total wages (K'000)
0 - 80	205	10250
80 – 120	200	22000
120 – 160	35	4900
160 – 200	30	5700
200 – 240	20	4400
240 - 280	10	2500
	500	49750

Construct a Lorenz curve and interpret it.

Solution

Wage group	f	cf	%cf	Total wages/(K'000)	cf	%cf
0 – 80	205	205	41	10250	10250	21
80 – 120	200	405	81	22000	32250	65
120 – 160	35	440	88	4900	37150	75
160 – 200	30	470	94	5700	42850	86
200 – 240	20	490	95	4400	47250	95
240 - 280	10	500	100	2500	49750	100
	500			49750		

- The Lorenz curve is as follows:

Percentage cumulative frequency (wages)

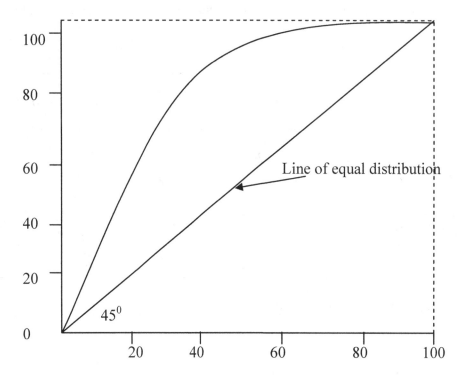

Percentage cumulative frequency (workers)

Interpretation: The further the Lorenz curve is away from the line of equal distribution, the more unevenly distributed is the wages. Luckily, for this bank the inequality is in favour of the low wage earners (poor) as the Lorenz curve is above the line of equal distribution.

Note: Any economist will tell you that one purpose of our taxation systems or any taxation system which is progressive is to reduce the inequality of incomes, and naturally we would like to know how far the system is succeeding in this objective.

THE Z CHART

A diagram which is often used in industry and commerce, although it seems to be less popular among statisticians, is the Z-chart, so called because the completed diagram takes the form of the letter Z. This is merely the devise to enable management to show concisely three different aspects of a time series plotted on one graph. It can show:

- How things are doing from month to month or week to week? (Time series).
- How does the current year's performance to date compare with the target or programme? (Cumulative target line).

- How does the present performance compare with that of the same period last year (moving annual total).

CONSTRUCTING THE Z-CHART

One the bottom of the Z chart we plot time series of monthly or weekly sale's or output or whatever variable we are considering. On the diagonal bar of the Z we plot the cumulative total to date, that is, the total sales or output we have achieved since the beginning of the year. Finally, at the top of the bar, we plot the total sales achieved in the last year: The first or January figure is the total sales achieved during the period 1st February last to 31st last March until the end of February this year, and so on.

Example 13

The following table summarizes the airtime sales for two years (2006 and 2007) for Mr. Kantemba who operates a payphone booth in Kamwala Residential area.

Month	2006 sales(K'000)	2007 sales(K'000)
January	430	450
February	365	340
March	365	400
April	680	680
May	560	610
June	800	760
July	630	700
August	760	800
September	540	570
October	635	590
November	630	420
December	415	430

Construct the Z chart for Mr. Kantemba.

Solution

We first complete the table showing the cumulative for 2007 and moving annual total columns.

Month	2006 sales (K'000)	2007 sales (K'000)	Cumulative for 2007 (K'000)	Moving annual total (K'000)
January	430	450	450	6830
February	365	340	790	6805
March	365	400	1190	6840
April	680	680	1870	6840
May	560	610	2480	6890
June	800	760	3240	6950
July	630	700	3940	6920
August	760	800	4740	6960
September	540	570	5310	6990
October	635	590	5900	6945
November	630	620	6520	6935
December	415	430	6950	6950

Notes:

1. 2006 figures are needed to enable us calculate the moving annual totals (MATs).

2. Each MAT is the sum of the twelve monthly figures up to and including the present month i.e. MAT for January is the sum of the sales figures from February 2006 up to and including January 2007. Quick calculation is as follows: For June, take the May figure of 6890, add sales for the month of June (760) and deduct the sales for the month of June 2006 (800) which gives MSAT of 6850.

3. Each December MAT is the same as the cumulative figure for that month.

4. The cumulative line starts at the beginning of each year.

5. Although the chart is shown as complete, it would in practice be kept up-to-date each month as the figures become available.

6. The value of the Mat is that it shows a t a glance how the current month compares with the same month last year. If the MAT line scopes up, as it does from August to September, then it shows that this September is better than the previous

September. For instance, MAT goes up from 6960 to 6990 showing that this September sales are 30 units higher than the last September.

The MAT line acts as a trend line in time series and gives the general trend for the series.

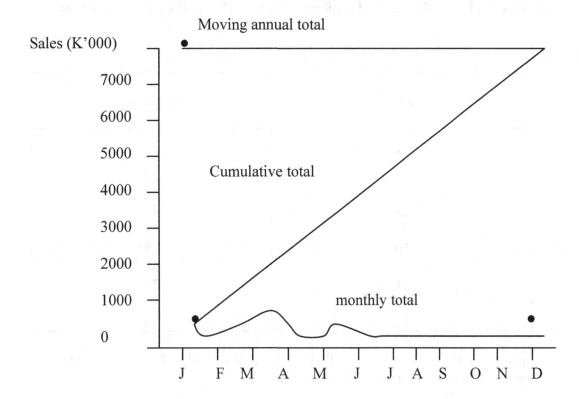

THE SCATTER DIAGRAM

This diagram covered in this chapter is not a graph at all. It is simply a series of dots placed haphazardly on the sheet of graph paper. The basic aim underlying the scatter diagram is to try to ascertain if there is a relationship between two variables, x and y, such that when one is high the other is high; when one is low the other is low. Or perhaps the relationship is inverse –when one variable is low, the other is high and vice versa. Notice that it may be necessary to determine which of the two variables is responsible for causing charges in the other variable (dependent).

Example 14

An educational economist wants to establish the relationship between an individual's income and education. He takes a random samples of 10 individuals and asks for their income (in K'000 000) and education (in years). The results are shown below.

X (education	Y (income)
11	25
12	33
11	22
15	41
8	18
10	28
11	32
11	24
17	53
11	26

Construct a scatter diagram for these data, and describe the relationship between the number of years of education and income level.

Solution

Income (K'000)

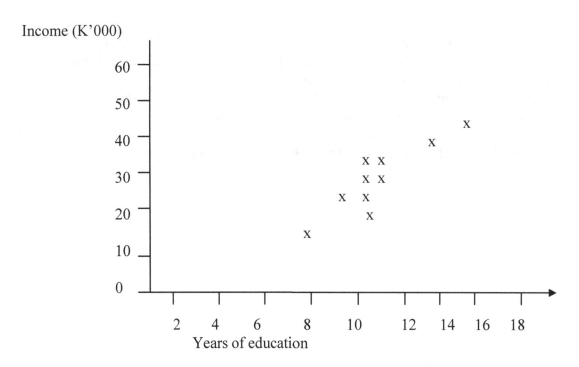

Years of education

There is a position relationship between an individual's income and education i.e. an individual's income increases with an increase in education.

PICTOGRAMS

Yet another less utilized technique for describing data is by way of pictorials. Pictures carefully drawn with an accompanying key can visibly illustrate maps, designs, and so on.

Example 15

Given that the symbol  represent 100 people, a journalist recorded the number of

people in attendance at a political party rally as

How many people were in attendance?

Solution

There were 450 people in attendance. (Notice the difficulties with pictograms, how would you represent 25 people, 80 people?)

CONCLUDING REMARKS

Since we want to use sample data to make inferences about the population from which it is drawn, it is important for us to be able to describe the data. Graphical methods are important and useful tools for describing both qualitative and quantitative data. Graphs must be presented neatly and legibly.

Our ultimate goal is to use the sample to make inferences about the population. We must be wary of using graphical techniques to accomplish this goal since they do not lend themselves to a measure of reliability for an inference. Therefore, we need to develop numerical measures to describe a data set. That is the purpose of the next Chapter.

PROGRESS TEST TWO

1. The weights in kilograms of a group of bank clerks at a named are as follows:

173	165	171	175	188
183	177	160	151	169
163	179	145	171	175
168	158	186	182	162
154	180	164	166	157

    (a) Construct a stem and leaf display for these data
    (b) Construct a frequency distribution for these data
    (c) Construct a relative frequency histogram for the data
    (d) Construct a relative frequency polygon for the data
    (e) Construct an Ogive for the data.

2. The census of population conducted in Zambia in the year 2000 produced the following results for the four cities.

City	Number of people
Lusaka	10 000
Livingstone	2 000
Ndola	3 000
Kitwe	2 000

    (a) Depict above data using a pie chart and a simple bar chart.
    (b) Using the simple bar chart, how can you approximate the mode?
    (c) Discuss the suitability of a compound bar chart, a pie chart and a pictogram for the presentation of data to:
    (i)   Top management
    (ii) Lower management
    (iii) The public. Give examples of data which could be satisfactorily presented in each case.

3. A random sample is taken of 50 employees of a bank. There ages were:

35	48	79	37	34	50	53	70	42	69
46	68	33	63	53	45	60	40	64	60
74	57	46	43	46	44	52	54	59	84
56	43	52	61	45	32	73	66	56	70
48	72	49	41	55	59	62	34	53	57

(a) Construct a stem and leaf diagram for these data.

(b) Construct a frequency table, and a cumulative and relative cumulative frequency for these data.

(c) Comment on the shape of the distribution of data.

4.   Construct a stem and leaf display for the following data (measurements).

2.6,   3.3,   2.4,   1.1,   0.8,   3.5,   1.6,   2.8,   2.6
3.4,   4.1,   2.0,   1.7,   2.9,   1.9,   2.9,   2.5,   5.0

5.   The popularity of automated bank tellers has been steadily increasing since their inception in the early 1970s. Although they are popular as a means of withdrawing cash, bank officials have become concerned about the public's general reluctance to deposit funds through the machines. The table illustrates the problem.

Type of transaction	Number of transactions During 2007 (billions)
Withdrawal	2.35
Deposit	0.59
Transfer or other transaction	0.16

(a)   Construct a relative frequency bar chart for the data.
(b)   Construct a pie chart for the data.

6.   Business is booming in the banking industry. Gross revenues for a named bank grew from K108 billion for the year 2006 to K192 billion for the year 2007. The revenues sources for 2007 as summarised in the following pie chart.

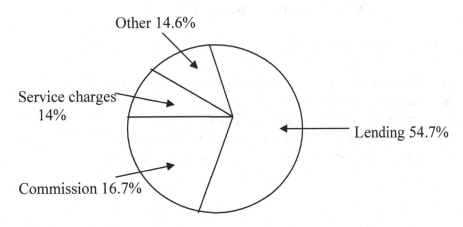

(a) Describe the information being conveyed by the pie chart.

(b) What proportion of the bank's gross revenues for the year 2007 were derived commissions?

(c) How much money did the bank receive from lending?

(d) Construct a component bar chart for the bank's gross revenue for 2007.

7.   Twenty-four economists were asked to project the percentage change in inflation rate between now (may) and September. The following are their projections:

$^+$2%	$^-$5%	+7%	$^+$4%	$^+$0%	$^+$1%	+4%	$^{+3\%}$
$^-$1%	$^-$1%	$^-$2%	$^+$4%	$^-$1%	$^+$5%	-2%	$^+$6%
$^+$6%	$^+$5%	$^+$2%	$^+$8%	$^+$12%	$^+$3%	+6%	$^-$4%

(a) How might you summarise these 24 predictions without using a graph or a table?

8.   The distance traveled (in kilometers) by a Courier Service Motorcycle on 30 trips were recorded by the drive.

24	19	21	27	20	17	17	32	22	26
18	13	23	30	10	13	18	22	34	16
18	23	15	19	28	25	25	20	17	15

(a) Define the random variable, the data type, and the measurement scale.

(b) From the data set, prepare"

i)   An absolute frequency distribution.

ii)   A relative frequency distribution.

iii)   The (relative) less than Ogive

(c) Construct the following graphs.

i)   a histogram of the relative frequency distribution

ii)   the cumulative frequency polygon

(d) From the graphs, read off:

i)   What percentage of trips were between 25 and 30 km long?

ii) What percentage of trips were under 25 km long?

iii) What percentage of trips were 22km or more?

iv) Below which distance were 55% of the trips made?

v) Above which distance were 20% of the trips made?

Chapter Three

NUMERICAL DESCRIPTIVE MEASURES: MEASURES OF CENTRAL TENDENCY

There is a major drawback to using a graphical descriptive method for making inferences about a population from which a sample was selected. Namely, it is difficult to provide a measure of the reliability of the inference. How similar will the graphical description of the sample data be to the corresponding figure for the population? To answer this question, statisticians use one or more numbers to create a mental image of a data set. These numbers, called numerical descriptive measures, are the topic of this and the next chapter.

THE SUMMATION (Σ) SIGN

The summation (Σ) sign implies that all the figures in the data set must be summed. It is necessary to take note of what range of figures are being considered by looking at the value of n (simple size) and i (the first of the figure). To use summation principles, the position of each figure is cardinal. For example, given 5, 6, 10, 20, 15, the respective positions are:

$x_1 = 5$, $x_2 = 6$, $x_3 = 10$, $x_4 = 20$, $x_5 = 15$ (note that position are **not** arranged in any order).

IMPORTANT SUMMATION RULES

1. $\displaystyle\sum_{i=1}^{n} a\, x_i = a \sum_{i=1}^{n} x_i$, where a = constant number

2. $\displaystyle\sum_{i=1}^{n} \frac{x_i}{n} = \frac{1}{n} \sum_{i=1}^{n} x_i$

3. $\displaystyle\sum_{i=1}^{n} \left(\frac{\bar{x}}{x_i} \right) = \left(\frac{\bar{x}}{1} \sum_{i=1}^{n} \frac{1}{x_i} \right)$

4. $\displaystyle\sum_{i=3}^{7} x_i = x_3 + x_4 + x_5 + x_6 + x_7$

5. $\displaystyle\sum_{i=1}^{4} x_i = x_1 + x_2 + x_3 + x_4$

6. $\displaystyle\sum_{i=1}^{4} (x_i)^2 = (x_i)^2 + (x_2)^2 + (x_3)^2 + (x_4)^2$

Example 1

Given $x_1 = 5$, $x_2 = 6$, $x_3 = 10$, $x_4 = 20$, $x_5 = 15$, find:

(a) $\displaystyle\sum_{i=1}^{5} x_i$

(b) $\displaystyle\sum_{i=3}^{5} x_i$

(c) $\displaystyle\sum_{i=3}^{5} (x_i)^2$

(d) $\displaystyle\sum_{i=1}^{5} \left(\dfrac{\bar{x}}{x_i} \right)$

(e) $\displaystyle\sum_{i=1}^{4} 2x_i$

Solution

(a) $\displaystyle\sum_{i=1}^{5} x_i = x_1 + x_2 + x_3 + x_4 + x_5$

$\qquad = 5 + 6 + 10 + 20 + 15$

$\qquad = \underline{56}$

(b) $\displaystyle\sum_{i=3}^{5} x_i = x_3 + x_4 + x_5$

$$= 10 + 20 + 15$$

$$= \underline{45}$$

(c) $\displaystyle\sum_{i=3}^{5} (x_i)^2 = (x_3)^2 + (x_4)^2 + (x_5)^2$

$$= (10)^2 + (20)^2 + (15)^2$$

$$= 100 + 400 + 225$$

$$= \underline{725}$$

(d) $\displaystyle\sum_{i=1}^{5} \left(\frac{\bar{x}}{x_i} \right) = \frac{\bar{x}}{1} \left(\sum_{i=1}^{5} \frac{1}{x_i} \right)$

- $\bar{x} = \dfrac{5 + 6 + 10 + 20 + 15}{5} = \dfrac{56}{5}$

- $\displaystyle\sum_{i=1}^{5} \frac{1}{x_i} = \frac{1}{5} + \frac{1}{6} + \frac{1}{10} + \frac{1}{20} + \frac{1}{15}$

$$= \frac{12 + 10 + 6 + 3 + 4}{60} = \frac{35}{60}$$

- $\displaystyle\sum_{i=1}^{5} \left(\frac{\bar{x}}{x_i} \right) = \frac{56}{5} \div \frac{35}{60} = \frac{56}{5} \times \frac{60}{35} = \frac{3360}{175} = \underline{19.2}$

(e) $\displaystyle\sum_{i=1}^{4} 2\, x_i = 2 \sum_{i=1}^{4} x_i$

$$= 2 (x_1 + x_2 + x_3 + x_4)$$

$$= 2(5 + 6 + 10 + 20)$$

$$= 2 (41)$$

$$= \underline{82}$$

GROUPED AND UNGROUPED DATA SETS

When working with numerical descriptive measures, it is always necessary to distinguish between grouped data and ungrouped data. This is because the formula to be applied in each situation is different. Grouped data is data that has been summarized into classes i.e. frequency table while ungrouped data is data that is not arranged into classes i.e. raw data.

ARITHMETIC MEAN ($\bar{X}$)

The arithmetic mean which simply called the mean is defined as the sum of all scores divided by the total number of scores. It is the most important of all numerical descriptive measurements.

Thus, $\boxed{\bar{x} = \dfrac{\text{Sum of all scores}}{\text{Total number of scores}}}$

CALCULATING THE MEAN: UNGROUPED DATA

This is calculated using the following formula:

$$\boxed{\bar{x} = \frac{\sum x}{n}}$$

Where $\bar{x}$ = mean

$\sum$ = summation of a set of values
x = variable used to represent raw scores
n = the number of scores being considered

Note: we use $\bar{x}$ to denote the sample mean and μ (mμ) to denote the population mean.

Example 2

Given $x_1 = 5$, $x_2 = 6$, $x_3 = 10$, $x_4 = 20$, $x_5 = 15$

Find the mean

Solution

$$\bar{x} = \frac{\sum x}{n} = \frac{5 + 6 + 10 + 20 + 15}{5} = \frac{56}{5} = \underline{11.2}$$

Example 3

Given $x_1 = 5$, $x_2 = 6$, $x_3 = 10$, $x_4 = 20$, $x_5 = 15$ and $f_1 = 4$, $f_2 = 2$, $f_3 = 3$, $f_4 = 1$, $f_5 = 2$. Find the mean

Solution

This is still ungrouped data. The frequencies simply show how many times the given x variable appears. Above data can be presented as follows:

x	f
5	4
6	2
10	3
20	1
15	2
	12

i.e. 5, 5, 5, 5, 6, 6, 10, 10, 10, 20, 15, 15. (now you can see that it is ungrouped data).

$$\bar{x} = \frac{\sum x}{n} = \frac{5\,(4) + 6\,(2) + 10\,(3) + 20\,(1) + 15\,(2)}{12}$$

$$= \frac{20 + 12 + 30 + 20 + 30}{12}$$

$$= \frac{112}{12}$$

$$= \underline{9.33}$$

CALCULATING THE MEAN GROUPED DATA

The mean from a frequency table or grouped data is calculated using the following formula:

$$\bar{x} = \frac{\sum f x}{\sum f} \quad \text{or} \quad \frac{\sum f x}{n}$$

Where $\bar{x}$ = mean

f = frequency

$\sum$ = summation of

x = midpoint of x variables

Note: midpoint (x) = $\dfrac{\text{Lower value} + \text{higher value in class}}{2}$

Example 4

The times when the bank's ATM equipment is not operating as a result of breakage are recorded for a sample of 100 breakdowns and summarized in the following table:

Time (minutes)	Frequency (f)
0 – 10	3
10 – 20	13
20 – 30	30
30 – 40	25
40 – 50	14
50 – 60	8
60 – 70	4
70 – 80	2
80 – 90	1
	100

Find the mean time in minutes

Solution

$$\bar{x} = \frac{\sum f x}{\sum f} = \frac{3400}{100} = 34 \text{ minutes}$$

Class	f	x	fx
0 – 10	3	5	15
10 – 20	13	15	195
20 – 30	30	25	750
30 – 40	25	35	875
40 – 50	14	45	630
50 – 60	8	55	440
50 – 60	4	65	260
70 – 80	2	75	150
80 90	1	85	85
	$\sum f = 100$		$\sum f x = 3400$

$$\bar{X} = \frac{3400}{100} = 34 \text{ minutes}$$

The following steps are followed in the above calculation:

- Compute the midpoint (x) for each class
- Multiply each midpoint by the respective frequency of that class (f x) and sum the product ($\sum f x$).
- Sum the frequency column, $n = \sum f$
- Divide the $\sum f x$ by n or $\sum f$.
- Note: working should always be in a tabular format as given above.

ADVANTAGES OF ARITHMETIC MEAN

1. It is easy to calculate as the only information required is the sum of all observations and the number of observations.
2. It is a well known statistic and it is easily manipulated to calculate other useful statistical measures.
3. It uses the values of all the observations.

DISADVANTAGES OF ARITHMETIC MEAN

1. A few extreme values can cause distortion which makes it unrepresentative of the data set. For example, the salary of four workers A, B, C, D earning K100 000, K150 000, K250 000 and K10 000 000 respectively is K2, 625, 000! This is really unrepresentative of the worker's earnings.

2. When the data is discrete it may produce a value which appears to be unrealistic. For example, the mean number of children per family may be calculated to be 2.86 children!

3. It cannot be read from a graph.

THE MEDIAN

The median of a set of scores is the middle value when the scores are arranged in either ascending or descending order. In other words, the median is the value of the item which lies exactly half way along the data set arranged in order of size.

After first arranging the original data set in order of size, the median will be either of the following:

*   If the number of observations is odd, the median is the number that is exactly in the middle of the list.

*   If the number of observations is even, the median is found by computing the mean of the two middle numbers.

CALCULATING THE MEDIAN: UNGROUPED DATA

The following are the steps:

*   Arrange the data in array
*   Determine the position of the median using

$$\text{Median position} = \frac{n + 1}{2}$$

*   Read the value of the medium from the number list.

Example 5

Given $x_1 = 5$, $x_2 = 6$, $x_3 = 10$, $x_4 = 20$, $x_5 = 15$, find the median

Solution

- Data set is odd

- Rearranging in ascending order gives 5, 6, 10, 15, 20

- Median position $= \dfrac{n+1}{2} = \dfrac{5+1}{2} = \dfrac{6}{2} = 3^{rd}$ position

- Median is therefore 10.

Example 6

Find the median of $x_1 = 5$, $x_2 = 6$, $x_3 = 18$, $x_4 = 10$, $x_5 = 20$, $x_6 = 15$

Solution

- Data set is even

- Rearranging we have 5, 6, 10, 15, 18, 20

- Median position $= \dfrac{n+1}{2} = \dfrac{6+1}{2} = \dfrac{7}{2} = 3.5^{th}$ position

- Median is the average of the 3rd and 4th values $\dfrac{10+15}{2} = 12.5$

CALCULATING THE MEDIAN: GROUPED DATA

The median can be determined either graphically or by calculation. With grouped data, we are unable to determine where the true middle value falls, but we can estimate the median by using a formula and assuming that the median value will be $\dfrac{n}{2}$ value.

Formula:

$$\text{Median} = L + \left(\frac{\frac{n}{2} - f_{m-1}}{f_m} \right) \times c$$

Where L = lower boundary of the median class.

f_{m-1} = sum of the frequencies up to, but not including the median class i.e. cumulative frequency immediately prior to median class.

F_m = frequency of the median class

c = class width or interval

$n = \sum f$

The following are the steps to the computation:

- Determine the location of the median using $\dfrac{n}{2}$

- Construct the cumulative frequency (i.e. less than) column.

- Compare the position of the median $\left(\dfrac{n}{2}\right)$ with the cumulative frequency column to determine which of the classes contains the median . The median class is the class where the cumulative frequency is equal to or exceeds $\dfrac{n}{2}$ for the first time.

- Estimate the value of the median using the formula for grouped data.

Example 7

The times when the bank's ATM equipment is not operating as a result of breakage are recorded for a sample of 100 breakdowns and summarized in the following table:

Time (minutes)	Frequency
0 – 10	3
10 – 20	13
20 – 30	30
30 – 40	25
40 – 50	14
50 – 60	8
60 – 70	4
70 – 80	2
80 – 90	1
	100

Find the median breakdown time in minutes.

Solution

Class	f	cf
0 – 10	3	3
10 – 20	13	16
20 – 30	30	46
30 – 40	**25**	**71**
40 – 50	14	85
50 – 60	8	93
60 – 70	4	97
70 – 80	2	99
80 – 90	1	100
	100	

- Median position = n/2 = 100/2 = 50th position
- From the cumulative frequency column of the table, 50 is first reached in the 4th class which has a c f of 71
- Thus, L = 30, f = 25, f_{m-1} = 46, n = 100, c = 10

- Median = $L + \left(\dfrac{\dfrac{n}{2} - f_{m-1}}{f_m} \right) \times c$

$$= 30 + \left(\dfrac{\dfrac{100}{2} - 46}{25} \right) \times 10$$

$$= 30 + \left(\dfrac{50 - 46}{25} \right) \times 10$$

$$= 30 + \dfrac{4}{25} \times 10$$

$$= 30 + 1.6$$

$$= \underline{31.6}$$

Thus, the median is 31.6 minutes. Note that the median value should always be within the median class and should never be negative. This is used to verify the calculations.

ADVANTAGES OF THE MEDIAN

1.   Its value is not distorted by extreme values open-ended classes or classes of irregular width for example, the median salary of four workers A, B, C, D each earning K100 000, K150 000, K250 000 and K10 000 000 respectively is

$$\frac{K150\ 000 + K250\ 000}{2} = K200\ 000 \text{ which is a reasonable estimate.}$$

2.   All the observations are used to order the data even though only the middle one or two observations are used in the calculation.

3.   It can be illustrated graphically in a very simple way.

DISADVANTAGES OF THE MEDIAN

1. In a grouped frequency distribution, the value of the median within the median class can only be an estimate, whether it is calculated or read from a graph.

2. Although the median is easy to calculate it is difficult to manipulate arithmetically. It is of little use in calculating other statistical measures.

THE MODE

The mode is obtained from a collection of observations by selecting the score that occurs most frequently.

- If the variable is discrete, the mode is that value of the variable which occurs most frequently. This value can be found by ordering the observations or inspecting the sample frequency distribution or its histogram.

- If the variable is continuous, the mode is located in the class with the largest frequency, and its value must intervals to have the same frequency, a set of data may have the modes.

- A set of data with one mode is called unimodal

- A set of data with two modes is called bimodal.

- A set of data with more than two modes is called multimodal

- A set of data with no observation repeated indicates no mode.

CALCULATING THE MODE: UNGROUPED

Example 8

Given $x_1 = 5$, $x_2 = 6$, $x_3 = 10$, $x_4 = 20$, $x_5 = 15$, find the mode

Solution

There is no mode as each value occurs only once!

Example 9

Suppose the data set in example 8 were $x_1 = 5$, $x_2 = 6$, $x_3 = 5$, $x_4 = 10$, $x_5 = 6$, what is the mode now?

Solution

- Ordered list is 5, 5, 6, 6, 10
- The mode is 5 and 6 as they both occur twice hence a bimodal data set.

CALCULATING THE MODE: GROUPED DATA

It is not possible to calculate the exact value of the mode of the original data in a grouped frequency distribution, since information is lost when data are grouped. However, it is possible to make an estimate of the mode. The class with the highest frequency is the modal class.

Formula

$$\text{Mode} = L + \left(\frac{D_1}{D_1 + D_2} \right) X\ C$$

Where L = lower boundary of the modal class.
 D_1 = frequency of modal minus frequency of previous class
 D_2 = frequency of modal class minus frequency of next class i.e. below modal class.
 C = class width of the modal class

The steps to the above computation are as follows:

- Select the class with the highest frequency as the modal class.
- Use the formula to estimate the modal value.

Example 10

The times when the bank's ATM equipment is not operating as a result of breakage are recorded for a sample of 100 breakdowns and summarized.

Time (minutes)	Frequency
0 – 10	3
10 – 20	13
20 – 30	**30**
30 – 40	25
40 – 50	14
50 – 60	8
60 – 70	4
70 – 80	2
80 – 90	1
	100

Compute the modal breakdown time in minutes.

Solution

- Choose class with highest frequency which is 20 – 30.

- Use formula mode $= L + \left(\dfrac{D_1}{D_1 + D_2} \right) \times C$

- Mode $= 20 + \left[\dfrac{30 - 13}{(30 - 13) + (30 - 25)} \right] \times 10$

$$= 20 + \left(\frac{17}{17 + 5} \right) \times 10$$

$$= 20 + \left(\frac{17}{22} \right) \times 10$$

$$= 20 + 7.72727272$$

$$= \underline{27.73}$$

Thus, modal breakdown time is 27.73 minutes. Again the mode must fall within the modal class.

ADVANTAGE OF THE MODE

1. it is not distorted by extreme values of the observations

2. it is easy to calculate

3. it can easily be estimated from a graph

DISADVANTAGES OF THE MODE

1. it cannot be used to calculate any further statistic

2. it may have more than one value (although this feature helps to show of the distribution.

THE BEST MEASURE OF CENTRAL TENDENCY

The different averages have different advantages and disadvantages, and there are no objective criterions that determine the most representative average of all data sets. Each researcher has to use his/her own discretion and a set of data.

- The mean is the most familiar average. It exists for each data set, takes every score into account, is affected by extreme scores, and works well with many statistical methods.

- The median is commonly used. It always exists, does not take every score into account, is not affected by extreme values, and is often a good choice if there are some extreme values in a data set.

- The mode is sometimes used. It might not exist, or there may be more than one mode. It does not take into account every score, is not affected by extreme scores and is approximate for data at the nominal level.

- For a data set that is approximately symmetric with one mode, the mean the median and the mode tend to have the same value. For a data set that is obviously asymmetric, it would be good to report both the mean and the median. The mean is relatively reliable, that is, when samples are drawn from the same population, the sample means tend to be more consistent than any the averages. A comparison of the mean and the median can reveal information about skewness.

Finally, if you are asked to comment on a result, you can often give a better answer if you compare several measures. Remember that all these measures of location replace the details of the raw data by one number, which summarizes the details to tell you one characteristic of the distribution. To get a good summary of the data you will need other statistics as well. Meanwhile, work through the progress clinic that follows to cement your understanding of measures of central tendency.

PROGRESS CLINIC THREE

1. The duration of the telephone calls made by an employee of PCBF Limited in a month were recorded. The results are shown in the table.

Duration (minutes)	Number of class
Under 3	45
3 and under 6	59
6 and under 9	38
9 and under 12	31
12 and under 15	19
15 and under 18	8
18 and above	0

Calculate:

(a) The mean number of calls.
(b) The median number of calls.
(c) The modal number of calls.
(d) The standard deviation of calls.
(e) The coefficient of variation of calls.
(f) Interpret your result.

2. The table below gives the distances (in kilometers) traveled by a Courier Service Vehicle for randomly selected trips.

20	26	30	32	35	37
23	27	31	32	35	37
23	27	31	33	36	38
25	27	31	34	37	40
25	30	32	34	37	44

(a) Using class interval of width 5 units, construct a less than cumulative frequency distribution of the above data. Let 20 units be the lower limit of the smallest class.

(b) For the grouped data of question (a), calculate:

(i) Mean, median and modal distances.
(ii) The inter quartile range.
(iii) Coefficient of variation.
(iv) Coefficient of skew ness.

3. The following data represents the percentage scores obtained by 20 students in a BF260 test at PCBF.

| 26 | 33 | 24 | 11 | 08 | 35 | 39 | 16 | 28 | 26 |
| 34 | 41 | 20 | 27 | 29 | 19 | 29 | 25 | 45 | 50 |

(a) Construct a stem and leaf display for the test results.
(b) Find, using the display, the mode, median and mean scores.
(c) How many students scored above 50%?
(d) What percentage scored between 20 and 39%?

4. (a) If $x_1 = 2$, $x_2 = 3$, $x_3 = 5$, $x_4 = 3$, $x_5 = 6$ and $x_6 = 8$. All the values of x are equally likely.
(i) Give the mode of these values.
(ii) Give the median of these values

(iii) Give $\sum_{i=2}^{5} xi^3$

(iv) Give $\sum_{i=2}^{5} \dfrac{\overline{x}}{xi}$

(v) Give $\sum_{i=2}^{5} 2 \dfrac{1}{xi}$

(b) You are given the following observations $x_1 = 1$, $x_2 = 2$, $x_3 = 3$, $x_4 = 4$, $x_5 = 5$, with the corresponding frequencies $f_1 = 3$, $f_2 = 4$, $f_3 = 5$, $f_6 = 6$.

(i) Give the mode, median, mean and the total observations.

(ii) Write down the cumulative frequency distribution and use it to find the median. Compare the two median values obtained.

5. In each of the following list and briefly explain which measure of central tendency is more appropriate.

(a) To determine the average salary at a bank.
(b) To determine which size of shoes should be produced the most by a shoe manufacturing company.

(c) To determine the average percentage score in a BF 260 test.
(d) To determine the average number of children per family in a given locality.
(e) What are the advantages and disadvantages of the mean, mode and median as measures of central tendency?

6. Given the following data set 5, 9, 6, 3, 7 compute

(a) $\sum\limits_{i=1}^{n} x_i$

(b) $\sum\limits_{i=1}^{n} x_i^2$

(c) $\left(\sum\limits_{i=1}^{n} x_i \right)^2$

(d) $\sum\limits_{i=1}^{4} \bar{x}_i$

(e) Suppose there was a mistake on the figure 6, it should have been 19, compute

$$\sum\limits_{i=2}^{4} \bar{x}_i.$$

(f) One of the principal properties of the mean is the fact that the sum of deviations from the mean of an ungrouped data set is equal to zero. Prove this by using the data set 5, 9, 6, 3, 7.

7. Of the ten different tests that a student wrote during the semester, the following were her results (%): 76, 38, 48, 59, 82, 60, 72, 50, 42, 42.

Find:

(a)   The mean percentage score.
(b)   The median percentage score
(c)   The modal score
(d)   Range score.

Chapter Four

NUMERICAL DESCRIPTIVE MEASURES: MEASURES OF DISPERSION (VARIABILITY) AND RELATIVE STANDING

In the previous chapter, we defined ways of describing distributions by calculating measures of central tendency (location). However, one value of a measure can represent several sets of data. Data sets may have the same mean, median and mode yet different in many respects. So we need another number to show the difference, and this number is called a measure of dispersion. It describes the way in which the observations are "spread" about the "center" i.e. it is a measure of the variability of data.

Consider the following groups of data

Data A   65, 66, 67, 68, 71, 73, 74, 77, 77, 77
Data B   42, 54, 58, 62, 67, 77, 77, 85, 93, 100

The averages computed are:

Mean (data A) = $\dfrac{715}{10}$ = 71.5

Mean (data B) = $\dfrac{715}{10}$ = 71.5

- Median (data A) = 72
- Median (data B) = 72
- Mode (data A) = 72
- Mode (data B) = 72

Note: Although there is no difference in the computed averages between the two data sets the scores of data B, are much more widely scattered than the scores for data A.

There are several different measures of dispersion. The most important of these described in this chapter are:

- Range
- Quartile deviation
- Mean deviation
- Standard deviation and variance
- Coefficient of skewness
- Coefficient of variation

THE RANGE (R)

The range of a distribution is the difference between the values of the largest and the smallest observations in the set of data. Thus, the range as a rough measure of spread depends only on the maximum and minimum observation.

CALCULATING THE RANGE: UNGROUPED DATA

- If the data is given in the form of a simple frequency distribution, the range is the difference between the largest and smallest values of the variable.

Range = maximum value – minimum value

Example 1

The daily withdraws from personal accounts at a named bank was recorded for a week as summarized below:

Day	Amount withdrawn
Monday	K20 000 000
Tuesday	K18 000 000
Wednesday	K 7 000 000
Thursday	K10 000 000
Friday	K13 000 000
Saturday	K15 000 000
Sunday	K 4 000 000

Find the range withdrawal for the branch

Solution

- Maximum withdrawal = K20 000 000
- Minimum withdrawal = K4 000 000
- Range = K20 000 000 – K4 000 000 = K16 000 000

Interpretation: K16 000 000 separates the smallest withdrawal from the largest withdrawal for the branch.

CALCULATING THE RANGE: GROUPED DATA

If the data is given in the form of a grouped frequency distribution, the range is the difference between the highest upper class boundary and the lowest lower class boundary.

> Thus, range = upper limit (highest class) – lower limit (lowest class

Example 2

The following frequency table summarizes the net monthly earnings of selected workers at friendly micro-finance institution located in Lusaka.

Salary K'000	Number of workers
500 and under 1000	15
100 and under 1500	10
1500 and under 2000	7
2000 and under 2500	4
2500 and under 3000	2
3000 and under 3500	1
3500 and under 4000	1
4000 and under 4500	0
	40

Compute the range of monthly salaries at the financial institution.

Solution

- Upper limit (highest class) = K4500 000
- Lower limit (lowest class) = K500 000
- Range = K4500 000 – K500 000 = K4000 000

ADVANTAGES OF THE RANGE

1. it is easy to understand
2. it is simple to calculate
3. it is a good measure for comparison as it spans the whole distribution.

DISADVANTAGES OF THE RANGE

1. it uses only two of the observations and so can be distorted by extreme values
2. it does not indicate any concentrations of the observations
3. it cannot be used in calculating other functions of the observations.

QUARTILE DEVIATION (QD)

The quartile deviation (QD) is half the difference between the third quartile (Q_3) and the first quartile (Q_1) and for this reason it is often called the **Semi-Inter-quartile Range** (SIQR). Quartiles divide the data into 4 equal parts. The first quartile (Q_1) is a value such that 25% of the observations and smaller, and the third quartile (Q_3), is the value such75% of the observations are smaller.

CALCULATING THE QUARTILE DEVIATION: UNGROUPED DATA

To calculate the quartile deviation, we must order the set of observations first, so this measure of dispersion is related to the median. In fact the median is the second quartile (Q_2) and represents 50% of the observations on either side.

- For data set whose number of observations are divisible by 4, the quartiles are found by computing the average of the relevant observations.
- However, if the data set has the number of observations not divisible by 4, the quartiles a picked directly?
- Position of quartile is given by $Q_j = \dfrac{jn + 2}{4}$ or $\dfrac{j(n+1)}{4}$

Example 3

The daily withdrawals from personal accounts at a named bank was recorded for a week as summarized below:

Day	Amount withdrawal K'000
Monday	20 000
Tuesday	18 000
Wednesday	7 000
Thursday	10 000
Friday	13 000
Saturday	15 000
Sunday	4 000

Compute the following:

(a) inter-quartile range of withdrawals
(b) quartile deviation of withdrawals

Solution

- Ordered data in thousand of Kwacha becomes: 4000, 7000, 10 000, 13 000, 15 000, 18 000, 20 000

- Position $Q_1 = \dfrac{1(7) + 2}{4} = 2.25$

- Value $Q_1 = 7000 + 0.25(10\ 000 - 7000) = \underline{7750}$

- Position $Q_3 = \dfrac{3(7) + 2}{4} = 5.75$

- Value $Q_3 = 15\ 000 + 0.75(18\ 000 - 15\ 000) = 17250$

(a) Inter-quartile range $= 17250 - 7750 = 9500$

(b) Quartile deviation $= \dfrac{17250 - 7750}{2} = 4750$

- Thus, inter-quartile range is K9500 000 while the quartile deviation is K4 750 000.

CALCULATING THE QUARTILE DEVIATION: GROUPED DATA

The quartile deviation and hence the inter-quartile range for a grouped data can be calculated using the following formula:

$$Q_D = \left[\left(L + \left(\dfrac{\dfrac{3n}{4} - f_{m-1}}{f_{Q3}} \right) \times C \right) - \left(L + \left(\dfrac{\dfrac{n}{4} - f_{m-1}}{f_{Q1}} \right) \times C \right) \right] \div 2$$

The above formula simply states that Q_D is the difference between Q_3 and Q_1 divided by 2.

The following are the steps to the computation:

- Determine the position of the quartile using: Position $Q_j = \dfrac{jn}{4}$

- Construct the cumulative frequency column.
- Compare the position of the quartile with the cumulative frequencies to determine which one of the classes contains the quartile. It will be the classes where the cumulative frequency is equal to or exceeds the position for the first time.

- Assume that the frequencies in the quartile class are evenly distributed, and estimate the value of the quartile (fractile) using the quartile formula.

Alternative formula for determining quartiles is:

$$L + \frac{R}{f} \times C$$

Where L = lower limit of the quartile class
  f = frequency of occurrences of the quartile class
  C = class width of the quartile class
  R = quartile member less the cumulative frequency above the quartile class.

Example 4

The following table summarizes the net monthly earnings for selected workers at friendly micro-finance institution located in Lusaka

Salary K'000	Number of workers
500 but under 1000	8
1000 but under 1500	15
1500 but under 2000	10
2000 but under 2500	7
2500 but under 3000	4
3000 but under 3500	2
3000 but under 4000	1
4000 but under 4500	1
	48

Compute the following:

(a) inter-quartile range
(b) quartile deviation

Solution

The table including cumulative frequency is as follows:

Salary K'000	f	cf
Less than 500	8	8
500 – 1000	15	23
1000 – 1500	10	33
1500 – 2000	7	40
2000 – 2500	4	44
2500 – 3000	2	46
3000 – 3500	1	47
3500 – 4000	1	48
4000 – 4500	0	48
	48	

- position $Q_1 = \dfrac{1n}{4} = \dfrac{1}{4} \times 48 = 12^{th}$ value

$$\text{Using } Q_1 = L + \left(\frac{\dfrac{1n}{4} - f_{m-1}}{f_{Q1}} \right) \times C$$

$$= 500 + \left(\frac{\dfrac{1(48)}{4} - 8}{15} \right) \times 500$$

$$= 500 + \frac{(12 - 8)}{15} \times 500$$

$$= 500 + 133.33$$

$$= \underline{K633.33}$$

- Position of $Q_3 = \dfrac{3n}{4} = \dfrac{3(48)}{4} = 36^{th}$ value

$$Q_3 = 1500 + \left(\frac{\dfrac{3(48)}{4} - 33}{7} \right) \times 500$$

$$= 1500 + \frac{3}{7} \times 500$$

$$= \underline{K1714.29}$$

(a) Inter-quartile range = 1714.29 – 633.33 = 1080.96 i.e. <u>K1,080,960</u>

(b) quartile deviation = $\dfrac{Q_3 - Q_1}{2}$

$$= \frac{1714.29 - 633.33}{2}$$

$$= 540.48 \text{ i.e. } K540, 480$$

- Using alternative formula:

$$L + \frac{R}{f} \text{ X C}$$

$$Q_1 = 500 + \frac{(12 - 8)}{15} \text{ X } 500 = 633.33$$

$$Q_3 = 1500 + \frac{(36 - 33)}{7} \text{ X } 500 = 1714.29$$

- Inter-quartile range 1714.29 – 633.33 = 1080.96

- Quartile deviation = $\dfrac{1714.29 - 633.33}{2}$ =K540.48

As calculated earlier

Note: The values for quartiles can also be determined graphically by making use of the cumulative frequency curve (Ogive). All that is needed is to locate the position of the quartile on the y-axis and read off the value from the x-axis.

ADVANTAGES OF QUARTILE DEVIATION

1. The calculations are simple and quick to do.
2. It covers the distorted by extreme values
3. It can be illustrated graphically.

DISADVANTAGES OF QUARTILE DEVIATION

1. The lower and upper 25% of the observations are not used in the calculation so it may not be representative of all the data.

2. Although it is related to the median, there is no direct arithmetic connection between the two.

3. It cannot be used to calculate any other functions of the data.

MEAN DEVIATION (MD)

Another measure of dispersion is the deviation. This is a measure of the average amount by which the values in a distribution differ from the arithmetic mean.

CALCULATING THE MEAN DEVIATION: UNGROUPED DATA

The MD for ungrouped data set is calculated using the following formula:

$$MD = \frac{\sum |x - \bar{x}|}{n}$$

Where n = number of items in the data set.
$\sum$ = summation
| | = absolute values i.e. ignoring negatives

$\sum |x - \bar{x}|$ = sum of the differences between the mean and the x variable.

The steps for the computation are as follows :

*   Calculate the arithmetic mean $(\bar{x})$ of the data set.

*   For each x, find $x - \bar{x}$

*   Now find $|x - \bar{x}|$ for each x.

*   Find the mean of the quantities in the above step, i.e. add them up $(\sum |x - \bar{x}|)$

Example 5

Refer to data set on personal accounts withdrawals at a branch which is reproduced here:

Day	Amount withdrawn (K'000)
Monday	20 000
Tuesday	18 000
Wednesday	7 000
Thursday	10 000
Friday	13 000
Saturday	15 000
Sunday	4 000
	87 000

Compute the mean deviation of withdraws.

Solution

$$\bar{x} = \frac{\sum x}{n} = \frac{2000 + 18000 + 7000 + 10000 + 13000 + 15000 + 4000}{7}$$

$$= \frac{87000\ 000}{7}$$

$$= \underline{K12,\ 428,571.43}$$

X	$(x - \bar{x})$	$|x - \bar{x}|$
20 000 000	7 571 428.57	7 57 428.57
18 000 000	5 571 428.57	5 571 428.57
7 000 000	¯5 428 571.43	5 428 571.43
10 000 000	¯2 428 571.43	2 428 571.43
13 000 000	571 428.57	571 428.57
15 000 000	2 571 428.57	2 571 428.57
4 000 000	¯8 428 571.43	8 428 571.43
	¯0.01	32571428.57

$$MD = \frac{32571428.57}{7}$$

$$= K4,653,061.22$$

Calculating the mean deviation: Grouped Data

$$MD = \frac{\sum f|x - \bar{x}|}{n}$$

Where $|x - \bar{x}|$ = difference between each value (x) in the distribution and the mean of the distribution. When calculating the mean deviation for grouped data the deviation should be measured to the mid-point of each class.

f = frequency
| | = all differences are taken as positive.

The steps for calculating the mean deviation from a grouped frequency distribution are as follows:

- Calculate the arithmetic mean of the distribution

- Determine the deviation of each midpoint from the mean $(\bar{x})$ without regard to the algebraic sign: $|x - \bar{x}|$.

- Multiply the absolute deviation in each class by the frequency of that class:

  $f|x - \bar{x}|$

- Add the absolute values of the deviations: $\sum f|x - \bar{x}|$.

- Divide the sum by the number of values (n).

ADVANTAGES OF THE MEAN DEVIATION

1. It uses all the observations in the set of data
2. It is directly related to the mean, i.e. a measure of location.
3. It is useful for simple comparisons between sets of data.

DISADVANTAGES OF THE MEAN DEVIATION

1. Absolute values are difficulty to manipulate arithmetically

2. It is not used in any further statistical analysis.

Example 6

The net monthly salaries of selected employees at a named institution were recorded and summarized in the following table:

Salary K'000	Number of workers
0 – 500	8
500 – 1000	15
1000 – 1500	10
1500 – 2000	7
2000 – 2500	4
2500 – 3000	2
3000 – 3500	1
3500 – 4000	1
4000 – 4500	0
	48

Compute the mean deviation of salaries

Solution

Salary	f	x (mid point)	Fx	$\lvert x - \overline{x} \rvert$	$f \lvert x - \overline{x} \rvert$
0 – 500	8	250	2000	989.58	7916.64
500 – 1000	15	750	11250	489.58	7343.7
1000 – 1500	10	1250	12500	10.42	104.2
1500 – 2000	7	1750	12250	510.42	3572.94
2000 – 2500	4	2250	9000	1010.42	4041.68
2500 – 3000	2	2750	5500	1510.42	3020.84
3000 – 3500	1	3250	3250	2010.42	2010.42
3500 – 4000	1	3750	3750	2510.42	2510.42
4000 - 4500	0	4250	0		0.00
	48		59500		30520.84

- Mean $= \dfrac{\sum f x}{\sum f} = \dfrac{59500}{48} = $ K1239.58

- MD $= \dfrac{\sum f \lvert x - \overline{x} \rvert}{n} = \dfrac{30520.84}{48} = $ K635.85 $= $ <u>K635, 850</u>

THE STANDARD DEVIATION (SD)

A standard deviation (SD) is a statistical measure which expresses the average deviation about the mean in the original units of the random variable (i.e. in squared units of measure).

CALCULATING THE STANDARD DEVIATION: UNGROUPED DATA.

The standard deviation for ungrouped data can be computed using any of the following:

$$SD = \sqrt{\frac{\sum (x - \bar{x})^2}{n - 1}} \quad \ldots \ldots \ldots \ldots \text{Mathematical formula}$$

Or

$$SD = \sqrt{\frac{n(\sum x^2) - (\sum x)^2}{n(n - 1)}} \quad \ldots \ldots \ldots \ldots \text{Computational formula}$$

The following steps are followed when using the mathematical formula:

- Compute the arithmetic mean $(\bar{x})$.

- Subtract the mean from each data value: $(x - \bar{x})$

- Square each difference: $(x - \bar{x})^2$

- Sum the squared differences: $\sum (x - \bar{x})^2$

- Calculating the average by dividing the sum by $(n - 1)$. Division by $(n - 1)$ is to correct the bias in estimating the population standard deviation using the sample standard deviation

- The standard deviation is the square root of this total.

Note: The standard deviation for ungrouped data can also be calculated using the following formula:

$$SD = \sqrt{\frac{\sum x^2}{n} - \bar{x}^2}$$

Example 7

Refer to data set on personal accounts withdrawals at a branch which reproduced here

Day	Amount withdrawal K'000
Monday	20 000
Tuesday	18 000
Wednesday	7 000
Thursday	10 000
Friday	13 000
Saturday	15 000
Sunday	4 000
	87 000

Compute the standard deviation of cash withdrawals at a branch in a week.

Solution

- $\bar{x} = \dfrac{\sum x}{n} = \dfrac{87\,000\,000}{7} = K12,428,571.43$

- $n = 7$

X	$(x - \bar{x})$	$(x - \bar{x})^2$
20 000 000	7 571 428.57	57 326 530 590 000
18 000 000	5 571 428.57	31 040 816 310 000
7 000 000	⁻5 428 571.43	29 469 387 770 000
10 000 000	⁻2 428 571.43	5 897 959 191 000
13 000 000	571 428.57	326 530 610 600
15 000 000	2 571 428.57	6 612 244 891 000
4 000 000	⁻8 428 571.43	71 040 816 350 000
		201 714 285 700 000

$$SD = \sqrt{\dfrac{201\,714\,285\,700\,000}{7-1}}$$

$$= \sqrt{33,619,047,620,000}$$

$$= \underline{K5,798,193.48}$$

Note: Care must be exercised when working with huge numbers like the example above where the calculator will always give you figures in scientific notation. These have to be converted into decimal notation. Alternatively, you can work with small number by taking 20 000 000 to be 20 and taking care of the million in your final answer.

CALCULATING THE STANDARD DEVIATION: GROUPED DATA

If data have been grouped into a frequency distribution, each class is represented by its midpoint (x) and the standard deviation is calculated using either of the following:

$$SD = \sqrt{\frac{\sum f(x - \overline{x})^2}{n-1}} \quad \ldots\ldots\ldots\ldots\ldots\ldots\ldots\text{Mathematical formula}$$

Or

$$SD = \sqrt{\frac{n(\sum f x^2) - (\sum f x)^2}{n(n-1)}} \quad \ldots\ldots\ldots\ldots\ldots\ldots \text{Computation formula}$$

Where x = midpoint of each class
f = frequency
n = sample size

Example 8

The net monthly salaries of selected employees at a named institution were recorded and summarized as follows:

Salary K'000	Number of workers
Less than 500	8
500 – 1000	15
1000 – 1500	10
1500 – 2000	7
2000 – 2500	4
2500 – 3000	2
3000 – 3500	1
3500 – 4000	1
4000 – 4500	0
	48

Compute the standard deviation of monthly salaries

Solution

Salaries	f	x	f x	$(x - \bar{x})^2$	$f(x - \bar{x})^2$
0 – 500	8	250	2000	979 268. 5764	834 148.611
500 – 1000	15	750	11250	239 688. 5764	3 595 328.646
1000 – 1500	10	1250	12500	108.5764	1 085. 764
1500 – 2000	7	1750	12250	260 528.5764	1 823 700.035
2000 – 2500	4	2250	9000	1 020 948.576	4 083 794.306
2500 – 3000	2	2750	5500	2 281 368.576	4 562 737.153
3000 – 3500	1	3250	3250	4 041 788.576	4 041 788. 576
3500 – 4000	1	3750	3750	6 302 208.576	6 302 208.576
4000 - 4500	0	4250	0	9 062 628.576	0.00
	48		59500		32 44 791.67

$$\bar{x} = \frac{\sum fx}{\sum f} = \frac{59500}{48} = 1239.58$$

$$SD = \sqrt{\frac{\sum f(x - \bar{x})^2}{n - 1}} = \sqrt{\frac{32\ 244\ 791.67}{47}} = 828.29$$

ADVANTAGES OF THE STANDARD DEVIATION

1. It uses all the observations
2. It is closely related to the most important and commonly used measure of location, i.e. the mean.
3. It is easy to manipulate arithmetically
4. It is used for further statistical analysis.

DISADVANTAGES OF THE STANDARD DEVIATION

1. It is rather complicated to define and calculate
2. Its value can be distorted by extreme values

THE VARIANCE (S^2)

The variance is the square of the standard deviation. The variance takes every observation into account and it is based on an average deviation from the central value.

CALCULATING VARIANCE: UNGROUPED DATA

The variance for ungrouped data can be calculated using either of the following formula:

$$S^2 = \frac{\sum (x - \bar{x})^2}{n - 1} \quad \dots\dots\dots\dots\dots\text{Mathematical formula}$$

or

$$S^2 = \frac{\sum x^2 - n(\bar{x})^2}{n - 1} \quad \dots\dots\dots\dots\text{Computation formula}$$

- The steps when using the mathematical formula are as follows:
- Compute the sample mean

- Find the squared deviation of each observation from the sample mean. Since $\sum(x - \bar{x}) = 0$, the deviation must first be squared to avoid the plus and minus deviations canceling each other: $(x - \bar{x})^2$.

- Sum the squared deviations: $\sum(x - \bar{x})^2$
- Compute variance by dividing the average squared deviations by $(n - 1)$.

Example 9

Refer to data set on personal accounts withdrawals at a branch which is reproduced here.

Day	Amount withdrawn K'000
Monday	20 000
Tuesday	18 000
Wednesday	7 000
Thursday	10 000
Friday	13 000
Saturday	15 000
Sunday	4 000

Compute the variance of the data set.

Solution

- Since the standard deviation was already calculated in example 16 to be K5, 798, 193.48 the variance $(S\ 2) = (SD)^2$

$$S\ 2 = (5\ 798\ 193.48)^2$$

$$= \underline{K33,\ 619,047,\ 630,000}$$

CALCULATING VARIANCE: GROUPED DATA

For grouped data, the variance is calculated using either of the following:

$$S^2 = \frac{\sum f(x - \overline{x})^2}{n-1} \quad \dots\dots\dots\dots\dots\text{Mathematical formula}$$

Or

$$S^2 = \frac{\sum f x^2 - n(\overline{x})^2}{n-1} \quad \dots\dots\dots\dots\dots\text{Computation formula}$$

The necessary steps when suing the mathematical formula are as follows:

- Compute the mean for the sample

- Find the squared deviations of the midpoint from the mean for each class interval i.e. $(x - \overline{x})^2$

- Multiply each squared deviation by its class frequency i.e. $f(x - \overline{x})^2$

- Sum the total squared deviations from each class over all classes i.e. $\sum (x - \overline{x})^2$

- The variance is found by dividing the total squared deviation by $(n-1)$.

Example 10

Refer to example 17, data set on net monthly earnings, compute the variance.

Solution

Since the standard deviation has already been calculated to be 828.29, we use this figure to find the variance since $S^2 = (SD)^2 = (828.29)2 = \underline{686\ 064.32}$.

ADVANTAGES OF THE VARIANCE

1. It uses all the observations in the set of data
2. It is directly related to the mean
3. It is easy to manipulate arithmetically

DISADVANTAGES OF THE VARIANCE

1. It is rather complicated to define and calculate.

2. Its value is distorted by extreme values.

COEFFICIENT OF VARIATION (CV)

The standard deviation is an absolute measure of dispersion and is expressed in the units i.e. which the observations are measured. The coefficient of variation (CV) is a relative measure of dispersion, i.e. it is independent of the units in which the standard deviation is expressed. The coefficient of variation is mainly used to compare two or more sets of data with different means, sample sizes or measurement units. The lower the CV, the lower the dispersion/variability.

CALCULATING THE COEFFICIENT OF VARIATION

The coefficient of variation is calculated by expressing the standard deviation as a percentage of the mean, regardless of whether, we have ungrouped or grouped data.

$$CV = \frac{SD \times 100}{\bar{X}}$$

Where SD = standard deviation

$\bar{x}$ = mean

Example 20

Refer to example 17, data on net monthly earnings and compute the coefficient of variation.

Solution

$$CV = \frac{SD \times 100}{\overline{X}}$$

$SD = 828.29$

$\overline{X} = 1239.58$

$$= \frac{828.29 \times 100}{1239.58}$$

$$= \underline{66.87\%}$$

Interpretation: If we had another data set with a CV less than 66.87%, we would conclude that the second data set is less variable i.e. more consistent.

ADVANTAGES OF COEFFICIENT OF VARIATION

1.   It is easy to calculate provided the mean and the standard deviation are known .

2.   It is a percentage or relative measure of dispersion hence unaffected by changes in absolute values or units of measurements.

DISADVANTAGES OF COEFFICIENT OF VARIATION

1.   It does not make sense for a single data set.
2.   It is not used in further statistical analysis.

COEFFICIENT OF SKEWNESS (CS)

Skewness is the asymmetric of the frequency distribution curve. It shows whether data is tilted towards the left or right of the centre or concentrated at, the centre.

Frequency distribution may be categorized into the following:

- The distribution is symmetrical if the mean = median = mode

- The distribution is positively skewed, if the mean > median > mode i.e. mean is greater than the median greater than the mode.
- The distribution is negatively skewed, if the mean > median > mode i.e. mean is less than the median less than the mode.
- Thus, the (+) or (-) must always be reported when calculating skewness.

CALCULATING THE COEFFICIENT OF SKEWNESS

The coefficient of skewness can be calculated using either Pearson's first or second coefficient of skewness as follows:

$$\text{Pearson's First Coefficient of Skewness} = \frac{\text{Mean} - \text{Mode}}{\text{Standard Deviation}}$$

Or

$$\text{Pearson's Second Coefficient of Skewness} = \frac{3 \,(\text{Mean} - \text{Median})}{\text{Standard Deviation}}$$

The more skewness distribution, the more spread out are measures of location.

Example 11

Refer to example 17 data set on net monthly earnings but assume that the median is 1241.42, calculate the coefficient of skewness and interpret your result.

Solution

Since the mean = 1238.58, standard deviation = 828.29 and the median = 1241.42, we can use Pearson's second coefficient of skewness formula:

$$CS = \frac{3\,(\text{mean} - \text{median})}{\text{Standard devotion}} = \frac{3\,(1238.58 - 1241.42)}{828.58}$$

$$= \frac{3\,(-2.84)}{828.58} = {}^{-}0.01$$

Interpretation: Data set is negatively skewed i.e. the mean is less than the median.

ADVANTAGES OF SKEWNESS

1. It is the only measure of dispersion
2. It is to calculate provided other measures are known.

DISADVANTAGES

1.   It can be complicated to calculate especially where measures are not known.
2.   It is not easily manipulated mathematically

PERCENTILES AND FRACTILES: AN ADDENDUM

- Percentiles divide the data into 100 equal parts and each percentile (P_j) is a value such that j% of the observations are smaller. The value of j will be between 1% and 100%.
- A fractile is a value that occupies a specific position, such as the median. The median is the middle quartile (Q_2). The exact location must therefore be determined before the value can be calculated.

CALCULATING THE PERCENTILE: UNGROUPED DATA

The position of the percentile for ungrouped data is calculated using the following formula

$$\text{Position } P_j = \frac{jn + 50}{100} \quad \text{or} \quad \frac{j(n+1)}{100}$$

Where Pj = required percentile
        n = sample size
        j = the given percentage

The steps for such a calculation are as follows:

- Arrange the numbers in an array
- Determine the position of the percentile
- Read the value of the percentile from the array.

Example 12

Calculate the 50th percentile for 5,6,10,20,15.

Solution

- Rearrange in ascending order we have 5,6,10,15,20
- Position $\frac{50(5+1)}{100}$ = 3rd

- P_{50} = 10. Note that this is the same calculated earlier on for the median or the same data set. Thus the other name for the 50th percentile is the median. Similarly, the 75th percentile is the upper quartile and 25th percentile is the lower quartile.

CALCULATING THE PERCENTILE: GROUPED DATA

The percentile number for a grouped data is determined using the following formula:

$$\text{Position } P_j = L + \left(\frac{\frac{jn}{100} - f_{m-1}}{f_{pj}} \right) X \ C$$

Where L = lower of class with the percentile

F_{m-1} = cumulative frequency of the prior class immediately
f_{pj} = frequency of the percentile class
C = class width of the percentile class

The following steps are followed:

- Determine the position of the percentile number using $\underline{P_j} = \frac{jn}{100}$

- Construct the cumulative frequency column.
- Compare the position of the percentile with the cumulative frequencies to determine which one of the classes contains the percentile. It will be the class where the cumulative frequency is equal to or exceeds the position for the first time.
- Assume that the frequencies in the percentile class are evenly spread and estimate the value of the percentile using the percentile formula.

Example 13

The branch manager conducted a survey of the number of days customer complaints lodge with the branch took to be addressed by members of staff. The results are summarized below.

Days	Frequency	Cumulative frequency
0.5 – 3.5	32	32
3.5 – 6.5	108	140
6.5 – 9.5	67	207
9.5 – 12.5	28	235
12.5 – 15.5	14	249
15.5 – 18.5	6	255
	255	

Calculate the 85th percentile i.e. P_{85}

Solution

- Position of P_{85} $= \underline{jn} = \underline{85\ (255)} = 216.75$
  $\qquad\qquad\qquad 100 \qquad\ 100$

- From the cumulative frequency column, this occurs in the interval 9.5 – 12.5, with C = 3, f_{pj} = 28, fm – 1 = 207 n = 255
- Using the formula:

$$P_j = L + \left(\frac{\dfrac{jn}{100} - f_{m-1}}{f_{pj}} \right) \times C$$

$$= 9.5 + \left(\frac{\dfrac{85\ (255)}{100} - 207}{28} \right) \times 3$$

$$= 9.5 + \left(\frac{9.75}{28} \right) \times 3$$

$$= \underline{10.54\ days}$$

Example 14

The following table is summary of the heights of employees at a named bank:

Height (cm)	Number of employees
160 but under 165	7
165 but under 170	11
170 but under 175	17
175 but under 180	20
180 but under 185	16
185 but under 190	9
	80

Using above 95th percentile e table compute the following
(a)   Mean height
(b)   Median height
(c)   Modal height
(d)   The standard deviation
(e)   The variance
(f)   The mean deviation
(g)   The quartile deviation
(h)   The range
(i)   Coefficient of variation
(j)   Coefficient of skewness
(k)   95th pecentile

Solution

Class	f	c f	x	f x	$(x - \bar{x})$	$(x - \bar{x})^2$	$f(x - \bar{x})^2$
160 – 165	7	7	162.5	1137.5	‾13.375	178.890625	1252.234375
165 – 170	11	18	167.5	1842.5	‾8.375	70.14625	771.546875
170 – 175	17	35	172.5	2932.5	‾3.375	11.390625	193.640625
175 – 180	20	55	177.5	3550.0	1.625	2.640625	52.8125
180 – 185	16	71	182.5	2920.0	6.625	43.890625	702.25
185 - 190	9	80	187.5	1687.5	11.625	135.140625	1216.265625
	80			14070.0			4188.75

(a) $\bar{x} = \dfrac{\sum f x}{\sum f} = \dfrac{14070}{80} = 175.875$ cm

(b) Median $\quad = \quad L + \left(\dfrac{\dfrac{n}{2} - f_m - 1}{f_m} \right) X\, C$

$$= \quad 175 + \left(\dfrac{\dfrac{80}{2} - 35}{20} \right) X\, 5$$

$$= \quad \underline{176.25 \text{ cm}}$$

(c) Mode $\quad = \quad L + \left(\dfrac{D_1}{D_1 + D_2} \right) X\, C$

$$= \quad 175 + \left[\dfrac{20 - 17}{(20 - 17) + 20 - 16} \right] X\, 5$$

$$= \quad \underline{177.14 \text{cm}}$$

(d) Standard deviation (SD) $\quad = \quad \sqrt{\dfrac{\Sigma f(x - \bar{x})^2}{n - 1}}$

$$= \quad \sqrt{\dfrac{4188.75}{80 - 1}}$$

$$= \quad \sqrt{\dfrac{4188.75}{79}}$$

$$= \quad \sqrt{3.0221519}$$

$$= \quad \underline{7.28 \text{ cm}}$$

(e) Variance $(S^2) = (SD)^2$

$$= (7.28)^2$$

$$= \underline{53 \text{ cm}}$$

(f) Mean deviation

Class	F	x	$|x - \bar{x}|$	$f|x - \bar{x}|$
160 – 165	7	162.5	13.375	93.625
165 – 170	11	167.5	8.375	92.125
170 – 175	17	172.5	3.375	57.375
175 – 180	20	177.5	1.625	32.5
180 – 185	16	182.5	6.625	106.0
185 - 190	9	187.5	11.625	104.625
	80			48.25

- Mean deviation $= \dfrac{\sum f|x - \bar{x}|}{n} = \dfrac{486.25}{80} = 6.08 \text{ cm}$

(g)   Quartile deviation (QD)

Position $Q_1 = \dfrac{1n}{4} = \dfrac{1(80)}{4} = 20$

$Q_3 = \dfrac{3n}{4} = \dfrac{3(80)}{4} = 60$

$Q_1 = 170 + \left(\dfrac{\frac{1(80)}{4} - 18}{17} \right) X5 = 170.588 \text{ cm}$

$Q_3 = 180 + \left(\dfrac{\frac{3(80)}{4} - 55}{16} \right) X 5 = 180.3125 \text{ cm}$

$Q_D = \dfrac{Q_3 - Q_1}{2} = \dfrac{180.3125 - 170.588}{2} = 4.86 \text{ cm}$

(h)   Range = Maximum limit (highest class) – Minimum limit (lowest class)

= 190 – 160 = 30cm

(i)   CV = S X 100 = $\dfrac{7.28}{}$ X 100 = 4.14%

$$\overline{x} \qquad 175.875$$

(j) $\quad CS = \dfrac{3 \text{ (mean - median)}}{\text{Standard deviation}} = \dfrac{3(175.875 - 176.25)}{7.28} = \underline{^-0.15}$

(k) $\quad P_{95} = 185 + \left[\dfrac{95\,(80)}{100} - 71 \right] \times 5 = \underline{187.78 \text{ cm}}$

NOTE: The Variance can be calculated using any of the following;

Ungrouped Data

$\qquad$ (a) $S^2 = \dfrac{\sum (x - {}^-x)^2}{N}$

$\qquad$ (b) $S^2 = \dfrac{\sum x^2}{N} - {}^-x^2$

$\qquad$ (c) $S^2 = \dfrac{\sum x^2}{N} - \dfrac{\sum x}{n}$

PROGRESS CLINIC FOUR

1. As well as head count, the ages of employees at a company is cardinal to human resource planning. The head of the Human Resources section of a named bank wanted to determine the ages of the 80 randomly selected employees. The following resulted:

160	166	170	173	176	179	181	184
162	166	171	174	176	179	181	185
163	167	171	174	177	179	181	186
163	168	172	174	177	179	182	186
164	168	173	174	177	179	182	187
164	169	173	175	177	180	182	187
164	169	173	175	178	180	183	188
165	169	173	175	178	180	183	188
165	170	173	176	178	181	183	188
165	170	173	176	179	181	183	189

Note: The ages were in years and the survey was conducted when average lifespan was in hundreds!

(d) Using a class interval of 5, construct a frequency and cumulative frequency table.

(e) Using the grouped frequency distribution, calculate:

    i)   the mean age
    ii)   the median age
    iii)   the modal age
    iv)   the standard deviation of the ages
    v)   the coefficient of variation of ages
    vi)   the coefficient of skewness
    vii)   the interquartile range
    viii) the quartile deviation
    ix)   the range

2. The following frequency distribution gives the annual wages of 200 employees at a bank (in thousands Kwacha

Wages	Number of employees
5000 – 5500	4
5500 – 6000	26
6000 – 6500	133
6500 – 7000	35
7000 – 7500	2
	200

(a) Calculate the mean, median and modal wages.
(b) Calculate the quartile deviation of the wages.
(c) Range of the wages

3. (a) Hours of overtime worked in the last quarter by 60 bank employees are as follows:

More than	not more than	Number of employees
0	10	3
10	20	6
20	30	11
30	40	15
40	50	12
50	60	7
60	70	6

Calculate the mean deviation of the data set.

(b) What is the 50th percentile of a given data? What is the other name for a 50th percentile?

4. (a) Given 15, 15, 2, 6, 12, and 100, 0, 0, 2 as two separate measurements from the two variables, compute :

  i) the standard deviation
  ii) the variance
  iii) the inter quartile range
  iv) coefficient of variation and use it to explain which data set shows much variability.

  (b) Compute the standard deviation for data sets with the following characteristics.

  a) $\sum_{i=1}^{n} xi^{2} = 246, \sum_{i=1}^{n} xi = 63, n = 22$

  b) $\sum_{i=1}^{n} xi^{2} = 666, \sum_{i=1}^{n} xi = 106, n = 25$

  c) $\sum_{i=1}^{n} xi^{2} = 76, \sum_{i=1}^{n} xi = 11, n = 7$

  d) $\sum_{i=1}^{n} xi^{2} = 246, \sum_{i=1}^{n} xi^{2}fi = 630, n = 22, \sum_{i=1}^{n} xifi = 10$

5. Seven workdays in June were selected, and the number of machine breakdowns per in the woodworking shop of a furniture company was recorded. This procedure was repeated in August after the firm has replaced ten of its oldest machines. The data are listed here:

June	8	3	0	0	10	4	9
August	0	3	4	11	3	3	2

  (a) Which month exhibits more variability in the number of machines that break down per day as measured by the range? As measured by the standard deviation? In this case, which measure, S^2 or range do you feel better represents the variability of the data sets? Explain.

  (b) Add 3 to each of the numbers of breakdowns per day in June and recomputed S^2 for June. Compare your result to that obtained in part (a). What is the effect on S^2 of adding a constant number to each of the sample measurements?

(c) Multiply each of the numbers of breakdowns per day in June by 3 and recomputed S^2 for June. Compare your result with that obtained in part (a). What is the effect on S^2 of multiplying each sample measurement by a constant?

6. Twelve beauty conscious females who purchased a particular brand of perfume gave the following ratings (based on the 5 – point Likert scale) to each of the two statements concerning brand preferences. The Likert rating scale is as follows:

1 – Strongly disagree
2 – Disagree
3 – Neutral
4 – Agree
5 – Strongly agree

Response ratings to each statement are:

Statement 1	2	2	3	4	2	3	2	1	3	3	2	4
Statement 2	3	3	2	4	3	3	2	4	4	5	3	4

(a) Determine the mean response rating per statement.
(b) Find the standard deviation of response ratings per statement.

(c) Find $\bar{x} \pm 20$ for each statement and explain its meaning.
(d) Compute the coefficient of variation for responses to each statement. On which statement is there less consensus? Explain.

Chapter Five

PROBABILITY

This chapter introduces the basic concepts of probability. It outlines the rules and techniques for assessing probabilities to events. Probability plays a critical role in the theory of statistics. All of us form simple probability conclusions in our daily lives. Sometimes these determinations are based on facts while at other times they are subjective. Probabilities can be assigned to events using the classical approach, the relative frequency approach, or the subjective approach.

Thus, probability may be defined as chance of something happening.

EVENTS, SAMPLE SPACES AND PROBABILITY

1. An experiment is an act or process that leads to a single outcome that cannot be predicted with certainty.

2. A simple event is an outcome of an experiment that cannot be decomposed into a simpler outcome it is a "single outcome" of an experiment.

The following illustrates the meanings of an experiment and simple events:

1. **Experiment**: Toss a coin and observe up face.

   Simple events:

   i) observe a head
   ii) observe a tail

2. **Experiment**: Throw a die and observe an even number.

   Simple events:

   i) Observe a 1
   ii) Observe a 2
   iii) Observe a 3
   iv) Observe a 4
   v) Observe a 5
   vi) Observe a 6

3. **Experiment**: Toss two coins and observe the up faces.

   Simple events:

   (i) Observe H_1, H_2
   (ii) Observe T_1, T_2

(iii)   Observe H_1, H_2
(iv)   Observe T_1, T_2

Where H_1 means" Head on coin 1", H_2 means "Head or coin 2", etc.)

4. An event is a collection of one or more simple events e.g. if the experiment is counting the number of errors on a page of an accountant's ledger, three examples of events are (a) observe no errors, (b) observe fewer than five errors (c) observe more than ten errors. Only the first observe no errors, is also a simple event.

5. The sample space of an experiment is the collection of all its simple events. For example, in the experiment of throwing a die, the six simple events comprise the sample space for the experiment. A sample space is usually represented by way of a Venn diagram

6. The union of two events A and B is the event that occurs if either A and B or Both occur on a single performance of the experiment. We denote the union of events A and B by the symbol A U B.

7. The intersection of two events A and B is the event that occurs if both A and B occur on a single performance of the experiment, we denote A∩B for the intersection of events A and B.

CALCULATING PROBABILITIES

No matter how we assign probabilities to simple events, the probabilities assigned must obey two rules:

1. All simple events probabilities must lie between 0 and 1, inclusive

- Probability of 1 indicates certainty
- Probability of 0 indicates impossibility
- Probability of 0.5 indicates 50% chance.

2. All probabilities of all the simple events in the sample space must sum to 1.

SIMPLE PROBABILITY

Simple probability is calculated using the following formula:

$$\text{Probability of achieving desired result} = \frac{\text{Number of ways of achieving desired result}}{\text{Total number of possible outcomes}}$$

Example 1

Suppose a coin is tossed in the air. What is the probability that it will come down heads?

Solution

- Total number of possible outcomes (sample space) is is "head" or "tail " = 2.
- Total number of ways of achieving desired result (which is "head") = 1
- Probability of head = ½,

Alternatively,

Probability of head $P(H) = \dfrac{Head}{Head + Tail}$ = ½ Or 0.5 or 50%

Example 2

When an unbiased die is thrown, calculate the probability that the outcome of a single throw is:

a) the number 4
b) an event number
c) a number less than 3
d) a number greater than 6
e) a number less than 7

Solution

Sample space = 1, 2, 3, 4, 5, 6.

a) $P(4) = \dfrac{1}{6}$ i.e. one of the six simple events is a number 4.

b) $P(even) = \dfrac{3}{6}$ or ½ i.e. 2, 4, and 6

c) $P(<3) = \dfrac{2}{6}$ or $\dfrac{1}{3}$ i.e. 1, and 2.

d) $P(>6) = 0$ i.e. none

e) $P(<7) = 1$ or 6 i.e. 1, 2, 3, 4, 5 and 6.

COMPLEMENTARY PROBABILITY

The complement of any event A is the event that A does not occur. We denote complement of event A by $\bar{A}$.

$$\text{Note } P(\bar{A}) = 1 - P(\bar{A}), \text{ where A is 'not A'}$$

The complementary rule above is very useful for many probability computations. Team when and how to use it?

Example 3

If there is a 25% chance of PF winning the next general election, use the law of complementary events to calculate the probability of PF not winning the next election?

Solution

P (winning) = 25% = 0.25

P (not wining) = 1 – 0.25 = <u>0.75</u> 0r <u>75%</u>

THE SIMPLE ADDITION or (OR) LAW: MUTUALLY EXCLUSIVE EVENTS

- The simple addition law for two mutually exclusive events, A and B, is as follows:

P (A or B) = P(A) + P(B)

- Mutually exclusive outcomes are outcomes where the occurrence of one of the outcomes excludes the possibility of any of the others happening. In other words, events A and B are mutually exclusive if A ∩ B contains no simple events i.e. $P(A \cap B = 0$

- Examples of mutually exclusive events are:

(a) being male and being female
(b) passing an exam and failing an exam
(c) Being black and being white
(d) Being tall and being short

In all the above, there is only one possibility and no middle possibility.

Example 4

Find the probability of observing a 4 or 5 from a die throw experiment.

Solution

In a die experiment, only one outcome is possible from a total of six. Thus, outcomes are mutually exclusive.

Example 5

The delivery of an item of raw material from a supplier may take up to six weeks from the time the order is placed. The probabilities of the various delivery times are as follows:

Delivery time	Probability
≤ 1 week	0.10
$>1, \leq 2$ weeks	0.25
$> 2, \leq 3$ weeks	0.20
$>3, \leq 4$ weeks	0.20
$> 4, \leq 5$ weeks	0.15
$> 5, \leq 6$ weeks	0.10
	1.00

Calculate the probability that a delivery will take the following times.

      a) two weeks or less
      b) more than three weeks.

Solution

These are mutually exclusive outcomes.

  a) $P (\leq 1$ or $>1, \leq 2$ weeks$) = P(\leq 1$ week $+ P (>, \leq 2$ weeks$)$

$$= 0.10 + 0.25$$

$$= \underline{0.35}$$

  b) $P(> 3, \leq 6$ weeks$) = P (> 3, \leq 4$ weeks$) + > 4, \leq 5$ week$) + P(>5, \leq 6$ weeks$)$

$$= 0.20 + 0.15 + 0.10$$

$$= \underline{0.45}$$

Alternatively, using complementary rule:

P ($\leq$3 weeks = P ($>$2, $\leq$ 3 weeks) + P($>$ 1, $\leq$2 weeks) + P($\leq$ 1 week)

$$= 0.20 + 0.25 + 0.10$$

$$= \underline{0.55}$$

Thus, P($>$ 3 weeks) = 1 – 0.55 = 0.45

THE GENERAL RULE OF ADDITION:NON_MUTUALLY EXCLUSIVE EVENTS

The general rule of addition for two events, A and B, which are not mutually exclusive, is as follows

$$P \text{ (A or B)} = P(A) + P \text{ (B)} - P \text{ (A and B)}$$

Note: Non-mutually exclusive events are those events where, the occurrence of one event does not exclude the possibility of another event occurring e.g. being a male and passing an exam. In such a case P (A $\cap$ B) # 0. This implies the two events have some common elements which must be subtracted in our addition rule to avoid double counting. Thus, P(A and B) represent the common elements to both events A and B and must be subtracted to avoid double counting.

Example 6

Twenty identical discs are marked 1 to 20 and placed in a box, one is drawn at random from a box. Calculate the probability that the number on the disc is:

   (a) a multiple of 2
   (b) a multiple of 5
   (c) a multiple of 2 or 5

Solution

   (a) P (multiples of 2) = P (2,4, 6, 8, 10, 12, 14, 16, 18, 20) = $\underline{10}$ 0r $\underline{0.5}$
    20

   (b) P (multiples of 2 or 5) = P (5, 10, 15, 20) = $\underline{4}$ = $\underline{0.2}$
    20

   (c) P (multiples of 2 or 5) = P(2, 4, 5, 6, 8, 10, 12, 14, 15, 16, 18, 20) 10 and 20 are common elements hence need not be counted twice.

$$P \text{ (2 and 5)} = P \text{ (10 or 20)} = \frac{2}{20} \text{ or } 0.1$$

Using $P \text{ (A or B)} = P \text{ (A)} + P \text{ (B)} - P \text{ (A and B)}$

$P \text{ (multiples 2 or 5)} = P \text{ (multiples of 2)} + P\text{(multiples of 5)} - P \text{ (multiples of 2 and 5)}$

$$= \frac{10}{20} + \frac{4}{20} - \frac{2}{20}$$

$$= \frac{12}{20} \text{ or } 0.6$$

This can be verified from the fact that there will be twelve such discs (2, 4, 5, 6, 8, 10, 12, 14, 15, 16, 18, 20)

Example 7

Calculate the probability of selecting a heart or a queen when one card is drawn at random from a pack of playing cards

Solution

The probability of selecting a heart or a queen is an overlap situation, as the queen of hearts would be included in both events. To avoid including this probability twice, it must be subtracted.

$$P \text{ (any heart)} = \frac{13}{52}$$

$$P \text{ (any queen)} = \frac{4}{52}$$

$$P \text{ (queen of hearts)} = \frac{1}{52}$$

Thus, $P \text{ (heart or queen)} = P \text{ (heart)} + P \text{ (Queen)} - P \text{ (Queen of hearts)}$

$$= \frac{13}{52} + \frac{4}{52} - \frac{1}{52}$$

$$= \frac{16}{52} \text{ or } 0.31$$

Above result can also be confirmed using "normal" counting.

THE SIMPLE MULTIPLICATION OR (AND) LAW: INDEPENDENT EVENTS

The simple multiplication law for two independent events, A and B, is as follows:

$$P (A \text{ and } B) = P (A) \times P (B)$$

Note: P (A and B) = 0 when A and B have mutually exclusive outcomes.

- Independent events are where the outcome of one event in no way affects the outcome of the other events. In other words, events A and B are independent, if the probability of the intersection of A and B equals the product of the intersection of A and B equals the product of the probabilities of A and B:

$$P (A \cap B) = P (A) \times P (B)$$

- Examples of independent events are:

(a) Tossing a coin and throwing a die
(b) Passing a exam and being female
(c) Being a parent and being a manager

Note: independent events can occur at the same time

Example 8

A die is thrown and a coin is tossed simultaneously. What is the probability of throwing a 5 and getting heads on the coin?

Solution

Above are independent events.

- Probability of throwing a 5 is $\frac{1}{6}$
- Probability of a tossed coin coming up heads is ½
- The probability of throwing a 5 and getting heads on a coin is $\frac{1}{2} \times \frac{1}{6} = \frac{1}{12}$

i.e. P(5 and head) = $\frac{1}{6} \times \frac{1}{2} = \frac{1}{12}$

Note: that in probability language "or" is for addition while "and" is for multiplication

THE GENERAL MULTIPLICATION LAW: DEPENDENT EVENTS

The general multiplication rule for two dependent events A and B is as follows:

$$P (A \text{ and } B) = P (A) \times P \left(\frac{B}{A}\right)$$

$$= P (B) \times P \left(\frac{A}{B}\right)$$

- Dependent events or conditional events are events where the outcome of one event depends on the outcome of the others
- Examples include:

(a) passing an exam is conditional upon sitting for that exam
(b) being female is conditional upon being "Human Being"

Note: When A and B are independent events, then $P (B/A) = P (B)$ since, by definition, the occurrence of B (and therefore $P (B)$ does not depend upon the occurrence of A. Similarly $P (A/B) = P (A)$

Example 9

The board of directors of Inefficient Ltd has warned that there is a 60% probability that a factory will be closed down unless its workforce improves its productivity. The factory's mangers, Mr. Careful has estimated that the probability of success in agreeing a productivity deal with the workforce is only 30%. Determine the likelihood that the factory will be closed.

Solution

If outcome A is the shutdown of the factory and outcome B is the failure to improve productivity.

$P (A \text{ and } B) = P(B) \times P(A/B)$

$$= 0.7 \times 0.6 = \underline{0.42}$$

Note: $P (B) = 1 - P (A) = 1 - 0.30 = 0.7$

Thus, the close down is dependent upon failure to improve productivity, so we cannot use the simple multiplication law since events are not independent.

MARGINAL, JOINT AND CONDITIONAL PROBABILITIES UNDER CONDITIONS OF STATISTICAL INDEPENDENCE

The events are statistically independent if the occurrence for one event has no effect on the probability of the occurrence of any other event. i.e. $P(B/A) = P(B)$.

There are three types of probabilities under statistical independence:

(a)   marginal
(b)   joint
(c)   conditional

- A marginal or unconditional probability is the simple probability of the occurrence of an event. In other words, a marginal probability is the probability of any single event occurring e.g. $P(A)$. For example, in a fair coin toss, $P(A) = 0.5$ and $P(T) = 0.5$ that is, the probability of heads equals 0.5 and the probability of tails equals 0.5 this is true for every toss, no matter how many tosses have been made or what their outcomes have been. Thus, the outcome of each toss of a fair coin is an event that is statistically independent of the outcomes of every other toss of the coin

- Thus, marginal probability of event A is written as $P(A)$.

A joint probability is the probability of both event A and event B occurring simultaneously on a given trial of a random experiment. A joint event describes the behaviour of two or more variables simultaneously. It is the intersection of two simple events in a Venn diagram and is written as $P(A \cap B)$.

Thus, the probability of two or more independent events occurring together or in succession is the product of their marginal probabilities. Mathematically, this is stated as:

$$P(A \cap B) = P(A) \times P(B).$$

Where $P(A \cap B)$ = Probability of events A and B occurring together or in succession: this is called joint probability.

$P(A)$ = marginal probability of event A occurring

$P(B)$ = marginal probability of event B occurring.

For example, in terms of a fair coin example, the probability of heads on two successive tosses is the probability of heads on the first toss (H_1) times the probability of heads on the second toss (H_2). That is, $P(H_1, H_2) = P(H_1) \times P(H_2)$
$$= 0.5 \times 0.5$$
$$= \underline{0.25}$$

A conditional probability is the probability of one event A occurring given information about the occurrence of another event B. The essential feature of the conditional probability is that the sample space is reduced to the outcomes describing event B (the given prior event) only, and not all possible outcomes as for marginal and joint probabilities.

Symbolically, conditional probability is written:

P (B/A) read "the probability of event B given that event A has occurred".

Thus, conditional probability is the probability that a second event (B) will occur if a first event (A) has already happened.

For statistically independent events, the conditional probability of event B given that event A has occurred is simply the probability of event B.

$$P (B/A) = P (B)$$

MARGINAL, JOINT AND CONDITIONAL PROBABILITIES UNDER CONDITIONS OF STATISTICAL DEPENDENCE

Statistical dependence exists when the probability of some event is dependent upon or affected by the occurrence of some other event. Here we have conditional, joint and marginal probabilities as well.

The formula for conditional probability under statistical dependence is:

$$P (B/A) = \frac{P (B \cap A)}{P (A)} \text{ or } P (A/B) = \frac{P (A \cap B)}{P (B)}$$

Example 10

The following contingency table shows the company size and industry type from a sample of 150 companies listed on the Lusaka Stock Exchange.

Industry type	Company	size (in million Kwacha turnover)		Row total
	Small (0 ≤10)	medium (10 ≤ 50)	large (≤ 50)	
Mining	0	0	35	35
Banking	9	21	42	72
Service	6	3	1	10
Retail	14	13	6	33
Total column	29	37	84	150

Find the probability of selecting a company from LUSE sample which is large given that the company is known to be a retail company.

Solution

- Let A = event (large company)
- Let B = event (retail company

Then, P (A/B) = $\dfrac{P (A \cap B)}{P (B)}$

$= \dfrac{6}{13}$ = 0.1818 i.e. there are six companies out of 33 retail companies.

Using the formula

- P (A ∩ B) = $\dfrac{6}{150}$ i.e. $\dfrac{6}{33}$ X $\dfrac{33}{150}$ (a joint probability)

- P (B) = $\dfrac{33}{150}$ (a marginal probability)

- P(A) = $\dfrac{6}{33}$

- P (A/B) = $\dfrac{P(A \cap B)}{P(B)}$ = $\dfrac{\frac{6}{150}}{\frac{33}{150}}$ = 0.1818

Note: The key to recognizing a conditional probability is to look for words "given that" or their equivalent. For example, the statement of a conditional probability might read" The probability that A will occur when B occurs" or "the probability that A will occur if B occurs". In each of these cases, you can reword the statement using" given that" instead of "when" or "if". Therefore, both of these statements refer to conditional probabilities.

Example 11

A bank's employees have been classified according to age and salary, as shown in the following table.

Age	SALARY			
	under K2500 000	K2500 000 – K4500 000	over K4500 000	Total
Under 30	32	3	0	35
30 – 45	10	18	21	49
Over 45	1	10	5	16
Total	43	31	26	100

One employee is selected at random, and two events are defined as follows:
   i. The employee is under 30
   ii. The employee's salary is under K2500 000.
   iii. Express each of the following probabilities in words, and find its numerical values:

(a) P (A/B)   (b) P (A/B)   (c) P (A/$\bar{B}$)   (d) P ($\bar{A}$ /B)

Solution

(a) Given that the employees salary is under K2500 000, the probability that the employee is under 30 is:

$$P (A/B) = \frac{P (A \cap B)}{P(B)} = \frac{32/100}{(32 + 10 + 1)/100} = \frac{32}{43} = 0.74$$

Answer could be got directly from the table i.e. 32/43.

(b) Given that the employee is under 30, the probability that the employee's salary is under K2500 000 is :

$$P(A/B) = \frac{P(A \cap B)}{P(B)} = \frac{32/100}{(32 + 3 + 0)/100} = \frac{32}{35} = 0.91$$

(c)   Given that the employee's salary is at least K25000 000, the probability that the employee is under 30 is:

$$P(\bar{B}/A) = \frac{P(A \text{ and } B)}{P(B)} = \frac{(30 + 0)/100}{(31 + 26)/100} = \frac{3}{57} = \underline{0.05}$$

(d)   Given that the employee's salary is under K2500 000, the probability that the employee is at least 30 is:

$$P(A/B) = \frac{P(A \text{ and } B)}{P(B)} = \frac{(10 + 1)/100}{43/100} = \frac{11}{43} = 0.26$$

- The formula for joint probability under conditions of statistical dependence is:

$$P(B \cap B) = P(B/A) \times P(A)$$

- The marginal probabilities under statistical dependence are computed by summing up the probability of all the joint events in which the simple event occurs.

BAYE'S THEOREM

At the beginning of a semester, the college principal may think his college has a good chance of recruiting more students based on last semester's results. However, as the semester progresses, reduced inquiries, will make him alter his prior probabilities of recruiting students. Thus, certain probabilities are altered after people involved get additional information.

The new probabilities are known as **revised** or "**posterior**" probabilities. Because probabilities can be revised as more information is gained, probability theory is more useful in managerial decision making. The origin of the concept of obtaining posterior probabilities with limited information is attributable to the Reverend Thomas Baye (1702 – 1761), and the basic formula for conditional probability under dependence is.

$$P(B/A) = \frac{P(B \cap A)}{P(A)} \quad \text{is called Baye's Theorem.}$$

- Baye's theorem offers a powerful statistical method of evaluating new information and revising our prior estimates (based upon limited information only) of the probability that things are in one state or another. If correctly used, it makes it unnecessary to gather masses of data over long periods in order to make decisions based upon probabilities.

Example 12

Given that P(A∩B) = 0.4 and P(A | B) = 0.8, find P(A).

Solution

Using $P(A | B) = \dfrac{P(A \cap B)}{P(A)}$

$0.8 = \dfrac{0.4}{P(A)}$

Therefore, P(A) = 0.5

Example 13

Are mutually exclusive events also dependent events? Explain.

Solution

Yes. Mutually exclusive events can also be dependent events but not independent events.

Example 14

Given that event A and event B are mutually exclusive with P(B) 0.4 and P(A) = 0.5, find the following probabilities

      (a) P(A⁻)

      (b) P(B⁻)

      (c) P(AUB)

      (d) P(AUB)

      Solution

          (a) 1- 0.5 = 0.5

          (b) 1 – 0.4 = 0.6

          (c) P(A) + P(B) =0.4 + 0.5 = 0.9

          (d) 0 for mutually exclusive events

PROBABILITIES AND EXPECTED VALUES

An expected value (EV) is a weighted average value, based on probabilities. The expected value for a single event can offer a helpful guide for management decisions: a project with a positive EV should be accepted and a project with a negative EV should be rejected.

$$EV = \sum X \, P(x)$$

Example 14

A bank plans to introduce a new product to the market. There is a 0.4 probability that the profit from the product will be K1 billion and a 0.6 probability that the profit will be K2 billion. What is the expected value of the product?

Solution

- Expected value = K1 billion X 0.4 = 400 000 000
- Expected value = K2 billion X 0.6 = 1200 000 000
  - Expected value = K1, 600, 000, 000

Example 15

A supermarket is opening a new store and two sites are available to them: A and B. From past experience, they calculate that the probability of success on site A is 0.8 with an annual profit of K500 000 000. If not successful, the annual loss is estimated at K80 000 000. For site B, the corresponding figures are 0.6 for success with annual profit of K600 000 000 or an annual loss of K120 000 000. Where should the branch be located in order to maximize profits.

Solution

We calculate the expected profit on each site.

Site A

P (success) = 0.8, expectation = 0.8 X 500 000 000

P (failure) = 0.2, expectation = 0.2 X ⁻80 000 000)

Thus, the expectation = K400 000 000 – K16 000 000 = K384 000 000 p.a.

Site B

P (success) = 0.6, expectation = 0.6 X 600 000 000 = 360 000 000
P (failure) = 0.4, expectation = 0.4 X (-120 000 000) = 48000 000
Expected profit   K312 000 000 000 p.a.

Site A should be selected because of the higher expected value. Note that in the above calculation, it has been assumed that the only outcomes are profit or loss.

PERMUTATIONS AND COMBINATIONS

Sometimes items can be selected from a larger group of items where the order in which the items are selected is significant or not significant.

FACTORIAL NOTATION (!)

All computations involving permutation and combination require the use of factorial notation.

The following are standard factorial rules:

1. $0! = 1$
2. $1! = 1$
3. $5! = 5 \times 4 \times 3 \times 2 \times 1$

Further, it should be noted that factorials are subject to normal mathematical operations of multiplication, division, addition and subtraction

Example 16

Simplify the following:

(a) $\dfrac{10!}{3! \, 2!}$

(b) $3! \, 2!$

(c) $\dfrac{10!}{7!}$

Solution

(a) $\dfrac{10!}{3! \, 2!} = \dfrac{10 \times 9 \times 8 \times 7 \times 6 \times 5 \times 4 \times 3 \times 2 \times 1}{3 \times 2 \times 1 \times 2 \times 1}$

$= \dfrac{3628\ 800}{12}$

$$= \underline{302\ 400}$$

(b) $3!\ 2! = 3 \times 2 \times 1 \times 2 \times 1 = \underline{12}$

(c) $\dfrac{10!}{7!} = \dfrac{10 \times 9 \times 8 \times 7 \times 6 \times 5 \times 4 \times 3 \times 2 \times 1}{7 \times 6 \times 5 \times 4 \times 3 \times 2 \times 1}$

$$= 10 \times 9 \times 8$$

$$= \underline{720}$$

Note that normal canceling has been used.

PERMUTATIONS

A permutation is a number of items, selected from a larger group of items, where the order in which the items are selected is **significant**.

The number of permutations of a given size is calculated using the following formula:

$$^nP_r = \dfrac{n!}{(n-r)!}$$

where n = total number of items
r = Number of items per arrangement
! = factorial

COMBINATIONS

A combination is a number of items, selected from a larger group of items where the order in which those items are selected is **not significant**.

The number of combinations of a given size is given by the following formula.

$$^nC_r = \dfrac{n!}{(n-r)!\,r!}$$

where n = total number of items
r = Number of items per arrangement
! = factorial

Example 17

The Board of Directors is to be formed from a group of 10 Senior Managers.

(a) How many different ways can this be achieved?
(b) If the board above consists of Managing Director, Chairman and Secretary, plus one other board member. How many different ways are possible now?

Solution

(a) Four specific candidates will constitute the same board irrespective of the order in which they are chosen, hence combinations rather than permutations are required.

$$^{n}C_r = \frac{n!}{(n-r)!\,r!} \qquad n = 10, r = 4$$

$$^{10}C_4 = \frac{10!}{(10-4)!\,4!} = \frac{10 \times 9 \times 8 \times 7}{4 \times 3 \times 2 \times 1} = \underline{210}$$

(b) Here the order is significant hence a permutation is required.

$$^{n}P_r = \frac{n!}{(n-r)!} \qquad n = 10, \quad r = 4$$

$$^{10}P_4 = \frac{10!}{(10-4)!} = 10 \times 9 \times 8 \times 7 = \underline{5040}$$

Example 18

A class of 15 students is about to sit a statistics examination. They will subsequently be listed in descending order by reference to marks scored. Assume that there are no tied positions with two or more students having the same mark.

Calculate:

a) The number of different possible results for the top three places
b) The number of different possible orderings for the whole class.
c) The number of different possible ways of having three people taking the top three places (irrespective of order).

Solution

(a) The number of different possible orderings for the whole class is:

$$^{15}P_{15} = \frac{15!}{(15-15)!} = \frac{15!}{0!} = 15! = \underline{1,307,674,3680,000}$$

(b) The number of different possible results for the top three is given by the number of permutations of 3 out of 15.

$$^{15}P_3 = \frac{15!}{(15-3)!} = \frac{15!}{12!} = 15 \times 14 \times 13 = \underline{2,730}$$

(c) The number of ways of having three people taking the top three places is given by the combinations of 3 out of 15.

$$^{15}C_3 = \frac{15!}{(15-3)!3!} = \frac{15 \times 14 \times 13}{3 \times 2 \times 1} = \underline{455}$$

SCIENTIFIC CALCULATOR AND PERMUTATIONS AND COMBINATIONS

If the total number of items (n) is large, it becomes a very tedious exercise to carry out the normal multiplications as presented above. Fortunately, scientific calculators have the necessary functions for permutations, combinations and factorials.

Example 19

Simplify

(a) $^{100}P_{10}$ (b) $^{100}C_{10}$

Solution

(a) The following steps are needed:
· Enter 100
· Press shift
· Press ^nC_r function
· Enter 10
· Press = to get the answer.

Using above steps, the display on your calculator should be as follows:

$$^{100}P_{10} = 6.281565096 \times 10^{19}$$

$$= \underline{62,815,650,960,000,000,000}$$

(b) The following steps are needed:
· Enter 100
· Press ^nC_r
· Enter 10
· Press = to get the answer

The display should be as follows:

$$^{100}C_{10} = 1.731030946 \times 10^{13}$$

$$= \underline{17,310,309,460,000}$$

Note: The above steps relate to a specific calculator. You need to know the type of calculator you are using very well.

Example 20

(a) $^{15}C_3$ (b) $^{15}P_{15}$ (c) $^{15}P3$ (d) $^{10}C_4$ (e) $^{10}P_4$

Solution

(a) $^{15}C_3 = 455$
(b) $^{15}P_{15} = 1.307674368 \times 10^{12} = 1,307,674,368,000$
(c) $^{15}P_3 = 2730$
(d) $^{10}C_4 = 210$
(e) $^{10}P_4 = 5040$

These are the same results as calculated earlier.

Example 21

How many different permutations can be formed from all the letter of each of the following words;

(a) Run
(b) Mumba
(c) Look

Solution

(a) $^3P_3 = \dfrac{3!}{(3-3)!} = 3 \times 2 \times 1 = 6$

(b) N= 5, n(m) =2, n(u) = 1, n(b) = 1, n(a) = 1

$$\frac{5!}{3!2!1!1!1!} = 10$$

(c) N = 2, n(o) = 2, n(l) = 1, n(k) = 1

$$\frac{4!}{2!1!1!} = 12$$

Note: In the above example, we count the number of times each letter occurs.

Example 22

Compute the number of permutations of the letters a,b,c and d taken 3 at a time.

Solution

$N = 4, r = 3$

$$^4P_3 = \frac{4!}{(4-3)!} = 4! = 24$$

Example 23

Compute the number of combinations of the letters a,b, c and d taken 3 at a time.

Solution

$N = 4, r = 3$

$$^4C_3 = \frac{4!}{(4-3)!3!} = 4$$

CONCLUDING REMARKS

Probability is a key topic in any statistics syllabus and you have to make sure you understand it. It is the building block to statistical inference which is the ultimate goal of statistical analysis. Probability results can be determined using the Venn diagrams or Tree diagrams. However, for convenient safe, these have not being covered in this chapter. I hope you have enjoyed the topic for once!

PROGRESS CLINIC FIVE

1. Suppose you plan to invest equal amounts of money in each of 5 business ventures. If you have 20 ventures from which to make a selection, how many different samples of 5 ventures can be selected from the 20?

2. The population of the amounts of 500 automobile loans made by a bank last year can be described as follows:

Amount of loan in K' million			
Under 1000	1000 – 3999	4000 – 5999	6000 or more
27	99	298	76

For the purpose of checking the accuracy of the bank's records, an auditor will randomly select one of these loans for inspection i.e. each loan has an equal probability of being selected.

(a) List the simple events in this experiment.
(b) What is the probability that the loan selected will be for K6000 million or more?
(c) What is the probability that the loan will be for less than K4000 million?

3. Refer to question (2) above, in which loan records were being audited. Suppose each of the 500 automobile loans made by the bank last year is now classified according to two characteristics amount of loan and age of loan.

As before an auditor is planning to choose one loan at random for inspection.

	Amount of loan K' million			
	Under 1000	1000 – 3999	4000 – 5999	6000 or more
Length o f loan (months) 12	25	4	0	0
24	2	15	1	0
36	0	23	92	2
42	0	53	93	50
48	0	0	112	24

(a) List the simple events in this experiment.
(b) What is the probability that the loan selected will be for K6000 million or more? Does your answer agree with your answer to part b in question 2?
(c) What is the probability that the loan selected is a 3 year loan for more than K5999 million?
(d) What is the probability that the loan selected is a 3 – or – 4 year loan?
(e) What is the probability that the loan selected is a 42-month loan for K1000 million or more?

4. Businesses that give credit to their customers are inevitably faced with the task of collecting unpaid bills. Suppose a study is conducted of collection remedies used by creditors. As part of the study asked samples of creditors in four towns about how they deal with past-due bills. Their responses are tallied in the table. "Tough actions" included filing a legal action, turning the debts over to a third party such as collection agency, garnishing wages, and repossessing security.

	Kitwe	Ndola	Lusaka	Livingstone
Take tough action early	0	1	5	1
Take tough action late	37	23	22	21
Never take tough action	9	11	6	15

Suppose one of the creditors is selected at random.

  (a) What is the probability that the creditor is from Kitwe or Livingstone?
  (b) What is the probability that the creditor is not from Kitwe or Livingstone?
  © What is the probability that the creditor never takes tough action?
  (d) What is the probability that the creditor is from Lusaka and never takes tough action?
  (e) What is the probability that the creditor is from Lusaka, given the creditor never takes tough action?

5. The set of securities (stocks, bonds, etc) held by an individual or organization is referred to as its portfolio. An investor wants to invest K2000 000 in each of the five different common stocks and has identified ten different stocks that she believes would be sound investment. How many different portfolios of five stocks could she form from among her list of ten stocks?

6. A company produces plastic elephants for the novelty trade market. Production in the factory is on three machines. 10% is on machine A, 40% is on machine B and the remainder on machine C. Machine A's production consists of 40% blue elephants and 60% pink elephants. Machine B's production consists of 30% blue elephant and 70% pink elephants. Machine C's production consists of 80% pink elephants, the remainder being blue"

  (a) What proportion do blue elephants form of the total?
  (b) If a particular elephant is pink, what is the probability it was made by chine B?

7. Six light bulbs are chosen at random 25 bulbs of which 15 are defective. Find the probability that:

  (a) at least one is defective
  (b) none is defective
  (c) exactly one is defective.

8. A bank's records show that 70% of its male employees have a college education, while only 50% of its female employees have a college's education. Forty percent of the bank's employees are male. What is the probability that an employee selected randomly:

  (a) is a male without college education?
  (b) has a college education.

9. Write down and illustrate the use in probability of the addition rule.

10. Consider the following population of savings accounts at a new bank.

ACCOUNT NUMBER	ACCOUNT BALANCE(k,000)
0001	K1 000
0002	12 500
0003	850
0004	1 000
0005	3 500

Suppose you wish to draw a random sample of two accounts from this population.

(a) List all possible different pairs of accounts that can be obtained
(b) What is the probability of selecting accounts 0001 and 0004?
(c) What is the probability of selecting two accounts that each have a balance of k1 000 000? That each have a balance other than k1 000 000?

Chapter Six

PROBABILITY DISTRIBUTIONS

Probability distributions are classified as either discrete or continuous, depending on the random variable.

· A random variable is discrete if it can assume only a countable number of possible values (0, 1, 2, 3, etc).

· A continuous random variable can assume any value in 1 or more intervals of values. It can take fractions, decimals, etc.

· A probability function , denoted P(x), specifies the probability that a random variable is equal to a specific value. More formerly, P(x) is the probability that random variable x takes on the value x.

The two key properties of a probability functions are:

· $0 \leq P(x) \leq 1$

·$\sum P(x) = 1$, i.e. the sum of the probabilities of all possible outcomes, x for a random variable, x, equals one.

PROBABILITY DISTRIBUTIONS FOR DISCRETE RANDOM VARIABLES

The probability distributions for discrete random variables are Binomial distributions, Poisson distribution to mention the most commonly used ones.

THE BINOMIAL RANDOM VARIABLE

A common source of business data is an opinion or preference survey. Many of these surveys result in dichotomous responses i.e. responses that admit one of two possible alternatives, such as Yes–No. The number of yes responses (or no responses) will usually have a binomial probability distribution. For example, suppose a random sample of consumers is selected from the totality of potential consumers of a particular product. The number of consumers in the sample who prefer the product to its competition is a random variable that has a binomial probability distribution. All experiments that have the characteristics of the coin-tossing experiments yield binomial random variables.

CHARACTERISTICS OF A BINOMIAL RANDOM VARIABLE

In general, to decide whether a discrete random variable has a binomial probability distribution, check it against the following characteristics:

The experiment consists of n identical trials.
1.   An event has only two recognizable outcomes on each trial (e.g. success and failure

or processing and not possessing an attribute). Examples are tossing a coin, rolling a die, consumer survey, etc.

2. The values of P and q can be calculated. P is the probability of success while q is the probability of failure. Note that $p + q = 1$

3. The values of P and q remain constant throughout the trial. This implies sampling with replacement.

4. The trials are independent statistically

5. It is applicable to discrete variables in the sample which can be 0, 1, 2, …….. but never a decimal or fraction.

6. The binomial random variable x is the number of success in n trials.

THE BINOMIAL PROBABILITY DISTRIBUTION

The probability of r successes in n trials is calculated using the following formula

$$P(r) = \binom{n}{r} P^r q^{n-r} \quad \text{or} \quad P(r) = \frac{n!}{(n-r)!r!} P^r q^{n-r}$$

where P = probability of a success on a single trial.
  q = 1 – P i.e. probability of a failure on a single trial
  n = Number of trials undertaken
  r = Number of successes in n trials

Note that r = 0, 1, 2 …n)

MEAN, VARIANCE AND STANDARD DEVIATION FOR A BINOMIAL RANDOM VARIABLE

The mean, variance and standard deviation for the binomial random variable x can be calculated using the following formulae:

$$\text{Mean: } \mu = np$$

$$\text{Variance: } \sigma^2 = npq$$

$$\text{Standard deviation: } \sigma = \sqrt{npq}$$

Where P = probability of a success on a single trail
  q = 1 – P i.e. probability of a failure on a single trial

n = Number of trials under taken

Example 1

A machine that produces stampings for automotive engines is malfunctioning and producing 10% defectives. The defective and non-defective stampings proceed from the machine in a random manner. If the next five stampings were tested:

   (a) find the probability that three of them are defective
   (b) calculate the mean and standard deviation
   (c) find the values of P(0), P(1), P(4) and P(5) and interpret your results.

Solution

This is a binomial situation with only two possible outcomes of success (defective) and failure (non-defective)

(a) $n = 5, r = 3, P = \dfrac{10}{100} = 0.1, q = 1 - 0.1 = 0.9$

using $P(r) = \dfrac{n!}{(n-r)!r!} P^r q^{n-r}$

$P(3) = \dfrac{5!}{2!3!} (0.1)^3 (0.9)^2$

$= \dfrac{120}{12} (0.001)(0.81)$

$= 10 (0.001)(0.81)$

$= \underline{0.0081}$

Note that the binomial formula us that there are ten simple events having three defectives, each with probability $(0.1)^3 (0.9)^2$

(b) $n = 5, \ P = 0.1, \ q = 0.9$

mean, $\mu = np = 5 \times 0.1 = 0.5$

Standard deviation $= \sqrt{npq} = \sqrt{5(0.1)(0.9)}$

$= \sqrt{0.45} \qquad = \underline{0.67}$

(c) again n = 5, P = 0.1, q = 0.9

Using $P(r) = \dfrac{n!}{(n-r)!r!} \, P^r q^{n-r}$

· $P(0) = \dfrac{5!}{(5-0)!0!} (0.1)^0 (0.9)^{5-0} = 0.59049$

· $P(1) = \dfrac{5!}{(5-2)!2!} (0.1)^1 (0.9)^{5-1} = \underline{0.32805}$

· $P(2) = \dfrac{5!}{(5-2)!2!} (0.1)^2 (0.9)^{5-2} = \underline{0.07290}$

· $P(4) = \dfrac{5!}{(5-4)!4!} (0.1)^4 (0.9)^{5-1} = \underline{0.00045}$

· $P(5) = \dfrac{5!}{(5-5)!5!} (0.5)^5 (0.9)^{5-5} = \underline{0.00001}$

Above are the probabilities that 0, 1, 2, 4 and 5 defective stampings.

Example 2

The probability that anyone of a batch of 2000 transistors is faulty is constant but its value is not known. The probability that a random sample of 10 will contain exactly zero faulty transistors is 0.048. What is the expected number of defective transistors in the original batch of 2000?

Solution

Above is a binomial situation probability of a transistor being faulty is P. Probability of it being good is q i.e. 1 – P using the binomial distribution.

$P(r) = \dfrac{n!}{(n-r)!r!} \, P^r q^{n-r}$

With P (r) = 0.048, n = 10, r = 0

$\dfrac{10!}{(10-0)!0!} \, P^0 q^{10-0} = 0.048$

$\dfrac{10!}{10!} \, q^{10} = 0.048$

Using q = 1 – P

- 124 -

$(1 - P)^{10} = 0.048$

Getting the 10th root on both sides

$$\sqrt[10]{(1 - P)\,10} = \sqrt[10]{0.048}$$

$1 - P = 0.738115157$

$P = \underline{0.261884842}$

Therefore, the expected number of defective transistors in a batch of 2000 is

$= 2000 \times 0.26188444842$

$= 523.7696853$

$= \underline{524 \text{ transistors}}$

Example 3

A named bank has found from experience that only 20% of the people applying for bank teller job are qualified for the work. If 5 people are interviewed, what is the probability of finding at least two qualified persons?

Solution

This is a binomial situation. An applicant can either be qualified or unqualified for the work. Note that the term "at least two" implies two and above.
Using the binomial formula;

$$P(r) = \frac{n!}{(n - r)!\,r!}\ P^r q^{n-r}$$

$P = \frac{20}{100} = 0.2, \ q = 1 - 0.2 = 0.8, \ n = 5, r = 0, 1, 2, 3, 4, 5$

$\cdot\ P(0) = \frac{5!}{(5 - 0)!\,0!}\ (0.2)^0 (0.8)^{5-0} = 0.3277$

$\cdot\ P(1) = \frac{5!}{(5 - 1)!\,1!}\ (0.2)^1 (0.8)^{5-1} = 0.4096$

$\cdot P(2) = \dfrac{5!}{(5-2)!2!} (0.2)^2 (0.8)^{5-2} = 0.2048$

$\cdot P(3) = \dfrac{5!}{(5-3)!3!} (0.2)^3 (0.8)^{5-3} = 0.2048$

$\cdot P(4) = \dfrac{5!}{(5-4)!4!} (0.2)^4 (0.8)^{5-4} = 0.0064$

$\cdot P(5) = \dfrac{5!}{(5-5)!5!} (0.2)^5 (0.8)^{5-5} = 0.0003$

Therefore, the probability that at least two will be qualified is:

$P(r = 2, 3, 4 \text{ or } 5) = 1 - P(r = 0 \text{ or } 1)$

$= 1 - (0.3277 + 0.4096)$

$= \underline{0.2627}$

Note that the above probability has been computed using the complementary rule of probability. The complementary rule should always be used whenever statements like at least 2, 3, or 4 successes are required. Remember at least 2 technically mean 2 and more successes which may go up to hundreds!

Alternatively, the probability of at least 2 being qualified can be computed using the simple addition rule of probability because there are only 5 people as follows:

$P(\text{at least } 2) = P(2) + P(3) + P(4) + P(5)$

$= 0.2048 + 0.0512 + 0.0064 + 0.0003$

$= \underline{0.2627}$ as calculated above

THE POISSON RANDOM VARIABLE

A type of probability distribution useful in describing the number of events that will occur in a specific period of time or in a specific area or volume is the Poisson distribution (named after the eighteenth-century physicist and mathematician. Simeon Poisson).
The following are typical examples of random variables for which the Poisson probability distribution provides a good model.

1. The number of industrial accidents in a given manufacturing plant per month observed by a plant safety supervisor.
2. The number of noticeable surface defects (scratches, dents, etc) found by quality inspectors on a new manufactured product.

3. The number of arithmetic errors per 100 invoices in the accounting records of a company.
4. The number of customer arrivals per unit time at a service counters (service station, hospital, a school, a bank etc).
5. The number of death claims per day received by an insurance company.
6. The number of ATM breakdowns at a bank per month

CHARACTERISTICS OF A POISSON RANDOM VARIABLE

The characteristics of the Poisson random variable are difficult to verify for practical examples. The previous examples satisfy them well enough that the Poisson distribution provides a good model in many instances. As with all probability models, the real test of the adequacy of the Poisson model is whether it provides a reasonable approximation to reality-that is, whether empirical data support it.

The following are the characteristics of a Poisson random variable.

1. The experiment consists of counting the number of times a particular event occurs during a given unit of time or in a given area or volume (weight, distance or any other unit of measurement)

2. The probability that an event occurs in a given unit of time, area, or volume is the same for all the units.

3. The number of events that occur in one unit of time, area or volume is independent of the number that occurs in other units.

4. The mean (or expected) number of events in each unit will be denoted by the Greek letter lambda, λ.

5. An important feature of the Poisson distribution is that the mean is equal to the variance. This is not true of other probability distributions and is therefore one way of testing whether a given distribution is Poisson.

6. It has very small P and very large n. It is always difficult to define what is meant by very small and very large, and the following are given as indicators: P less than 0.01 and n of the order of several hundreds or even thousands.

PROBABILITY DISTRIBUTION, MEAN, AND VARIANCE FOR A POISSON RANDOM VARIABLE

$$P(x) = \frac{\lambda^x e^{-\lambda}}{x!} \text{ or } P(x) = \frac{1}{(2.718)^m} \times \frac{m^x}{x!}$$

where x = 0, 1, 2, ……………………..

λ or m = the average number of successes occurring in the given time or measurement.

e = 2.71828 (the base of natural logarithms)

Mean: $\mu = \lambda$

Variance: $\sigma^2 = \lambda$

Note: The Poisson distribution also provides a good approximation to a binomial probability distribution with the mean $\lambda = np$ where n is large and P is small.

Example 4

Suppose the number, x, of a bank's employees who are absent on Mondays has approximately a Poisson probability distribution. Further, assume that the average number of Monday absentees is 2.6

  (a) Find the mean and standard deviation of x, the number of employees absent on Monday.

  (b) Find the probability that fewer than two employees are absent on a given Monday.

  (c) Find the probability that more than five employees are absent on a given Monday.

  (d) Find the probability that exactly five employees are absent on a given Monday

Solution

(a) The mean and variance of a Poisson random variable are both equal to λ. Thus, $\mu = \lambda = 2.6$, $\sigma^2 = 2.6$

Then standard deviation of x is

$$\sigma = \sqrt{\sigma^2} = \sigma = \sqrt{2.6} = \underline{1.61}$$

Note, the mean measures the central tendency of the distribution (2.6 absences) while the standard deviation measures the variability of Monday absences (1.61).

(b) P (x = 0, or 1) = P (0) + P (1)

Using $P(x) = \dfrac{1}{2.718^m} \times \dfrac{m^x}{x!}$

· $P(0) = \dfrac{1}{(2.718)2.6} \times \dfrac{(2.6)^0}{0!} = 0.074$

· $P(1) = \dfrac{1}{(2.718} \times \dfrac{(2.6)^1}{1!} = 0.193$

Thus, P (x < 2) = 0.074 + 0.193

$$= \underline{0.267}$$

(c) To find the probability that more than five employees are absent on a given Monday, we consider the complementary event.

P (x > 5) = P (x ≤ 5)

1 − {P(0) + P(1) + P(2) + P(3) + P (4) + P (5)]

Since we already have P (0) and P (1), we need to compute P (2), P (3), P (4) and P (5).

· $P(2) = \dfrac{1}{(2.718)^{2.6}} \times \dfrac{(2.6)^2}{2!} = \underline{0.251}$

· $P(3) = \dfrac{1}{(2.718)^{2.6}} \times \dfrac{(2.6)^3}{3!} = 0.218$

· $P(4) = \dfrac{1}{(2.718)^{2.6}} \times \dfrac{(2.6)^4}{4!} = 0.141$

· $P(5) = \dfrac{1}{(2.718)^{2.6}} \times \dfrac{(2.6)^5}{5!} = 0.074$

Thus, P (x > 5) = 1 − (0.074 + 0.193 + 0.251 + 0.218 + 0.1=141 + 0.074

$$= 1 - 0.951$$

$$= \underline{\mathbf{0.049}}$$

(d) To find the probability that exactly five employees are absent on a given Monday, this can be written as:

$P (x = 5) = P (x \le 5) - P (x \le 4)$

$= 0.951 - (0.074 + 0.193 + 0.251 + 0.218 + 0.141)$

$= 0.951 - 0.877$

$= \underline{\textbf{0.074}}$

Example 5

Seismography record of a number of years indicates that in a particular place, the average number of earth quakes over a given length is two a year.

Calculate the probability that in the next year there will be at least three earthquakes.

Solution

$P \text{ (at least 3)} = 1 - P (0) + P (1) + P (2)$

Mean $(m) = 2$

$$P (0) = \frac{1}{(2.718)^2} \quad X \quad \frac{2^0}{0!}$$

$$= \frac{1}{7.388} = 0.1353466290$$

$$= \underline{0.135}$$

$$P (1) = 0.135354629 \quad X \quad \frac{2^1}{1!} = 0.27079258$$

$$= \underline{0.271}$$

$$P (2) = 0.135354629 \quad X \quad \frac{2^2}{2!} = 0.2709258$$

$$= \underline{0.271}$$

Thus, $P \text{ (at least 3)} = 1 - (0.135 + 0.271 + 0.271)$

$$= 1 - 0.677$$

$$= \underline{0.323}$$

Example 6

Assembly line produces approximately 3% defective items. In a batch of 150 items, find the probability of obtaining;

(a) At least one is defective
(b) None is defective
(c) Exactly one is defective

Solution

Poisson distribution because n is very large and P is very small i.e. 0.03

$$P(x) = \frac{\lambda^x e^{-\lambda}}{X!}, \quad \lambda = np = 150(0.03) = 4.5$$

(a) $P(x \geq 1) = 1 - P(x=0) = 1 - \frac{4.5^0 e^{-4.5}}{0!} = 1 - 0.011 = 0.9889$

(b) $P(x=0) = \frac{4.5^0 e^{-4.5}}{0!} = 0.0111$

(c) $P(x=1) = \frac{4.5^1 e^{-4.5}}{1!} = 4.5(0.0111) = 0.04999$

Example 7

Customers arrive randomly at a bank branch at an average rate of 3.5 per minute. Assuming the customer arrivals form a poisson distribution , calculate the probability that;

(a) No customer arrives in any particular minute
(b) Exactly one customer arrives
(c) Two or mor customers arrive
(d) One or more customers arrive

Solution

(a) $\lambda = 3.5$, $x = 0$

$$P(x = 0) = \frac{3.5^0 e^{-3.5}}{0!} = 0.030$$

(b) $P(x = 1) = \frac{3.5^1 e^{-3.5}}{1!} = 0.106$

(c) $P(x \geq 2) = 1 - P(x=0) + P(x=1)$

$$1 - 0.030 + 0.106$$

$$= 0.864$$

(d) For 1 minute or 60 seconds $\lambda = 3.5$, hence for 30 seconds $\lambda = 1.75$

$$P(x \geq 1) = 1 - P(x = 0)$$

$$P(x = 0) = \frac{1.75^0 e^{-1.75}}{0!} = 0.174$$

Thus, $P(x \geq 1) = 1 - 0.174 = 0.826$

CONTINUOUS RANDOM VARIABLES

A Continuous random variable is one that can assume any value within some interval or intervals. The graphical form of the probability distribution for a continuous random variable, x is a smooth curve. This curve, a function of x, is denoted by the symbol $f(x)$ and is variously called a probability density function, a frequency function, or a probability distribution. The areas under a probability distribution correspond to probabilities for x.

There are three specific types of continuous probability distributions that are used in making business decisions. These are:

- The normal probability distribution, which plays a basic and important role in both theory and applications of statistics and is essential, is the study of the most of the subsequent chapters.

- The uniform probability distribution

- The exponential probability distribution.

Since both the uniform and exponential distributions have specialized applications to business problems, they are briefly treated for convenience's sake.

THE NORMAL DISTRIBUTION

The normal distribution is a probability distribution which usually applies to continuous variables, such as time and distance. The normal distribution is important because in the practical application of statistics, it has been found that many probability distributions are close enough to a normal distribution to be treated as one without any significant loss of accuracy.

CHARACTERISTICS OF THE NORMAL DISTRIBUTION

The properties or characteristics of the normal distribution are as follows.

1. The distribution is symmetrical around its mean, and bell-shaped in appearance.

2. The x-axis represents the possible values of the x-variable, which are infinite.

3. The left and right hand tails of the distribution approach the x-axis but never touch it. This is the major difference of the normal distribution from the naturally occurring distributions.

4. The total area under the curve is equal to 1 or 100%. This means that the areas to the left and the right of the mean will each comprise 0.5 or 50% of the total area.

5. The two parameters necessary to construct the normal distribution are the mean (μ) and standard deviation (σ). The centre of the distribution is determined by μ, and the spread by σ.

6. It is a mathematical curve calculated using a formula and closely fits with many natural occurring distributions.

GRAPHING THE NORMAL DISTRIBUTION

The graph of the normal distribution is bell-shaped as shown below.

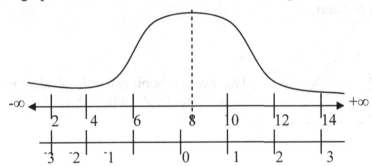

In the above curve, the mean (μ) always corresponds to 0 i.e. zero standard deviations from the mean. On the other hand, 1, 2, 3………... above represent the number of standard deviations to the right of the mean and ˉ1,ˉ2,ˉ3 … represent the number of standard deviations to the left of the mean. The area to the left = the area to the right of the mean.

STANDARDIZING THE NORMAL DISTRIBUTION

It is possible to convert the normal distribution into a standard form (z), by expressing the difference between the value of interest (x) and the mean (μ) in units of standard deviations (σ). This z-score as it is called will show the number of standard deviations that a particular value lies to the right or left of the mean. Any x-value greater or left of the mean will standard normal distribution are contained in published tables. Normal distribution tables only have simply indicates that value is to the left of the mean (I.e.

below the mean) while a positive indicates that it is to the right of the mean (i.e. above the mean).

Standardizing is achieved by calculating the z-scores using the following formula:

$$Z = \frac{x - \mu}{\sigma}$$

where x = random variable
μ = mean of the population
σ = standard deviation of the population

Since population figures are difficult to capture, we use the sample figures and the formula changes to the following:

$$Z = \frac{x - \bar{x}}{s}$$

where x = random variable

$\bar{x}$ = sample mean
s = sample standard deviation

RULES APPLIED TO THE USE OF NORMAL DISTRIBUTION

The following rules are critical to finding the area under a normal distribution curve. Make sure you learn them by heart.

1.
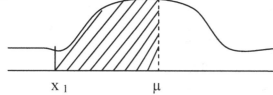

·The area (probability) of the shade portion is got directly from the table.

2.
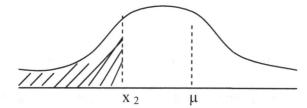

· To find the shaded area we first find the area between μ and x_2 and subtract this from 0.5.

3.
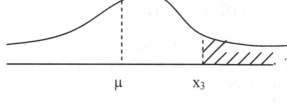

· To find shaded area, we First find area between μ and x_3 and subtract this from 0.5.

4.

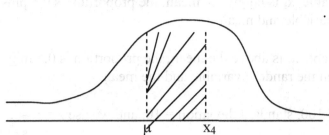

· To find the shaded area between μ and x4, pick the figure directly from the table.

5.

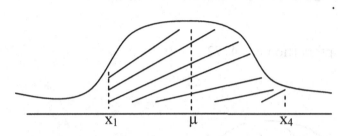

· To find the shaded area, we find areas' between x_1 and μ and x_4 and μ and <u>add</u> them (i.e. different sides of the mean, we add).

6.

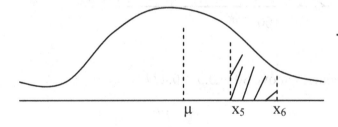

· To find the shaded area, Between μ and x5, and μ And x6, then subtract the Two (i.e. same side of the mean we subtract).

Note: it is advisable to practice to sketch your solutions for simplifications whenever dealing with the normal distribution problems!

Example 6

A frequency distribution is normal, with a mean of 100 and a standard deviation of 10. Calculate the proportion of the total frequencies which will be:

    (a) above 80
    (b) above 90
    (c) above 100
    (d) above 115
    (e) below 85
    (f) below 95
    (g) below 108
    (h) in the range 80 – 110
    (i) in the range 90 – 95

Solution

- If the random variable, x, is <u>below</u> the mean, the proportion is 0.5 plus proportion between random variable and mean.

- If the random variable x, is above the mean, the proportion is 0.5 <u>minus</u> proportion between the random variable and the mean

- In all case mean = 100, standard deviation = 10, and we use $z = \dfrac{x - \bar{x}}{s}$

(a) $z = \dfrac{80 - 100}{10} = {}^-2$ i.e. 2 standard deviations below the mean

- From tables z = 2, proportion is 0.4772.

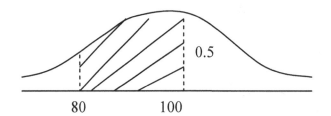

- Proportion of frequencies above 80 is 0.5 + 0.4772

$$= \underline{0.9772}$$

(b) $z = \dfrac{90 - 100}{10} = {}^-1$ i.e. 1 standard deviation below the mean.

- From table z = 1, gives a proportion of 0.3413

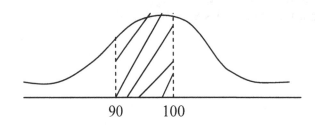

- Proportion of frequencies above 90 is 0.5 + 0.3413

$$= \underline{0.8413}$$

(c) z = $\dfrac{100 - 100}{10}$ = 0 standard deviations

100 is the mean and the random variable

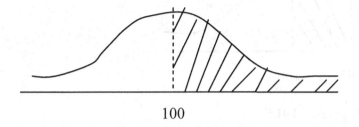

100

- Proportion above 100 is <u>0.5</u>

(d) z = $\dfrac{115 - 100}{10}$ = 1.5 standard deviation above the mean.

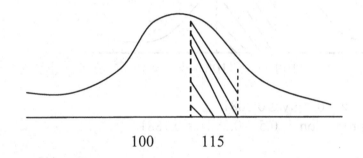

100   115

- From tables, z = 1.5, gives 0.4332
- The required proportion is 0.5 – 0.4332 = 0.0668

(e) z = $\dfrac{85 - 100}{10}$ = 1.5 standard deviations below the mean.

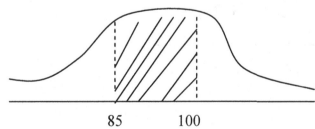

85   100

- Required proportion is the same as in (d) above i.e. 0.0668

(f) z = $\underline{95 - 100}$ = 0.5 standard deviation below the mean.

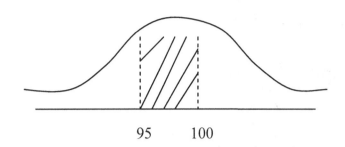

95   100

- From tables, z = 0.5, gives 0.1915
- Required proportion is 0.5 – 0.1915 = 0.3085

(g) z = $\underline{108 - 100}$ = 0.8 standard deviations above mean
           10

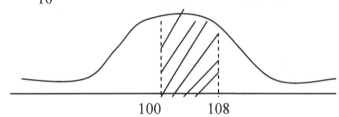

100   108

- From tables, z = 0.8 gives 0.2881
- Required proportion is 0.5 + 0.2881 = 0.7881

(h) Proportion in the range 80 to 100   =   0.4 772
- proportion range 100 to 110   =   0..3413
- Proportion in the   total range 80 to 110 (0.4747 – 3413 = 0.8185

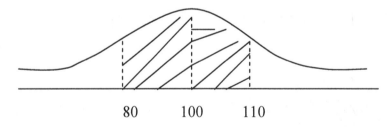

80   100   110

Note: Opposite sides we <u>add</u>

(i) Range 90 to 95

- Proportion above 90 and below mean = 0.3415
- Proportion above 95 and below mean = 0.1915
- Proportion between 90 and 95   = 0.1498

Note: Same side we subtract.

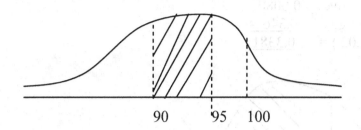

90   95   100

Example 7

From the table, find and sketch:

   (a) $P(z < 0.01)$
   (b) $P(z < 0.52)$
   (c) $P(z < 1.00)$
   (d) $P(0.02 < z < 1.02)$
   (e) $P(z > 0.51)$

(a) From tables, $z = 0.01$, gives 0.0040

   Thus, $P(z < 0.01) = 0.5 + 0.0040$

                $= \underline{0.5040}$

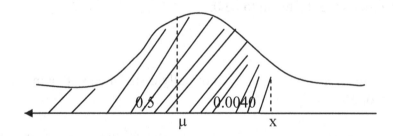

(b) From tables, $z = 0.52$ gives 0.1985

   Thus, $P(z < 0.52) \; 0.5 + 0.1985 = \underline{0.6985}$

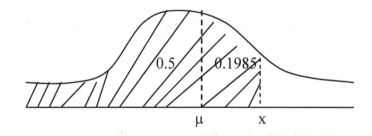

(c) From tables, z = 1.00 gives 0.313
Thus P (z < 1.00) = 0.5 + 0.3413 = 0.8413

(d) From tables z = 0.02 gives   0.0080
z = 1.02 gives   0.3461-
Thus, P (0.02 < z 1.02) =   0.3381

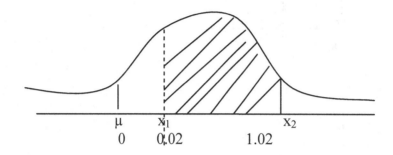

(e) From tables z = 0.51 gives 0.1950
Thus, P (z > 0.51) = 0.5 - 0.1950 = 0.3050

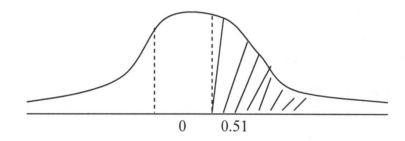

Note: In the above example, take the mean to be 0.

Example 8

In a certain test where scores were approximately normally distributed with a mean of 75 and a standard deviation of 20.

(a) If you achieved a score of 55, how far, in standard deviation did your score depart from the mean?
(b) What percentage of candidates scored higher than 55?

Solution

(a) $Z = \dfrac{x - \mu}{\sigma} = \dfrac{55 - 75}{20} = {}^-1$, which means 1 standard deviation below the mean

(b) $P(z > 55) = \dfrac{55 - 75}{20} = 0.3413$

Thus 0.3413 + 0.5 = 0.8413 or 84% scored higher than 55.

Example 9

The salaries of employees at a named bank are normally distributed with a mean of K1 400 000 and a standard deviation of K270 000.

Calculate:

(a) the proportion of employees who earn less than K1200 000

(b) The proportion of employees who earn between K1100 000 and K1900 000.

(c) The proportion of employees who earn more than K1900 000.

(d) The proportion of employees who earn exactly k1500 000

(e) In a group of 200 employees, how many would you expect to earn more than k1900 000

(f) Approximately 30% earn less than the recommended minimum basic salary. What is this minimum rate?

Solution

$\overline{X}$ = K1400 000, s = K270 000.

(a) $Z = \dfrac{K1200\ 000 - K1400\ 000}{K270\ 000} = ^-074$

Z = 0.74 gives 0.2704

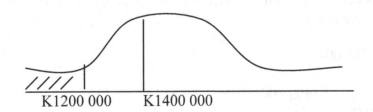

K1200 000   K1400 000

- Thus employees earning less than K1200 000 is 0.5 – 0.2704 = 02296 or 23% of them.

(b) Proportion earning between K1100 000 and K1400 000

$Z = \dfrac{K1100\ 000 - K1400\ 000}{K270\ 000} = ^-1.11$ standard deviations below the mean which gives 0.3665

- Proportion earning between K140 000 and K190 000

$$Z = \frac{K1900\ 000 - K1400\ 000}{K270\ 000} = 1.85 \text{ standard deviations above the mean which gives } 0.4678.$$

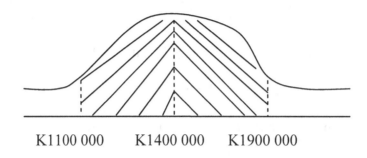

K1100 000   K1400 000   K1900 000

- Required proportion is 0.3665 + 0.4678 = 0.8343 or 83% of the employees.

(c) Above K1900 000

$$Z = \frac{K1900\ 000 - K1400\ 000}{K270\ 000} = 1.85, \text{ which gives } 0.4678$$

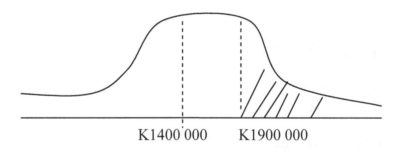

K1400 000   K1900 000

- Proportion of earnings above K1900 000 is 0.5 – 0.4678 = 0.0322 0r 3% of the employees.

(d) Exactly k1500 000

$$Z = \frac{k1500\ 000 - k1400\ 000}{K270\ 000} = 0.37, \text{ which gives } 0.1443$$

(e) 200 x 0.0322 = 6 employees are expected to earn above k1900 000.

(f) Here we need to find the value of x. The first step is to determine the Z- score using the data given. Change 30% into decimal which gives 0.3.Now each half of the normal distribution is has area of 0.5, therefore, we need to subtract 0.3 from 0.5 which gives 0.2000.In the mass of figures in the normal distribution table look for this area (0.2000) or the area closest to it. For 0.2000 we have 0.1985 which corresponds to a z- score of -0.52 and 0.2019 which corresponds to a Z-score of 0.53. Using these Z-scores we can now determine the value of x as follows:

$$Z = \frac{x - \mu}{\sigma}$$

$$-0.53 = \frac{x - 1400\ 000}{270\ 000} \qquad \text{or} \ -0.52 = \frac{x - 1400\ 000}{270\ 000}$$

$$X = k1\ 256\ 900 \qquad\qquad x = k1\ 259\ 600$$

Example 10

A firm of stockbrokers will on average handle 2500 shares a day with a standard deviation of 250 shares. If the number of shares sold is normally distributed, find the following:

(a) The probability that more than 2700 shares will be sold in any day?
(b) The probability that the stockholders will sell between 2300 and 2550 shares a day?
(c) The probability they will sell either more than 3125 or less than 2000 shares in a day?

Solution

$$\overline{X} = 2500,\ s = 250$$

$$Z = \frac{x - 2500}{250}$$

(a) $P\ (x > 2700) = P\left[z > \dfrac{2700 - 2500}{250}\right]$

$$= P\ (z > 0.8) = 0.5 - 0.2881$$

$$= \underline{0.2119}$$

(b) $P\ (x < 1900) = P\left[z < \dfrac{1900 - 2500}{250}\right]$

$$= P\ (z < -2.4) = P\ (z > 2.4)$$

$$= 0.05 - 0.4918$$

$$= \underline{0.0082}$$

(c) $P (2300 < X < 2550 = P\left(\dfrac{2300 - 2500}{250} < z < \dfrac{2550 - 2500}{250} \right)$

$$= P\ (^{-}0.8 < X < 0.2)$$

$$= 0.2881 + 0.793$$

$$= \underline{0.3674}$$

(d) $P\ (x > 3125) = P\left(z > \dfrac{3125 - 2500}{250} \right) = P\ (z > 2.5)$

$$0.5 - 0.4938 = 0.0062$$

$$P\ (\ x < 2000) = P\left(z < \dfrac{2000 - 2500}{250} \right) = P\ (z < ^{-}2)$$

$$= 0.228 + 0.0062$$

$$= \underline{0.029}$$

Note: these are mutually exclusive events.

Example 11

Computers consist of a number of components including what is called a memory. These memories, produced by an automatic process, have a useful life length of which is normally distributed with a mean of 500 hours and a standard deviation of 30 hours. If one thousand of these memories are selected at random from the production line:

(a) How many of the memories would you expect to last longer than 550 hours?
(b) How many memories you expect to have a life between 480 and 510 hour?
(c) How many memories would you expect to have a useful life of more than 560 hours or less than 440 hours?

Solution

(a) $P\ (x > 550) = P\left(z > \dfrac{550 - 500}{30} \right) = 1.67$

$$0.5 - 0.4525 = 0.0475$$

Thus, $0.0475 \times 1000 = 475$ memories

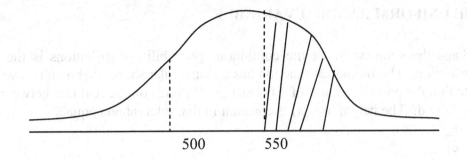

(b) P (450 < X < 510) = P (z = 0.33) + P (z = -0.67)

$$= 0.1293 + 0.2486$$

$$= \underline{0.3779}$$

Thus, 0.3779 X 1000 = <u>377.9</u> memories

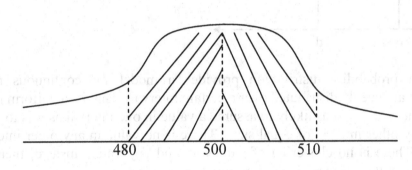

(c) P (x > 560) = P (z > 2)

P (x < 440) = P (z < ˉ2)

$$= 2 (0.0228) = 0.0456$$

Thus, 0.0456 X 1000 = 45.6 memories

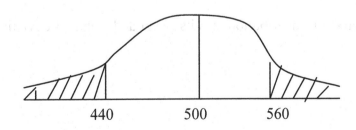

Thus, P (x > 560) = 0.5 − 0.4772 = 0.0228
P (x < 440) = 0.5 − 0.4772 = <u>0.0228</u>
<u>0.0456</u> as above

THE UNIFORM RANDOM VARIABLE

Perhaps the simplest of all the continuous probability distributions is the uniform distribution. The frequency function has a rectangular shape as shown below:
Note that the possible values of x consist of all points on the real line between point c and point d. The height of f (x) is constant in that interval and equals

$$\frac{1}{(d-c)}.$$

Therefore, the total area under f(x) is given by the area of the rectangle:
  A =(d-c)(1/d-c)

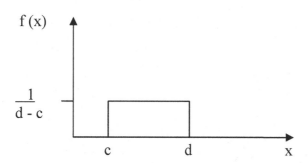

The uniform probability distribution provides a model for continuous random variables that are evenly distributed over a certain interval. That is, a uniform random variable is one that is just as likely to assume a value in one interval as it is to assume a value in any other interval of equal size. There is no value in any other interval of equal size. There is no clustering of values around any value, instead, there is an even spread over the entire region of possible values.

The uniform distribution is sometimes referred to as the **randomness distribution**, since one way of generating a uniform random variable is to perform an experiment in which a point is randomly selected on the horizontal axis between point's c and d. If the experiment is repeated infinitely, we would create a uniform probability distribution.

PROBABILITY DISTRIBUTION, MEAN AND STANDARD DEVIATION OF A UNIFORM RANDOM VARIATION X

The formula for the probability distribution and its mean and standard deviation are given below:

- $f(x) = \dfrac{1}{d-c}$ $\qquad (c \le x \le d)$

- $\mu = \dfrac{c-d}{2}$

- $\sigma = \dfrac{d-c}{\sqrt{12}}$

Suppose the interval $a < x < b$ lies within the domain of x: i.e. it falls within the larger interval $c < x < d$. Then the probability that x assumes a value within the interval $a < x < b$ is the area of a rectangle over the interval – namely $\dfrac{b-a}{d-c}$

Note: the student who has knowledge of calculus should note that

$$P(a < x < b) = \int_a^b f(x)\, dx = \int_a^b \frac{1}{(d-c)}\, dx = (b-a)/(d-c)$$

Example 12

Suppose the research department of a steel manufacturer believes that one of the company's rolling machines is producing sheets of varying thickness. The thickness is a uniform random variable with the values between 150 and 200 millimeters. Any sheets less than 160 millimeters thick must be scrapped because they are unacceptable to buyers.

(a) Calculate the mean and standard deviation of x, the thickness of the sheets produced by the machine. Then graph the probability distribution and show the mean on the horizontal axis. Also show 1 and 2 standard deviation intervals around the mean.

(b) Calculate the fraction of steel sheets produced by this machine that have to be scrapped.

Solution

(a) mean, $\mu = \dfrac{c+d}{2} = \dfrac{150+200}{2} = 175$ millimeters

Standard deviation, $\sigma = \dfrac{d-c}{\sqrt{12}} = \dfrac{200-150}{\sqrt{12}} = \dfrac{50}{3.464} = 14.43$

- 147 -

The uniform probability distribution is

$$f(x) = \frac{1}{d-c} = \frac{1}{200-150} = \frac{1}{50}$$

The graph is shown below:

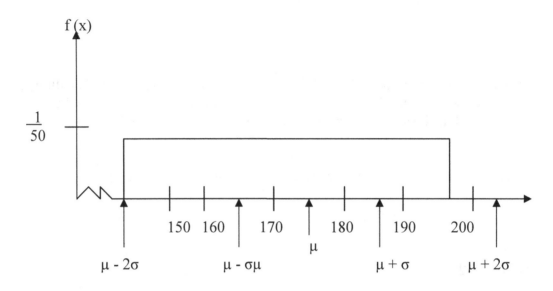

b) To find the fraction of steel sheets produced by the machine that have to be scrapped, we must find the probability that x, the thickness, is less than 160 millimeters. We need to calculate the area under the frequency function f (x) between x = 150 and 160. This is the area of a rectangle with 160 – 150 = 10 and height 1. The fraction that has to be scrapped is then: 50.

$$P(x < 160) = (Base)(height) = (10) \left[\frac{1}{50}\right] = \frac{1}{5}$$

That is, 20% of all the sheets by this machine must be scrape

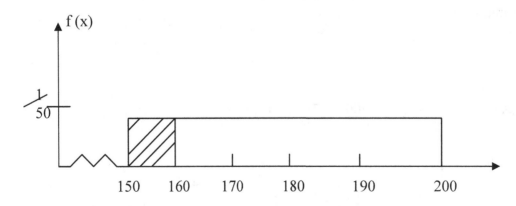

Example 13

The ages of a group of executives attending a convention are uniformly distributed between 40 years and 75 years. If x standards for ages in years, the probability density function is:

$$f(x) = \begin{cases} \dfrac{1}{35} & \text{for } 40 < x < 75 \text{ otherwise.} \end{cases}$$

(a) Draw the probability density function for this random variable x.

(b) Find and draw the cumulative distribution function for this random variable.

(c) Find the probability that the age of a randomly chosen executive in this group is between 45 and 60 years

(d) Find the mean and standard deviation age of the executives in the groups.

Solution

Above depicts a uniform probability distribution

a) $f(x) = \dfrac{1}{d-c} = \dfrac{1}{75-40} = \dfrac{1}{35}$ as given in the question.

Hence the domain of x is $40 < x < 75$ and the height of the rectangle is $\dfrac{1}{35}$

The probability density function is therefore:

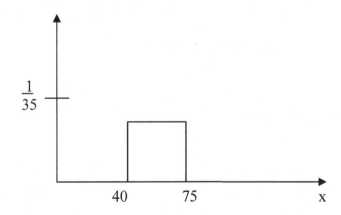

b) The cumulative distribution function of this random variance can be represented as shown below:

$$f(x) = \int_{40}^{x} \frac{1}{35}\ dx \quad = \frac{x}{35}$$

$$f(x) = \begin{cases} \dfrac{x}{35} & 40 < X < 75 \\ \\ 0 & \text{otherwise} \end{cases}$$

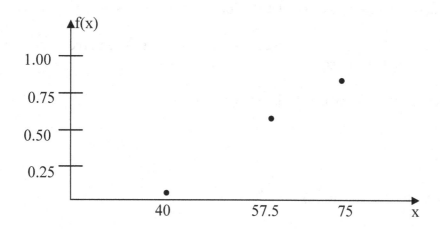

c) The probability that the age of a randomly chosen executive in this group is between 45 and 60 years is given by the area of the rectangle with x = 45 and x = 60.

$$\text{Area} = \frac{b-a}{d-c} = \frac{60-45}{75-40} = \frac{15}{35} = 0.428571428 = \underline{0.4286}$$

Alternatively,

$$\text{or} \quad P(45 < X < 60) = \frac{1}{35} \int_{45}^{60} dx = \frac{60-45}{35} = \underline{0.4286}$$

a) Mean age of executives is given by:

$$\mu = \frac{c+d}{2} = \frac{40+75}{2} = \frac{115}{2} = \underline{\mathbf{57.5}}$$

Alternatively:

$$\mu = \frac{1}{35} \int_{40}^{75} x\,dx = \frac{x^2}{70}\Big|_{40}^{75} = \frac{(75)^2 - (40)^2}{70}$$

$$= \frac{(75 - 40)\ (75 + 40)}{70}$$

$$= \underline{\mathbf{57.5}} \text{ as before}$$

$$\frac{60 - 45}{75 - 40} = \frac{15}{35} = \mathbf{0.428571428}$$

Standard deviation is given by:

$$\sigma = \frac{d - c}{\sqrt{12}} = \frac{75 - 40}{\sqrt{12}} = \frac{35}{3.464101615}$$

$$= 10.10362971$$

$$= \underline{\mathbf{10.10}}$$

Alternatively:

$$\text{Standard deviation} = \sqrt{\frac{1}{35} \int_{40}^{75} x^2\,dx - (57.5)^2}$$

$$= \sqrt{\frac{x^3}{105}\Big|_{40}^{75} - 3306.25}$$

$$= 3408.33 - 3306.25$$

$$= \sqrt{102.08}$$

$$= 10.10346475$$

$$= \underline{\mathbf{10.10}} \text{ as before}$$

Example 14

The distribution of random variable x has a density function $f(x) = \dfrac{1}{5}$ where $1 \le x \le = 6$.

(a) Find by integration the mean of x
(b) Find also the variance of x
(c) What is P (x > 2 | x < 3)?

Solution

a) Mean $= \dfrac{c + d}{2} = \dfrac{1 + 6}{2} = 3.5$

Alternatively:

$$\text{Mean} = E(x) = \int_{a}^{b} x \, f(x) \, dx$$

$$= \int_{1}^{6} x \cdot \frac{1}{5} \, dx$$

$$= \left. \frac{x^2}{10} \right|_{1}^{6} = \frac{36 - 1}{10} = \frac{35}{10} = \underline{3.5}$$

b) Variance = (standard deviation)^2

Standard deviation $= \dfrac{d - c}{12} = \dfrac{6 - 1}{12} = \dfrac{5}{3.464101615}$

$$= \underline{1.443375673}$$

c) Variance = $(1.443375673)^2 = 2.083333333$

$$= \textbf{2.08}$$

$$\text{Variance} = \text{var} \ (x) = \int_a^b x^2 \ f(x) \ dx - \mu^2$$

$$= \int_1^6 x^2 \ dx \ - 12.25$$

$$= \frac{x^2}{15} \ \Big|_1^6 \ - \ 12.25$$

$$= \frac{216 - 1}{15} \ - 12.25$$

$$= \ 14.33 \ - 12.25$$

$$= \ \textbf{2.08} \quad \text{as before.}$$

(c) $P \ (x > 2 \mid x < 3 \mid \ = \dfrac{b - c}{a - c} = \dfrac{3 - 2}{3 - 1} = \dfrac{1}{2} = \textbf{0.5}$

Alternatively:

- $\dfrac{P(\ x > 2 \cap x < 3)}{P\ (\ x < 3)}$

$$= \ \frac{\displaystyle\int_2^3 \frac{1}{5} \ dx}{\displaystyle\int_1^3 \frac{1}{5} \ dx} \qquad = \ \frac{\displaystyle\int_2^3 \ dx}{\displaystyle\int_1^3 \ dx}$$

$$= \ \frac{3 - 2}{3 - 1} = \frac{1}{2} \ = \textbf{0.5} \ \text{as before}$$

THE EXPONENTIAL RANDOM VARIABLE

Another important probability distribution that is useful for describing business data is the exponential probability distribution. Two business phenomena with frequency functions that might be well approximated by the exponential distribution are the length of time between the filings of claims in a small insurance office, the length of time between arrivals at a bank counter. Note that in each of the above examples, the measurements are the lengths of time between certain events. For this reason, the exponential distribution is sometimes called the waiting time distribution.

PROBABILITY DISTRIBUTION, MEAN AND STANDARD DEVIATION FOR AN EXPONENTIAL VARIABLE X

- $f(x) = \lambda e^{-\lambda x} \quad (x > 0)$

- $\mu = \dfrac{1}{\lambda}$

- $\sigma = \dfrac{1}{\lambda}$

Unlike the normal distribution, which has a shape and location determined by the values of the two quantities, μ and σ, the shape of the exponential distribution is governed by a single quantity, λ. Further, it is a probability distribution with the property that the mean equals its standard deviation.

FINDING THE AREA, A, TO THE RIGHT OF A NUMBER, a, FOR AN EXPONENTIAL DISTRIBUTION

To calculate probabilities for exponential random variables, we need to find the areas under, the exponential probability distribution   if we want to find the area, A, to the right of some number a, this can be calculated by using the following formula:

$$A = P(x \geq a) = e^{-\lambda a}$$

This area is calculated by integration:

$$\int_{a}^{\infty} \lambda e^{-\lambda x}\, dx = e^{-\lambda x}\Big|_{a}^{\infty} = e^{-\lambda a}$$

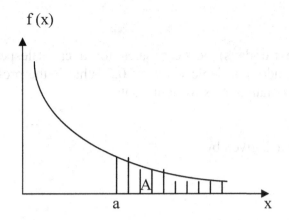

f(x)

a   x

Above show the area, A, to the right of a number, a, for an Exponential Distribution.

Example 15

A microwave oven manufacturer is trying to determine the length of warranty period it should attach to its magnetron tube, the most critical component in the oven. Preliminary testing has shown that the length of life (in years), x, of a magnetron tube has an exponential probability with $\lambda = 0.16$
(a) Find the mean and standard deviation of x
(b) If a warranty period of 5 years is attached to the tube, what fraction of tubes must the manufacturer plan to replace(assuming the exponential model wth $\lambda=0.16$ is correct?
(c) Find the probability that the length of life of a magnetron tube will fall within the interval $\mu\pm2\sigma$.

Solution

(a) $\mu = \dfrac{1}{\lambda} = \dfrac{1}{0.16}$ = 6.25 years,

Also since $\mu = \sigma$ = 6.25 years.

(b) $P(x>5) = e^{-\lambda 5} = e^{(-0.16)(5)} = 0.449329$.
    To find the area A we use the complimentary rule
    Thus, $P(x>5) = 1 - P(x>5) = 1 - 0.449329 = 0.550671$ i.e. approximately 55% of the tubes will be replaced during the 5 year warranty period.

(c) We would expect the probability of the tube, x, fall within the interval μ -2σ to μ = 2σ. Since the point μ - 2σ lies below x = 0, we need to find only the area between x = 0 and a = μ +2σ = 6.25 + 2(6.25) = 18.75.
    Therefore, A = 1 − P(x >18.75), $1 - e^{-(0.16)(18.75)} = 1 - e^{-3} = 1 - 0.049787 = 0.950213$

Example 16

Suppose the length of time (in days) between sales for a car salesperson is modeled as an exponential random variable with $\lambda = 0.5$. What is the probability that the salesperson goes more than 5 days without a sale?

Solution
Area to the right of a number a is given by:
$$A = P(x \geq a) = e^{-\lambda a}$$
$$= e^{-(0.5)(5)} = 0.082085$$

Example 17

A professor sees students during regular office hours. Time spent with the students follow an exponential distribution with mean 4 minutes.

(a) Find the probability that a given student spends less than 10 minutes with the professor.
(b) Find the probability that a given student spends more than 6 minutes with the professor
(c) Find the probability that a given student spends between 12 and 20 minutes with the professor.

Solution

$$\text{Mean} = E(x) = \frac{1}{\lambda} = 4 \text{ therefore } \lambda = \frac{1}{4}$$

(a) $P(x < 10) = 1 - e^{-1/4(10)} = 1 \, e^{-2.5} = 1 - 0.082084998 = 0.917915001$

(b) $P(x > 6) = e^{-1/4(6)} = e^{-(0.25)(6)} = e^{-1.5} = 0.22313016$

(c) $P(12 \leq x \leq 20) = e^{-(1/4)(12)} - e^{-(1/4)(20)} = e^{-3} - e^{-5} = 0.049787068 - 0.006737946999 = 0.043049121$

PROGRESS CLINIC SIX

1. The number of train passengers who fail to pay for their ticket in a certain region is, on average 4 per day. If there are 4800 trains per month in the region, find the expected number of trains with more than three non fare-paying passengers. Calculate the average cost to the train company if the average cost of a ticket is K10. Assume independent, random occurrences of non fare-payments.

2. Twenty percent of the population is thought to be carriers of a certain disease, although they themselves may show no symptoms. If this is true, evaluate the following probabilities for a sample of five people drawn at random from the population:

   (a) that all five are carriers
   (b) that at least 2 are carriers
   (c) that no more than 4 are carriers

3. An industrial oven used to cure sand cores for a manufacturing engine blocks for small cars is able to maintain fairly accurate temperatures. The temperature range of the oven follows a normal distribution with a mean of 450^0F and a standard deviation of 25^0F. If the oven gets hotter than 475^0F, the core is defective. What is the probability that the oven will cause a core to be defective? What is the probability that the temperature of the oven will range from 460^0F to 470^0F?

4. A company receives a very large shipment of components. A random sample of ten (10) of these components are checked, and the shipment is accepted if fewer than three (3) of these components are defective. What is the probability of accepting a shipment containing 2% defects?

5. A bank's records indicate that 90% are error free. If 8 records are randomly selected, what is the probability that at least 2 records have errors?

6. On an average one motor-vehicle accident per week occurs at a busy road intersection. What is the probability that at least two accidents occur over a 4 week period?

7. In an aptitude test administered to 1000 job applicants for Management Training position, the average score was 42 and the standard deviation 24. Assuming normal distribution, find:

   (a) the number of candidates with scores between 30 and 60
   (b) the score exceeded by the top 100 candidates

8. Suppose x is uniformly distributed on (c, d):

   (a) Find the density function for x.
   (b) What is the expected value for x?
   (c) Find the variance of x.

9. Most computer languages have a function that can be used to generate random numbers. In Microsoft's Quick BASIC, the RND function can be used to generate random numbers between 0 and 1. If we let x denote the random number generated, then x is a continuous random variable with the following probability density function.

$$f(x) = \begin{cases} 1 \\ 0 \text{ for } 0 \leq X \leq 1 \text{ elsewhere} \end{cases}$$

(a) Graph the probability density function
(b) What is the probability of generating a random number between .25 and .75?
(c) What is the probability of generating a random number with a value less than or equal to .30?
(d) What is the probability of generating a random number with a value greater than 0.60?

Chapter Seven

SAMPLING DISTRIBUTION AND ESTIMATION

INTRODUCTION TO SAMPLING DISTRIBUTIONS

Any probability distribution (and, therefore, any sampling distribution can be described (partially) by its mean and standard deviation. A probability distribution of all the possible means of the samples is a distribution of the sample means. Statisticians call this a sampling distribution of the mean. In the like manner, we have the sampling distribution of the proportion.

Rather than say "standard deviation of the means" to describe a distribution of sample means, statisticians refer to the **standard error of the mean**. Similarly, the "standard deviation of the distribution of the sample proportions" is shortened to the **standard error of the proportion**. The term standard error is used because it conveys a specific meaning. Suppose we wish to learn something about the height of new students at PCBF. We would take a series of samples and calculate the mean height for each sample. It is highly unlikely that all of these sample means would be the same: we expect to see some variability in our observed means. This variability in the sample statistic results from **sampling error** due to chance; that is, there are differences between each sample and the population, and among the several samples, owing solely to the elements we happened to choose for the samples. The standard error indicates not only the size of the chance error that has been made but also the accuracy we are likely to get if we use a sample statistic to estimate a population parameter. A distribution of sample means that is less spread out (that has a small standard error) is a better estimator of the population mean than a distribution of sample means that is widely dispersed and has a larger standard error.

The standard error is calculated using the following formula:

$$\sigma \bar{x} = \frac{\sigma}{\sqrt{N}}$$

Where σ = population standard deviation
n = sample size

$\sigma\bar{x}$ = standard error of the mean
Or

$$Se = \frac{s}{\sqrt{n}}$$

Where S = sample standard deviation
      n = sample size
      Se = standard error of the mean

PROPERTIES OF THE SAMPLING DISTRIBUTION OF THE MEAN

The properties of the sampling distribution of the mean when the population is normally distributed are:

1. The sampling distribution has a mean equal to the population mean

   i.e. $\bar{\mu}x = \mu$

2. The sampling distribution has a standard deviation (a standard error) equal to the population standard deviation divided by the square root of the sample size

   i.e. $\bar{\sigma}x = \dfrac{\sigma}{\sqrt{n}}$

3. The sampling distribution is normally distributed.

Note that the Z score is now calculated using $Z = \dfrac{\bar{x} - \mu}{\bar{\sigma}x}$ instead of

$Z = \dfrac{\bar{x} - \mu}{\sigma}$ where $\bar{x}$ = sample mean
                    μ = population mean
                    σ = standard deviation

                    $\bar{\sigma}x$ = standard error of the mean

Further, note that the concept of standard error is very important in statistical analysis hence the need to appreciate its role.

Example 1

A bank calculates that its individual savings accounts are normally distributed with a mean of K200 000 and a standard deviation of K60 000. If the bank takes a random sample of 100 accounts, what is the probability that the sample mean will lie between K190 000 and K205 000?

Solution

This is a question about the sampling distribution of the mean; hence we must first calculate the standard error of the mean.

$$\text{Standard error of the mean} \qquad Se \longrightarrow \bar{O}x = \longrightarrow \frac{O}{\sqrt{n}}$$

Where

        O = population standard deviation

        n = sample size

Applying above formula, we get:

$$\bar{O}x = \frac{K60\,000}{\sqrt{100}} = \frac{K60\,000}{10} = K6\,000$$

Next, we calculate the Z scores using the formula

$$Z = \frac{x - \mu}{\bar{O}x}$$

Where x = sample mean

    u = population mean

    $\bar{O}x$ = standard error of the mean

Thus, for $\bar{x}$ = K190 000

$$Z = \frac{K190\,000 - K200\,000}{K6\,000}$$

        = ⁻1.67   Standard deviations from the mean of a standard normal probability distribution

For $\bar{x}$ = K205 000

$$Z = \frac{K205\,000 - K200\,000}{K6\,000}$$

= 0.83 standard deviations from the mean of the standard normal
probability distribution

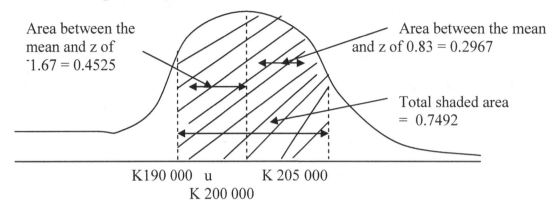

Area between the mean and z of ⁻1.67 = 0.4525

Area between the mean and z of 0.83 = 0.2967

Total shaded area = 0.7492

K190 000 u   K 205 000
K 200 000

Thus, the normal distribution table gives us an area of 0.4528 corresponding to a z-score of ⁻1.67, and it gives us an area of 0.2967 for a z-score of 0.83. Since these are on opposite side of the mean, we add them together to get 0.7492 as the probability that the sample mean will lie between K190 000 and K205 000.

THE CENTRAL LIMIT THEOREM

The relationship between the shape of the population distribution and the shape of the sampling distribution of the mean is called *the central limit theorem*. The central limit theorem is perhaps the most important theorem in all of statistical inference.

- It assures us that the sampling distribution of the mean approaches normal as the sample size increases.

- The significance of the central limit theorem is that it permits us knowing anything about the shape of the frequency distribution of that population other than what we can get from the sample

Example 2

The distribution of annual earnings of all bank tellers with five year's experience is skewed negatively. The distribution has a mean of K150, 000 and a standard deviation of K200, 000. If we draw a random sample of 30 tellers, what is the probability that their earnings will average more than K1, 575,000 annually.

Solution

First, we calculate the standard error of the mean

$$\sigma \bar{x} = \frac{\sigma}{\sqrt{n}} = \frac{K200\ 000}{\sqrt{30}} = \frac{K200\ 000}{5.477225575}$$

$$= \underline{K36, 514.84}$$

For $\bar{x}$ = K1, 575, 000

$$Z = \frac{\text{K1575 000} - \text{K1500 000}}{\text{K36 514.84}}$$

$$= \underline{2.053959431}$$

$$= \mathbf{2.05}$$

From normal distribution tables 2.05 gives us an area of **0.4798**.

Since half or 0.5000 of the area under the curve lies between the mean and the right-hand tail, the required area must be:

```
   0.5000      Area between the mean and right hand tail
 - 0.4798   Area between the mean and K1575 000
   0.0202   Area between the right hand tail and K1575 000
```

Thus, there is slightly more than a 2% chance of average earnings being more than K1575 000 annually in a group of 30 teller

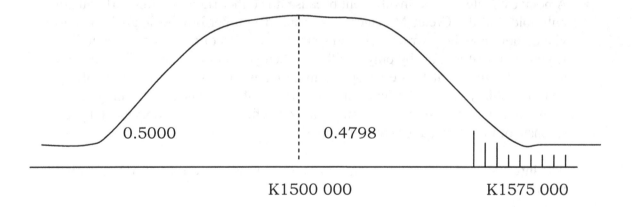

ESTIMATION

Everyone makes estimates. When you get ready to cross a street, you estimate the speed of any car that is approaching, the distance between you and that car, and your own speed. Having made these quick estimates, you decide whether to wait, walk or run.

All managers must make quick estimates, too. The outcome of these estimates can affect their organizations as seriously as the outcome of your decision as to whether to cross the street. Credit managers estimate whether a purchaser will eventually pay his bills. Prospective home buyers make estimates concerning the behaviour of interest rates in the mortgage market. College principals make estimates of the next semester's enrollment in banking. All these people make estimates without worry about whether they are scientific but with the hope that the estimates bear a reasonable resemblance to the outcome.

Managers use estimates because in all but the most trivial decisions, they must make rational decisions without complete information and with a great deal of uncertainty about what the future will bring.

How do managers use sample statistics to estimate population parameters? For example, the credit manager attempts to estimate the credit worthiness of prospective customers from a sample of their past payment habits. Thus, a manager is trying to infer something about a population from information taken from a sample.

TYPES OF ESTIMATES

Generally, there are two types of estimates about a population namely: a point estimate and an interval estimate.

- **A point estimate** is a single number that it's used to estimate an unknown population parameter. An example of a point estimate is when the Credit Manager says" our current data indicate this year the figure for non-performing loans is K200 000 000".

- A point estimate is often insufficient because it is either right or wrong. If you are only told that the Credit Manager's estimate of non-performing loans is wrong, you do not know how wrong it is and cannot be certain of the estimate reliability. If you learn that it is off by only K100 000, then you would accept K200 000 000 as a good estimate of future non-performing loans. But if the estimate is off by K90 000 000, you would reject it as an estimate of future non-performing loans. Therefore, a point estimate is much more useful if it is accompanied by an estimate of the error that might be involved.

- **An interval estimate** is a range of values used to estimate a population parameter.

  It indicates the error in the two ways; by the extent of its range and by the probability of the true population parameter lying within that range. In this case, the Credit Manager would say something like," I estimate that the true non-performing loans this year will be between K150 000 000 and K250 000 000 and that it is very likely that the exact figure will fall within this interval". The Credit Manager has a better idea of the reliability of his estimate.

ESTIMATORS AND ESTIMATES

- Any sample statistic that is used to estimate a population parameter is called **an estimator**; that is, an estimator is a sample statistic used to estimate a population mean µ.

- **An estimate** is a specific observed value of a statistic. For example, if we calculate the mean odometer reading (mileage) from a sample of used cars to be 98 000 miles. If we use this specific figure to estimate mileage of used cars, 98 000 miles would be an estimate.

CRITERIA OF A GOOD ESTIMATOR

Some statistics are better estimators than others. Fortunately we can evaluate the quality of a statistic as an estimator by using four criteria.

1. **Unbiasedness** – This is a desirable property for a good estimator to have. The term unbiasedness refers to the fact that a sample mean is an unbiased estimator of a population mean because the mean of the sampling distribution of sample is equal to the population mean itself.

2. **Efficiency** – Efficiency refers to the size of the standard error of the statistic. If we compare two statistics from a sample of the same size and try to decide which one is the more efficient estimator, we would pick a statistic that has the smaller standard error, or standard deviation of the sampling distribution.

3. **Consistency** – A statistic is a consistent estimator of a population parameter if as the sample size increases, it becomes almost certain that the value of the statistic comes very close to the value of the population parameter. If an estimator is consistent, it becomes more reliable with large samples size. To get more information about a population parameter, find out first whether your statistics is a consistent estimator. If it is not, you will waste money and time by taking larger samples.

4. **Sufficiency** – An estimator is sufficient if it makes so much use of the information in the sample that no other estimator could extract from the sample additional information about the population parameter being estimated.

Note: The above four criteria are presented to make you aware of the care that statisticians must use in picking an estimator.

EXPECTED VALUES OF DISCRETE RANDOM VARIABLES

A random variable is a rule that assigns one and only one numerical value to each simple event of an experiment.

- Random variables that can assume a countable number of values are called discrete while those that can assume values corresponding to any of the points contained in one or more intervals are called continuous.

- Example of discrete random variables are:

1. The number of students in statistics class in a given day; x = 1, 2, 3, …………

2. The number of people who have bank accounts; x = 5101, 200, ……………..

3. The number of bids received in a bond offering; x = 0, 1, 2, …………………

4. The number of errors on a page of an accountant's ledger, x = 0, 1, 2, ………..

5. The number of customers waiting to be served in a bank hall at a particular time; x = 0, 1, 2……………..

Note that each of the examples of discrete random variables begins with the word "the number of". This is very common because the discrete random variables most frequently observed are countables.

- Examples of continuous random variables are:
1. The length of time between arrivals at a bank: $0 \leq x \leq \infty$ (infinity).
2. The weight of a food item bought in a supermarket: 3.052 kg

Mean or expected value of a discrete random variable x is

$$M = E(x) = \sum_{all\ x} x\, p(x)$$

The formula above states that the mean or expected value is simply the product of the discrete random variable and its probability.

Example 3

Suppose you work for an insurance company and you sell a K1000 000 whole life insurance policy at an annual premium of K290 000. Actuarial tables show that he probability of death during the next year for a person of your customer's age, sex, health, etc is 0.001. What is the expected gain (amount of money made by the company) for a policy of this type?

Solution

The experiment is to observe whether the customer survives the upcoming year. The probabilities associated with the two simple events, Live and Die, are 0.999 and 0.001

respectively. The random variable you are interested in is the gain x, which can assume the following values:

Gain x	Simple event	Probability
K290 000	Customer lives	0.999
K290 000 – K1000 000	Customer dies	0.001

M=(290 000)(0.999) + (290 000 - 10 000 000(0.001)
   = 290 000(0.999+ 0.001) – 10 000 000(0.001)
   = 290 000 – 10 000
   = k280 000

Distance traveled by a bank sales representative per working day: 30.35km.

THE PROBABILITY DISTRIBUTION FOR DISCRETE RANDOM VARIABLES

The probability distribution of a discrete random variable is a graph, table or formula that specifies the probability associated with each possible value the random variable can assume. The requirements for the probability distribution of a discrete random variable x are:

1. $p(x) > 0$ for all values of x

2. $\sum_{\text{all } x} p(x) = 1$

EXPECTED VALUES OF DISCRETE RANDOM VARIABLES

The term 'expected' is a mathematical term and should be interpreted as it is typically used. Specifically, the expected value is the mean of the probability distribution, a measure of its central tendency.

If a discrete random variable, x were observed a very large number of times, the probability distribution of x possesses mean μ and a variance σ^2 that are identical to the corresponding descriptive, measures for the population.

If the customer lives, the company gains K290 000 premium as profit. If the customer dies, the gain is negative because the company must pay K1000 000, for a net gain of K290 000 – K1000 000). The expected gain is:

$\mu = E(x) = \sum_{\text{all } x} x P(x)$

$= K290\ 000\ (0.999) + (290\ 000 – 1000\ 000)\ (0.001)$

$= K289\ 710 + (\overline{7}10)$

$= \underline{\textbf{K289 000}}$

POPULATION VARIANCE σ^2

The population variance, σ^2, is defined as the average squared distance of x from the population mean, μ. Since x is a random variable, the squared distance, $(x - \mu)^2$, is also a random variable. Applying the same logic used to find the mean value of x, we find the mean value of $(x - \mu)^2$ by multiplying all possible values of $(x - \mu)^2$ by p (x) and then summing over all possible x values as follows:

$$E\left[(x - \mu)^2 \right] = \sum_{all\ x} (x - \mu)^2\ p\ (x)$$

Note that $E\ (x - \mu)^2 = E\ (x)^2 - \mu^2$

Where $E(x^2) = \sum_{all\ x} x^2\ p\ (x)$

Standard deviation of x is defined as the square root of the variance $\sigma = \sqrt{\sigma}$

Example 4

Suppose you invest a fixed sum of money in each of five business ventures. Assume you know that 70% of such ventures are successful, the outcomes of the ventures are independent of one another and the probability distribution of the number, x of successful ventures out of five is:

x	0	1	2	3	4	5
P (x)	0.02	0.29	0.132	0.309	0.360	0.168

(a) Find $\mu = E\ (x)$
(b) Find $\sigma = E\ [(x - \mu)^2]$

Solution

$$(a)\ \mu = E\ (x) = \sum x\ p\ (x)$$

$$= 0.\ (0.002) + 1\ (0.29) + 2(0.132) + 3(0.309) + 4(0.360) + 5(0.168)$$

$$= 3.50$$

$$(b)\ \sigma^2 = E\ [(x - \mu)^2] = \sum (x - \mu)^2\ p\ (x)$$

$$= (0 - 3.5)^2\ (0.002) + (1 - 3.5)^2\ (0.29) + (2 - 3.5)^2\ (0.132) + (3 - 3.5)^2$$
$$(0.304) + (4 - 3.5)^2\ (0.360) + (5 - 3.5)^2\ (0.168) = \underline{\textbf{1.05}}$$

The standard deviation, $\sigma = \sqrt{\sigma^2}$

$$= \sqrt{1.05}$$

$$= \underline{\mathbf{1.02}}$$

RULES OF ALGEBRA OF EXPECTATIONS

The rules of summation have very close parallels in the rules for the algebraic treatment of expectations. These rules apply either to discrete or continuous random variables if particular boundary conditions exist: for our purposes these rules can be used without our going further into these special qualifications.

RULE 1: If **a** is some constant, then

$$E(a) = a$$

That is, if the same constant value **a** were associated with each and every elementary event in some sample space, the expectation or mean of the values would most certainly be **a**.

RULE 2: If **a** is some constant real number and x is a random variable with expectation E
      (x), then

$$E(ax) = a\,E(x)$$

RULE 3: If **a** is constant real number and x is a random variable then

$$E(x + a) = E(x) + a$$

This can be shown very simply for a discrete random variable. Here,

$$E(x + a) = \sum_x (x + a) \, p(x + a)$$

$$= \sum_x xp(x + a) + a\sum_x p(x + a)$$

However, $P(x + a) = P(x)$ for each value of x, so that

$$E(x + a) = E = (x) + a \sum_x P(x) = E(x) + a$$

The expectations of functions of random variables such as:

$$E[(x + 2)^2]$$

$$E(\sqrt{x + b})$$

$$E(b^x),$$

To give only a few examples, are subject to the same algebraic rules as summations. That is, the operation indicated within the punctuation is to be carried out before the expectation is taken. It is most important that this can be kept in mind during any algebraic argument involving summations.

In general:

- $E[(x + 2)] \neq [E(x) + E(2)]$

- $E(\sqrt{x}) \neq (\sqrt{E(x)})$

- $E(b^x) \neq b^{E(x)}$ and so forth.

The next two rules concern two or more random variables, symbolized by x and y.

RULE 4: If x is a random variable with the expectation $E(x)$, and y is a random variable with the expectation $E(y)$, then $E(x + y) = \sum_x \sum_y (x + y) \, p \, x, y$

Notice that here the expectation involves the sum over all possible joint events (x, y). This could be written as:

$$E(x+y) = \sum_x \sum_y xp(x,y) + \sum_x \sum_y (x+y) P(x,y).$$

However, for any fixed x, $\sum_y p(x,y) = P(y)$.

and for any fixed y, $\sum_x p(x,y) = p(x)$.

Thus, $p(x+y) = \sum_x x(px) + \sum_y yp(y) = E(x) + E(y)$.

In particular, one of the random variables may be in a functional relation to the other. For example, let $y = 3x^2$, then

$$E(x+y) = E(x+3x^2)$$

$$E(x) + E(3x^2)$$

$$= E(x) + 3E(x^2).$$

This principle lets one distribute the expectation. Over an expression which itself has the form of a sum. This may be extended to any finite number of random variables as given by rule 5.

RULE 5: Given the finite number of random variables, the expectation of the sum of those variables is the sum of their individual expectations. Thus, $E(x+y+z) = E(x) + (y) + E(z)$, and so on.

For example, given $y = 6x^4$ and $z = \sqrt{2x}$, then $E(x + 6x^4 + \sqrt{2x}) = E(x) + 6E(x^4) + E(\sqrt{2x})$.

RULE 6: Given random variable x with expectation $E(x)$ and random variable y with expectation $E(y)$, then if x and y are independent.

$$E(xy) = E(x) E(y)$$

This rule states that if random variables are statistically independent, the expectation of the product of these variables is the product of their separate expectations. This rule applies to independent random variables only. An important corollary to this principle is:

If E (xy) # E (x) E (y), the variables x and y are independent.

RULE 7:   Given the finite number of random variables if all the variables are independent of each other, the expectation of their product is the product of their separate expectations. Thus,

$$E(xyz) = E(x) E(y) E(z)$$

and so on. Incidentally, we will have occasion to use the idea of the **covariance** of two random variables defined by Cov. $(x,y) = E [(x – E (x)] (y – E (y)]$When x and y are independent, Cov. $(x, y) = E (x – E (x)] E [y – E (y)]$ by the rule given above. Since it is obvious that: $E [x – E (x)] = E (x) – E (x) = 0$ from rule 1 and rule 3, it follows that when random variables are independent, their covariance is zero. However, it is not necessarily true that zero covariance implies that the variables are independent.

RULE 8:   If **a** is some constant real number, and if x is a random variance with expectation (E (x) and variance σ_x^2, then the random variable (x + a) has variance σ_x^2. This can be shown as follows:

Var.$(x + a) = E [(x + a)^2] – [E (x + a)]^2$. By rule 3 above, and expanding the squares, we have:

$E [(x + a)^2] – [E (x + a)]^2 = E[(x^2 + 2x a + a^2] – [E (x) + a]^2 = E [x^2 + 2ax + a^2] - [E (x)^2 – 2aE (x0 – a^2$.

Var. $(x + a) = E (x)^2 + 2aE (x) + a^2 – [E (x)]^2 – 2aE (x) – a^2$.

$$= E (x)^2 – [E (x)]^2.$$

$$= \sigma_x^2.$$

RULE 9: If **a** is some constant real number, and if x is a random variable with variance σx^2, the variance of the random variable ax is Va. $(ax) = a^2 \sigma_x^2$.

In order to show this we take:

Var. $(ax) = E [(ax)^2] – [E (xa)]^2$

$$= a^2 E (x)^2 – a2 [E (x)]^2$$

$$= a^2 (E(x^2) – [E (x)]^2.$$

$$= a^2 \sigma_x^2.$$

In short, adding a constant value to each value of a random variable leaves the variance unchanged, but multiplying each value by a constant multiplies the variance by the square of the constant.

Note the last two use rules (8 and 9) involve the variance of a random variable. The variance is defined by Var. $(x) = \sigma_x^2 = E[x - E(x)]^2$

$$\sigma_x^2 = E(x^2) - [E(x)]^2.$$

Quiet involving not so? The most important thing here is to grasp the principles and then apply them in solving questions.

Example 4

If $x_1 = 5$, $x_2 = 4$, $x_3 = 6$, $x_4 = 4$, $x_5 = 7$, and all are equally likely values for x. What is $E[x(x-1)]$?

Solution

Using the above rules:

$E[x(x-1)] = E(x^2 - x)$

$\qquad = E(x^2) - E(x)$

$\qquad = \sum x^2 p(x) - \sum x p(x)$

$\qquad = \dfrac{5^2 + 4^2 + 6^2 + 4^2 + 7^2}{5} - \dfrac{5 + 4 + 6 + 4 + 7}{5}$

$\qquad = \dfrac{131}{5} - \dfrac{26}{5}$

$\qquad = \dfrac{105}{5}$

$\qquad = \underline{\mathbf{21}}$

Example 5

X is a random variable, which $[E(x^2)]^2$ or $E(x^4)$ is the smaller

Solution

Let $x_1 = 1$, $x_2 = 2$ x_3, $= 4$ are equally likely random numbers,

Then $E(x^2) = \sum x^2 p(x) = \dfrac{1^2 + 2^2 + 4^2}{3} = \dfrac{21}{3} = \underline{7}$

$[E(x^2)]^2 = (7)^2 = \underline{49}$

$E(x^4) = \sum x^4 p(x) = \dfrac{1^4 + 2^4 + 4^4}{3} = \dfrac{273}{3} = \underline{91}$

Therefore $[E(x^2)]^2$ is smaller than $E(x^4)$.

Example 6

X is a random variable with $p(x = 1) = 0.25$, $p(x = 2) = 0.30$, $p(x = 3|) = 0.20$, x can also take the 4, but no other values.

      (a) What is the probability that x is even.
      (b) What is $E(x^2)$?
      (c) What is $p(x > 2 \mid x$ is an odd number)?

Solution

Given data may be summarized as follows:

X	1	2	3	4
P (x = x	0.25	0.30	0.20	0.25

      (a) $p(x$ is even$) = P(x = 2) + p(x = 4)$

$$= 0.30 + 0.25$$

$$= 0.55$$

      (b) $E(x^2) = \sum = x^2 p(x)$

$$= 1^2 (0.25) + 2^2 (0.30) + 3^2 (0.20)\ 4^2 (0.25)$$

$$= 0.25 + 1.2 + 1.8 + 4$$

$$= \underline{7.25}$$

      (c) $P(x \geq 2 | x$ is odd$)$ is an example of conditional probability.

Thus, P (x ≥ 2 ∩ x is odd)

P (x is odd

$\{x| \geq 2\} = \{2, 3, 4\}$

X is odd = $\{1, 3\}$

$\{x| x \geq 2\} \cap \{x| \text{is odd}\}$

$= \{2, 3, 4\} \cap \{1, 3\} = \{3\}$

$= \dfrac{0.20}{0.25 + 0.20}$

$= \dfrac{0.20}{0.45}$

$= \underline{\mathbf{0.4444}}$

Example 7

Find $E[x(x – 2)]$ given $x_1 = 2, x_2, = 3, x_3 = 5, x_4 = 3, x_5 = 6, x6 = 8$

Solution

$E [x(x – 2)] = E [x^2 – 2x] = E [x^2] – 2E (x)$

$E(x^2) = \sum_{\text{all x}} x^2 p(x)$

$= \dfrac{(2)^2 + (3)^2 + (5)^2 + (3)^2 + (6)^2 + (8)^2}{6} = \dfrac{147}{6}$

$= 24.5$

$E (x) = \sum_{\text{all x}} xp(x)$

$= \dfrac{2 + 3 + 5 + 3 + 6 + 8}{6} = \dfrac{27}{6} = 4.5$

∴ $E [(x^2 – 2)] = 24.5 – 2 (4.5) = \underline{\mathbf{15.5}}$

PROGRESS CLINIC SEVEN

1.   Banks and microfinance companies compete for personal loans customers. For purposes of product design and marketing, it is important for these financial institutions to understand the similarities and differences of the customers they attract. To further such understanding, a credit analyst sampled and questioned 488 bank borrowers and 87 microfinance companies. One of the characteristics he investigated was the credit worthiness of borrowers. He evaluated each borrower using a credit scoring system of a large commercial bank. (Credit score is inversely related to credit risk). The table summarizes the scores he obtained. The relative frequencies can be thought of as the approximate probabilities of a randomly selected borrower having an associated credit score.

Credit score	Relative frequency	
	Bank customers'	Microfinance customers
210	0.109	0.000
200	0.117	0.023
190	0.109	0.034
180	0.113	0.034
170	0.219	0.184
160	0.102	0.069
150	0.102	0.161
140	0.074	0.172
130	0.035	0.105
120	0.020	0.218

(a)Find the expected credit score for bank borrowers. Find the expected credit score for micro-finance company customers. Interpret both these values in the context of the problem

(b) Find the standard deviation for the credit scores of bank borrowers and for micro-finance company borrowers.

(c)   Using the probability distributions in the table and your results from parts (a) and (b), compare the credit, worthiness of bank borrowers and micro-finance company borrowers.

2.   A bank's marketing and accounting departments have determined that if the bank markets its newly development line of lending facilities, the probability distribution shown below will describe the contribution of the new line to the bank's profit during the next 6 months. The bank has decided it should market the new line if the expected contribution to profit for the next 6 months in over K10 000 000. Based on the probability distribution, should the bank market the new line?

Profit contribution X	P(x)
ˉK5 000 000	0.2
K10 000 000	0.5
K30 000 000	0.3

3. Suppose you own a company that bonds financial managers. Based on past experience, your assess the probability that you will have to forfeit any particular bond to be 0.001. How much should you charge for a K1000 000 000 bond in order to break even on all such bonds?

4. A music promoter has scheduled an outdoor concert for Saturday, January 24. If it does not rain, the promoter expects to make K20 000 000 profit form the concert. If it does rain, the promoter will be forced to cancel the concert and will lose K12 000 000 (musician's fee, advertising costs, stadium rental, administrative costs, etc). The promoter has learned from the Meteorological Department that the probability of rain on January 24 is 0.4.

    (a) Find the promoters expected profit from the concert.

    (b)For a fee of K1000 000, an insurance company has offered to insure the promoter against all loses resulting from a rained-out concert. If the promoter buys the insurance, what is his expected profit from the concert?

    (c) Assuming the Meteorological Department's forecast is accurate; do you believe the insurance company has charged too much or too little for the policy? Explain.

5. The economic risks taken by business can be defined as being either pure risks or speculative risks. A pure risk is faced when there is a chance of incurring an economic loss but no chance of gain. A speculative risk is faced when there is a chance of gain as well as a chance of loss. Risk is sometimes measured by computing the variance or standard deviation of the probability distribution that describes the potential gains or losses of the firm. This follows form the fact that the greater the variation in potential outcomes, the greater the uncertainty faced by the firm; the smaller the variation, the more predicable the firm's gains or losses.

    The two discrete probability distributions given in the table were developed from historical data. They describe the potential total physical damage losses next year to the fleets of delivery trucks of two different firms. Both firms have ten trucks, and both have the same expected loss next year.

	Firm A			Firm B	
	Loss next year	probability		Loss next year	probability
K	0	0.01	K	0	0.00
	500	0.01		200	0.01
	1000	0.01		700	0.02
	1500	0.02		1200	0.15
	2000	0.35		1700	0.30
	2500	0.30		2200	0.30
	3000	0.25		2700	0.15
	3500	0.20		3200	0.02
	4000	0.01		3700	0.02
	4500	0.01		4200	0.01
	5000	0.01	4700		

(a) Verify that both firms have the same expected total physical damage loss.

(b) Computer the standard deviation of both probability distributions, and determine which firm faces the greater risk of physical damage to its fleet next year.

(c) Was part (b) concerned with measuring speculative risk or pure risk? Explain.

6.   A stock market analyst believes that the probability of stock ABC increasing in price by close of the business tomorrow is 0.6, the probability of decreasing in prices is 0.2, and the probability of tomorrow's price remaining the same as today's is 0.2. Assume that the ABCs price changes it does so exactly by K2.

(a) Based on the analyst's assumptions, what is the business tomorrow?

(b) Can the change in ABC's price at the close of the business tomorrow actually equal its expected value? Explain.

7. Consider the following probability distribution of the random variable x.

X	10	20	30	40	50	60
P (x)	0.10	0.25	0.30	0.20	0.10	0.05

Find:

(a) E (x)

    (a) variance (σ^2)
(b) standard deviation

(c) construct the interval $\mu \pm 2\sigma$

8. Let x^1, x^2 and x^3 be random sample from a population with mean μ and variance $\sigma2$. Consider the following two point estimating of μ:

$$\hat{\mu_1} = \frac{3x_1 + x_2 + 5x_3}{9}, \qquad \hat{\mu_2} = \frac{x_1 + 7x_2 + x3}{9}$$

(a) Show that both estimates are unbiased.
(b) Which estimates is more efficient
(c) Find the relative efficiency.
(d) Find an biased estimator of the population mean that is more efficient than either of these estimators

9. What are the four properties of a good estimator?

10. (a) What is the difference between the standard error and the standard deviation?

(b) Given that a certain sample has a mean of 60, a standard deviation of 12 and a sample size of 25. Find the standard error of the mean.

11. Critical to sampling distribution is the concept of "Central Limit Theorem" Define and explain the importance of central limit theorem in statistical analysis.

12. Define the following statistical terms

(a) point estimate
(b) interval estimate
(c) an estimator
(d) an estimate

Chapter Eight

INFERENTIAL STATISTICS: HYPOTHESIS TESTING

Hypothesis testing is the statistical assessment of a statement or idea regarding a population. For example, a statement could be as follows:
"The mean salary for a bank clerk in Zambia is greater than K1500 000 per month." Given the relevant salaries data, hypothesis testing procedures can be employed to test the validity of this statement at a given significance level for a sample of the Zambian banking industry. On the basis of results found at a sample level, an inference can be made about the population as a whole.

THE KEY CONCEPTS IN HYPOTHESIS TESTING

In order to undertake hypothesis testing, you need to have and demonstrate clear understanding of the following concepts.

1. Parameter – This is a descriptive measure of a population e.g. population mean.

6. **Statistic** – this is a descriptive measure of a sample e.g. sample mean, sample standard deviation, etc.

3. **Standard error** – This is the value that describe the characteristics of the sampling distribution of the statistic.

4. **Standard error of the mean** – This is the standard deviation of the sampling distribution. It is a measure of the extent to which we expect the mean from the different samples to vary from the population mean owing to the chance error in the sampling process.

5. **Central Limit Theorem** – This is a rule assuring that the sampling distribution of the mean approaches normal as the sample size increases, regardless of the shape of the population distribution from which the sample is selected.

6. **Point Estimate** – This is a single number that is used to estimate an unknown population parameter.

7. **Interval Estimate** – This is a range of values used to estimate the population parameter.

8. **Confidence Interval** – This is a range of values that has some designated probability of including the true population parameter value.

9. **Confidence level** – This is the probability that statistician associate with an interval estimate of a population parameter indicating how confident they are the interval estimate will include the true population parameter.

It is the probability of committing a type I error and is represented by Alpha (α). The common values of α are 0.01 (1%), 0.05 (5%) and 0.10 (10%). An alpha is determined before the experiment.

10. **Confidence Limits** – These are the lower and upper boundaries of a confidence interval. The following results must be learnt by heart:

(a) 95% confidence limit = $\bar{x} \pm 1.96$ standard errors.

(b) 99% confidence limit = $\bar{x} \pm 2.58$ standard errors

(c) 68% confidence limit = $\bar{x} \pm 1$ standard error

$$\text{Standard error} = \frac{\text{Standard deviation (sample)}}{\sqrt{\text{Sample size}}} = \frac{S}{\sqrt{n}}$$

i.e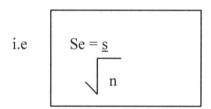

$$Se = \frac{s}{\sqrt{n}}$$

11. **Type I error** – This is an error committed by rejecting a true null hypothesis. The probability of committing type I error is represented by Alpha (α).

12. **Type II error** – This is an error committed by failing to reject a false null hypothesis. The probability of committing type II error is represented by beta (β). Whereas alpha is determined before the experiment, beta is computed using the alpha. Further, note that there is an inverse relationship between beta and alpha. For a given sample size, β increases as the researcher decreases α and vice versa.

13. **Power of a test** – Power of a test is the probability of a test rejecting the null hypothesis when the null hypothesis is false. Power of a test = $1 - \beta$.

Summary

Accept Ho	Reject Ho
Ho is true – correct decision made Ho is false – type II error	Type I error Correct decision made

14. **Critical value** – This is a value that divides the acceptance rejection from the rejection region. Commonly used values of $Z\alpha$ which you should learn by heart are summarized below. $\qquad 2$

Confidence level			
$100 (1 - \alpha)$	α	$\alpha/2$	$Z\alpha/2$
90%	0.10	0.05	1.645
95%	0.05	0.025	1.96
99%	0.01	0.005	2.58

15. **Acceptance Region** – It is any portion of a distribution that is not in the rejection region. If the observed/calculated statistic falls in this region, the decision is to fail to reject the null hypothesis i.e. to accept the null hypothesis.

16. **Rejection region** – If a computed statistic falls in this region or portion of a distribution, the null hypothesis is rejected.

17. A **One – Tailed test** – This is a statistical test where in the researcher is only interested in testing one side of the distribution.

18. A **Two-Tailed Test** – This is a statistical test where in the researcher is interested in testing both sides of the distribution.

Note: It is always important to identify whether the question refers to a one tailed or two tailed test. Look for key phrases such as "not equal to", the greater than". "Less than", etc. Always remember that the alternative hypothesis is set up to answer the question. If the question asks you to determine whether there is enough statistical evidence that the mean is "not equal to ", then you perform a two-tailed test otherwise perform a one-tailed test.

The critical Z values dependent on the type of test and the level of significance which are commonly used are given below. Memorize the results

Level of significance	Right-Tailed Test	Left Tailed – Test	Two Tailed Test
5%	1. 645	-1. 645	-1 .96 and 1. 96
1%	2. 326	-2. 326	-2. 58 and 2. 58
0.1%	3. 09	-3. 09	-3. 29 and 3. 29

19. **Null and Alternative Hypothesis** – The null hypothesis (Ho) must always specify that the parameter is "equal to" some particular value. Thus, Ho, maintains the status quo. Since it is not possible to establish the equality using statistical methods, it falls to the alternative hypothesis (Ha) to answer the question. Hence in order to specify Ha, you must determine what the question asks.

20. .**Large and small sample** – A small sample is one where the sample size is less than 30 whereas a large sample is one where the sample size is greater than 30. For small samples, a t – distribution is used while for large samples, a normal distribution (z – table) is used. Note that it is critical for you to know which of the two distributions is appropriate in a given situation.

HYPOTHESIS TESTS ABOUT ONE MEAN: LARGE SAMPLE

The important thing to remember about hypothesis tests is that there should be no personal bias in the decision i.e. the test must be set up so that the same decision is reached whoever carries out the test. With this in mind, a procedure has been designed that should be followed for every test. The steps listed below are for tests about means but could be applicable to any measure.

1. State the null hypothesis, Ho.
2. Decide on the alternative hypothesis, Ha.
3. Choose the level of significance, thus fixing the critical region.
4. Calculate the mean and standard deviation of the sample, if these are not given in the question, and the standard error of the mean.
5. Calculate the standardized Z statistic.
6. Accept or reject the null hypothesis.

CONFIDENCE INTERVAL: MEAN

Example 1

A large automobile parts wholesaler needs an estimate of the mean life it can expect from windshield wiper blades under typical driving conditions. Already management has determined the standard deviation of the population life to be 6 months, with a mean of

21 months. Using a sample of 100 randomly selected wiper blades, find the interval estimates with a confidence level of 95%.

Solution

a. First, we find the standard error of the mean

$$Se = \frac{s}{\sqrt{n}} = \frac{6 \text{ months}}{\sqrt{100}} = \frac{6}{10} = 0.6 \text{ months}$$

Thus, 0.6 months is the standard error of the mean for an infinite population.

b. Next, we consider the confidence level with which we are working. Since a 95% confidence level includes $\frac{47.5\%}{2}$ I.e. 95% area on both sides of the mean of the sampling distribution, from tables, we find $\frac{0.475}{2}$ i.e. 47.5% to be 1.96 standard errors.

c. The interval is, therefore $\bar{x} \pm 1.96 Se$

Where $\bar{x} + 1.96$ Se is the upper confidence limit

$\bar{x} - 1.96$ Se is the lower confidence limit

Thus, 21 months $\pm$ 1.96 (0.6 months)

$$= 21 \text{ months} \pm 1.176$$

$$= \underline{19.82 \text{ and } 22.18 \text{ months}}$$

Thus, the estimated mean life of the population of wiper blades is between 19.82 months and 22.18 months with 95% confidence.

Note: We can find the number of standard errors for any given confidence level by dividing the given confidence level by 2 and then changing the result into decimal by dividing by 100, and finally picking the figure equal to or slightly greater than the calculated decimal from the normal distribution table.

E.g. 99% confidence level $= \frac{99\%}{2} = \underline{49.5\%}$

$$\frac{49.5\%}{100} = 0.495 \text{ area}$$

From the table 0.4950 corresponds to 2.58 standard errors. (Note: we used 0.4951 as being the closest to 0.4950)

Using the same principles, we can find the standard errors for any confidence level.

e.g. $90\% = \dfrac{90\%}{2} = \dfrac{45\%}{100} = 0.4500 = 1.65$ standard errors for any confidence level

$86\% = \dfrac{86\%}{2} = \dfrac{43\%}{100} = 0.4300 = 1.48$ standard errors

- Therefore, do not say you don't know how to determine the standard errors for any given level of confidence!

Example 2

A sample of 100 fluorescent tubes used by Lotti House gives a mean length of life 20.5 hours with a standard deviation of 1.6 hours.

Find, (a) a 95% confidence interval
    (b) a 99% confidence for the average length of life of those tubes.
    (c) interpret the result in each case

Solution

(a) Given x = 20.5, S = 1.6, n = 100, Z = 1.96

- 95% confidence interval = X $\pm$ 1.96 Se

$$Se = \dfrac{1.6}{\sqrt{100}} = \dfrac{1.6}{\sqrt{10}} = 0.16$$

Thus, 20.5 $\pm$ 1.96 (0.16)

   20.5 $\pm$ 1.95 (0.16)

   20.5 $\pm$ 0.3136

   20.19 to 20.81 hours

This means that we are 95% confident that the true population parameter lies between these values.

(b) Given $\bar{X} = 20.5$, S = 1.6, n = 100, Z = 2.58

99% confidence interval = $\bar{X} \pm 2.58$ Se

$$Se = \frac{1.6}{\sqrt{100}} = \frac{1.6}{\sqrt{10} =} = 0.16$$

$$20.5 \pm 2.58 \, (0.16)$$

$$20.5 \pm 0.4128$$

$$\underline{20.09 \text{ to } 20.91 \text{ hours}}$$

We are 99% confidence that the true value of population mean lies between 20.09 to 20.91 hours.

Note: Increasing the confidence level from 95% to 99% increases the interval from 0.62 to 0.82!

SAMPLE SIZE FOR A GIVEN ERROR

1.96 Se and 2.58Se are called errors in the estimate of the population mean. It is possible to reduce the size of this error by increasing the value of n, the sample size. This is in line with the Central Limit Theorem.

Example 3

In measuring the reaction time in individuals, a Psychologist estimates that the standard deviation of all such times is 0.05 seconds. Calculate the smallest sample size necessary in order to be:

(a) 95% and (b) 99% confident that the error in the estimate will not exceed 0.01 second

Solution

(a) 95% confidence, $1.96Se \leq 0.01$

$$= 1.96 \times \frac{0.05}{\sqrt{n}} \leq 0.01$$

$$= \frac{1.96 \times 0.05}{0.01} \leq \sqrt{n}$$

$$= (9.8)2 \leq (\sqrt{n})^2$$

$$= 96.04 \leq n$$

Thus, the sample size should be 97 since n must be greater than or equal to 96.04

(b) For 99% confidence level, $2.58\ Se \leq 0.01$

$$= 2.58 \times \frac{0.05}{\sqrt{n}} \leq 0.01$$

$$= \frac{2.58 \times 0.05}{0.01} \leq \sqrt{n}$$

$$= (12.9)2 \leq (\sqrt{n})^2$$

$$= 166.41 \leq n$$

The sample size must be 167

Note: By increasing the sample size from 97 to 167, we can be more confident that the mean reaction time is within the required limits.

PROPORTIONS: CONFIDENCE INTERVAL

Sometimes it is necessary to estimate a population proportion from a sample, rather than estimating a mean. This type of sampling is called **sampling for attributes**, as the object is to estimate the proportion of the population who possess the attribute under investigation such as in consumer research, public polls, etc.

The confidence limits of proportions are obtained in the same way as those of the mean.

(a) 95% confidence level = proportion $\pm$ 1.96se.
(b) 99% confidence level = proportion $\pm$ 2.58se
(c) 68% confidence level = proportion $\pm$ 1se

The standard error of a proportion is given by:

$$Se = \sqrt{\frac{pq}{n}}$$

Or

$$\sqrt{\frac{P(1-p)}{n}}$$

Where p = proportion of population possessing the attribute.
    q = proportion of population not possessing the attributes
    n = sample size

Example 4

In a sample of 200 voters, 80 were in favour of re-introducing the death penalty. Find a 95% confidence interval for the promotion of all voters who are in favour of this measure.

Solution

$P = \frac{80}{200} = 0.4$, $q = 1 - P = 0.6$

$$Se = \sqrt{\frac{Pq}{n}} = \sqrt{\frac{0.4 \times 0.6}{200}} = \sqrt{\frac{0.24}{200}} = \sqrt{0.0012}$$

= 0.0346

Thus, a 95% confidence interval $= P \pm 1.96$ Se

$$= 0.4 + 1.96 \, (0.0346)$$

$$= 0.4 + 0.67816$$

$$\underline{= 0.332 \text{ to } 0.468}$$

Therefore, the proportion of voters in favour of the measure lies between 33% and 47%

Example 5

Past experience with an exam in Statistics has shown that only 50% of the students pass. Find the probability that 55% or more of a group of 200 students will pass the exam.

Solution

- Proportion is $50\% = \dfrac{50}{100} = 0.5$

- $q = 1 - 0.5 = 0.5$, $n = 200$

$$\text{Se} = \sqrt{\frac{pq}{n}} \quad = \sqrt{\frac{0.5 \times 0.5}{200}} \quad = \underline{0.03536}$$

- Given sample proportion is $55\% = \dfrac{55}{100} = 0.55$

- Standardizing the value 0.55

$$Z = \frac{0.55 - 0.5}{0.03536} = 1.41 \text{ which give area of } 0.4207 \text{ from tables}$$

Thus, the required probability is $0.5 - 0.4207 = \underline{0.0793}$. Therefore, chances of 55% or more passing are 8 in 100 i.e. 8%

SAMPLE SIZE AND PROPORTIONS

The standard error and hence the error in the estimate can again be reduced by increasing the sample size, n

Example 6

A manufacturer of electric light bulbs needs to estimate the average "burning life" of the bulbs he makes. A random sample of 100 bulbs was found to have a mean life of 340 hours with a standard deviation of 30 hours.

Calculate the size of the sample necessary to provide a degree of accuracy within 3 hours at the 95% confidence level.

Solution

- The error of the estimate = 3 hours

Thus, $1.96 \times \dfrac{5}{\sqrt{n}} = 3$ hours

$$= 1.96 \times \frac{30}{\sqrt{n}} = 3$$

$$= \frac{1.96 \times 30}{3} = \sqrt{n}$$

$$= 19.6 = n$$

$$n = \underline{384.16}$$

Thus, the manufacturer must use at least 385 sample.

SMALL SAMPLE INFERENCES ABOUT POPULATION MEAN

A small sample is one whose sample size is less than 30 i.e. n < 30. For small samples, we use the t-distribution also called the student distribution discovered by W.S. Gosset.

Note that unlike the normal distribution, the t-distribution has degrees of freedom (df). The degrees of freedom are calculated using (n – 1) where n is the sample size.

Thus, t_α values are listed for degrees of freedom from 1 to 29, 30, 40, ------00 where α refers to the tail area to the right of t_α. For example, if we want to find the t value with an area of 0.025 to its right and 4 degrees of freedom, we look in the table under the column t.025 for the entry in the row corresponding to 4 df. This entry is t.025, 4 = 2.776.

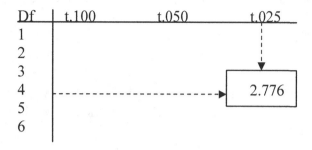

SMALL SAMPLE CONFIDENCE INTERVAL ABOUT A POPULATION MEAN

We can use a t-distribution to form a small sample confidence interval for a population mean, μ, if the population is approximately normally distributed.

The confidence interval is determined using the following formula:

$$\bar{X} \pm t_{\frac{\alpha}{2}} \left(\sqrt{\frac{s}{n}} \right)$$

Where $t_{\frac{\alpha}{2}}$ is based on (n – 1) degrees f freedom

Assumption: The sampled population is approximately normal.

Example 7

Some quality control experiments require destructive sampling in order to measure some particular characteristics of the product. Suppose a manufacturer of printers for PCs wishes to estimate the mean number of characters printed before the print head fails. The cost of destructive sampling often dictates small samples. Suppose the print manufacturer tests n = 15 print heads and calculates the following statistics.
X = 1.23 million characters
S = 0.27 million characters

Form a 99% confidence interval for the mean number of characters printed before the head fails.

Solution

- Thus, $t\frac{\alpha}{2} = \frac{0.01}{2} = 0.005$

- Degrees of freedom $= n - 1 = 15 - 1 = 14$

- Thus, $t\frac{\alpha}{2}, 14 = t.005, 14 = 2.977$ form the table.

- Interval is $\bar{x} \pm t\frac{\alpha}{2}\left(\frac{s}{\sqrt{n}}\right)$

$$= 1.23 \pm 2.977 \left(\frac{0.27}{\sqrt{15}}\right)$$

$$= 1.23 \pm 2.977 \left(\frac{0.27}{3.87}\right)$$

$$= 1.23 \pm 0.21$$

$$= \underline{1.02 \text{ million to } 1.44 \text{ million}} \text{ characters}$$

- Thus, the manufacturer can be 99% confident that the print head has a mean life between 1.02 and 1.44 million characters. If the manufacturer were to advertise that the mean life of its print heads is (at least) 1 million characters, the interval would support his claim!

Note: we don't have standard t values for a given confidence level as we do for z values. This is because the t value or tα is determined by the sample size which in turn determines the degrees of freedom. For example, if n = 20, a 99% confidence level gives t value of t α = 0.01, df = 20 - 1 = 19

This gives t.01, 19 = 2.539 from the table!

LARGE SAMPLE TEST OF HYPOTHESIS ABOUT A POPULATION MEAN (μ).

In this section we advance by undertaking the actual hypothesis test. Earlier on, we alluded to the steps involved in a hypothesis test. In summary form, these steps are given below:

One tailed test	Two tailed test
1. Ho: $\mu = \mu_o$ Ha: $\mu > \mu_o$ Or $\mu < \mu_o$ 2. Test statistics: $Zc = \dfrac{\bar{x} - \mu}{\dfrac{s}{\sqrt{n}}}$ 3. Rejection region: $Zc < -Z\alpha$ Or $Zc > Z\alpha$	1. Ho: $\mu = \mu_o$ Ha: $\mu \# \mu$ 2. Test statistics: $Zc = \dfrac{\bar{x} - \mu}{\dfrac{s}{\sqrt{n}}}$ 3. Rejection region: $Zc < -Z\frac{\alpha}{2}$ or $Zc > Z\frac{\alpha}{2}$

Remember always to use the correct critical Z values for the given significance level depending on whether the test is one tailed or two tailed!

Example 8

A sample of 100 florescent light tubes has a mean life of 20.5 hours and a standard deviation of 1.6 hours. Test:

(a) At the 1% level whether the sample comes from the population with mean 23.2 hours
(b) At the 5% level whether it comes from a population with mean 20.8 hours
(c) At the 5% level whether it comes from a population with mean less than 20.8 hours.

Solution

(a) This is a two-tailed test.
- Ho: $\mu = 23.2$
- Ha: $\mu \neq 23.2$
- $\alpha = 0.01$ or 1%
- Critical Z values are $^-2.576$ and 2.576
- Rejection or critical region is either $Z < ^-2.576$ or $Z > 2.576$

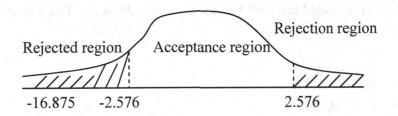

Rejected region   Acceptance region   Rejection region

-16.875   -2.576   2.576

- Test statistics: $\dfrac{\bar{x} - \mu}{\dfrac{S}{\sqrt{n}}}$

where $\dfrac{s}{\sqrt{n}}$ = standard error = $\dfrac{1.6}{\sqrt{100}}$ = $\dfrac{1.6}{10}$ = 0.16

$\therefore$ Z = $\dfrac{20.5 - 23.2}{0.16}$ = $\dfrac{-2.7}{0.16}$ = -16.875

Conclusion: since the calculated Z value falls in the rejection region, we reject Ho i.e. the population mean is not 23.2 hours.

(b) This is also a two-failed test.

- Ho: μ = 20.8
- Ha: $\mu \neq$ 20.8
- α = 0.05 or 5%
- Critical Z values are ⁻1.96 and 1.96
- Rejection region is Z < ⁻1.96 or Z > 1.96

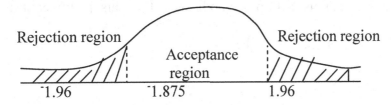

Rejection region   Rejection region

Acceptance region

⁻1.96   ⁻1.875   1.96

- Test statistics = $\dfrac{\bar{x} - \mu}{\dfrac{S}{\sqrt{n}}}$ = $\dfrac{20.5 - 20.8}{0.16}$ = ⁻1.875

- Conclusion: The calculated Z value does not lie in the rejection region. We accept Ho i.e. the sample suggests that the population mean is 20.8 hours.

(c) This is a one-tailed test (left hand side of distribution). The Key word is "less than".

- Ho: $\mu = 20.8$
- Ha: $\mu < 20.8$
- $\alpha = 0.05$ or 5%
- Critical Z value is ‾1.645
- Rejection region is Z < ‾1.645

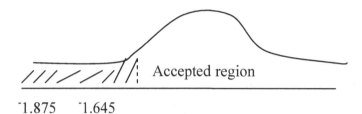

‾1.875   ‾1.645

- Test statistics: $Z = \dfrac{\overline{x} - \mu}{\dfrac{S}{\sqrt{n}}} = \dfrac{20.5 - 20.8}{0.16} = {}^{-}1.875$

- Conclusion: since the calculated Z value lies in the rejection region, we reject H; i.e. the result is significant i.e. population mean is 20.8 hours

Example 9

A manufacturer of cereal wants to test the performance of a filling machine. The machine is designed to discharge a mean amount of $\mu = 12$ grams per box, and the manufacturer wants to detect any departure from this setting. The quality control experiment calls for sampling of 100 boxes to determine whether the machine is performing to specifications. Set up a hypothesis test for this quality control experiment

using $\alpha = 0.01$,   s = 2, $\overline{x}$ = 10,

Solution

Since the manufacturer wishes to detect a departure from the setting $\mu = 12$, in either direction, $\mu < 12$ or $\mu > 12$, we conduct a two-tailed test.

Ho: $\mu = 12$ Hypothesis (i.e. machine is operating properly).
Ha: $\mu \neq 12$ (i.e. $\mu < 12$ or $\mu > 12$) (i.e. machine not operating properly).

Test statistic

This measures the number of standard deviations between observed value of $\overline{x}$ and the Ho value $\mu = 12$.

Test statistics: $Z = \dfrac{\bar{x} - \mu}{\sqrt{\dfrac{S}{n}}} = \dfrac{10 - 12}{\sqrt{\dfrac{2}{100}}} = {}^{-}10$

Rejection region

To determine the precise values of Z that comprise the rejection region, we divide α equally between the lower and upper tails of a distribution.

Thus, $Z\alpha = 0.01$, $\dfrac{Z\alpha}{2} = \dfrac{0.01}{2} = 0.005$ which corresponds to Z = -2.576 and Z = 2.576

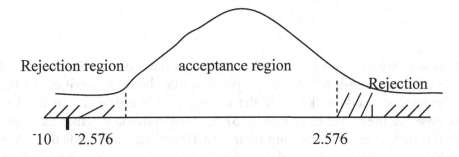

Rejection region   acceptance region   Rejection

${}^{-}10$ ${}^{-}2.576$ 2.576

Conclusion: The calculated test statistic z = ${}^{-}10$ falls in the rejection region, hence we reject Ho.

Example 10

You take a sample of 240 people in Lusaka Central Business and get a mean of 15 and a standard deviation of 5.Test the null hypotheses that the mean adult savings account holding for Lusaka Central Business district is less than your original population.

The original population is 17.5. Test using $\alpha = 0.05$ and explain your results.

Solution

This is a one-tailed test on the left hand side of a distribution (key word "less than").

Given n = 240, $\bar{x} = 15$, s = 5

- Ho: $\mu = 17.5$
- Ha: $\mu < 17.5$

- Test statistic: $Z = \dfrac{\bar{x} - \mu}{\sqrt{\dfrac{S}{n}}} = \dfrac{15 - 17.5}{\sqrt{\dfrac{5}{240}}} = \dfrac{{}^{-}2.5}{0.3227} = {}^{-}7.75$

- Rejection region: Reject if Z < ⁻1.645

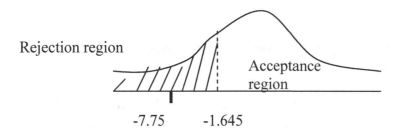

Rejection region

Acceptance region

-7.75   -1.645

Conclusion: Reject Ho since the calculated Z value falls in the rejection region.

Example 11

A statistical analyst who works for a large bank is in the process of examining several pension plans. Because the length of life of the pension plan holders is critical to the plan's integrity, the analyst needs to know if the mean age has changed. In the last census (2000), suppose the mean age of retirees is 67.5. To determine whether the mean age has increased, the analyst selects a random sample of 100 retirees and finds that X = 68.2. If we assume that the population standard deviation $\sigma = 3.1$, can we conclude with $\alpha = 0.05$ that there is evidence to indicate the mean age of retirees has increased since 2000?

Solution

The question asks if there is sufficient evidence to conclude that μ (the mean age at present) is greater than the mean age in 2000 (67.5). As a result this is a one-tailed test to the right.

Ho: $\mu = 67.5$
Ha: $\mu > 67.5$

Test statistic: $Z = \dfrac{x - \mu}{\sqrt{\dfrac{S}{n}}} = \dfrac{68.2 - 67.5}{\sqrt{\dfrac{3.1}{100}}} = 2.26$

Rejection region at $\alpha = 0.05$ if $Z > 1.645$ i.e. we reject Ho in favour of the alternative hypothesis (Ha) only if the test statistic is too large. The rejection region is.

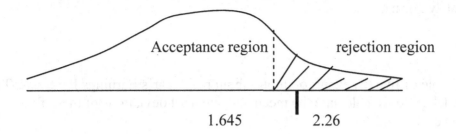

Conclusion: since the test statistic $Z = 2.26$ falls in the rejection region, we reject Ho.

Note: The P-value is simply the probability that Z is greater than 2.26, that is P – value = $P(Z > 2.26) = 0.5 - 0.4881 = 0.0119$. The test statistic falls into the reject region (and the P-value is small) hence there is sufficient evidence to indicate that $\mu > 67.5$

Finally, the above examples provide all the essentials of hypothesis tests involving large samples i.e. $n > 30$. Learn them by practicing until they become second nature.

SMALL SAMPLE TEST OF HYPOTHESIS ABOUT A POPULATION MEAN

For surveys involving a sample size of less than 30, the tests of hypothesis principles applied to large samples are still applicable here except that the test statistics is now the t-value. The following summarizes the steps involved in conducting a small sample test of hypothesis about a population mean.

One-tailed test	two-tailed test
1. Ho: $\mu = \mu_0$ Ha: $\mu < \mu_0$ or $\mu > \mu_0$ 2. Test statistic: $t = \dfrac{\bar{x} - \mu_0}{\sqrt{\dfrac{s}{n}}}$ 3. Rejection region: $t < ^-t\alpha$ Or $t > t\alpha$ Where $t\alpha$ and $t\alpha$ are based on $(n-1)$ df.	1. Ho: $\mu = \mu_0$ Ha: $\mu \# \mu_0$ 2. Test statistic: $t = \dfrac{\bar{x} - \mu_0}{\sqrt{\dfrac{s}{n}}}$ 3. Rejection region: $t < ^-\dfrac{t\alpha}{2}$ or $\dfrac{t\alpha}{2}$

ASSUMPTION

A random sample is selected from a population with a relative frequency distribution that is approximately normal.

Example 12

Suppose a sample of five (5) expert opinions about next year's Earnings Per Share (EPS) for a stock is take and we calculate the mean and standard deviations of these five projection to be $\bar{x}$ = K2.63 and S = K0.72

If last year's earnings were K2.01 per share, is there enough evidence to indicate that the mean expert projection, µ, exceeds last year's figure. Test using α = 0.05 level.

Solution

This is a one tailed test to the right hand side of the distribution (key word "exceeds")

- Ho: µ = K2.01
- Ha: µ > K2.01
- α = 0.05
- Test statistics: $t = \dfrac{\bar{x} - \mu}{\sqrt{\dfrac{S}{n}}} = \dfrac{K2.63 - K2.01}{\sqrt{\dfrac{0.72}{5}}} = \dfrac{0.62}{\dfrac{0.72}{2.24}} = 1.93$

- Rejection region: df = n – 1 = 5 – 1 = 4, α = 0.05 t0.05, 4 = 2.132

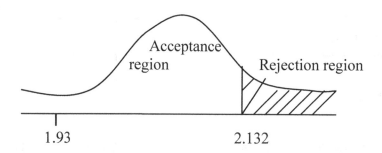

Thus, we reject Ho, if t > 2.132.

Conclusion: Since the calculated t value (1.93) does not exceed the tabulated value (2.132), we cannot conclude that the mean projection of all experts exceeds last year's earnings of K2.01.

Example 13

A car manufacturer wants to test a new engine to determine whether it meets new air pollution standards. The mean emission, µ, of all engines of this type must be less than

20 parts per million of carbon. 10 engines are manufactured for testing purposes and the mean and standard deviations of the emissions for this sample are determined to

$\overline{X}$ = 17.1 parts per million, S = 3.0 parts per million.

Do data supply sufficient evidence to allow the manufacturer to conclude that this type of engine meet the pollution standard? Assume that error with probability α = .0.1

Solution

This is a lower end one tailed test. The manufacturer wishes to have $\mu < 20$.

- Ho: $\mu = 20$
- Ha: $\mu < 20$

- Test statistic: $t = \dfrac{\overline{x} - \mu}{\dfrac{S}{\sqrt{n}}} = \dfrac{17.1 - 20}{\dfrac{30}{\sqrt{10}}} = {}^-3.06$

Rejection region: df = n – 1 = 10 – 1 = 9, α = .01, hence t.01, 9 = 2.821

We reject Ho, if t < ¯2. 821 i.e. if the calculated t-value is less than ¯2.821.

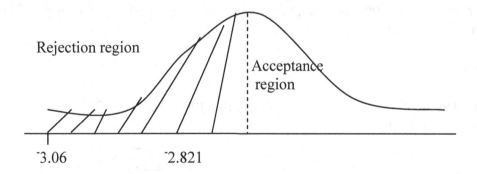

Rejection region

Acceptance region

¯3.06   ¯2.821

Conclusion: Since the calculated t falls in the rejection region, the manufacturer concludes that $\mu < 20$ parts per gallon and the new engine type meets the pollution standard i.e. we reject Ho.

LARGE PROPORTION TEST OF HYPOTHESIS ABOUT A POPULATION PROPORTION

As alluded to earlier on, sometimes a proportion lends itself to better statistical analysis than the mean. Hence we need to carry out hypothesis tests about one proportion. The procedures are basically the same as those involving one mean.

One tailed test	Two tailed test

1. Ho: $P = P_0$
     Ha: $P > P_0$ or $P > P_0$
 	
 2. Test statistics: $Z = \dfrac{P - P_0}{\sqrt{\dfrac{P(1-P)}{n}}}$
 	
 3. Rejection region: $Z < {}^-Z\alpha$
     or $Z > Z\alpha$
	1. Ho: $P = P_0$
	     Ha: $P \# P_0$
	
	 2. test statistics: $Z = \dfrac{P - P_0}{\sqrt{\dfrac{P(1-P)}{n}}}$
	
	 3. Rejection region : $Z < {}^-Z\dfrac{\alpha}{2}$ or
	        $Z > Z\dfrac{\alpha}{2}$

Example 14

The proportion of drivers who plead guilty to driving offences is usually 60%. Out of 750 prosecutions 400 pleaded guilty. Is this proportion significantly different from usual? Use $\alpha = .05$.

Solution

- Ho: $p = 0.6$
- Ha: $P \# 0.6$

Notes $P = \dfrac{400}{750} = 0.53$, $n = 750$

$$Se = \sqrt{\dfrac{0.6 \times 0.4}{750}} = 0.018$$

- Test statistic: $Z = \dfrac{P - P0}{\sqrt{\dfrac{P(1-P)}{n}}}$

$$= \dfrac{0.53 - 0.6}{0.018}$$

$$= \dfrac{\bar{}0.07}{0.018}$$

$$= \bar{}3.89$$

- Rejection Region: $\alpha = 0.05$, critical Z values are $\bar{}1.96$ and 1.96

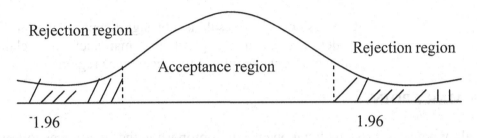

Thus, we reject Ho if $Z < -1.96$ or $Z > 1.96$.

Conclusion: Calculated value falls in the rejection region hence we reject Ho. i.e. the result is significant to reject Ho i.e. the sample of prosecutions suggests that the proportion of driver pleading guilty is changing.

Example 15

The manufacturer of computers claims that his computers are operational for at least 80% of the time. During the course of a year one computer was operational for 270 days. Test, at the 1% level whether the manufacturer's claim was justisfied.

Solution

$$P = \dfrac{270}{365} = 0.74, \ n = 365, \ Se = \sqrt{\dfrac{0.8 \times 0.2}{365}} = 0.021$$

- Ho: $P = 0.8$
- Ha: $P > 0.8$
- Test statistics: $Z = \dfrac{P - P_0}{\sqrt{\dfrac{P(1-P)}{n}}} = \dfrac{0.74 - 0.8}{0.021} = -2.86$

- Rejection region: $\alpha = 0.01$, critical Z value is 2.326.

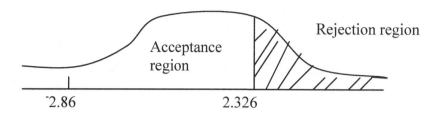

Thus, we reject Ho if the calculated Z value is Z > 2.326.

■   Conclusion: The result is not significant so accept Ho i.e. the evidence does not support the manufacturer's claim. (The calculated Z value falls in the acceptance region).

SUMMARY POINTS

For all hypothesis tests involving one mean or proportion the steps are as follows:

    1. Determine the hypotheses i.e. Ho and Ha

    2. Determine the test statistics using:

- $Z = \dfrac{\bar{x} - \mu}{\sqrt{\dfrac{S}{n}}}$ for large sample

- $t = \dfrac{\bar{x} - \mu}{\sqrt{\dfrac{s}{n}}}$ for small sample

(a) $Z = \dfrac{P - P_0}{\sqrt{\dfrac{P_0(1 - P_0)}{n}}}$ for large proportions

2. Identify the rejection region

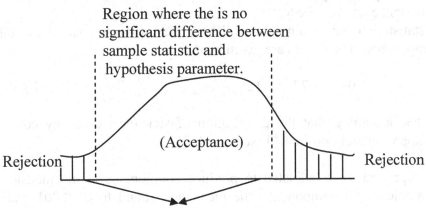

Region where the is no
significant difference between
sample statistic and
hypothesis parameter.

(Acceptance)

Rejection

Rejection

In the two regions, there is a significant
difference between sample statistic and population
Parameter (Reject)

3. State conclusion – This should be stated in the context of the problem and the level of significance should be included.

PROGRESS CLINIC EIGHT

1. When introducing new products into the market place a particular company has a policy that a minimum of 40% of those trying the product at the test market stage should express their approval of it. The new product was tested using a random sample of 200 people of whom 70% expressed their approval of it. Investigate the company's policy at the 5% level of significance.

2. Samples of 500 transistors are tested and twenty are found to be defective. Find a 95% confidence interval P, the true fraction of defective transistors.

3. Shopping is an escalating problem for retailers one Lusaka based store randomly selected 500 shoppers and observed them while they were in the store. Two in twenty-five were seen stealing. How accurate is this estimate? To help you answer this question, construct a 95% confidence interval for P, the proportion of all the store's customers who are shoplifters.

4. A company is interested in estimating μ, the mean number of days of sick leave taken by all its employees. The firm's statistician selects at random 100 personnel files and notes the number of sick days taken by each employee. The following sample statistics are computed:

S = 10 days $\bar{x}$ = 12.2 days

(a) Estimate μ using a 90% confidence interval.
(b) How many personnel files would the statistician have to select in order to estimate μ within 2 days with 99% confidence?

(c) Do the data support the alternative hypothesis that, the mean number of sick days taken by the employees is greater than 10.9 days? Test at $\alpha = 0.05$ report the observed significance level of the test.

(d) Suppose the statistician can obtain data on the number of days of sick leave taken by only six employees. The values are given here:

11   15   4   0   22   12

Conduct the test assuming that the distribution of sick days taken by company employees is approximately normal. Test at $\alpha = 0.05$

5. A machine is supposed to be adjusted to produce components to a dimension of 2.0cm. In a sample of 50 components, the mean was found to be 2.001 and the standard deviation to be 0.003 cm. Is there evidence to suggest that the machine is set too high? Use $\alpha = 0.05$.

6. It is important for airlines to know the approximate total weight of the baggage carried on each airplane. An airline researcher believes that the mean baggage weight for each adult is 60kg. To test his belief, he draws a random sample of 50 adult passengers and weighs their baggage. He finds the sample mean to be 57.1kg. If he knows that the population standard deviation is 10kg, can he conclude at the 5% significance level that his belief is incorrect?

7. The scores of candidates in statistical analysis over the years have followed a distribution that is skewed to the right with a mean of 65% and a standard deviation of 12.5%. A random sample of 30 candidates from PCBF Ltd scored an average of 71.0% Is this evidence suggest that PCBF students performed any differently from other candidates? Test at $\alpha = 0.01$.

8. Chicken and Chips is very popular menu among the working class in Lusaka. The quantity of the one piece chicken and small chips sold at different outlets is usually known to follow a normal distribution with a mean of 18 grammes. An inspector from Zambia Competition Commission is investigating complaints that the quantity in recent packets has been less than expected. To test this he selected a random sample of 9 packets and weighted them. The results were: 14 12   20   16   15 15 17   18   13. Are the complaints justified? Use a one-sized test at $\alpha = 0.05$.

9. A mobile phone provider claims that his market share is 60%. However a random sample of 500 customers reveals that only 275 are user of his product. Test the providers' claim at the 1% level of significance.

10. In a training process, the average time taken is 6.4 hours with a standard deviation of 1.1 hours. Eight employees were trained using a new method and they had an average training time of 6.2 hours Use a 5% level of significance to determine if the new process reduced the average training time.

Chapter Nine

COMPARING TWO OR MORE POPULATION MEANS AND PROPOTIONS

Many experiments involve a comparison of two or more population means. For example, a Sales Manager for a Steel Company may want to estimate the difference in mean sales per customer between two different sales people. A consumer group may want to test whether two brands of food freezers differ in the mean amount of electricity they use. |In this section, we consider techniques for solving these two sample inference problems.

LARGE SAMPLE INFERENCES ABOUT THE DIFFERENCE BETWEEN TWO POPULATION MEANS: INDEPENDENT SAMPLING

Since the shape of the sampling distribution is approximately normal for large samples, we can use the z statistic to make inferences about

$(\bar{x}_1 - \bar{x}_2)$ just as we did for a single mean. The procedures for forming confidence intervals and testing hypotheses are summarized below:

PROPERTIES OF THE SAMPLING DISTRIBUTION OF $(\bar{X}_1 - \bar{X}_2)$

1. The sampling distribution of $(\bar{x}_1 - \bar{x}_2)$ is approximately normal for large samples.

2. The mean of the sampling distribution of $(\bar{x}_1 - \bar{x}_2)$ is $(u_1 - u_2)$.

3. If the two samples are independent, the standard deviation of the sampling distribution is:

$$\sigma(\bar{x}_1 - \bar{x}_2) = \sqrt{\frac{\sigma_1^2}{n_1} + \frac{\sigma_2^2}{n_2}}$$

Where σ_1^2 and σ_2^2 are the variances of the two properties being sampled, and n_1 and n_2 are the respective sample sizes.

LARGE SAMPLE CONFIDENCE INTERVAL FOR ($U_1 - U_2$)

$$(\bar{x}_1 - \bar{x}_2) \pm z\,\alpha/2\ \bar{O}\ (\bar{x}_1 - \bar{x}_2 = (\bar{x}_1 - \bar{x}_2) \pm z\alpha/2 \sqrt{\frac{O_1^2}{n_1} + \frac{O_2^2}{n_2}}$$

Assumptions:1. The two samples are randomly selected in an independent manner from the two populations.

2.The sample sizes n_1 and n_2 are large enough so that $\bar{x}_1$ and $\bar{x}_2$ each have approximately normal sampling distributions and so that
S_1^2 and S_2^2 provide good approximations to O_1^2 and O_2^2. This will generally be time if $n_1 \geq 30$ and $n_2 \geq 30$.

LARGE SAMPLE TEST OF HYPOTHESIS FOR ($U_1 - U_2$)

One – Tailed Test

Ho: $(u_1 - u_2) = Do$
Ho: $(u_1 - u_2) < Do$
(or Ha: $(u_1 - u_2) > Do$

Two – Tailed Test

Ho: $(u_1 - u_2) = Do$
Ho: $(u_1 - u_2) \neq Do$

Where Do Hypothesized difference between the means (this is often 0).

. Test statistic: $z = \dfrac{(\bar{x}_1 - \bar{x}_2) - Do}{O = (\bar{x}_1 - \bar{x}_2)}$ Test statistic: $z = \dfrac{(x_1 - x_2) - Do}{O = (x_1 - x_2)}$

Where $O\ (\bar{x}_1 - \bar{x}_2) =$ $\dfrac{O_1^1}{n_1} + \dfrac{O_2^2}{n_2 O}$

. Rejection region: $z < -z\,\alpha$ (or $z > z\,\alpha$. Rejection region: $z < -z\alpha/2$ or $z > z\,\alpha/2$

When Ha: $(u_1 - u_2) > Do)$

Assumptions: Same as for the large sample confidence interval above.

Example 1

Suppose a bank is considering two suburbs of Lusaka as alternatives for locating a new branch. The final decision about location to choose is to be based on a comparison of the mean incomes of families living in the two suburbs. The branch is to be located in the suburb that has the higher mean income per household.

Suppose the means and standard deviations of the incomes of the sampled households from the two suburbs are as follows:

Suburb 1 (Chawama)   Suburb 2 (Matero)

$\bar{x}_1$ = K18 750 $\bar{x}_2$ = K15 150
S_1 = K3200 S_2 = K2 700
n_1 = 100 n_2 = 100

Form a 95% confidence interval for the difference $(u_1 - U_2)$ between the two mean suburban incomes and advice where a branch should be located.

Solution

95% confidence interval

$$(\bar{x}_1 = \bar{x}_2) \pm 1.96 \sqrt{\frac{\sigma_1^2}{n_1} + \frac{\sigma_2^2}{n_2}} = (18\,750 - 15150 \pm 1.96 \sqrt{\frac{\sigma_1^2}{100} + \frac{\sigma_2^2}{100}}$$

We need to estimate σ_1^2 and σ_2^2. Since the samples are both relatively large, the sample variances S_1^2 and S_2^2 will provide reasonable approximations.

Thus, $3600 \pm 1.96 \sqrt{\frac{(3200)^2}{100} + \frac{(2700)^2}{100}}$

$= 3600 \pm 821$

$= $ K2779 and K4421

Thus we are 95% confidence that the mean income of households in suburb 1 (Chawama) is between K2779 and K4421 higher than the mean income of households in suburb 2 (Matero). Based on this information, the bank should build a new branch suburb 1.

Example 2

The management of a bank wants to determine whether a new advertising campaign has increased its daily income (gross). The daily incomes for 50 business days prior to the campaign's beginning were recorded. After conducting the advertising campaign and allowing a 20 – day period for the advertising to take effect, the bank management recorded the income for 30 business days. These two samples will allow management to make an inference about the effect of the advertising campaign on the bank's daily income. A summary of the result of the two samples is shown below:

Before campaign   After campaign

$n_1 = 50$ $n_2 = 30$

$\bar{x}_1 = K1255$ $\bar{x}_2 = K1330$
$S_1 = K215$ $S_2 = K238$

Do these samples provide sufficient evidence for the management to conclude that the mean income has been increased by the advertising campaign? Test using $\alpha = 0.01$.

Solution

We can best answer this question by performing a test of hypothesis. Defining u_1 as the mean daily income before the campaign and u_2 as the mean daily income after the campaign, we will attempt to support the alternative (research) hypothesis that $u_2 > u_1$ (i.e. that $(u_1 - u_2) < 0$). Thus, we will test null hypothesis $(u_1 - u_2) = 0$, rejecting this hypothesis if

$(\bar{x}_1 - \bar{x}_2)$ equals a large negative value. The elements of the test are as
follows:

Ho: $(u_1 - u_2) = 0$ i.e. $u_1 - u_2$: note Do = for this are as follows:
Ha: $(u_1 - u_2) < 0$ (i.e. $u_1 < u_2$).

Test statistics: $\dfrac{(\bar{x}_1 - \bar{x}_2) - Do}{\sigma(\bar{x}_1 - \bar{x}_2)} = \dfrac{(\bar{x}_1 - \bar{x}_2) - 0}{\sigma(\bar{x}_1 - \bar{x}_2)}$

Rejection region: $z < {}^-z\alpha = {}^-1.645$

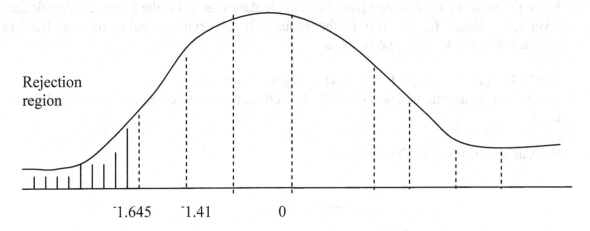

Rejection
region

$^-1.645$ $^-1.41$ 0

$\alpha = 0.05$

Assuming the sample before and after the campaign are independent, we now calculate.

$$Z = \frac{(\bar{x}_1 - \bar{x}_2) - 0}{\sigma(\bar{x}_1 - \bar{x}_2)} = \frac{(1255 - 1330)}{\sqrt{\dfrac{\sigma_1^2 + \sigma_2^2}{n_1 \quad n_2}}} = \frac{^-75}{\sqrt{\dfrac{S_1^2 + S_2^2}{n_1 \quad n_2}}}$$

$$= \frac{^-75}{\sqrt{\dfrac{(215)^2 + (238)^2}{50 \quad\quad 30}}} = \frac{-75}{53.03}$$

$$= ^-1.41$$

The calculated z value does not fall in the rejection region. The samples do not provide sufficient evidence, at $\alpha = 0.05$, for the bank management to conclude that the advertising campaign has increased the mean daily income.

Example 3

Find the observed significance level for the test in Example 2.

Solution

The alternative hypothesis in example 2: Ha: $(u_1 - u_2) < 0$ required a lower one-tailed test using:

$$Z = \frac{\bar{x}_1 - \bar{x}_2}{\sigma(\bar{x}_1 - \bar{x}_2)} \quad\quad \text{as a test statistic}$$

Since the value of z calculated from the sample data was $^-1.41$, the observed significance level (p – value) for the test is the probability observing a value of z at least as contradictory to the null hypothesis as

z = $^-1.41$: i.e. P – value = P (z $\leq$ $^-1.41$). The area corresponding to z = $^-1.41$ from normal tables is 0.4207. Therefore, the observed significance level for the test is:

P – Value = 0.5000 – 0.4207 = 0.0793

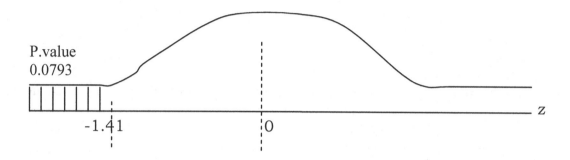

Example 4

Find a 95% confidence interval for the difference in mean daily incomes before and after advertising campaign in Example 2 and discuss the implications of the confidence interval.

Solution

The 95% confidence interval for $(u_1 - u_2)$ is $(\overline{x}_1 - \overline{x}_2) \pm z\alpha/2$

$$\sqrt{\frac{\sigma_1^2}{n_1} + \frac{\sigma_2^2}{n_2}}$$

Once again, we will substitute S_1^2 and S_2^2 for σ_1^2 and σ_2^2 for samples as large as $n_1 = 50$ and $n_2 = 30$. Then 95% confidence interval for $(u_1 - u_2)$ is

$$(1255 - 1330) \pm 1.96 \sqrt{\frac{(215)^2}{50} + \frac{(238)^2}{30}} = {}^-75 \pm 103.94$$

= $^-$K178.94 to K28.94

Thus, we estimate the difference in mean daily income to fall in the interval –K178.94 to K28.94. In other words, we estimate that u_2, the mean daily income after campaign, could be larger than u_1, the mean daily income before the campaign, by much as K178.94 per day, or it could be less than u_1 by K28.94 per day. Note that the large sample sizes collected in the experiment were not large enough to detect a difference between u_1 and u_2. To be able to detect a difference, management will have to repeat the experiment and increase the sample sizes. Thereafter, management will decide whether to continue the experiment or reject the new advertising programme as a poor investment.

SMALL-SAMPLE INFERENCES ABOUT THE DIFFERENCE BETWEEN TWO POPULATION MEANS: INDEPENDENT SAMPLING.

Recall that a small-sample is one whose sample size is less than 30. And when dealing with a small-sample we use the t-distribution.

The t-statistic can also be used to construct confidence intervals for the difference between population means. Both the confidence interval and the test of hypothesis procedures are as follows:

SMALL SAMPLE CONFIDENCE INTERVAL FOR $(U_1 - U_2)$

$$(\bar{x}_1 - \bar{x}_2) \pm t\alpha/2 \sqrt{S_p^2 \left(\frac{1}{n_1} + \frac{1}{n_2} \right)}$$

Where $S_p^2 = \dfrac{(n1 - 1)\ S_1^2 + (n_2 - 1)\ S_2^2}{n_1 + n_2 - 2}$

and $t\alpha/2$ is based on $(n_1 + n_2 - 2)df$

Assumptions: 1. Both sampled populations have relative frequency distributions that are approximately normal.

2. The population variances are equal

3. The samples are randomly and independently selected from the populations.

Recall that the term degree of freedom is defined as 1 less than the sample size for each sample – i.e. $(n_1 - 1)$ for sample 1 and $(n_2 - 1)$ for sample 2. Since we are pooling the information O^2 obtained from both samples, the degree of freedom associated with the pooled variance S_p^2 is equal to the sum of the degrees of freedom for the two samples, namely the denominator of S_p^2 – i.e. $(n_1 - 1) + n_1 + n_2 - 2$

SMALL SAMPLE TEST OF HYPOTHESIS FOR $(U_1 - U_2)$ (INDEPENDENT SAMPLE)

One-tailed test	Two-tailed test
Ho: $(u_1 - u_2) = Do$	Ho: $(u_1 - u_2) = Do$
Ha: $(u_1 - u_2) < Do$	Ha: $(u_1 - u_2) \neq Do$
(or $(u_1 - u_2) > Do$)	

Test statistic:

$$t = \frac{(\bar{x}_1 - \bar{x}_2) - Do}{\sqrt{S_p^2 \left(\frac{1}{n_1} + \frac{1}{n_2}\right)}}$$

Test statistic:

$$t = \frac{(\bar{x}_1 - \bar{x}_2) - Do}{\sqrt{S_p^2 \left(\frac{1}{n_1} + \frac{1}{n_2}\right)}}$$

Rejection region:

$t < -t\alpha$
(or $t > t\alpha$ when
Ha: $(u_1 - u_2) > Do$)

Rejection region:

$t < -t\alpha/2$ or $t > t\alpha/2$
where $t\alpha/2$ is based on
$(n_1 + n_2 - 2)$df.

Assumptions: same as for the small sample confidence interval for $(u_1 - u_2)$ above.

Example 5

Suppose ZNBC TV wanted to determine whether major sports events or first-run movies attract more viewers in the prime time hours. It selected 28 prime-time evenings; of these, 13 had programmes devoted to major sports events, and the remaining 15 had first – run movies. The number of viewers (estimated by a television viewer rating firm) was recorded for each programme. The results are as follows:

Sports	Movie
$n_1 = 13$	$n_2 = 15$
$\bar{x}_1 = 6.8$ million	$\bar{x}_2 = 5.3$ million
$S_1 = 1.8$ million	$S_2 = 1.6$ million

Detect a difference between u_1 and u_2 if such a difference exists. Use $\alpha = 0.05$.

Solution

This is an example of a two-tailed test.

Ho: $(u_1 - u_2) = 0$

Ha: $(u_1 - u_2) \neq 0$ (i.e. either $u_1 > u_2$ or $u_1 < u_2$)

$$t = \frac{(\bar{x}_1 - \bar{x}_2) - Do}{\sqrt{S_p^2 \left(\frac{1}{n_1} + \frac{1}{n_2}\right)}}$$

$$S_p^2 = \frac{(n_1 - 1) S_1^2 + (n_2 - 1) S_2^2}{n_1 + n_2 - 2}$$

$$= \frac{(13 - 1)(1.8)^2 + (15 - 1)(1.6)^2}{13 + 15 - 2}$$

$$= \frac{74.72}{26}$$

$$= 2.87$$

Thus, $t = \dfrac{(6.8 - 5.3) - 0}{\sqrt{2.87 \left(\dfrac{1}{13} + \dfrac{1}{15}\right)}}$

$$= \frac{1.5}{0.64}$$

$$= 2.34$$

Rejection region at $\alpha = 0.05$

$t < \bar{t}\alpha/2$ or $t > t\alpha/2$

Note: For two tailed test $t\alpha/2 = t\dfrac{0.05}{2} = t\,0.025$

$df = 13 + 15 - 2 = 26df$

The value for $-t\,0.025$ with $df = 26$, from the tables $= 2.056$. Thus, the rejection region for the television example is:

t < -2.056 or t > 2.056

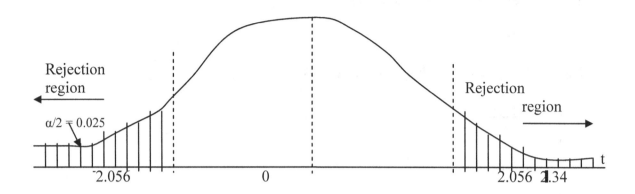

Since the observed value of t, t = 2.34, falls in the rejection region, the samples' provide sufficient evidence to indicate that the mean number of viewers differ for major sports events and first – run movies shown in prime time. Dr, we say the test results are statistically significant at the $\alpha = 0.05$ level of significance. Because the rejection was in the positive or upper tail of the t-distribution, the indication is that the mean number of viewers for sports events exceeds that for movies.

Example 6

Suppose you want to estimate the difference in annual operating costs for automobiles with rotary engines and those with standard engines. You randomly select 8 owners of cars with rotary engines and 12 owners of cars with standard engines who have purchased their cars within the last 2 years and are willing to participate in the experiment. Each of the 20 owners keeps accurate records of the amount spent on operating his or her car (including gasoline, oil, repairs, etc) for a 12 – month period. All costs are recorded on a per-thousand mile basis to adjust for differences in mileage driven during the 12 - month period. The results are summarized as follows:

Rotary   Standard

$n_1 = 8$ $n_2 = 12$

$\bar{x}_1 = K56.96$ $\bar{x}_2 = K52.73$

$S_1 = K4.85$ $S_2 = K6.35$

Estimate the true difference $(u_1 – u_2)$ in the mean operating costs per thousand miles between cars with rotary and cars with standard engines. Use a 90% confidence interval.

Solution

The objective of this experiment is to obtain a 90% confidence interval for $(u_1 - u_2)$, the following assumptions must be satisfied:

1. The operating cost per thousand miles is normally distributed for cars with both rotary and standard engines. Since these costs are averages (because we observe them on a per-thousand-mile basis), the central limit theorem lends credence to this assumption.

2. The variance in cost is the same for the two types of cars. Under these circumstances, we might expect the variation in cost from automobile to automobile to be about the same for both types of engines.

3. The samples are randomly and independently selected from the two populations. We have randomly chosen 20 different owners for both two samples in such a way that cost measurement for one owner is not dependent on the cost measurement for any other owner. Therefore, this assumption would be valid.

The first step in performing the test is to calculate the pooled estimate of variance:

$$S_p^2 = \frac{(n_1 - n1)S_1^2 + (n_2 - n_1)S_2^2}{n1 + n_2 - 2}$$

$$= \frac{(8 - 1)(4.85)^2 + (12 - 1)(6.35)^2}{8 + 12 - 2}$$

$$= 33.7892$$

Where S_p^2 possesses $(n_1 + n_2 - 2) = (8 + 12 - 2) = 18$ df. Then the 90% confidence interval for $(u_1 - u_2)$, the difference in mean operating costs for the two types of automobiles, is

$$(\bar{x}_1 - \bar{x}_2) \pm t\alpha/2 \sqrt{S_p^2\left(\frac{1}{n_1} + \frac{1}{n_2}\right)}$$

$$= (56.96 - 52.73) \pm t0.05 \sqrt{33.7892\left(\frac{1}{8} + \frac{1}{12}\right)}$$

$$= 4.23 \pm 1.734 \ (2.653)$$

$$= 4.23 \pm 4.60$$

$$= (\ ^{-}0.37, 8.83)$$

This means that, with 90% confidence, we estimate the difference in mean operating costs per thousand miles between cars with rotary engines and those with standard engines fall in the interval ⁻K0.37 td K8.83.

INFERENCES ABOUT THE DIFFERENCE BETWEEN TWO POPULATION MEANS: PAIRED DIFFERENCE EXPERIMENTS

This is the kind of experiment in which observations are paired and the differences analyzed.

In many cases a paired difference experiment provides more information about the difference between population means than an independent samples experiment. The differencing removes the variability due to the dimension on which the observations are paired. The removal of the variability due to this extra dimension is called **blocking**, and the paired difference experiment is a simple example of **randomized block experiment**.

Examples for which the paired difference experiment might be appropriate are the following:

1. To compare the performance of two automobile sales people, we might test a hypothesis about the difference $(u_1 - u_2)$ in their respective mean monthly sales. By taking the difference in monthly sales for the two sales people for each of the months, the month-to-month variability (seasonal variation) in sales can be eliminated and the probability of detecting a difference between u_1 and u_2, if it exists, is increased.

2. To estimate the difference $(u_1 - u_2)$ in mean price between two major brands of premium gasoline. If you were to choose two independent random samples of stations for each brand, the variability in price due to geographical location may be large. To eliminate this source of variability, you could choose pairs of stations, one station for each brand, in close geographic proximity and use the sample of differences between the prices of the brands to make an inference about $(u_1 - u_2)$.

3. Suppose a college placement centre wants to estimate the difference $(u_1 - u_2)$ in mean starting salaries for men and women graduates who seek jobs through the centre. If it independently samples men and women, the starting salaries may vary due to their different college majors and difference in grade-point averages. To eliminate these sources of variability, the placement centre could match male and female job-seekers according to their majors and grade-points averages.

Then the difference between the starting salaries of each pair in the sample could be used to make an inference about ($u_1 - u_2$).

SMALL SAMPLE PAIRED DIFFERENCE CONFIDENCE INTERVAL

The confidence interval based on a paired difference experiment is given below:

$$\overline{X}_D \pm t_{\alpha/2} \frac{S_D}{\sqrt{n_D}}$$

Where $\overline{X}_D$ = sample mean of differences

S_D = Sample standard deviation of differences

n_D = Number of differences

Assumptions: 1. The relative frequency distribution of the population of differences is normal.

2. The differences are randomly selected form the population of differences.

PAIRED DIFFERENCE TEST OF HYPOTHESIS

The hypothesis test based on a paired difference experiment is set out below:

One-Tailed Test	Two-Tailed Test
Ho: $(u_1 - u_2) = Do$ i.e. $(u_D = Do)$	Ho: $(u_1 - u_2) = Do$ I.e. $(M_D = Do)$
Ha: $(u_1 - u_2) < Do$ i.e. $(u_D < Do)$	Ha: $(u_1 - u_2) \neq Do$ i.e. $(M_D \neq Do)$
(or $(u_1 - u_2) > Do$ i.e. $(M_D > Do)$	
Test statistic: $t = \dfrac{\overline{X}_D - Do}{SD/\sqrt{n_D}}$	Test statistic: $t = \dfrac{\overline{X}_D - Do}{SD/\sqrt{n_D}}$
Rejection region: $t < {}^-t\alpha$ or $t > t\alpha$ Where $t\alpha$ has $(n_D - 1)$ df.	Rejection region: $t < {}^-t\alpha/2$ or $t > t\alpha/2$ Where $t\alpha/2$ has $(n_D - 1)$ df.

Example 7

Suppose the MD of a named bank wants to compare the mean daily withdrawals of cash of two branches located in Lusaka. If he were to record the branches' total withdrawals for each of the 12 days, and found the following tabulated results:

Day	Branch 1	Branch 2
1 (Monday)	K 759 000	K 678 000
2 (Tuesday)	981 000	933 000
3 (Wednesday)	1 005 000	918 000
4 (Thursday)	1 449 000	1 302 000
5 (Friday)	1 905 000	1 782 000
6 (Saturday)	2 073 000	1 971 000
7 (Monday)	693 000	639 000
8 (Tuesday)	873 000	825 000
9 (Wednesday)	1 074 000	990 000
10 (Thursday)	1 338 000	1 281 000
11 (Friday)	1 932 000	1 827 000
12 (Saturday)	2 106 000	2 049 000

$$\overline{X}_D = K82\ 000$$
$$S_D = K32\ 000$$

Test the null hypothesis that the mean daily cash withdrawals, u_1 and u_2 for the two branches are equal against the alternative that they differ. Use $\alpha = 0.05$. Form a confidence interval.

Solution

Critical examinations of the pairs of daily cash withdraw shows that they tend to rise and fall together over the days of the week. This pattern suggests a strong daily dependence between the two samples and a violation of the assumption of independence required for the two-sample t test discussed earlier. To test the hypothesis, we need to add a column for differences as follows:

Day	Branch 1	Branch 2	Branch 1 and Branch 2
1	K759 000	K678 000	K81 000
2	981 000	933 000	48 000
3	1005 000	918 000	87 000
4	1449 000	1302 000	147 000
5	1905 000	1782 000	123 000
6	2073 000	1971 000	102 000
7	693 000	639 000	54 000

8	873 000	825 000	48 000
9	1074 000	999 000	75 000
10	1338 000	1281 000	57 000
11	1932 000	1827 000	105 000
12	2106 000	2049 000	57 000

$$\overline{X}_D = K82\ 000$$
$$S_D = K32\ 000$$

Ho: $U_D = 0$ (i.e. $U_1 - u_2 = 0$)

Ha: $u_D \neq 0$ (i.e. $U_1 - u_2 \neq 0$)

Rejection region: $t < \ ^-t\ \alpha/2$ or $t > t\alpha/2$

At $\alpha = 0.05$, $t0.05 = \underline{t0.025}$
$$2$$

$df = (n_D - 1) = 12 - 1 = 11$

From tables, $t0.025, 11 = 2.201>$

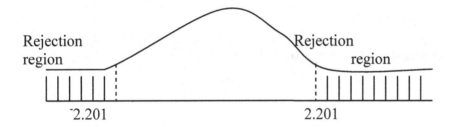

Rejection region   Rejection region

$^-2.201$ 2.201

Test statistic: $t = \dfrac{\overline{X}D - Do}{SD/\sqrt{n_D}}$

$$= \left(\frac{82\ 000}{32000/\sqrt{12}} \right)$$

$$= \left(\frac{82000}{32000/3.464101615} \right)$$

$$= 8.876760388$$

$$= \underline{8.88}$$

Conclusion: Because this value of t falls in the rejection region, we conclude that the two branches differ from 0. The fact that

$\bar{X}_1 - \bar{X}_2 = K82\ 000 = \bar{X}_D$ strongly suggests that the mean daily cash withdrawals for branch 1 exceeds the mean daily cash withdrawals for branch 2.

The confidence interval is:

$$\bar{X}_D \pm t\ \alpha/2 \frac{S_D}{\sqrt{n_D}}$$

$$K82\ 000 \pm 2.201 \frac{K32000}{12}$$

$$K82\ 000 \pm 2.201 \frac{K32\ 000}{3.464101615}$$

$$K82\ 000 \pm 2.201\ (K9237.604307)$$

$$K82\ 000 \pm K20331.96708$$

K61 668.03292 to K102 331.9671

Thus, interval is K61.668.03 to K102 331.97

Example 8

The Human Resource Specialist of a named bank in Lusaka conducts a paired difference experiment to compare the starting salaries of male and female college graduates in Banking and Finance. Pairs are formed by choosing a male and a female with the same grade-point averages. A random sample of ten pairs is formed in this manner where the starting annual salary for each person is recorded. The results are given below. Test to see whether there is evidence that the mean starting salary, u_1, for males exceeds the mean starting salary, u_2, for females.
Use $\alpha = 0.05$. Form a 95% confidence interval.

Pair	Male	Female	Difference (Male-Female)
1	K14 300 000	K13 800 000	K500 000
2	16 500 000	16 600 000	-100 000
3	15 400 000	14 800 000	600 000
4	13 500 000	13 500 000	0
5	18 500 000	17 600 000	900 000
6	12 800 000	13 000 000	ˉ200 000
7	14 500 000	14 200 000	300 000
8	16 200 000	15 100 000	1100 000
9	13 400 000	13 200 000	200 000
10	14 200 000	13 500 000	700 000

Solution

Since we are interested in determining whether the data indicate that u_1 exceeds u_2, we will choose a one-tailed test. The elements of the paired difference test are:

Ho: $u_D = 0$ (i.e. $u_1 - u_2 = 0$)

Ha: $U_D > 0$ (i.e. $u_1 - u_2 < 0$)

Rejection region: since the test is upper-tailed, we will reject Ho if t > t&.

$$t\alpha = t0.05$$

$$df = (n_D - 1) = 10 - 1 = 9$$

From table's t0.05, 9 gives 1.833

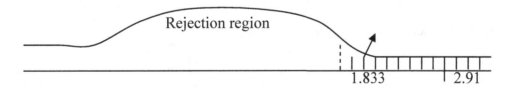

Test statistic: $t = \dfrac{\overline{X}_D - 0}{S_D / \sqrt{n_D}}$

Since $\overline{X}_D$ and S_D are not given, we need to compute them. We can either use the table above by squaring the differences column or calculate them straight away as follows:

$$\sum_{i=1}^{10} X_{Di} = 500\ 000 + (ˉ100\ 000) + 600\ 000 + \ldots\ldots + 700\ 000 = 4000\ 000$$

$$\sum_{i=1}^{10} X^2_{Di} = 3\ 300\ 000\ 000$$

Then $X_D = \dfrac{\sum_{i=1}^{10} X_{Di}}{n_D} = \dfrac{4000\ 000}{10} = 400\ 000$

$$S^2_D = \dfrac{\sum_{i=1}^{nD} (X_{Di} - \bar{X_D})^2}{n_D - 1} = \dfrac{\sum_{i=1}^{10} X^2_{Di} - (\sum X_{Di})^2/10}{10 - 1}$$

$$= \dfrac{3\ 300\ 000\ 000 - (4000\ 000)2/10}{9}$$

$$= 188\ 888\ 889$$

$$S_D = \sqrt{S^2_D} = \sqrt{188\ 888\ 889} = K434\ 610.$$

Then $t = \dfrac{X_D - 0}{S_D/\sqrt{n_D}} = \dfrac{400\ 000}{434610/\sqrt{10}} = 2.91$

Conclusion: The calculated t falls in the rejection region. Thus, we conclude at $\alpha = 0.05$ that the mean starting salary for males exceeds the mean starting salary for females.

A 95% percent confidence interval for $(u_1 - U_2)$ is $X_D + t\alpha/2 \dfrac{S_D}{\sqrt{n_D}}$

$400\ 000 \pm 2.62 \dfrac{(434610)}{\sqrt{10}}$

$= 4000\ 000 \pm 310880$

$= 400\ 000 \pm 311000$

$= \underline{K89\ 000\ \text{to}\ K711\ 000}$

INFERENCES ABOUT THE DIFFERENCE BETWEEN POPULATION PROPORTIONS

Many experiments are conducted in business to compare two or more population proportions. Those conducted to sample the opinions of people are called sample surveys. For example, a bank might wish to estimate the difference in the proportion of customers in two branches who prefer their services over the competition. Or, after an innovative process change, a customer services manager might wish to determine whether the proportion of customer complaints before the change. This section looks at how to test hypothesis about the difference between two population proportions based on independent random sampling.

PROPERTIES OF THE SAMPLING DISTRIBUTION OF $(\hat{P}_1 - \hat{P}_2)$

The following are the key properties of the sampling distribution of the difference between two samples, proportions.

1. If the sample sizes n, and n_2 are large, the sampling distribution of $(\hat{P}_1 - \hat{P}_2)$ is approximately normal.

2. The mean of the sampling distribution of $(\hat{P}_1, P_2)$ is $(P_1 - P_2)$ i.e. $E(\hat{P}_1 - \hat{P}_2) = P_1 - P_2$

    Thus, $(\hat{P}_1 - \hat{P}_2)$ is an unbiased estimator of $(P_1 - P_2)$

3. The standard deviation of the sampling distribution of $(\hat{P}_1 - \hat{P}_2)$ is

$$\sigma(\hat{P}_1 - \hat{P}_2) = \sqrt{\frac{P_1 q_1}{n_1} + \frac{P_2 q_2}{n_2}}$$

LARGE SAMPLE TEST OF HYPOTHESIS ABOUT $(P_1 - P_2)$

The large sample test of hypothesis about $(P_1 - P_2)$ is:

One-tailed test   Two-tailed test

(b)   Ho: $(P_1 - P_2) = 0$ Ho: $(P_1 - P_2) = 0$
         Ha: $(p_1 - P_2) < 0$ Ha: $(P_1 - P_2) \neq 0$
             (or $(P_1 - P_2) > 0$)

(c) Test statistic: $Z = \dfrac{(\hat{P}_1 - \hat{P}_2)}{\sigma(\hat{P}_1 - \hat{P}_2)}$ Test statistic: $Z = \dfrac{(\hat{P}_1 - \hat{P}_2)}{\sigma(\hat{P}_1 - \hat{P}_2)}$

Where $\sigma(P_1 - P_2) = \sqrt{\dfrac{P_1 q_1}{n_1} + \dfrac{P_2 q_2}{n_2}}$

$$= \sqrt{\hat{P}\,\hat{q}\left(\dfrac{1}{n_1} + \dfrac{1}{n_2}\right)}$$

(d) Rejection region: $Z < Z_{\frac{\alpha}{2}}$ or $Z > Z_{\frac{\alpha}{2}}$

Where $\hat{P} = \dfrac{x_1 + x_2}{n_1 + n_2} = \dfrac{n_1 \hat{P}_1 + n_2 \hat{P}_2}{n_1 + n_2}$

(e) Rejection region: $Z < -Z\alpha$

                        (or $Z > Z\alpha$ when Ha: $(P_1 - P_2) > 0$)

Assumption: The two samples are independent random samples from binomial distribution. Both samples should be large enough to allow the use of the normal distribution.

LARGE SAMPLE CONFIDENCE INTERVAL FOR $(P_1 - P_2)$

This is given by:

$$(\hat{P}_1 - \hat{P}_2) \pm Z_{\frac{\alpha}{2}}\ \sigma(P_1 - P_2) = (\hat{P}_1 - \hat{P}_2) \pm Z_{\frac{\alpha}{2}} \sqrt{\dfrac{P_1 q_1}{n_1} + \dfrac{P_2 q_2}{n_2}}$$

$$= (P_1 - P_2) + Z_{\frac{\alpha}{2}} \sqrt{\dfrac{P_1 q_1}{n_1} + \dfrac{P_2 q_2}{n_2}}$$

Assumptions: Same as for large sample test of hypothesis about $(P_1 - P_2)$

Example 9

A consumer agency wants to determine whether there is a difference between the proportions of the two leading automobile models that need major repairs within two years of their purchase. A sample of 400 two-years owners of model 1 are contacted and a sample of 500 two-year owners of model 2 are contacted. The numbers x_1 and x_2 of owners who report their cars needed major repairs within the first two years are 53 and 78, respectively. Test the null hypothesis that no difference exists between the proportions in populations 1 and 2 needing major repairs against the alternative that a difference does exist. Use $\alpha = .10$. Also find the observed significance level (P-value) for the test.

Solution

If we define P_1 and P_2 as the true proportions of model 1 and model 2 owners, respectively, whose cars need major repairs within two years, the elements of the test are:

Ho: $(P_1 - P_2) = 0$
Ha: $(P_1 - P_2) \neq 0$

Test statistic: $Z = \dfrac{(\hat{P}_1 - \hat{P}_2)}{\sigma (\hat{P}_1 - \hat{P}_2)}$

Rejection region: ($\alpha = .10$): $Z > Z\dfrac{\alpha}{2} = Z.05 = 1.645$

$$\text{Or } Z < {}^{-}Z\frac{\alpha}{2} = {}^{-}Z.05 = \underline{{}^{-}1.645}$$

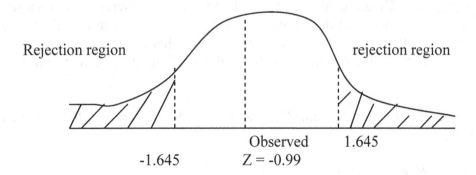

Rejection region   rejection region

-1.645   Observed   1.645
                      Z = -0.99

- 227 -

We now calculate

$$Z = \frac{(\hat{P}_1 - \hat{P}_2)}{\sigma(\hat{P}_1 - \hat{P}_2)} = \frac{(\hat{P}_1 - \hat{P}_2)}{\sqrt{\dfrac{\hat{P}_1 \hat{q}_1}{n_1} + \dfrac{\hat{P}_2 \hat{q}_2}{n_2}}} = \frac{(\hat{P}_1 - \hat{P}_2)}{\sqrt{\hat{P}\,\hat{q}\left(\dfrac{1}{n_1} + \dfrac{1}{n_2}\right)}}$$

$$\text{where } \hat{P}_1 = \frac{x_1}{n_1} = \frac{53}{400} = 0.1325$$

$$\hat{P}_2 = \frac{x_2}{n_2} = \frac{78}{500} = 0.1560$$

$$\text{and } \hat{P} = \frac{n_1 \hat{P}_1 + n_2 \hat{P}_2}{n_1 + n_2} = \frac{400\,(0.1325) + 500\,(0.1560)}{400 + 500} = 0.1456$$

Thus, $\hat{P}$ is a weighted average of $\hat{P}_1$ and $\hat{P}_2$, with more weight given the larger sample of model 2 owners. We substitute to obtain the approximate Z test statistic:

$$Z = \frac{0.1325 - 0.1560}{\sqrt{(0.1456)(0.8544)\left(\dfrac{1}{400} + \dfrac{1}{500}\right)}} = \frac{^-0.0235}{0.0237} = {}^-0.99$$

The samples provide insufficient evidence at $\alpha = .10$ to detect a difference between the proportions of the two models that need repairs within two years. Even though 2.35% more sampled owners of the model 2 found major repairs, this difference is only 0.99 standard deviations (Z = -0.99 form the hypothesized zero difference between the true proportions.

The observed value of Z for this two-tailed test was Z = $^-$0.99. Therefore, the observed significance level is:

P – value = P (Z< $^-$0.99 or Z > 0.99)

P – value = 2(0.5 – 0.3389) = 0.3222

Note: The area corresponding to Z = 0.99 from the table gives 0.3389.

Example 10

Market research organization carried out a sample survey on the ownership of washing machines in Lusaka and concluded that 64% of households owned a washing machine, out of 200 households sampled. Six months later they repeated the survey using the same questionnaire and concluded that 69% owned a washing machine, out of 150 households sampled. Is the difference due to significant increase in ownership or it is a random sampling error. Use $\alpha = 0.05$.

Solution

$$\hat{P}_1 = \frac{64}{100} = 0.64, \quad n1 = 200, \quad \hat{P}_2 = \frac{69}{100} = 0.69, \quad n_2 = \underline{150}$$

Ho: $P_1 - P_2 = 0$ i.e. $P_1 = P_2$
Ha: $P_1 - P_2 < 0$ i.e. $P_1 < P_2$

Critical Z value at $\alpha = 0.05$ is $^-1.645$

$$\hat{P} = \frac{200 (0.64) + 150 (0.69)}{200 + 150} = 0.66$$

$$\hat{q} = 1 - \hat{P} = 1 - 0.66 = \underline{0.34}$$

$$Se = \sqrt{\frac{\hat{P}\hat{q}}{n_1} + \frac{\hat{P}\hat{q}}{n_2}} = \sqrt{\frac{0.66 (0.34) + 0.66(0.34)}{200 + 150}} = \underline{0.051}$$

$$Z = \frac{\hat{P}_1 - \hat{P}_2}{Se} = \frac{0.64 - 0.69}{0.051} = {}^-0.98$$

Rejection region is $Z < {}^-1.645$

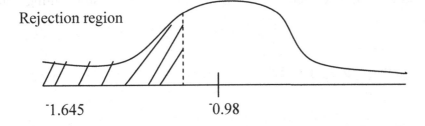

Rejection region

$^-1.645$ $^-0.98$

The calculated Z value does not lie in the critical region or rejection region hence the result is **not** significant so accept Ho.

DETERMINING THE SAMPLE SIZE FOR COMPARING TWO PROPORTIONS

The sample sizes n_1 and n_2 required to compare two population proportions can be found in a manner similar to the method for comparing sizes i.e. $n_1 = n_2$ and then choose n so that $\hat{\ }$ $\hat{\ }$

$(P_1 - P_2)$ will differ from $(P_1 - P_2)$ by no more than a bound B with a specified probability. To estimate $(P_1 - P_2)$ to a given bound B with probability $(1 - \alpha)$ or equivalently, with a 100 $(1 - \alpha)$ % confidence interval of width W = 2B, use the following formula to solve for equal sample sizes that will achieve the desired reliability:

$$n_1 = n_2 = \frac{\left(\frac{Z\alpha}{2}\right)^2 (P_1 q_1 + P_2 q_2)}{B^2} = \frac{4\left(\frac{Z\alpha}{2}\right)^2 (P_1 q_1 + P_2 q_2)}{W^2}$$

Example 11

A production manager suspects a difference exists between the proportions of defective items produced by two different machines. Experience has shown that the proportion defective for the two machines is in the neighbourhood of 0.03. If the manager wants to estimate the difference in the proportions using a 95% confidence interval with width 0.01 how many items must be randomly sampled from the production of each machine. (Assume $n_1 = n_2 = n$).

Solution

For the specified level of reliability, $Z_{\frac{\alpha}{2}} = Z_{\frac{0.05}{2}} = Z0.025 = 1.96$. Then letting $P_1 = P_2$

= 0.03 and $n_1 = n_2 = n$, we find the required sample size per machine by solving the following equation for n:

$$Z_{\frac{\alpha}{2}} \sqrt{\frac{P_1 q_2}{n_1} + \frac{P_2 q_2}{n_2}} = \frac{W}{2}$$

Where is the desired width of the confidence interval, i.e. W = 0.01. Substituting and solving for n, we obtain:

$$1.96 \sqrt{\frac{(0.03)(0.97)}{n} + \frac{(0.03)(0.97)}{n}} = 0.005$$

$$= 1.96 \sqrt{\frac{2(0.03)\,0.97)}{n}} = 0.005$$

$$= (1.96)^2 \frac{2(0.03)\,(0.97)}{n} = (0.005)^2$$

$$= \frac{3.8416 \times 0.0582}{n} = 0.000025$$

$$= 0.000025n = 0.22358112$$

$$n = \frac{0.22358112}{0.000025}$$

$$\underline{n = 8943.2448}$$

Thus, about 9000 items would have to be inspected for each machine if the manager insists on estimating $(P_1 - P_2)$ correct to within 0.005 with probability equal to 0.95. This may be a tedious sampling procedure.

DETERMINING THE SAMPLE SIZE FOR COMPARING TWO POPULATIONS MEANS $(\mu_1 - \mu_2)$.

We can find the appropriate sample size to estimate the difference between two population parameters with a specified degree of reliability. That is, to estimate the difference between two parameters correct to within B units with probability $(1 - \alpha)$, set $Z\alpha/2$ standard deviations of the sampling distribution of the estimator equal to B. Then Solve for the sample size. To do this we have to specify a particular ratio between n_1 and n_2. Most often, we want to have equal sample sizes i.e. $n_1 = n_2 = n$

INDEPENDENT RANDOM SAMPLES

To estimate $(\mu_1 - \mu_2)$ to within a given bound B with probability $(1 - \alpha)$ or, equivalently, with a 100 $(1 - \alpha)$ % confidence interval with width $W = 2B$, we use the following formula to solve for equal sample sizes that will achieve the desired reliability:

$$n_1 = n_2 = \frac{(Z\alpha/2)^2\,(\sigma^2_1 + \sigma^2_2)}{B^2} = \frac{4(z\alpha/2)\,(\sigma^2_1 + \sigma^2_2)}{W^2}$$

Note: We need to substitute the values of σ^2_1 and σ^2_2 before solving for the sample size. These might be sample variances S^2_1 and S^2_2 from prior sampling or from educated guess based on the range i.e. $S = R/$

PAIRED DIFFERENCE EXPERIMENT

To estimate n_D to within a given bound B with probability $(1 - \alpha)$, or, equivalently, with a $100(1 - \alpha)\%$ confidence interval of width $W = 2B$, use the following formula to solve for n_D that will achieve the desired reliability.

$$n_D = \frac{\left(Z_{\frac{\alpha}{2}}\right)^2 \sigma_D^2}{B^2} = 4 \frac{\left(Z_{\frac{\alpha}{2}}\right)^2 \sigma_D^2}{W^2}$$

We need to substitute an estimate for the value σ_D^2 before solving for the sample size. This estimate might be of sample variance S_D^2 from prior sampling or from an educated guess based on the range i.e. $S_D = \frac{R}{4}$

Example 12

The sales manager for a Chain of Super markets wants to determine whether store location, management, and other factors produce a difference in the mean meat purchase per customer (Zero purchases to be excluded) at two different stores. The estimate of the difference in mean purchase per customer is to be correct to within K2.00 with the probability equal to 0.95. If the two sample sizes are to be equal, find $n_1 = n_2 = n$, the number of customer meat sales to be randomly selected form each store.

Solution

To solve the problem, we have to know something about the variation in the Kwacha amount of meet sales a range of approximately K30 at each store, then we could approximate $\sigma_1 = \sigma_2$ by letting the range equal 4σ, and

$4\sigma = K30$
$\sigma = \frac{K30}{4} = K7.50$

The next step is to solve the equation

$$Z_{\frac{\alpha}{2}} \sqrt{\frac{\sigma_1^2}{n_1} + \frac{\sigma_2^2}{n_2}} = B$$

For n_1 where $n = n_1 = n_2$. Since we want the estimate to lie within $B = K2.00$ of $(\mu_1 - \mu_2)$ with probability equal to 0.95, $Z_{\frac{\alpha}{2}} = Z_{0.025} = 1.96$

Then letting $\sigma^1 = \sigma^2 = 7.5$ and solving for n, we have:

$$1.96 \sqrt{\frac{(7.5)^2}{n} + \frac{(7.5)^2}{n}} = 2.00$$

$$1.96 \sqrt{\frac{2(7.5)^2}{n}} = 2.00$$

$$\frac{112.5}{n} = 1.020408163$$

$$\frac{112.5}{n} = 1.04123282$$

$$n = \underline{108.045}$$

Thus, the sales manager has to randomly sample 108 meat sales per store to estimate the difference in meat sales per customer correct to within K2.00 with probability equal to 0.95.

Example 13

A laboratory manager wishes to compare the difference in the mean readings of two instruments, A and B, designed to measure the potency (in, parts per million) of an antibiotic. To conduct the experiment, the manager plans to select n_D specimens of the antibiotic from a vat and to measure each specimen with both instruments. The difference (μ_A - μ_B) will be estimated based on the n_D paired differences ($x_A - x_B$) obtained in the experiment. If preliminary measurements suggests that the differences will range between plus or minus 10 parts per million, how many differences will be needed to estimate (μ_A - μ_B) correct to within 1 part per million with confidence coefficient equal to 0.99?

Solution

The estimator for (μ_A - μ_B), based on a paired difference experiment, is $\bar{x}_D = (\bar{x}_A - \bar{x}_B)$ and

$$\sigma\bar{x}_D = \frac{\sigma_D}{\sqrt{n_D}}$$

Thus, the number n_D of pairs of measurements needed to estimate (μ_A - μ_B) to within 1 apart per million can be obtained by solving for n_D in the equation

$$Z_{\alpha/2} \frac{\sigma_D}{\sqrt{n_D}} = B$$

Where $Z_{0.005} = 2.58$ and $B = 1$. To solve this equation for n_D, we need to have an approximate value of σ_D.

We are given the information that the difference are expected to range from ⁻10 to 10 parts per million. Letting the range equal to $4\sigma_D$, we find:

Range = $20 = 4\sigma_D$

$$\sigma_D = 5$$

Substituting $\sigma_D = 5$, $B = 1$ and $Z_{0.005} = 2.58$ into the equation and solving for n_D, we obtain

$$2.58 \frac{5}{\sqrt{n_D}} = 1$$

$$\frac{5}{\sqrt{n_D}} = 0.387596899$$

$$0.387596899 \, n_D = 5$$

$$0.150231356 \, n_D = 25$$

$$n_D = \frac{25}{0.150231356} = 166.4100003$$

$$n_D = 166$$

Therefore, it will approximately $n_D = 166$ pairs of measurements to estimate (μ_A - μ_B) correct within 1 part per million using the paired difference experiments.

PROGRESS CLINIC NINE

1. A paper company conducted an experiment to compare the mean time to unload shipment of logs for two different unloading procedures. Random samples of 50 trucks each were unloaded using a new methods and the company's current method.. The objective of the experiment is to determine whether the new will reduce the mean unloading time. The sample means and standard deviations are shown.

New method	Current method
$n_1 = 50$	$n_2 = 50$
$\bar{x}_1 = 25.4$ minutes	$\bar{x}_2 = 27$ minutes
$S_1 = 3.1$ minutes	$S_2 = 3.7$ minutes

(a) Do the data provide sufficient evidence to indicate that the mean unloading time for the new method is less than the mean unloading time for the method currently in use? Test using $\alpha = 0.05$.

(b) Give the observed significance level for the test.

(c) Find a 90% confidence interval for the difference in mean unloading times between the two methods.

2. A study was carried out to compare the profiles of a sample of 44 firms that merged with those of a sample of 44 firms that did not merge. The table displays information obtained on the firms' price earnings ratios:

	Merged firms	Non-merged firms
Sample mean	7.295	14.666
Sample standard deviation	7.374	16.089

(a) The analysis of the study indicated that "merged firms generally have smaller price-earnings ratios". Do you agree? Test using $\alpha = 0.05$.

(b) Report the p – value of the test you conducted in part (a).

(c) What assumption(s) was it necessary to make in order to perform the test in part a?

(d) Do you think that the distribution of the price-earnings ration for the populations from which these samples were drawn are normally distributed? Why or why not? (Hint: Note the relative values of the sample means and standard deviations.)

3. One way corporations raise money for expansion is to issue bonds, which are loan agreements to repay the purchaser a specified amount of money with a fixed rate of interest paid periodically over the life of the bond. In a study described in the Harvard Business Review (July – August 1979), D. Logue and R .Rogalski asks the question, "Does it pay to shop for your bond underwriter?" The reason for the question is that the price of a bond may rise or fall after its issuance. Therefore, whether a corporation receives the market price for a bond depends on the skill of the underwriter. The change in the prices of 27 bonds handled over a 12-month period by one underwriter and in the prices of 23 bonds handled by another underwriter are given in the table.

	Underwriter 1	Underwriter 2
Sample size	27	23
Sample mean	‾0.0491	‾0.0307
Sample variance	0.009800	0.002465

(a) Do the data provide sufficient evidence to indicate a difference in the mean change in bond prices handled by the two underwriters? Test using $\alpha = 0.05$.

(b) Find a 95% confidence interval for the mean difference for the two underwriters, and interpret it.

4. We are given four populations with different means but the same variance σ^2. If the samples from these standard deviations as follows 0.02, 0.05, 0.15 and 0.12. What is the last unbiased estimator of σ^2?

5. In order to determine whether there is a difference in the performance of 2 training methods, samples of individuals from each of the methods were checked. For the 6 individuals from method 1, the mean efficiency score was 35, with a standard deviation of 6. for the 8 individuals from method 2 , the mean efficiency score was 27, with a standard deviation of 7. Set $\alpha = 0.02$.

6. A paired difference experiment yielded the data shown below:

Person	Before x_1	After x_2
1	83	92
2	60	71
3	55	56
4	99	104
5	77	89

(a) compute $\bar{x}_D$ and s_D

(b) Demonstrate that $\bar{x}_D = \bar{x}_1 - \bar{x}_2$.

(c) Is there sufficient evidence to conclude that $\mu_1 \# \mu_2$? Test using $\alpha = 0.05$

(d) What assumptions are necessary to the paired difference test will be valid.

(e) Construct a 95% confidence interval for μ_D.

7. In order to compare sales for two local fast-foods stores, a marketing researcher recorded the number of chicken and chips sold during the lunch hour for each day during a randomly selected week. The following results were obtained:

Day	Store 1	Store 2
Monday	140	100
Tuesday	95	60
Wednesday	75	65
Thursday	65	41
Friday	85	64
Saturday	155	114
Sunday	132	111

(a) Construct a 95% confidence interval for $\mu_1 - \mu_2$, where μ_1 and μ_2 are the mean lunch hour sales for fast food stores 1 and 2 respectively.

(b) Is there evidence (at $\alpha = 0.05$) to refute the claim of no difference in mean lunch hour sales for the two stores?

(c) What assumptions are required for the validity of the procedure used in part (a) and (b)?

(d) Frequently, a paired difference experiment provides more information about the difference between two population means than an independent random samples experiment. Explain. Also explain when it may not.

8. A paired difference experiment yielded the data shown below:

Pair	x_1	x_2
1	55	44
2	68	55
3	40	25
4	55	56
5	75	62
6	52	38
6	49	31

(a) Test Ho: $\mu_D = 10$ against Ha: $\mu_D \# 10$, where $\mu_D = (x_1 - x_2)$. Use $\alpha = 0.05$.

(b) Report the p – value for the test you conducted in part (a). Interpret the p – value.

9. A manufacturer of automobile shock absorbers was interested in comparing the durability of its shocks with that of the shocks produced by its biggest competitor.

To make the comparison, one of the manufacturer's and one of the competitor's shocks were randomly selected and installed on the rear wheel of each of six cars. After the cars had been driven 20 000 miles, coded and recorded. Results of the examination are shown in the table below.

Car number	Manufacturer's shock	Competitor shock
1	8.8	8.4
2	10.5	10.1
3	12.5	12.0
4	9.7	9.3
5	9.6	9.0
6	13.2	13.0

(a) Do that data present sufficient evidence to conclude that there is a difference in the mean length of the two types of shocks after 20 000 miles of use? Use $\alpha = 0.05$.

(b) Find the approximate observed significance level for the test, and interpret its value.

(c) What assumptions are necessary to apply a paired difference analysis to the data?

(d) Construct a 95% confidence interval for $(\mu_1 - \mu_2)$. Interpret the confidence interval.

(e) Suppose the above data are based on independent random samples.

(i) Do the data provide sufficient to indicate a difference between the mean strengths for the two types of shocks? Use $\alpha = 0.05$.

(ii) Construct a 95% confidence interval for $(\mu_1 - \mu_2)$. Interpret your result.

(iii) Compare the confidence intervals you obtained in (d) and part (ii) above. Which is wider? To what do you attribute the difference in width? Assuming in each case that the appropriate assumptions are satisfied, which interval provides you with more information about $(\mu_1 - \mu_2)$? Explain.

(iv) Are the results of unpaired analysis valid when the data have been collected from a paired experiment?

10. Two banks, bank 1 and bank 2, independently sampled 40 and 50 of their business accounts, respectively, and determined the number of the bank's services (loans,

chequing, savings, investment advisory services etc). Each sampled business was using. Both banks offer the same services. A summary of the data supplied by the samples is listed in the table.

Bank 1	Bank 2
$\bar{x}_1 = 2.2$	$\bar{x}_2 = 1.8$
$s_1 = 1.15$	$s_2 = 1.10$

(a) Do there samples provide sufficient evidence to conclude that the average number of services used by bank 1's business customers is significantly greater (at $\alpha = 0.10$) than the average number of services used by bank 2's business customers?

(b) Find a 99% confidence interval for $(\mu_1 - \mu_2)$. Does the interval include 0? Interpret the confidence interval.

11. Management training programmes are often instituted to teach supervising skills and thereby increase productivity suppose a company psychologist administers a set of examinations to each of the ten supervisors before a training programme begins and then administers similar examinations are designed to measure supervisory skills, with higher scores indicating increased skill. The results of the tests are shown below:

Supervisor	Before training programme	After training programme
1	63	78
2	93	92
3	84	91
4	72	80
5	65	69
6	72	85
7	91	99
8	84	82
9	71	81
10	87	80

(a) Do the data provide evidence that the training programme is effective in increasing supervisory skills, as measured by the examination scores? Use $\alpha = 0.10$

(b) Find and interpret the approximate p –value for the test.

12. Workers in two different banks were asked what they considered to be most important labour-management problem. In group A, 200 out of a random sample of 400 workers felt that a fair adjustment of grievances was the most important problem. In group B, 60 out of a random sample of 100 workers felt that this was the most important problem. ? Would you conclude that these two groups differed with respect to the proportion of workers who believed that fair adjustments of grievances was the most important problem. Test at $\alpha = 0.10$.

13. Marketing research has been defined by the American Marketing Association as the "systematic gathering< recording, and analyzing of data about problems relating to the marketing of goods and services "(American Marketing Association, 1961). Companies may have their own marketing research departments, or they may contract the services of a marketing research firm. The marketing research department of a large manufacturer of facial tissue paper was charged with the responsibility of determining consumer preferences regarding the softness of its newly developed product (brand A) relative to the industry leader (brand B). A random sample of 205 consumers was selected and asked to rank the softness of brands, A and B. in the results 119 ranked brand A as softer, and 86 ranked brand B as softer.

(a) Do the data indicate that brand A is perceived by consumers as being superior to brand B in terms of softness? Test using $\alpha = .05$.

(b) Find the P – value for the test and interpret its value.

14. Careful auditing is essential to all businesses, large and small. Suppose a firm wants to compare the performance of two auditors it employs. One measure of auditing performance is error rate, so the firm decides to sample 400 pages at random from the work of each auditor and carefully examine each page for errors. Suppose the number of pages on which at least one error is found is 50 for auditor A and 73 for auditor B.

(a) Dot he data provide evidence of a difference between the error rates for the two auditors? Use $\alpha = 0.01$.

(b) Find the P – value for the test and interpret it value.

Chapter Ten

TEST OF HYPOTHESIS USING THE CHI-SQUARE (X^2) DISTRIBUTION

Results obtained in a statistical study do not always correspond to what we would expect. To examine whether results deviate extensively from what may be expected, because of chance alone, we can perform a chi-square test.

CHARACTERISTICS OF THE CHI-SQUARE TEST

The type of test has the following characteristics

1. The chi-square (x^2) distribution is a continuous distribution, and because there is no assumption for normality, it can be applied more generally.

2. The distribution is positively skewed, but approaches the normal distribution as the number of degrees of freedom increases.

3. It is used to test whether the observed frequency corresponds with the expected frequency.

4. The x^2-value is always positive.

5. It may be utilized in conditions with a relatively small sample size.

6. It enables us to test a hypothesis concerning more than two distributions.

7. Three basic tests will be discussed: the test for independence of variables, the test for the difference between more than two proportions and a test to determine whether a specific pattern, does in fact conform to that pattern.

TEST OF INDEPENDENCE

It is often important to determine whether relationships exist between different variables, or whether the variable may be considered independent.

The null hypothesis states that the two variables are statistically independent. This means that knowledge of either variable does not help in predicting the other variable. In contrast, the alternative hypothesis states that the two variables are dependent i.e. knowledge of either variable does help in predicting the other variable.

The following are the steps for the test of independence between two variables

1. Ho: the variables are independent

2.   Ha: the variables are dependent

3.   Since two variables are involved, the observed frequencies (fo) are entered in a cell in a two-way classification table or contingency table. The dimensions of such a table are described by identifying the number of rows (r) and the number of columns (k) in the identity (r X k).

4.   In order to perform the chi-square test, expected frequencies are needed. A table of expected frequencies (fe) is determined, based on Ho being true. The (fe) for any given cell is in the product of total of the frequencies observed in the row and the total of the frequencies observed in that column, divided by the overall size of the sample.

5. fe = $\frac{\text{row total X column total}}{\text{overall total}}$

6.   The fo column total should be the same as the fe column total.

7.   There is a rule that no fe should be less than 5. when this happens combine adjacent classes.

8.   In order to determine if the differences between the fe and the fo, are significant, we use the chi-square test:

9. $x^2 = \frac{\sum (fo - fe)}{fe}$

10. Calculate the value of the chi-square by substituting, cell by cell, the values from the fo and fe table into the formula.

11. In order to determine how different the fo can be from the fe and still support the Ho, the calculated x^2 is compared with a critical chi-square value from the chi-square table. The top row of the table shows the significance level specified along with the Ho, and the first column contains the number of degrees of freedom (df).

   df =(number of rows – 1) X (number of columns – 1) = (r – 1) (k – 1).

12. Because the x^2 distribution is positively skewed, the critical value will always be positive and in the right-hand tail of the curve.

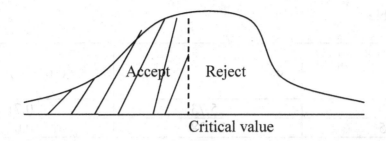

Accept / Reject

Critical value

13. Reject or accept Ho: The acceptance region for Ho goes from the left tail of the curve to the x^2 critical value. The rejection region/area lies to the right.

14. State your conclusion.

Example 1

A random sample of adults was selected from each of the four major tribes in Lusaka. Respondents were asked to specify their primary sources of news. The results were as tabulated below:

Source	Tribe				
	A	B	C	D	Total
T V	30	20	25	20	95
Radio	25	25	20	20	90
Newspaper	10	10	5	30	55
Total	65	55	50	70	240

Is there a relationship between the tribe and source of news, at a 2.5% level of significance?

Solution

14. Ho: There is no relationship between tribe and source of news
15. Ha: There is a relationship between tribe and source of news.
16. $\alpha = 0.025$
17. $df = (r - 1) \times (k - 1) = (3 - 1) \times (4 - 1) = 6$
18. From x^2–distribution table $\alpha = 0.025$ at $df = 6$ gives 14.449.
19. Reject Ho if the calculated x value > 14.449

Contingency table

fo	fe	$x^2 = \sum \dfrac{(fo - fe)^2}{fe}$
30	25.73	0.71
25	24.38	0.02
10	14.90	1.61
20	21.77	0.14
25	20.62	0.93
10	12.60	0.54
25	19.79	1.37
10	18.75	0.08
5	11.46	3.64
20	27.71	2.15
20	26.25	1.49
30	16.04	12.15
240	**240**	**24.83**

Because the test statistic exceeds the critical x_2 value, we reject the Ho that there is no relationship between tribe and source of news at the 2.5% level of confidence.

TEST FOR THE DIFFERENCE BETWEEN PROPORTIONS

This is the method for testing whether two or more proportions are statistically equal. The hypothesis of this kind of problem differs from the previous method, but is analyzed in the same way. It is still a chi-square test.

Example 2

The improvements in information technology has brought about the use of Automated Teller Machines (ATMs) in retail banks. These have a lot of advantages and disadvantages to both the bank and the customers. As a security requirements, customers are urged not to keep the ATM card and the account number (documents) together. Apparently, reported cases indicate that most customers keep the two together. The bank risk manager of a named bank wishes to determine whether there are any differences in recalling the NRC number, account number and ATM card number. The results of a study on a random sample were as follows:

Recall ability	Card number			
	NRC	Account	ATM	Total
Remember	94	96	95	285
Not remember	6	4	5	15
Total	100	100	100	300

At 0.10 level of significance, determine whether there is evidence of a difference, in recalling number between the cards.

Solution

- Ho: There is no difference in recalling numbers between the cards i.e. Ho: A = B = C

- Ha: There is a difference in recalling numbers between the cards i.e. Ha: A ≠ B ≠ C

- Calculate the degrees of freedom (df).

  df = (number of columns - 1) X (number of rows – 1) = (3 – 1) X (2 – 1) = 2

- State the decision rule (given that α = 0.10 and df = 2)

  Reject Ho if the calculated x^2 value > 4.60517.

- Compute the test statistic by making use of a contingency table. The sample resorts are known as the observed frequency (f_o). An expected frequency (f_e) is calculated for each f_o by making use of the following formula:

  $$f_e = \frac{\text{row total X column total}}{\text{grand total}}$$

- In order to determine whether the differences between f_o and f_e are significant, we use the x^2 – test.

  $$x^2 = \frac{\sum (f_o - f_e)^2}{f_e}$$

f_o	f_e	x^2
94	95	0.01
96	95	0.01
95	95	0
4	5	0.20
6	5	0.20
5	5	0
300	300	0.42

Conclusion: The calculated x^2 falls within the acceptance region. Therefore accept Ho at a 0.10 level of significance. The population proportion of recalling numbers is the same for each card tested.

Example 3

The percentage of sales of motor cars by a dealer in four areas A, B, C and D were 30, 20, 10 and 40 respectively in 2010. This year the actual sales in the four areas are 90, 65, 180 and 185 respectively. What inference can be made from these figures. Use α =0.05.

Solution

This is a test for the difference between proportions.

- Ho: A = B = C = D

- Ha : At least one is different

- df = (k -1)(r – 1) = (4 -1)(2 – 1) = 3

- Critical X^2 Value $X^2_{0.05,3}$ = 7.81473

- Reject Ho if X^2 > 7.81473

- Contingency table

Area	f_o	f_e	X^2
A	90	156	27.92307692
B	65	104	14.625
C	180	52	315.0769231
D	185	208	2.543269231
Total	520	520	**360.1682693**

- Reject Ho and conclude that one of them is different.

Note: f_e column is calculated as follows;

For A f_e = 30% of 520 = 156

For B f_e = 20% of 520 =104 and so on.

GOODNESS – OF- FIT- TEST

The x^2 goodness–of-fit-test is used to determine whether a set of sample data differs significantly from what is expected. The procedures are the same as given above. The examples that follow illustrate the technique.

Example 4

Suppose that the following were the respective bank's shares on the national market.

Bank	% of shares
Zanaco	37
Finance	30
Barclays	15
Standard charted	10
Stanbic	0

A random sample of 2,000 bank customers in Lusaka revealed the following pattern: Zanaco 758, Finance 680, Barclays 300, Standard Chartered 162 and Stanbic 100. Does the pattern in Lusaka differ significantly from the national pattern? Use $\alpha = 0.05$.

Solution

- Ho: The pattern in Lusaka is the same as the national pattern
- Ha: The pattern in Lusaka differs from the national pattern.
- $df = (r-1) \times (k-1) = (2-1) \times (5-1) = 4$
- x^2 at $\alpha = 0.05$ with 4 df from x^2 tables gives 9.488
- Reject Ho if the calculated x^2 test > 9.488.

Contingency table

Bank	National pattern (f_e)	Lusaka Pattern (f_o)	$f_o - f_e$	$(f_o - f_e)^2$	$x^2 = \sum \frac{(f_o - f_e)^2}{f_e}$
Zanaco	37% = 740	758	18	324	0.44
Finance	30% = 600	680	80	6400	10.67
Barclays	15% = 300	300	0	0	0
Standard	10% = 200	162	-38	1444	7.22
Stanbic	8% = 160	100	-60	3600	22.5
	2000	**2000**			**40.883**

- Decision: Because the first statistic is in the rejection region, Ho should be rejected at a 0.05 significance level.
- Conclusion: There is evidence that national pattern differs from the pattern in Lusaka. (Some banks do not have presence in some districts).

Notes to the calculation above:

- x^2 values have been rounded to 2 decimal places. This would not affect the decision whether we used 3 or 4 decimal places. However, the best approach is to use the same number of decimals as given by x^2 table.

- f_e has been calculated as a percentage of 2000 since in contingency theory $\sum f_e = \sum f_o$

- $f_e - f_o$ and $(f_e - f_o)^2$ columns have been included here but can be omitted as in a previous examples. They are included here to demonstrate the full set of columns normally involved.

Example 4

A lecture in BF 260 at PCBF wishes to know if students of BE 260 have topic preferences. To answer the question, a random sample of 200 students was offered a Statistics syllabus. The recipients chose from 4 topics. The choices were as follows:

- Descriptive statistics   66
- Probabilities   53
- Sampling distribution   45
- Hypothesis testing   36

Do the preferences in respect of topics among students differ? Use $\alpha = 0.01$.

Solution

- Ho: There is no preference (i.e. all topics are equal)
- Ha: There is a preference in respect of topics (i.e. not all topics are equal).
- $df = (2 - 1) \times (4 - 1) = 3$
- $\alpha = 0.01$
- From x^2 tables, α 0.01 with $df = 3$, gives 11.345
- Rejection if $x^2 > 11.345$

Topic	f_o	f_e	$x^2 = \sum\frac{(f_o - f_e)^2}{f_e}$
• Descriptive statistics	66	50	5.12
• probabilities	53	50	0.18
• Sampling distribution	45	50	0.50
• Hypothesis testing	36	50	3.92
	200	200	9.72

Decision: Because the calculated x^2 is in the acceptance region, Ho should be accepted at $\alpha = 0.01$ significance level.

Conclusion: There is no evidence to suggest that there is a preference with respect to topics.

Notes to calculation:

- If we expect no preference, the frequency for all topics should be equal ($200 \div 4 = 50$)

- $f_e = \dfrac{\text{row total X column total}}{\text{Grand total}}$

- $f_o - f_e$ and $(f_o - f_e)^2$ columns have been eliminated for convenience.

PROGRESS CLINIC TEN

1. A cellular telephone company conducts a survey to determine the ownership of cellular phones in different age groups. The results for 1000 households are shown in the table below.

	AGE GROUP (YRS)				
Cell phone	18 – 24	25 – 54	55 – 56	> 65	Total
Yes	50	80	70	50	250
No	200	170	180	200	750
Total	250	250	250	250	1000

Test at the 5% level of significance whether cellular telephone ownership is the same across the different age groups or not.

2. In an experiment a die is tossed 96 times yielding the following results.

Score	1	2	3	4	5	6
Frequency	10	16	21	15	18	16

Use the x^2 test at the 5% level of significance to investigate whether the die is biased.

3. The following table shows the responses from interviews of managers about career progression and their character. Test an appropriate hypothesis at the 5% level of significance.

	Slow	Average	Fast	Very fast
Aggressive	48	51	43	35
Moderate	22	42	59	57
Passive	15	22	33	13

4. Suppose that in for branches, the bank samples its employees' attitude job performance reviews. Respondents are given a choice between the present method (two reviews a year) and a proposed new method (quarterly reviews). The contingency table below illustrates the response to this question from the sample polled.

	Mazabuka	Kafue	Kitwe	Matero	Total
Prefer present method	68	75	57	79	279
Prefer new method	32	45	33	31	141
Total	100	120	90	110	420

Use the x^2 test at the 10% level of significance to investigate whether the preferences differ.

5. An economist is opposed to national health insurance. He argues that it would be too costly to implement, particularly since the existence of such a system would, among other effects, tend to encourage people to spend more time in hospitals. He believes that lengths of stays in hospitals are dependent on the types of health insurance that people have. He asked his junior statistician, to check the matter out. The junior statistician collected data on a random sample of 660 hospital stays and summarized it in the following table.

	Days in hospital			
	< 5	5 – 10	> 10	Total
Fraction of	40	75	65	180
Cost covered	30	45	75	150
By insurance	40	100	190	330
Total	110	220	330	660

Use the x^2 test at the 1% level of significance to investigate whether the length of hospital stay and insurance coverage are dependent on each other

Chapter Eleven

COMPARING MORE THAN TWO POPULATION MEANS: ANALYSIS OF VARIANCE (ANOVA)

More than two population means may be compared by using the analysis of variance (ANOVA). If we denote population means as μ_1, μ_2,.........μ_p, then the objective of an analysis of variance is to test the null hypothesis that the means are all identical against the alternative that at least two of the means differ:

Ho: $\mu_1 = \mu_2 = ...= \mu_p$.
Ha: At least one of the means differ

In order to conduct a statistical test of these hypotheses using an analysis of variance, we compute the p sample means.
The logic of this requires the definition and calculation of the following:

1. **Sum of squares for treatment (SST)** – This measures the variation between means.

$$SST = \sum_{i=1}^{P} ni \, (\overline{xi} - \overline{x})^2$$

Where ni = sample size

$\overline{x}$ = the mean of the combined samples.

2. **Sum of squares for Error (SSE)** – This measures the variability around the sample, means that is attributed to sampling error.

$$SSE = \sum_{j=1}^{n_1}(x_{1j} - \overline{x_1})^2 + \sum_{j=1}^{n_2}(x_{2j} - \overline{x_2})^2 + ...+ \sum^{np}(x_{pi} - \overline{x_p})^2$$

Where $x_{1j} = j^{th}$ measurement in sample
$x_{2j} = j^{th}$ measurement in sample 2, etc.

3. **Mean square for treatment (MST)** – This measures the variability among the sample means.

$MST = \dfrac{SST}{P-1}$ where number of degrees of freedom for the p samples is (p – 1)

4.   **Mean square for Error (MSE)** – This measures the sampling variability within the samples.

$$MSE = \frac{SSE}{n - p}$$

5.   **F – Statistic** – This is the test statistic used to test Ho: $\mu_1 = \mu_2 \ldots\ldots\ldots\mu_p$. Values of F near 1 indicate the two sources of variation, that between sample means and that within samples, are approximately equal. In this case, the difference between the sample means may well be attributable to sampling error, which provides little support for the alternative hypothesis that the population means differ. Values of F well in excess of 1 indicate that the variation among sample means well exceeds that within samples and therefore support the alternative hypothesis that the population means differ.

$$F = \frac{MST}{MSE}$$

Note that F depends on the degrees of freedom associated with MST and MSE and on the value of α selected for the test. We then compare the calculated F value to a value of the F distribution with $v_1 = (p - 1)\, df$ in the numerator and $v_2 = (n - p)\, df$ in the denominator, and a corresponding type 1 error probability of α.

ANALYSIS OF VARIANCE F TEST TO COMPARE P POPULATION MEANS: INDEPENDENT RANDOM SAMPLES

Ho: $\mu_1 = \mu_2 = \ldots\ldots\ldots\ldots\mu_p$.
Ha: At least one of the means differ.

Test statistic: $F = \dfrac{MST}{MSE}$

Rejection region: F > Fα, where Fα is based on (p – 1) numerator degrees of freedom (associated with MST) and (n – p) denominator degrees of freedom (associated with MSE).

Assumption: 1. All p population probability distributions are normal.

                    (d) The p population variances are equal
                    (e) Samples are selected randomly and independently from the respective populations.

Example 1

Suppose one selects independent random samples of five female and five male high school seniors, and record their SAT scores. The following are the ten measurements:

Female   490,   520,   550,   580,   610
Male   530,   560,   590,   620   650

Test the null hypothesis that the mean SAT score for female is equal to the mean SAT score for male against the alternative hypothesis that they differ. Use $\alpha = 0.05$.

Solution

Ho: $\mu_1 = \mu_2$
Ha: At least two means differ.

Test statistic: $F = \dfrac{MST}{MSE}$

Rejection region: $F > F\alpha$: $F_{.05} = 5.32$ for $v_1 = (2 - 1) = 1$ and $v_2 = (n - p) = 10 - 2 = 8$.

$$SST = \sum_{i=1}^{p} ni\, (\overline{xi} - \overline{x})^2$$

$$= 5(550 - 570)^2 + 5(590 - 570)^2 = 4000$$

Note: 570 is the combined mean of two samples

$$SSE = \sum_{j=1}^{ni}(x_{ij} - \overline{x_1})^2 + \sum_{j=1}^{n2}(x_{2j} - \overline{x_2})^2 + \ldots\ldots\sum_{j=1}^{np}(xpj - \overline{xp})^2$$

$SSE = (490 - 550)^2 + (520 - 550)^2 + (550 - 5550)^2 + (580 - 550)^2 + (610 - 550)^2 +$

$(530 - 590)^2 + (560 - 590)^2 + (590 - 590)^2 + (620 - 590)^2 + (650 - 590)^2 = \underline{18000}$

$$MST = \frac{SST}{P-1} = \frac{4000}{2-1} = 4000$$

$$MSE = \frac{SSE}{n-p} = \frac{18000}{10-2} = 2250$$

$$F = \frac{MST}{MSE} = \frac{4000}{2250} = 1.78$$

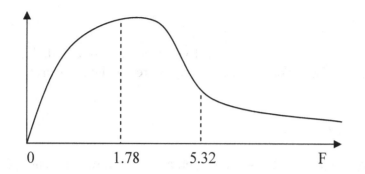

Since $F_c < F_{0.5, 1, 8} = 5.32$, we do not reject Ho at $\alpha = 0.05$.
There is insufficient information to conclude that mean SAT scores differ.

Alternatively, the above problem could have been worked out using the following approach:

Ho: $\mu_f = \mu_m$
Ha: $\mu_f \neq \mu_m$
Reject Ho $F_c > F_\alpha = 5.32$

Test statistic

Female	Male
490	530
520	560
550	590
580	620
610	650
2750	2950

$\Sigma Y = 2750 + 2950 = 5700$, $n = 10$, $p = 2$

$\Sigma Y^2 = (490)^2 + (520)^2 + (550)^2 + (580)^2 + (610)^2 + (530)^2 + (560)^2 + (590)^2 + (620)^2$

$+ (650)^2 = 3\ 271\ 000$

$SSTO = \Sigma Y^2 - \dfrac{(\Sigma Y)^2}{n} = 3\ 271\ 000 - \dfrac{(5700)^2}{10} = 3\ 271\ 000 - 3\ 249\ 000 = 22000$

$SS_{trt} = \dfrac{\Sigma T^2}{n_i} - \dfrac{(\Sigma Y)^2}{N} = \dfrac{(2750)^2}{5} + \dfrac{(2950)^2}{5} - \dfrac{(5700)^2}{10}$

$\qquad\qquad = 1\ 512\ 500 + 1\ 740\ 500 - 3\ 249\ 000$

$\qquad\qquad = 4000$

$SSE = SSTO - SS_{trt} = 22000 - 4000 = 18\ 000$

$MST = \dfrac{SS_{trt}}{} = \dfrac{4000}{} = 4000$

$$P -1 \quad 2 -1$$

$$MSE = \frac{SSE}{n-p} = \frac{18\ 000}{10-2} = 2250$$

$$F_c = \frac{MST}{MSE} = 1.78 \text{ as calculated earlier.}$$

Conlusion: Do not reject Ho at $\alpha = 0.05$

Example 2

Suppose the Lusaka Golf Club wants to compare the mean distances traveled by four different brands of golf balls design is employed, with a robotic golfer using a driver to hit a ransom sample of ten balls of each brand in a random sequence. The distance is recorded for each hit and the results are tabulated below:

	Brand A	Brand B	Brand C	Brand C
	251.2	263.2	269.7	251.6
	245.1	262.9	263.2	248.6
	248.0	265.0	277.5	249.4
	251.1	254.5	267.4	242.0
	265.5	264.3	270.5	246.5
	250.0	257.0	265.5	251.3
	253.9	262.8	270.7	262.8
	244.6	264.4	272.9	249.0
	254.6	255.9	275.6	247.1
	248.8	255.9	266.5	245.9
Means	251.3	261.1	270.0	249.4

Set up the test to compare the mean distances for the four brands. Use $\alpha = 0.10$.

Solution

To compare the mean distances of the four brands, we first specify the hypothesis to be tested.

Ho: $\mu_1 = \mu_2 = \mu_3 = \mu_4$
Ha: The mean distances differ for at least one of the brands.

Test statistic compares the variation among the four within each of the brands.

Test statistic: $F = \frac{MST}{MSE} = \frac{903.07}{25.22} = 35.81$

Rejection region: $F > F\alpha$: $F_{0.10,3,36} = 2.25$ for $v_1 = (p - 1) = 4 - 1 = 3$,
$v_2 = (n - p) = 40 - 4 = \underline{36}$

Since $F_c > F_\alpha = 2.25$, we reject Ho at $\alpha = 0.10$ and conclude that at least the distance travelled by one brand differs.

Note that the same procedure is used to find MST and MSE. Try it.

CONFIDENCE INTERVALS FOR MEANS

There are two types of confidence interval for means using ANOVA depending on the number of treatments. The term 'treatment' originates from the methods where the populations that are being compared represent experimental units subjected to different types of treatments. For example, the populations might correspond to yields of a variety of maize subjected to different types (treatments) of fertilizer.

Single treatment mean (say, treatment i): $\bar{x}i \pm t_{\frac{\alpha}{2}} \dfrac{s}{\sqrt{ni}}$

Differences between two treatment means (say treatment I and j):

$$(\bar{x}i - \bar{x}j) \pm t_{\frac{\alpha}{2}} \; S\sqrt{\dfrac{1}{ni} + \dfrac{1}{nj}}$$

Where s= MSE and $t_{\frac{\alpha}{2}}$ is the tabulated value of t from the t-distribution that locates $\dfrac{\alpha}{2}$ in

The upper tail of the t-distribution and has $(n - p)$ degrees of freedom (the degrees of freedom associated with error in the ANOVA).

RELATIONSHIP BETWEEN THE t AND F TESTS

The above confidence intervals show the important relationship between the t and F tests. Recall that we performed a hypothesis test for the difference between means in Chapter 9 using a two sample t-statistic for two independent samples. When two independent samples are being compared, the t and F tests are equivalent. To see this, consider the SAT scores for male and female of example1 and recall the following formula:

$$t = \dfrac{\bar{x}_1 - \bar{x}_2}{\sqrt{S^2_p\left(\dfrac{1}{n_1} + \dfrac{1}{n_2}\right)}} = \dfrac{590 - 550}{\sqrt{(62.5)\left(\dfrac{1}{5} + \dfrac{1}{5}\right)}} = \dfrac{40}{5} = 8$$

Where we used the fact that $S^2_p = MSE$, which you can verify by comparing the formulas. Note that the calculated F for these samples (F = 64) equals the square of the calculated t for the same samples (t = 8). Similarly, the tabled F value (5.32) equals the square of the tabled t value at the two-sided $\alpha = 0.05$ level of significance ($t0.025 = 2.306$ with 8df). Since both the rejection region and the calculated values are related in the same way, the tests are equivalent. Moreover, the assumptions that must be met to assure the validity of the t and F tests are the same.

In fact, the only real difference between the tests is that the F test can be used to compare more than two population means, while the t test is applicable to two samples only.

COMPUTER PRINTOUTS FOR ANOVA DATA

The results of an analysis of variance (ANOVA) can be summarised in a single tabular format. The general form of the table is shown below where the symbols df, SS and MS stand for degrees of freedom, sum of squares, and square respectively. Note that the two sources of variation, Treatments and Error, add to the Total Sum of Squares, SS (total).

Source	df	SS	MS	F
Treatments	$p - 1$	SST	$MST = \dfrac{SST}{p - 1}$	$\dfrac{MST}{MSE}$
Error	$p - 1$	SSE	$MSE = \dfrac{SSE}{n - p}$	
Total	$n - 1$	SS (total)		

The summary table for **Example 1** is given below

Source	df	SS	MS	F
Scores	1	4000	4000	1.78
Error	8	18000	2250	
Total	9	22000		

Similarly, the ANOVA summary table for **Example 2** is:

Source	df	SS	MS	F

Brands	3	2709.20	903.07	35.81
Error	36	907.86	25.22	
Total	39	3617.06		

As an exercise confirm the above summary results.

Computer printouts are often used to summarize ANOVA computations. The SAS printout for the analysis of variance of example 2 is given below. The top portion of the printout contains the SSE and MSE values in the row labeled "Error" under the column heading "Sum of Squares" and "Mean Square" respectively. The bottom part of the printout gives SST and MST in the row labeled "BRAND" under the columns "Type 1 SS" and "Mean Square," respectively.

Dependent variable: DISTANCE

Source	DF	Sum of Squares	Mean square	F value	Pr > F
Model	3	2790.19875	903.06625	35.81	0.0001
Error	36	907.86100	25.21836		
Corrected total	39	3617.05975			

	R-Square	C.V.	Root MSE	DISTANCE	Mean
	0.749006	1.9469768	5.021739	257.927500	

Source	DF	Type 1 SS	Mean Square	F value	Pr > F
BRAND	3	2709.20	903.07	35.81	

Generally, the values of the mean squares MST and MSE 903.07 and 25.22 respectively, are shaded in the printout together with the F ratio, 35.81. The F value exceeds the tabled value 2.25. We therefore reject the null hypothesis at the 0.10 level of significance, concluding that at least two of the brands differ with respect to mean distance traveled when struck by the driver. The observed significance level of the F test is also given on the printout: 0.0001. This is the area to the right of the calculated F value and implies that we would reject the null hypothesis that the means are equal at any α level greater than 0.0001.

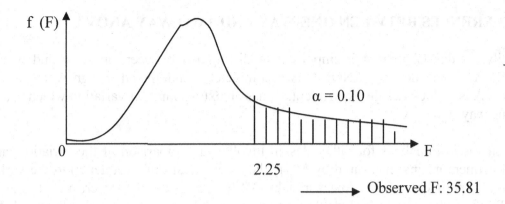

f (F)

α = 0.10

0

2.25

F

Observed F: 35.81

Example 3

Refer to example 2, in which it was concluded that at least two of the four brands of the golf balls are associated with different mean distances traveled when struck with a driver. Form a 95% confidence interval for the difference between the mean distances traveled by brands A and B. Interpret the result.

Solution

$$S = \sqrt{MSE} = \sqrt{25.22} = 5.02 \text{ which is also given in the SAS printout as "Root}$$

MSE". Also $\bar{x}_A = 251.3$ and $\bar{x}_B = 261.1$. The tabulated value, $t = 0.25$, for 36 df (the same as the MSE) is 1.96. so a 95% confidence interval for $(\mu_A - \mu_B)$, the difference between the mean distances traveled by the two golf ball brands is:

$$(\bar{x}_A - \bar{x}_B) \pm t_{\frac{\alpha}{2}} \ S \sqrt{\frac{1}{n_A} + \frac{1}{n_B}}$$

$$= (251.3 - 261) \pm 1.96 \ (5.02) \sqrt{\frac{1}{10} + \frac{1}{10}}$$

$$= \ ^-9.8 + 4.4$$

$$= \ ^-14.2, \ ^-5.4$$

Note that the interval includes only negative numbers. This implies that μ_B exceeds μ_A (since $\mu_A - \mu_B < 0$) with 95% confidence. More specifically, we can be 95% confident that the mean distance traveled by golf ball brand B exceeds the corresponding mean distance for brand A by an amount between 5.4 and 14.2 kilometers.

DIFFERENCES BETWEEN ONE-WAY AND TWO WAY ANOVA

Finally, in this Chapter it is important to distinguish between one-way and two way ANOVA. The one way ANOVA is a completely randomized design while two way ANOVA is a block design experiment. It has an extra source of variation which is absent in one way ANOVA.

The method of analysis for either design involves a comparison of the variation among the treatment means (measured by MST, the mean square of treatments) to the variation among experimental units (measured by MSE, the mean square error). If the ratio MST/MSE is large, we conclude that the means of at least two of the populations differ.

The following are the formulas used:

One way

- $SS_{trt} = \dfrac{\sum T_i^2}{n_i} - \left(\dfrac{\sum y}{N}\right)^2$

- $SS_{Total} = \sum xy^2 - \left(\dfrac{\sum y}{N}\right)^2$

- $SS_{Total} = SSE + SS_{trt}$

Alternatively: $SStrt = \sum_{i=1} n_i (\overline{x_i} - \overline{x})$

Where $\overline{x}$ is the grand mean

Two way ANOVA

$SSB = \dfrac{\sum B_i^2}{n_i} - \left(\dfrac{\sum y}{N}\right)^2$

$SS_{Total} = SSE + SS_{trt} + SSB$

PROGRESS CLINIC ELEVEN

1. A partially completed ANOVA summary of an independent samples design is shown in the table.

Source	df	SS	MS	F
Treatments	6	16.9		
Error				
Total	41	45.2		

(a) Complete the ANOVA table.
(b) How many treatments are involved in the experiment?
(c) Do the data provide sufficient evidence to indicate a difference among the population means? Test using $\alpha = 0.10$
(d) Find the approximate observed significance level for the test in part (c), and interpret it.

(e) Suppose $\bar{x}_1 = 3.7$ and $\bar{x}_2 = 4.1$. Do the data provide sufficient evidence to indicate a difference between μ_1 and μ_2? Assume that there are seven observations for each treatment. Test using $\alpha = 0.10$.
(f) Refer to part (e). Find a 90% confidence interval for (μ_1 and μ_2).
(g) Refer to part (e). Find a 90% confidence interval for μ_1.

2. The Minitab Printout for an experiment utilizing independent samples design is shown here (Note: Minitab uses "FACTOR" instead of "Treatments)"

ANALYSIS OF VARIANCE

Source	DF	SS	MS	F
FACTOR	3	57258	19086	14.80
ERROR	34	43836	1289	
TOTAL	37	101094		

(a) How many treatments are involved? What is the total sample size?
(b) Conduct a test of the null hypothesis that the treatment means are equal. Use $\alpha = 0.01$.
(c) What additional information is needed in order to be able to compare specific pairs of treatment means?
(d) Suppose the treatment means are 190.8, 260.1, 191.7, and 279.4, with sample sizes 8, 12, 10 and 8, respectively.

i.   Form a 95% confidence interval for μ_2.

ii. Form a 95% confidence interval for $(\mu_3 - \mu_4)$.

3. The application of Management by Objectives (MBO), a method of performance appraisal, is the subject of a study by Y.K. Shetty and H.M. Carlisle (1974) of Utah State University. The study dealt with the reactions of a university faculty to an MBO Programme.

One hundred nine faculty members were asked to comment on whether they thought the MBO Programme was successful in improving their performance within their respective departments and the university. Each response was assigned a score from 1 (significant improvement) to 5 (significant decrease). The table shows the sample sizes, sample totals, mean scores, and sum of squares of deviations within each sample for sample of scores corresponding to the four academic ranks. Assume that the four samples in the table can be viewed as independent random samples of scores selected from among the four academic ranks.

	Instructor	Assistant professor	Associate professor	professor
Sample size	15	41	29	24
Sample total	42.960	145.222	92.249	73.224
Sample mean	2.864	3.542	3.181	3.051
Within-sample sum of squared deviations	2.0859	14.0186	7.9247	5.6812

(a) Given that SST = 6.816 and SSE = 29.710, construct an ANOVA table for this experiment.

(b) Do the data provide sufficient evidence to conclude there is a difference in mean scores among the four academic ranks? Test using $\alpha = 0.05$

4. The SPSS Printout for an experiment utilizing an independent samples design is shown here.

Analysis of variance

Source	D.F.	Sum of Squares	Mean Squares	F Ratio	F Prob.
Between Groups	3	2.5187	0.8396	20.3000	0.000
Within Groups	19	0.7858	0.0414		
Total	22	3.3044			

Note: SPSS uses "Between groups" instead of "Treatments" and "Within groups" instead of "Error".

(a) Is there sufficient evidence to indicate that the means differ among the four treatments? Test using $\alpha = 0.01$

(b) What assumptions must be satisfied in order for the test in (a) to be valid?

5. How does flextime, which allows workers to set their individual work schedules, affect worker job satisfaction? Researchers recently conducted a study to compare a measure of job satisfaction for workers using a measure of job satisfaction for workers using three types of work schedules: flextime, staggered starting hours, and fixed hours. Workers in each group worked according to their specified work scheduling system for 4 months. Although each worker filled out job satisfaction questionnaires both before and after the 4-month test period, we will examine only the post-test-period scores. The sample sizes, means, standard deviations of the scores for the three groups are shown in the table below.

	GROUP		
	Flextime	Staggered	Fixed
Sample size	27	59	24
Sample mean	35.22	31.05	28.71
Standard deviation	10.22	7.22	9.28

(a) Assume that the data were collected according to a completely randomized design. Identify the response, the factor, the factor type, the treatments, and the experimental units.

(b) Use the sample means to calculate the sum of squares for Treatment, SST.

©Use the standard deviation to calculate the sum of squares for Error, SSE. Remember that SSE is the measurement in the experiment and the corresponding treatment mean.

(d) Construct an ANOVA table for this experiment.

(e) Do the data provide sufficient evidence that the three groups differ with respect to their mean job satisfaction? Test using $\alpha = 0.05$.

(f) For each of the three groups, construct a 99% confidence interval for the mean job satisfaction score.

6. Suppose the Lusaka Golf Club wants to compare the mean distances traveled by four different brands of golf balls when struck with a driver. An independent sampling design is employed, with a robotic golfer using a driver to hit a random sample of 10 balls of each brand in a random sequence. The distance is recorded for each hit and the results are tabulated below:

	Brand A	Brand B	Brand C	Brand D
	251.2	263.2	269.7	251.6
	245.1	262.9	263.2	248.6
	248.0	265.0	277.5	249.4
	251.1	254.5	267.4	242.0
	265.5	264.3	270.5	246.5
	250.0	267.0	265.5	251.3
	253.9	262.8	270.7	262.8
	244.6	264.4	272.9	249.0
	254.6	260.6	275.6	247.1
	248.8	255.9	266.5	245.9
Mean	**251.3**	**261.1**	**270.0**	**249.4**

(a) How many treatments are involved?
(b) What is the sample size?
(c) Set up a test to compare the mean distances for the four brands. Use $\alpha = 0.10$.

Chapter Twelve

LINEAR REGRESSION AND CORRELATION

REGRESSION ANALYSIS

Least squares regression is used to predict a linear relationship between two variables. It derives a line of best fit by a statistical method. The equation of the regression line of y on x is of the form.

$$Y = a + bx$$

Where

a = the y – intercept, i.e. the value of y when x=0
b = slope of the line, i.e. the rate of change x that causes changes
in y, changes as a result of changes in x.

To use the above equation, we must first calculate a and b as follows:

a) $a = \dfrac{\sum y}{n} - \dfrac{b\sum x}{n}$ or $a = \bar{y} - b\bar{x}$

b) $b = \dfrac{n\sum x\sum y - \sum x\sum y}{n\sum x^2 - (\sum x)^2}$

Where n = number of pairs of values

Note: the value of b must be calculated first as it is needed to calculate a

Example 1

The frequency table shows the number of units of goods produced and the total cost incurred.

Units (x) 00.	Total costs (y) 000
100	40 000
200	45 000
300	50 000
400	65 000
500	70 000
600	70 000
700	80 000
2800	420 000

Required

    (a) Calculate the regression of y on x

    (b) Find the fixed total

    (c) Find the variable cost/unit

    (d) Estimate the total costs when 450 units are produced

    (e) Determine which one is the independent variable

Solution

(a) $\quad b = \dfrac{n\sum y - \sum x \sum y}{n\sum x^2 - (\sum x)^2} = \dfrac{7(1870) - (28)(420)}{7(140) - (28)}$

$= \dfrac{13090 - 11760}{980 - 748}$

$= \dfrac{1330}{196}$

$b = 6.79$

$a = \dfrac{\sum y}{n} - \dfrac{b\sum x}{n}$

$= \dfrac{420}{7} - 6.79 \left(\dfrac{28}{7} \right)$

$= 60 - 6.79 \,(4)$

$= 32.84$

Prediction equation $= y = 32.84 + 6.79x$ units in hundreds and costs in thousands .

Therefore
$$y = 32840 + 6790x$$
(b) Total cost when units $= 450$
$$y = 32840 + 6790 \,(450)$$

(c) Total cost $= FC + VC \,(q)$

  FC $=$ value of a $=$ K32.84
(d) Variable cost $=$ value of b $=$ K6.79
(e) Units produced

INTERPOLATION AND EXTRAPOLATION

That are outside the limits of the original data. This is known as extrapolation. The problem with extrapolation is that it assumes that the relationship already calculated is still valid. This may or may not be so.

CORRELATION

Though regression analysis it is possible to derive a linear relationship between two variables and estimate a formula for the line. However, this does not measure the degree of correlation between the variables. Correlation measures how strong the connection is between the two variables. The degree of correlation is measured by Pearson's correlation coefficient at which is also called the product moment correlation coefficient.

Formula

$$r = \frac{n\sum xy - \sum x \sum y}{\sqrt{\left(n\sum x^2 - (\sum x)^2\right)\left(n\sum y^2 - (\sum y)^2\right)}}$$

INTERPRETATION OF r

The value of r ranges between $^+1$ and $^-1$
 A figure outs this range implies wrong calculation
If r = $^+1$ means perfect positive linear correlation
If r = $^-1$ means perfect negative linear correlation
If r = 0 means correlation

COEFFICIENT OF DETERMINATION

The coefficient of determination is the square of the coefficient of correlation and is the measure of how much of the variation in the dependent variables is explained by the variation of the independent variable. When x is output volume and y is total cost r2 will show how much of the variations in total cost can be explained by variations in the activity level. The variation not accounted for by variations in the independent variations or to other specific factors that have not been identified in considering two variable problems.

SPURIOUS CORRELATION

There is a big danger unsolved in correlation analysis two variables when compared may show a high degree of correlation but they may still have no direct connection. Such correlation is turned spurious or nonsense correlation and unless two variables can reasonably be assumed to have same direct connection, the correlation coefficient found will be meaningless however, high it maybe.

Example 2

Using the previous data in example 1, calculate,

(a) correlation coefficient
(b) coefficient of determination and interpret the results

Solution

DATA

$\sum x = 28,$ $\quad \sum y = 420,$ $\sum xy = 1870,$ $\sum x^2 = 140,$ $\quad n = 7,$ $\sum y^2 = 26\,550$

a) $r = \dfrac{n\sum xy - \sum x \sum y}{\sqrt{\left\{ (n\sum x^2 = (\sum x)^2\, n\sum y^2 - (\sum y)^2 \right\}}}$

$= \dfrac{7\,(1870) - (28)\,(420)}{\sqrt{7(140)^2 - (28)^2\ 7(26538) - (402)^2}}$

$= \dfrac{1330}{\sqrt{196 \times 9400}}$

$= \dfrac{1330}{\sqrt{1852\,200}} \qquad \dfrac{1330}{1360.96}$

$r = {}^{+}0.98$

b) $r = (0.98)^2$

$= 0.9604 \times 100$

$r = 96\%$

About 96% of changes in total cost is attributed to change in the units produced, 4% is attributed to other factors.

SCATTER GRAPHS

A scatter graph is simply a graph on which historical data is plotted. One advantage of a scatter graph is that, it is possible to see quite easily if the point indicate that a strong relation exist between the variables be to see if any correlation exist between them. However, it is not possible to measure the degree of correlation from a scatter graph.

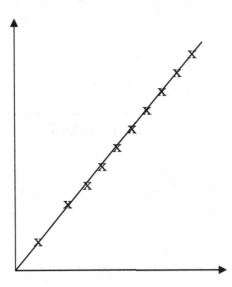

a) Perfect positive linear

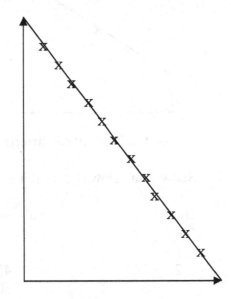

Perfect negative linear

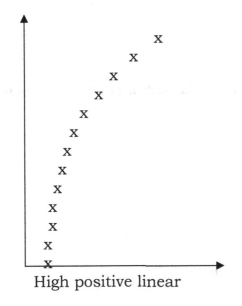

High positive linear

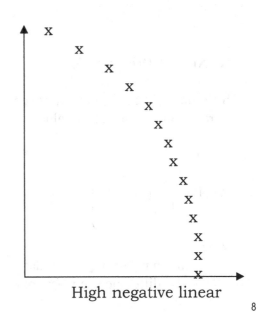

High negative linear

8

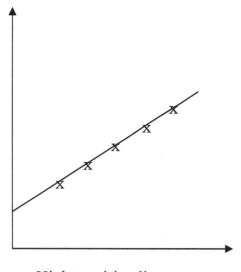

High positive linear

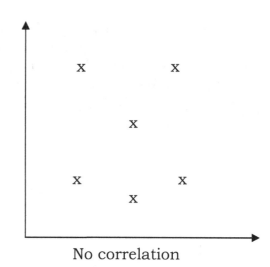

No correlation

Show data below in a scatter graph

Units	Total cost
1	40
2	45
3	50
4	65
5	70
6	70
7	80

RANK CORRELATION

Spearman's rank correlation (R) coefficient is used when data is given in terms of orders or rank rather than actual values

Formula

$$R = 1 - \left(\frac{b\sum d^2}{n(n^2 - 1)} \right)$$

Where

   n = number of pairs of data
   d = difference between ranking in each data set.

INTERPRETATION OF RANK

Rank correlation coefficient can be interpreted in exactly the same way as the ordinary correlation coefficient. Its value ranges from $^-1$ to $^+1$.

Example 3

Examination placing of 7 students were as follows

Students	Mathematics placing	Economics placing
A	3	1
B	1	3
C	4	7
D	6	5
E	5	6
F	3	2
G	7	4

Required judge whether the placing in mathematics correlate with the placing in economics

Solution

Students	Mathematics	Economics	d	d^2
A	3	1	2	4
B	1	3	$^-2$	4
C	4	7	$^-3$	9
D	6	5	1	1
E	5	6	$^-1$	1
F	3	2	1	1
G	7	4	3	9
				$\sum d^2 = 26$

$$R = 1 - \left(\frac{6 \times 26}{7(72 - 1)} \right)$$

$$= \frac{1 - 156}{3.36}$$

$$= 1 - 0.464$$

$$R = {}^+0.536$$

The correlation is positive though not very strong.

REGRESSION AND CORRELATION: AN ADDENDUM

In addition to the above analysis of regression and correction, there is an alternative viewpoint which is covered in this section.

REGRESSION MODEL

$y = a + bx$ or $y = B_0 + B_1 x$

Where in both cases:

y = dependent variable
x = independent or explanatory variable
$a + B_0$ = y – intercept i.e. the value of y when x = 0
b or B_1 = the slope or rate of change.

Formula for least squares estimates

Slope: $\hat{B}_1 = \dfrac{SS_{xy}}{SS_{xx}}$

y – intercept = $\hat{B}_0 = \bar{y} - \hat{B}_1 \bar{x}$

Where $SS_{xy} = \sum\limits_{i=1}^{n} x_i y_i \ - \ \dfrac{\left(\sum\limits_{i=1}^{n} x_i\right)\left(\sum\limits_{i=1}^{n} y_i\right)}{n}$

$SS_{xx} = \sum\limits_{i=1}^{n} x_i{}^2 \ - \ \dfrac{\left(\sum\limits_{i=1}^{n} x_i\right)^2}{n}$

n = sample size

Example 4

The following data relates to advertising expenditure and sales volume at a named company. Compute the least squares regression line.

xi	yi	xi^2	xi yi
100	100	10 000	10 000
200	100	40 000	20 000
300	200	90 000	60 000
400	200	160 000	80 000
500	400	250 000	200 000
1500	1000	550 000	370 000

Solution

- $SS_{xy} = 370\ 000 - \dfrac{(1500)}{5} - (1000) = 70\ 000$

- $SS_{xx} = 550\ 000 - \dfrac{(1500)^2}{5} = 100\ 000$

- $\hat{B}_1 = \dfrac{SS_{xy}}{SS_{xx}} = \dfrac{70\ 000}{100\ 000} = 0.7$

- $\hat{B}_0 = \dfrac{1000}{5} - (0.7)\left(\dfrac{1500}{5}\right) = {}^-10$

- Least squares line is therefore:

  $y = {}^-10 + 0.7x$

MAKING INFERENCES ABOUT THE SLOPE, β

. One Tailed Test

. Ho: $B_1 = 0$

. Ha: $B_1 < 0$ (or $B_1 > 0$)

. Test statistic:

$$t = \frac{\hat{B_1}}{S_{\hat{B_1}}} = \frac{\hat{B}}{S / \sqrt{SS_{xx}}}$$

. Rejection region:

$t < t \alpha$

or $t > t \alpha$

Where $t \alpha$ is based on $(n - 2)$ df

. Two Tailed Test

. Ho: $B_1 = 0$

. Ha: $B_1 \neq 0$

. Test statistic:

$$t = \frac{\hat{B}}{S_{\hat{B_1}}} = \frac{\hat{B}}{S / \sqrt{SS_{xx}}}$$

. Rejection region:

$t < -t \alpha_{/2}$ or $t > t \alpha_{/2}$

where $t \alpha_{/2}$ is based on $(n - 2)$ df

CONFIDENCE INTERVAL FOR THE SLOPE, β,

The confidence interval for the slope, B, is given by:

$$B_1 \pm t \alpha_{/2} \ S_{\hat{B_1}} \quad \text{or} \quad B_1 \pm t \alpha_{/2} \ \sqrt{\frac{S}{SS_{xx}}}$$

Where $t \alpha$ is based on $(n - 2)$ df

Example 5

Using the advertising and sales data given in example 1, above test using $\alpha = 0.05$ and come up with a 95% confidence interval for the slope, $\hat{B_1}$.

Solution

This is a two tailed test, hence:

. Ho: $B_1 = 0$

. Ha: $B_1 \neq 0$

. Test statistic: $t = \dfrac{\hat{B_1}}{S/\sqrt{SS_{xx}}}$

. Rejection region: $t\ 0.05 = 0.025$, $df = 5 - 2 = 3$

  $t\ 0.025, 3 = 3.182$ from the t – distribution table

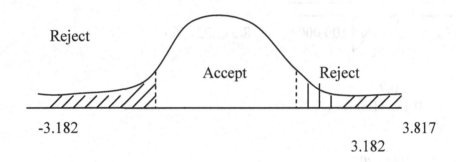

Reject   Accept   Reject

-3.182   3.817

3.182

Now, for us to compute, the test statistic, we need to know $\hat{B_1}$, S, and SS_{xx}.

$B_1 = 0.7$

$SS_{xx} = 100\ 000$

$S_2 = \dfrac{SSE}{n-2}$

Where $SSE = (y_1 - \hat{y_1})^2 = SS_{yy} - \hat{B_1}\ SS_{xy}$

$SS_{yy} = \sum (yi - yi)^2 = \sum y\,i^2 - \dfrac{(\sum yi)^2}{n}$

Thus $SS_{yy} = (100)^2 + (100)^2 + (200)^2 + (200)^2 + (400)^2 - \dfrac{(1000)^2}{5}$

$$= 10\,000 + 10\,000 + 40\,000 + 40\,000 + 160\,000 - 200\,000$$

$$= \underline{60\,000}$$

$SSE = 60\,0000 - 0.7\,(70\,000) = 11000$

$$S^2 = \frac{SSE}{n-2} = \frac{11000}{5-2} = \frac{11000}{3} = 3366.666667$$

Therefore $S = S^2 = \sqrt{3366.666667} = \underline{58}$

$$t = \frac{\hat{B_1}}{S/\sqrt{SS_{xx}}} = \frac{0.7}{58/\sqrt{100\,000}} = \frac{0.7}{58/316.227766}$$

$$= \frac{0.7}{0.18341204}$$

$$= 3.81664201$$

$$= \underline{\mathbf{3.817}}$$

Since the calculated t falls outside we reject Ho at $\alpha = 0.05$. i.e. the calculated t (3.817) falls in the upper tail rejection region.

Confidence interval for the slope then is:

$$\hat{B_1} + t\,\frac{\alpha}{2} \quad \frac{S}{\sqrt{SS_{xx}}}$$

$$0.7 + 3.182 \left(\frac{58}{100\,000} \right)$$

$$0.7 + 3.182\,(0.00058)$$

0.7 + 0.00184556

0.69815444 to 0.70184556

= <u>0.698 to 0.072</u>

Note: BOADMAS has to be carefully applied in all the above computations.

CORRELATION COEFFICIENT (r)

The strength of the relationship between two variables is explained by the correlation coefficient (r)

$$r = \frac{SS_{xy}}{\sqrt{SS_{xx} SS_{xy}}}$$

Where $SS_{xy} = \sum x_i y_i - \frac{(\sum x_i)(\sum y_i)}{n}$

$SS_{xx} = \sum x_i{}^2 - \frac{(\sum x_i)^2}{n}$

$SS_{yy} = \sum y_i{}^2 - \frac{(\sum y_i)^2}{n}$

COEFFICIENT OF DETERMINATION (r^2)

The coefficient of determination is the square of the correlation coefficient.

$r^2 = \frac{SS_{yy} - SSE}{SS_{yy}} = 1 - \frac{SSE}{SS_{yy}}$

Example 6

Using the advertising and sales data in example 1, compute the coefficient of correlation (r) and the coefficient of determination (r^2) and interpret your result.

Solution

$$R = \frac{SS_{xy}}{\sqrt{SS_{xx}SS_{xy}}} = \frac{70\ 000}{\sqrt{(100\ 000)\ (70\ 000)}}$$

$$= \frac{70\ 000}{\sqrt{7000\ 000\ 000}}$$

$$= \frac{70\ 000}{83666.00265}$$

$$= 0.836660026$$

$$\therefore r = \underline{0.84}$$

$$r^2 = 1 - \frac{SSE}{SS_{yy}} = 1 - \frac{11000}{60\ 000}$$

This simply means that about 82% of the changes in sales volume is attributable to advertising while about 18% is attributable to other factors.

HYPOTHESIS TEST FOR COEFFICIENT OF CORRELATION AND SPEARMAN'S RANK CORRELATION COEFFICIENT

One tailed test	Two tailed test
Ho: r = 0	Ho: r = 0
Ha: r > 0 (or r < 0)	Ha: r ≠ 0
. Test statistic	. Test statistic
$$t = \frac{r}{\sqrt{(1 - r^2)/(n-2)}}$$	$$t = \frac{r}{\sqrt{(1 - r^2)/(n-2)}}$$
. Rejection region:	. Rejection region:
$t < -t_\alpha$ or $t > t_\alpha$	$t < -t_{\alpha/2}$ or $t > t_{\alpha/2}$

Where t_α and $t_{\alpha/2}$ are based on (n – 2) df

Example 7

The following represents the scores of 65 students taking BF 150 and BF 260 at Premier College during one mock exam.

Name of student	BF 150	BF 260
Mortality	30	45
Regression	41	52
Progression	45	58
Probability	68	35
Protester	85	85
Brilliant	95	81

(i) Calculate the Spearman's rank correlation coefficient

(ii) Test against the alternative of positive association the null hypothesis of no association between BF 150 and BF 260. Use α = 0.05.

Solution

To calculate the Spearman's rank correlation coefficient we first need to rank the score, find the differences (d) and square those differences (d^2). The following formula is then applied.

$$r = 1 - \frac{6 \sum d^2}{n(n^2 - 1)}$$

Rankings areas follows

Name of students	BF 150	BF 260	d	d_2
. Mortality	6	5	1	1
. Regression	5	4	1	1
. progression	4	3	1	1
. Probability	3	6	⁻3	9
. Protester	2	1	1	1
. Brilliant	1	2	⁻1	1
				$\sum d^2 = 14$

(i) $r = 1 - \left(\dfrac{6 \sum d^2}{n(n^2 - 1)} \right)$

$$= 1 - \left(\frac{6(14)}{6(6^2 - 1)} \right)$$

$$= 1 - \left(\frac{84}{210} \right)$$

$\therefore \quad r = \underline{0.6}$

(ii) Test at $\alpha = 0.05$

Ho: $r = 0$

Ha: $r > 0$

Test statistic:

$$T = \frac{r}{\sqrt{(1 - r^2)/(n - 2)}}$$

$$= \frac{0.6}{\sqrt{(1 - 0.6^2)/(6-2)}}$$

$$= \frac{0.6}{\sqrt{(0.64)/4}}$$

$$= \frac{0.6}{\sqrt{0.16}}$$

$$= \frac{0.6}{0.4}$$

$$= \underline{1.5}$$

. Rejection region: t 0.05, 4 = 2.132

Rejection is the calculated t > 2.132.

Conclusion: Since calculated t (1.5) is less than the critical t value (2.132), we accept Ho.

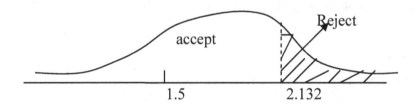

SAMPLING ERRORS FOR THE ESTIMATOR OF THE MEAN OF Y AND THE PREDICTOR OF AN INDIVIDUAL Y

1)   The standard deviation of the sapling distribution of the estimator $\hat{y}$ of the mean value of y at a particular value of x, say xp is:

$$\sigma \hat{y} = \sigma \sqrt{\frac{1}{n} + \frac{(xp - \bar{x})^2}{SS_{xx}}}$$

Where σ is the standard deviation of the random error E

2) The standard deviation of the prediction error for the predictor $\hat{y}$ of an individual y value for x = xp is:

$$\sigma(y - \hat{y}) = \sigma\sqrt{1 + \frac{1}{n} + \frac{(xP - \bar{x})^2}{SSxx}}$$

Where σ is the standard deviation of the random error E

CONFIDENCE INTERVAL FOR THE MEAN OF y FOR x = xp

$$\hat{y} \pm t_{\frac{\alpha}{2}}[(\text{estimated standard deviation of } \hat{y})]$$

$$\text{Or } \hat{y} \pm t_{\frac{\alpha}{2}}\sqrt{1 + (xp - \bar{x})^2}$$

Where t α is based on (n – 2) df.

A 100 (1 – α) % PREDICTION INTERVAL FOR AN INDIVIDUAL y FOR x = xp.

$$\hat{y} \pm t_{\frac{\alpha}{2}}[(\text{Estimated standard deviation of } (y - \hat{y}))]$$

$$\text{or } \hat{y} \pm t_{\frac{\alpha}{2}}\sqrt{1 + \frac{1}{n} + \frac{(xp - \bar{x})^2}{SS_{xx}}}$$

Where t $\frac{\alpha}{2}$ is based on (n – 2) df

Example 8

Find a 95% confidence interval for the monthly sales when the appliance store spends K400 on advertising.

Solution

For a K400 advertising expenditure, $xp = 4$ and since $n = 5$, $df \ n - 2 = 5 - 2 = 3$.

Then the confidence interval for the mean value of y is:

$$\hat{y} \pm t\alpha/2 \ \ S\sqrt{\frac{1}{n} + \frac{(xp - \bar{x})^2}{SS_{xx}}}$$

$$\hat{y} \pm t0.025 \ \ S\sqrt{\frac{1}{5} + \frac{(4 - \bar{x})^2}{SS_{xx}}}$$

Recall that $\hat{y} = 2.7$, $S = 0.61$, $\bar{x} = 3$, and $SS_{xx} = 10$

From the t distribution $t0.25 = 3.182$.

Thus, $2.7 \pm (3.182)(0.61)(0.55)$

$\quad = 2.7 \pm (3.182)(0.61)(0.55)$

$\quad = 2.7 \pm 1.1$

$\quad = \underline{1.6 \ \text{to} \ 3.8}$

We estimate that the interval from K1600 to K3800 encloses the mean sales revenue when the store spends K400 a month on advertising. Note that we used a small amount of data for purposes of illustration in fitting the least squares line and the width of the interval could be decreased by using a larger number of data points.

Example 9

Predict the monthly sales for next month if a K400 expenditure is to be made on advertising. Use a 95% prediction interval.

Solution

To predict the sales for a particular month for which $xp = 4$, we calculate 95% prediction interval as:

$$\hat{y} \pm t\alpha_{/2} \sqrt{1 + \frac{1}{n} + \frac{(xp - \bar{x})^2}{SS_{xx}}}$$

$$2.7 \pm (3.182)(0.61) \sqrt{1 + \frac{1}{5} + \frac{(4-3)^2}{10}}$$

$$2.7 \pm 2.2$$

0.5 to 4.9

As in the case for the confidence interval for the mean value of y1 the prediction interval of y is quite large. This is because we have been chosen a small number of data points to fit the least squares line. The width of the prediction interval could be reduced by using a larger number of data points.

USING THE COMPUTER FOR SIMPLE LINEAR REGRESSION

All of the examples of simple linear regression that we have presented thus for have required rather tedious calculations involving SS_{yy}, SS_{xx}, x^2, y^2, xy and so on. Even with the use of pocket calculators, the process is laborious and susceptible to error.

Fortunately, the use of computers can significantly reduce the labor involved in regression calculations. In this section, regression output from one statistical software package, the SAS system is presented though this is just one of the many statistical packages available that provide simple linear regression output, most produce essentially the same quantities differing only in format and labeling to SPSS.

The SAS output will be illustrated using the following example.

Example 10

Suppose a fire insurance company wants to relate the amount of fire damage in major residential fires to the distance between the residence and the nearest fire station. The study is conducted in Lusaka; a sample of 15 recent fires in the city is selected. The amount of damage, y, and the distance, x, between the nearest fire station and the fire are recorded for each fire. The results are:

Distance From Fire Station x (kilometers)	Fire Damage y (K'000)	Distance From Fire Station x (kilometers)	Fire Damage y (K'000)
3.4	26.2	2.6	19.6
1.8	17.8	4.3	31.3
2.3	31.3	2.1	24.0
3.1	23.1	1.1	17.3
5.5	36.0	6.1	43.2
0.7	14.1	4.8	36.4
3.0	22.3	3.8	26.1

Find the linear regression equation and check the usefulness of the hypothesized model i.e. whether x really contributes information for the prediction of y using the straight line model. Also forma 95% confidence interval for the scope and a 95% prediction interval when $x_p = 3.5$.

Solution

Once the x and y values have been input properly, the SAS printout for fire damage regression analysis is as follows:

RETALIATION INDEX VS. SALARY

Model: MODEL 1
Dep variable: R_INDEX

Analysis of Variance

Source	DF	Sum of Squares	Mean Square	F Value	Prob> F
Model	1	20853.93900	20853.93900	0.295	0.3538
Error	13	293208.46100	22554.49700		
C Total	14	314062.40000			

		Root MSE	150.18155	R-Square	0.0664

Root MSE   150.18155   R-Square 0.0664
Dep Mean   499.80000   Adj R-Sq -0.0054
C.V.   30.04833

Parameter Estimates

Variable	DF	parameter Estimates	Standard Error	T for Ho: Parameter = 0	Prob>| T|
INTERCEP	1	575.028672	87.31829499	6.585	0.0001
SALARY	1	-0.002186	0.00227386	ˉ0.962	0.3538

Obs	Salary	R_INDEX	Predict value	Residual	Lower 95% Mean	Upper 95% Mean
1	62000	301.0	439.5	ˉ138.5	280.1	598.8
2	36500	550.0	495.2	54.7770	410.8	579.6
3	17600	755.0	536.5	218.5	418.9	654.2
4	20000	327.0	531.3	ˉ204.3	421.6	641.0
5	30100	500.0	509.2	ˉ9.2163	422.8	595.6
6	35000	377.0	498.5	ˉ121.5	414.7	582.3
7	47500	290.0	471.2	ˉ181.2	365.6	576.8
8	54000	452.0	457.0	ˉ4.9600	329.4	584.6
9	15800	535.0	540.5	ˉ5.4827	416.5	664.5
10	44000	455.0	478.8	ˉ23.8246	382.7	574.9
11	46600	615.0	473.1	141.9	370.2	576.1
12	12100	700.0	548.6	151.4	370.2	686.5
13	62000	650.0	439.5	210.5	280.1	598.8
14	21000	630.0	529.1	100.9	422.6	635.7
15	11900	360.0	549.0	ˉ189.0	410.3	687.7

Now, how do we get meaning from the printout?

- First, the estimate of the y-intercept and the slope are found about halfway down the printout on the left-hand side, under the column labeled Parameter Estimate and in the rows labeled INTERCEPT and x, respectively. The values are

$$\hat{B}_0 = 10.277929 \text{ and } \hat{B}_1 = 4.919331.$$

- Next, we find the measures of variability: SSE, S^2, and S. They are shaded in the upper portion of the printout. SSE is found under the column heading sum of squares and in the row labeled Error: SSE = 69.75098. The estimate of the error variance σ^2 is under the column heading mean square and in the row labeled

Error: $S^2 = 5.36546$. The estimate of the standard deviation σ is directly to the right of the heading Root MSE: $S = 2.31635$.

- The coefficient of determination is shown (shaded) under the heading R-Square in the upper portion of the printout: $r^2 = 0.9235$. The coefficient of correlation r is not given on the printout.

The t statistic for testing Ho: $B_1 = 0$ versus Ha: $B_1 \neq 0$ is given (shaded) in the centre of the page under the column heading T for Ho: parameter = 0 in the row corresponding to x. The value $t = 12.525$ can be confirmed using

$$ t = \frac{\hat{B_1}}{S\hat{B_1}} = \frac{\hat{B_1}}{S/\sqrt{SS_{xx}}} $$

- To determine which hypothesis this test statistic supports, we can establish a rejection region using the t-table. However, the printout makes this unnecessary, because the observed significance level, or P-value, is shown (shade) immediately to the right of the t statistic, under the column heading Prob >|T|. Remember that if the observed significance level is less than the α value your select, then the test statistic supports the alternative hypothesis at that level. For example, if we select $\alpha = 0.05$ in this example, the observed significance level of 0.0001 given on the printout indicates that we should reject Ho. We can conclude that there is sufficient evidence at $\alpha = 0.05$ to infer that a linear relationship between fire damage and distance from the station is useful for predicting damage.

- If you wish to conduct a one-tailed test, the observed significance level is half that given on the printout (assuming the sign of the test statistic agrees with the alternative hypothesis). Thus, if we are testing Ho: $B_1 = 0$ versus Ha: $B_1 > 0$ in this example, the observed significance level would be ½ (0.0001) = 0.00005.

- The predicted y values and the corresponding prediction intervals are given in the lower portion of the SAS printout. To find the 95% prediction intervals for the fire damage y when the distance from the fire station is x = 3.5 kilometers, first locate the value 3.5 in the column labeled ID (the last value in the column) The prediction is given in the centre column labeled predict value in the row corresponding to 3.5:

$$ \hat{y} = 27.4956 $$

- The lower and upper confidence bounds (shaded) are given in the columns headed lower and upper 95%, respectively:

Lower = 22.3239

Upper = 32.6672

- Finally, although much more information is given on the SAS printout, we have discussed only those aspects that have been presented in the Chapter. The point is that the computer can alleviate much of the burden of calculation involved in a regression analysis, and enable us to spend more time on the interpretation of the model. The time spent in learning how to read computer regression output is a good investment.

6   Suppose a fire insurance company wants to relate the amount of fire damage in major residential fires to the distance between the residence and the nearest fire station. The study is to be conducted in Lusaka: a sample of 15 recent fires in the city are selected. The amount of damage, y, and the distance, x, between the fire and the nearest fire station are recorded for each fire. The results are given below:

Distance from Fire Station x (kilometers)	Fire Damage y (K'000)	Distance Form Fire Station x (kilometers)	Fire Damage y (K'000)
3.4	26.2	2.6	19.6
1.8	17.8	4.3	13.3
4.6	31.3	2.1	24.0
2.3	23.1	1.1	17.3
3.1	27.5	6.1	43.2
5.5	36.0	4.8	36.4
0.7	14.1	3.8	26.1
3.0	22.3		

Hypothesizing a straight-line probabilistic model:

(a) Find the least squares regression equation

(b) Test the null hypothesis that the slope B_1 = zero against the alternative that the slope B_1 $\neq$ zero. Use $\alpha = 0.05$.

(c) Find a 95% confidence interval for the slope B_1.

(d) Find r and r^2 and interpret the result.

(e) Find a 95% prediction interval when the distance is 3.5 kilometers from the nearest fire station.

7. A regression model relating x, number of salespersons at a branch office to y, annual sales at the office (K'000) has been developed. The computer output from a regression analysis of the data follows:

The regression equation is:

$$Y = 80.0 + 50.00x$$

Mediator	Coef.	Stdev	t-ratio
Constant	80.0	11.333	7.06
x	50.0	5.482	9.12

Analysis of variance

Source	DF	SS	MS
Regression	1	6828.6	6828.6
Error	28	2298.8	82.1
Total	29	9127.4	

(a) Write the estimated regression equation.

(b) How many branch offices were involved in the study?

(c) Compute the F statistic and test the significance of the relationship at $\alpha = 0.05$ level.

(d) Predict the annual sales at the branch if it has 12 salespersons.

(e) Did the estimated regression equation provide a good fit? Explain

(f) Develop a 95%confidence interval for the regression coefficient 0.

(g) Deduce the relationship between t and F tests. Confirm your deduction by calculation.

8. Based on an observational study of five chief executives, Mintzberg (1973) identified ten managerial roles that can be found in all managerial jobs: figurehead, leader, liaison, monitor, disseminator, spokesperson, entrepreneur, disturbance handler, resource allocator, and negotiator. In a recent observational study of 19 managers from a medium-sized manufacturing plant, Luthans, Rosenkrantz and Hannessey (1985) extended Mintzber's work by investigating which activities successful managers actually perform. Each manager was observed during eighty – 10 minutes intervals over a 2-week period and their activities recorded. The authors used regression analysis to investigate which of the recorded activities were related to managerial success. To measure success, Luthans, et al. devised an index based on the manager's length of time in the organization and his or her level within the firm: the higher the index, the more successful manager. The table presents data (which are representative of the data collected by Luthans, et al.) that can be used to determine whether managerial success can in part be explained by extensiveness of a manager's network- building interactions with people outside the manager's work unit. Such interactions include phone and face-to-face meetings with customers and suppliers, attending external meetings, and doing public relations work.

Manager	Manager Success Index	Number of interactions with outsiders	Manager	Manager success index	Number of interactions with outsiders
1	40	12	11	70	20
2	73	71	12	47	81
3	95	70	13	80	40
4	60	43	14	51	33
5	81	50	15	32	45
6	27	42	16	50	10
7	53	18	17	52	65
8	66	35	18	30	20
9	25	82	19		
10	63				

(a) Construct scatter gram for the data and comment.

(b) Given $SS_{yy} = 7006.6316$, $SS_{xx} = 10824.5263$, $SS_{xy} = 2561.2632$, $\bar{y} = 54.5789$, and $\bar{x} = 44.1579$, use the method of least squares to find the prediction equation for managerial success.

(c) Find SSE, S^2 and S for your prediction equation. Interpret the standard deviation, S, in the context of this problem.

(d) Conduct a formal statistical hypothesis test to determine whether the number of interactions with outsiders contributes information for the prediction of managerial success. Use $\alpha = 0.05$.

(e) Construct a 95% confidence interval for B_1. interpret the interval in the context of the problem

(f) The SAS simple linear regression printout for the above data is given below.

Source	DF	Sum of Squares	Mean Square	F value	prob.F
Model	1	606.03751	606.03751	1. 610	0.2216
Error	17	6400.59407	376.50553		
C Total	18	7006.63158			
Root MSE		19.40375	R-Square	0.0865	
Dep mean		54.57895	Adj. R-Square	0.0328	

Parameter Estimates

Variable	DF	Parameter Estimator	Standard Error	T for Ho: Parameter = 0	Pro> |T|
INTERCEP	1	44.130454	9.36159293	4.714	0.0002
INTERACT	1	0.236617	0.18650103	1.269	0.2216

(i)   Find the least squares equation, and compare it to that you calculated in (a) above.
(ii)   Find the standard deviation, S, and interpret the value in terms of this problem.
(iii) Find and interpret r^2.
(iv)   Is there sufficient evidence to indicate that the model is useful for predicting y? What is the observed significance level of the test?

9. A firm's demand curve describes the quantity of its product that can be sold at different possible prices, other things being equal. Over the period of a year, a tire company varied the price of one of its radial tires in order to estimate the demand curve for the tire. They observed that when the very low or very high, they sold few tires. The latter result they understood: the former they determined was due to consumer misconception that the tires low price must be linked to poor quality.   The data in the table describe the tire's sales over the experiment period.

Tire price (K'000)	Number sold
20	13
35	57
45	85
60	43
70	17

(a) Calculate a least squares line to approximate the firm's demand.
(b) Test Ho: $B_1 = 0$ using a two-tailed test at $\alpha = 0.05$. Draw the appropriate conclusion in the context of the problem.
(c) Does the non rejection of Ho in part (b) imply that no relationship exist between tire price and sales volume? Explain.
(d) Calculate the coefficient of determination for the least squares line of pat (a) and interpret its value in the context of the problem

PROGRESS CLINIC TWELVE

1. The demand for banker's drafts at a bank in Lusaka over a period 2000 – 2006 is shown below. Find the straight line trend to these data and forecast 2007 demand.

Year	2000	2001	2002	2003	2004	2005	2006
Drafts demanded	74	79	80	90	105	142	122

2. A manufacturer would like to develop a method for estimating direct labour cost for small-batch production orders. The following table gives a random sample of actual direct-labour cost for ten batches.

Batch size (units)	Direct labour cost
15	260
18	240
18	260
21	290
23	300
23	320
26	380
28	370
32	400
37	470

(a) Plot a scatter graph and comment.
(b) Determine the linear regression equation
(c) Determine r^2. What is the significance of this value?
(d) Calculate a statistic which will indicate how well the regression line explains the variability of data.
(e) Provide an estimate of the direct labour cost regarding an order for a batch size of 25 units.

3. Commercial banks primary objective is to maximize profits so as to maximize shareholder wealth. The most important source of profits is bank lending. In bank lending the interest rate to be charged is a paramount decision. Some loans are for 12 months, 36 months, and so on. The interest rate charged for a given period generally differs from interest charged for another period as given by the **yield curve**. One of the factors that strongly influence nominal interest rates is the rate if inflation. A lending officer wanted to determine the relationship between inflation rates and interest rates. He collected data on inflation rates and interest rates for the last 10 years.

Year	1998	1999	2000	2001	2002	2003	2004	2005	2006	2007
Inflation rate (%)	40	38	35	37	29	24	21	18	13	10
Base rate (%)	62	51	49	55	41	36	36	32	25	20

(a) Determine the predictor variable in the above table
(b) Determine the regression line.
(c) Use the regression line to predict what loan when the interest rate be for a 36 month loan when inflation is 8%.
(d) Compute the correlation coefficient
(e) Compute the coefficient of determination and interpret the result.
(f) What reservations would you have about the predicted interest rate in (c) ?

4. XYZ Ltd produces brakes for motor industry. Its management accountants are investigating the relationship between electricity costs and the volume of production. The frequency data for the last 10 quarters has been derived. The cost figures have been adjusted to take into account price changes.

Quarter	1	2	3	4	5	6	7	8	9	10
Electricity (y)	10	11	6	18	13	10	10	20	17	15
Production (x)	30	20	10	60	40	25	13	50	44	28

(a) Draw a scatter graph for the data and comment.
(b) Find the least squares regression line for electricity on production and explain this result.
(c) Find the correlation coefficient and the coefficient of determination and interpret your result.
(d) Test the validity of the slope at $\alpha = 0.05$.
(e) What assumptions are necessary when carrying out the test in (d)?
(f) Find a 95% confidence interval for the slope and comment

5. The management accountant at Nyati Milling in Mazabuka is trying to predict the quarterly total maintenance cost for a group of similar machines. She has extracted the following information for the eight quarters:

Quarter Number	1	2	3	4	5	6	7	8
Total maintenance cost (K'000)	265	302	222	240	362	295	404	400
Production units ('000)	20	24	16	18	26	22	32	50

The effects of inflation have been eliminated from the above costs.

The management accountant is using linear regression to establish an equation of the form y = a + bx and has produced the following preliminary calculations:

i) $\sum$ (total maintenance cost X production unit) = K61 250 million
ii) $\sum$ (total maintenance cost)^2 = K809 598 million
iii) $\sum$ (production units)^2 = K4 640 million

(a) Establish the equation which will allow the management accountant to predict quarterly total maintenance costs for a given level of production. Interpret your answer in terms of fixed and variable maintenance costs.

(b) Using the equation in (a), predict total maintenance cost for the next quarter when planned production is 44 000 units. Suggest a major reservation, other than the effect of inflation you would have about this prediction.

(c) What is the relationship between maintenance costs and production units? Explain.

6. Suppose a fire insurance company wants to relate the amount of fire damage in major residential fires to the distance between the residence and the nearest fire station. The study is to be conducted in Lusaka: a sample of 15 recent fires in the city are selected. The amount of damage, y, and the distance, x, between the fire and the nearest fire station are recorded for each fire. The results are given below:

Distance from Fire station x (kilometers)	Fire Damage y (K'000)	Distance from Fire station x (kilometers)	Fire Damage y (k'000)
3.4	26.2	2.6	19.6
1.8	17.8	4.3	31.3
4.6	31.3	2.1	24.0
2.3	23.1	1.1	17.3
3.1	27.5	6.1	43.2
5.5	36.0	4.8	36.4
0.7	14.1	3.8	26.1
3.0	22.3		

Hypothesizing a straight line probabilistic model.

   a. Find the least squares regression equations

   b. Test the null hypothesis that the slope B_1 = zero against the alternative that the slope $B_1 \neq$ zero. Use $\alpha = 0.05$.

   c. Find a 95% confidence interval for the slope B_1.

   d. Find r and r^2 and interpret the result

   e. Find a 95% prediction interval when the distance is 3.5 kilometers from the nearest fire station.

7. A regression model relating x, number of sales persons at a branch office to y, annual sales at the office (K000) has been developed. The computer output from a regression analysis of the data follows:

The regression equation is :

$$Y = 80.0 + 50.00x$$

Mediator	coef.	Stdev	t – ratio
Constant	80.0	11.333	7.06
x	50.0	5.482	9.12

Analysis of variance

Source	DF	SS	MS
Regression	1	6828.6	6828.6
Error	28	2298.8	82.1
Total	29	9127.4	

(h) Write the estimated regression equation.

(i) How many branch offices were involved in the study?

(j) Compute the F statistic and test the significance of the relationship at $\alpha = 0.05$ level.

(k) Predict the annual sales at the branch if it has 12 salespersons.

(l) Did the estimated regression equation provide a good fit? Explain

(m) Develop a 95% confidence interval for the regression coefficient 0.

(n) Deduce the relationship between t and F tests. Confirm your deduction by calculation.

8. Based on an observational study of five chief executives, Mintzberg (1973) identified ten managerial jobs: figure heard, leader, liaison, monitor, disseminator, spokesperson, and negotiator. In a recent observational study of 19 managers from a medium-sized manufacturing plant, Luthans, Rosenkrantz, and Hannessey (1985) extended Mintberg's work by investigating which activities successful managers actually perform. Each manager was observed during eighty – 10 minute interval over a 2-week period and their activities recorded. The authors used regression analysis to investigate which of the recorded activities were related to managerial success. To measure success, Luthans, et al. devised on index based on the manager's length of time in the organization and his or her level within the firm: the higher the index, the more successful manager. The table presents data (which are representative of the data collected by Luthans, et al.) that can be used to determine whether managerial success can in part be explained by extensiveness of a manager's network –building interactions with people outside the manager's work unit. Such interactions include phone and face-to-face meetings with customers and suppliers, attending external meetings, and doing public relations work.

Manager	Manager success Index	Number of interactions with with outsiders	Manager	Manager success index	Number of interactions with outsiders
1	40	12	11	70	20
2	73	71	12	47	81
3	95	70	13	80	40
4	60	80	14	51	33
5	81	43	15	32	45
6	27	50	16	50	10
7	53	42	17	30	65
8	66	18	18	42	21
9	25	35	19		
1.		63	82		

(a) Construct a scatter gram for the data and comment.

(b) Given $SS_{yy} = 7006.6316$, $SS_{xx} = 10824.5263$, $SS_{xy} = 2561.2632$,

$\bar{y} = 54.5789$, and $\bar{x} = 44.1579$, use the method of least squares to find the prediction equation for managerial success.

(c) Find SSE, S^2, and S for your prediction equation. Interpret the standard deviation, S, in the context of this problem.

(d) Conduct a formal statistical hypothesis test to determine whether the number of interactions with outsiders contributes information for the prediction of managerial success. Use $\alpha = 0.05$.

(e) Construct a 95% confidence interval for B_1. Interpret the interval in the context of the problem.

(f) The SAS simple linear regression printout for the above data is given below:

Source	DF	Sum of Squares	Mean square	F value	Prob. F
Model	1	606.03751	606.03751	1.610	0.2216
Error	17	6400.59407	376.50553		
C Total	18	7006.63158			

Root MSE		19.40375	R – Square	0.0865	
Dep. mean		54.57895	Adj. R. square	0.0328	
C.V.		35.55171			

Parameter Estimates

Variable	DF	Parameter Estimate	Standard Error	T for Ho: Parameter = 0	Prob > |T|
INTERCEP	1	44.130454	9.36159293	4.714	0.0002
INTERACT	1	0.236617	0.18650103	1.269	0.2216

    (i)   Find the least squares equation, and compare it to that you calculated in (a) above.

       i. Find the standard deviation, S, and interpret the value in terms of this problem.

     ii. Find and interpret r^2.

   iii. Is there sufficient evidence to indicate that the model is useful for predicting y? What is the observed significance level of the test?

9. A firm's demand curve describes the quality of its product that can be sold at different possible prices, other things being equal. Over the period of a year, a tire company varied the price of one of its radial tires in order to estimate the demand curve for the tire. They observed that when the very low or very high, they sold few tires. The latter result they understood: the former they determined was due to consumer misconception that the tire's low price must be linked to poor quality. The data in the table describe the tire's sales over the experimental period.

Tire price (k'000)	Number sold
20	13
35	57
45	85
60	43
70	17

(a) Calculate a least squares line to approximate the firm's demand.

(b) Test Ho: $B_1 = 0$ using a two-tailed test at $\alpha = 0.05$. Draw the appropriate conclusion in the context of the problem.

(c) Does the non-rejection of Ho in part (b) imply that no relationship exists between tire price and sales volume? Explain.

(d) Calculate the coefficient of determination for the least squares line of part (a) and interpret its value in the context of the problem

Chapter Thirteen

TIME SERIES ANALYSIS AND FORECASTING

A time series of figures or values recorded over time. The graph of a time series is called a histogram.

EXAMPLES OF TIME SERIES

- Output at a factory each day for the last month
- Monthly sales over the last two years
- Total annual costs for the last ten years
- The number of people employed by a company each year for the last 20 years.

There are four components of a time series: trend, seasonal variations, cyclical variations and random variations.

THE TREND

The trend is the underlying long-term movement over time in the values of the data recorded.

Example 1

	Output per labor hour Units	cost per unit K	Number of employees
20X4	30	1.00	100
20X5	24	1.08	103
20X6	26	1.20	96
20X7	22	1.15	102
20X8	21	1.85	103
20X9	17	1.25	98
	(A)	(B)	(C)

(a) In time series (A) there is a **downward trend** in the output per labour hour. Output per labour hour did not fall every year, because it went between 20X5 and 20X6, but long t-term movements clearly a downward on

Graph showing trend of output per labour hour in year 20X4-X9

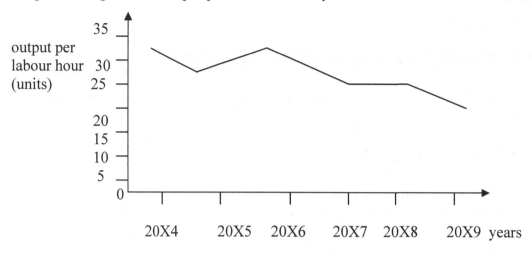

(b) In the series (B) there is an upward trend in the cost per unit. Although unit costs went down in 20X7 from a higher level in 20X6, the basic movement over time is one of rising costs.

Graph showing trend of costs per unit in year's 20X4-X9

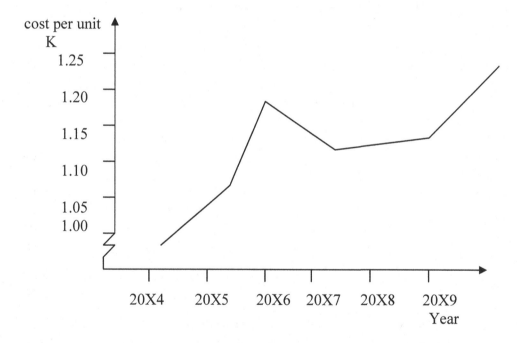

(c) In time series (C) there is no clear movement up or down, and the number of employees remained fairly constant around. The trend is therefore a **static** or **level one**.

Graph showing trend of number of employees in year's 20X4-X9

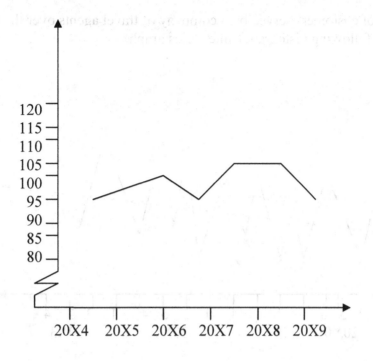

Year

SEASONAL VARIATIONS

Seasonal variations are short-term fluctuations in recorded values, due to different circumstances which affect results at different times of the year, on different days of the week, at different times of a day, or whatever.

EXAMPLES OF SEASONAL VARIATIONS

(a) Sales of ice cream will be higher in summer than in winter, and sales of overcoats will be higher in autumn than in spring.

(b) Shops might expect higher sales shortly before Christmas or in their winter and summer sales.

(c) Sales might be higher on Friday and Saturday than on Monday.

(d) The telephone network may be heavily used at certain times of the day (such as mid-morning and mid-afternoon) and much less used at other times (such as in the middle of the night).

Example 2

The number of customers served by a company of travel agents over the past four years is shown in the following histogram (time series graph).

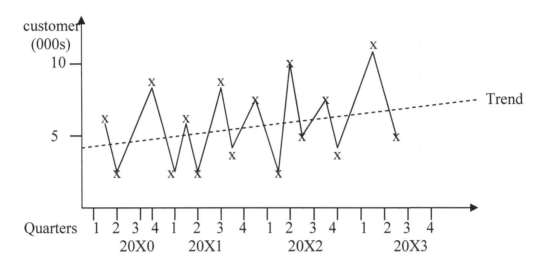

In this example, there would appear to be large seasonal fluctuations in demand, but there is also a basic trend.

CYCLICAL VARIATIONS

Cyclical variations are medium-term changes in results caused by circumstances which repeat in cycles.

In business, cycles variations are commonly associated with **economic cycles, successive booms** and **slumps** in the economy. Economic cycles may last a few years. Cyclical variations are longer term than **seasonal variations**.

SUMMARIZING THE COMPONENTS

The components of a time series can be summarized by the following equation.

$$Y = T + S + C + I$$

Where Y = the actual time series
      T = the trend series
      S = the seasonal component
      C = the cyclical component
      I = the random or irregular component

Though you should be aware of the cyclical component, you will not be expected to carry out any calculation connected with isolating it. The mathematical model which we will use, the **additive model** therefore excludes any reference to C.

$$\boxed{\begin{array}{l} \text{Additive model: Series = Trend + Seasonal + Random} \\ \qquad\qquad Y = T + S + I \end{array}}$$

FINDING THE TREND

METHODS OF FINDING THE TREND

The main problem we are concerned with in time series analysis is how to identify the trend and seasonal variations.

Main methods of finding a trend

- (a) A line of best fit (the trend line) can be drawn by eye on a graph. (we will cover this in section 4 of this chapter).
- (b) A statistical techniques known as linear regression by the least squares method can be used. (We will cover this in chapter 14).
- (c) A technique known as moving averages can be used.

FINDING THE TREND BY MOVING AVERAGES

One method of finding the trend is by use of **moving averages**.

- A moving average is an average of the results of a fixed number of periods.
- The moving averages method is a technique used to find the trend. This method attempts to remove seasonal variations from actual data by process of averaging.

Example 3

Year	Sales units
20X0	390
20X1	380
20X2	460
20X3	450
20X4	470
20X5	440
20X6	500

Required

Take a moving average of the annual sales over a period of three years.

Solution

(a) Average sales in the three-year period 20X0 – 20X2 were

$$\left(\frac{390 + 380 + 400}{3}\right) = \frac{1{,}230}{3} = 410$$

This average relates to the middle year of the period, 20X1

(b) Similarly, average sales in the three year period 20X1 – 20X3 were

$$\left(\frac{360 + 460 + 450}{3} = \frac{1{,}290}{3}\right) = 430$$

This average relates to the middle year of the period, 20X2.

(c) This average sales can also be found for the periods 20X2 – 20X4, 20X3 – 20X5 and 20X4 – 20X6, to five the following.

Year	Sales	Moving total of 3 years' sales	Moving average of 3 years' sales (÷ 3)
20X0	390		
20X1	380	1,230	410
20X2	460	1,290	430
20X3	450	1,380	460
20X4	470	1,360	453
20X5	440	1,410	470
20X6	500		

Note the following points

(i)   The moving average series has five relating to the years form 20X1 to 20X5. The original series had seven figures for the year from 20X0 to 20X6.

(ii)   There is an upward trend in sales, which is more noticeable form the series of moving averages than from the original series of actual sales each year.

OVER WHAT PERIOD SHOULD A MOVING AVERAGE BE TAKEN?

The above example averaged over a three-year period. Over what period should a moving average be taken? The answer to this question is that the **moving average which is most appropriate will depend on the circumstances and the nature of the time series**. Note the following points.

(a) A moving average which takes an average of the results in many time periods will represent results over a longer term than a moving average of two or three periods.

(b) On the other hand, with a moving average of results in many time periods, the last figure in the series will be out of date by several periods. In our example, the most recent average related to 20X5. With a moving average of five years' results, the final figure in the series would relate to 24X4.

(c) When there is a known cycle over which seasonal variations occur, such as all the days in the week or all the seasons in the year, the most suitable moving average would be one which covers one full cycle.

Example 4

Using the following data, complete the following table in order to determine the three-months moving average for the period January –June.

Month	No of new houses finished	Moving total 3 months new houses finished	Moving average of 3 months new houses finished
January	500		
February	450		
March	700		
April	900		
May	1,250		
June	1,000		

Solution

Month	No of new houses finished	Moving total 3 months new houses finished	Moving average of 3 months new houses finished
January	500		
February	450	1,650	550
March	700	2,050	683.33
April	900	2,850	950
May	1,250	3,150	1,050
June	1,000		

MOVING AVERAGES OF AN EVEN NUMBER OF RESULTS

When finding the moving average of an even number of results, a second moving average has to be calculated so that trend values relate to specific actual figures.

In the previous example, moving averages were taken of the results in an odd number of time periods, and the average then related to mid-point of the overall period. If a moving average were taken of results in an even number of time periods, the basic technique would be the same, but the mid-point of the overall period would not relate to a single period. For example, suppose an average were taken of the following four results.

		Volume of sales '000 units			
Spring		120			
Summer		90	average		
Autumn		180			
Winter		70			

Example 5

Calculate a moving average trend line of the following results.

Year	Quarter	Volume of sales '000 units
20X5	1	600
	2	840
	3	423
	4	720
20X6	1	640
	2	860
	3	420
	4	740
20X7	1	670
	2	900
	3	430
	4	760

Solution

A moving average of four will be used, since the volume of sales would appear to depend on the season of the year, and each year has four quarterly results.

The moving average of four does not relate to any specific period of time; therefore a second moving average of two will be calculated on the first moving average trend line.

Year	Quarter	Actual volume of sales '000 units (A)	Moving Total of 4 quarters' sales '000 units (B)	Moving average of 4 quarters' sales '000 units (B ÷ 4)	Mid-pint of 2 moving averages Trend line '000 units (C)
20X5	1	600			
	2	840			
			2,580	645.0	
	3	420			650.00
			2,650	655.0	
	4	720			657.50
			2,640	660.0	
20X6	1	640			

Year	Quarter	Value	Moving total	Moving average	Centred average
			2,640	660.0	
	2	860			662.50
			2,660	665.0	
	3	420			668.75
			2,690	672.5	
	4	760			677.50
			2,730	682.5	
20X7	1	670			683.75
			2,740	685.5	
	2	900			687.50
			2,760	690.0	
	3	430			
	4	760			

By taking a mid point (a moving average of two) **of the original moving averages, we can relate the results to specify quarters** (from the third quarter of 20X05 to the second quarter of 20X7).

FINDING THE SEASONAL VARIATIONS

SEASONAL VARIATIONS USING THE ADDITIVE MODEL

Once a trend has been established, by whatever method, we can find the seasonal variations.

Seasonal variations are the difference between actual and trend figures. An average of the seasonal variations for each time period within the cycle must be determined and then adjusted so that the total of the seasonal variations sums to zero. Seasonal variations can be estimated using the additive model. ($Y = T + S + I$, with seasonal variations – $Y – T$ or the proportional (multiplicative) model ($Y = T \times S \times I$, with seasonal variations = $Y \div T$).

FINDING THE SEASONAL COMPONENT

Step 1   The additive model for time series analysis is $Y = T + S + I$.

Step 2   If we deduct the trend from the additive model, we get $Y – T = S + I$

Step 3   If we assume that I, the random, or irregular component of the time series is relatively small and therefore negligible, then $S = Y – T$.

Therefore, the seasonal components, S = Y- T (the de-trended series).

Example 6

Output at a factory appears to vary with the day of the week. Output over the last three weeks has been as follows.

	Week 1 '000 units	Week 2 '000 units	Week 3 '000 units
Monday	80	82	84
Tuesday	104	110	116
Wednesday	94	97	100
Thursday	120	125	130
Friday	62	64	66

Required

Find the seasonal variation for each of the 15 days, and the average seasonal variation for each day of the week using the moving averages method.

Solution

Actual results fluctuate up and down according to the day of the week and so a moving average of live will be used. **The difference the actual result on any one day (Y) and the trend figure for that day (T) will be the seasonal variation (S) for the day**. The seasonal variations for the 15 days are as follows.

		Actual (Y)	Moving total of five days' output	Trend (T)	Seasonal variation (Y – T)
Week 1	Monday	80			
	Tuesday	104			
	Wednesday	94	460	92.0	$^+2.0$
	Thursday	120	462	92.4	$^+27.6$
	Friday	62	468	93.6	$^-31.6$
Week 2	Monday	82	471	94.2	$^-12.2$
	Tuesday	110	476	95.2	$^+14.8$
	Wednesday	97	478	95.6	$^+1.4$
	Thursday	125	480	96.0	$^+29.0$
	Friday	64	486	97.2	$^-33.2$
Week	Monday	84	489	97.8	$^-13.8$
	Tuesday	116	494	98.8	$^+17.2$
	Wednesday	100	496	99.2	$^+0.8$
	Thursday	130			
	Friday	66			

You will notice that the variation between the actual results on any one particular day and the trend line average is not the same from week to week. This is because **Y – T** **contains not only seasonal variations but random variations, and an average of these variations can be taken.**

	Monday	Tuesday	Wednesday	Thursday	Friday
Week 1			+2.0	+27.6	-31.6
Week 2	-12.2	+14.8	+1.4	+29.0	-33.2
Week 3	-13.8	+17.2	+0.8		
Average	**+13.0**	**+16.0**	**+1.4**	**+28.3**	**-32.4**

Variations around the basic trend line should cancel each other out, and add up to 0. At the moment they do not. **The average seasonal estimates must therefore be corrected so that they add up to zero** and so we spread the total of the daily variations (0.30) across the five days (0.3 ÷ 5) so that the final total of the daily variations goes to zero.

	Monday	Tuesday	Wednesday	Thursday	Friday	Total
Estimated average Daily variation	⁻13.00	⁺16.00	⁺1.40	⁺28.30	⁻32.40	0.30
Adjustment to reduce Total variations to 0	⁻0.06	⁻0.06	⁻0.06	⁻0.06	⁻0.06	⁻0.30
Final estimate of average Daily variation	**⁻13.06**	**⁺15.94**	**⁺1.34**	**⁺28.24**	**⁻32.46**	**0.00**

These might be rounded up or down as follows.

Monday -13; Tuesday +16; Wednesday +1; Thursday +28; Friday -32; Total 0

Example 7

Calculate a four-quarter moving average trend centered on actual quarter and then find seasonal variations from the following.

	Sales in K'000			
	Spring	Summer	Autumn	Winter
20X7	200	120	160	280
20X8	220	140	140	300
20X9	200	120	180	320

Solution

		Moving average total	Seasonal variation total	Sales (Y)	4-quarter (T)	8-quarter (Y –T)
20X7	Spring	200				
	Summer	120				
			760			
	Autumn	160		1,580	192.5	-32.5
			780			
	Winter	280		1,580	197.5	+82.5
			800			
20X8	Spring	220		1,580	197.5	+22.5
			780			
	Summer	140		1,580	197.5	-57.5
			800			
	Autumn	140		1,580	197.5	-57.5
			780			
	Winter	300		1,540	197.5	+107.5
			760			
20X9	Spring	200		1,560	197.5	+5.0
			800			
	Summer	120		1,620	202.5	-82.5
			820			
	Autumn	180				
		320				

We can now average the seasonal variations.

	Spring	Summer	Autumn	Winter	Total
20X7			⁻32.5	⁻82.5	
20X8	⁺22.5	⁻57.5	⁻57.5	⁺107.5	
20X9	⁺5.0	⁻82.5			
	⁺27.5	⁻140.0	⁻90.0	⁺190.0	
Average variations (in K'000)	⁺13.75	⁻70.00	⁻45.00	⁺95.00	⁻6.25
Adjustment so sum is zero	⁺1.5625	⁺1.5625	⁺1.5625	⁺1.5625	⁺6.25
Adjusted average variations	⁺15.3125	⁻68.4375	⁻43.4375	⁺96.5625	0

These might be rounded up or down to:

Spring K15, 000, Summer – K68, 000, Autumn – K43, 000, Winter K96, 000.

SEASONAL VARIATIONS USING THE MULTIPLICATIVE MODEL

The method of estimating the seasonal variations in the model is to use the differences between the trend and actual data. The **additive model assumes that the components of** the series are independent to each other, an increasing trend not affecting the seasonal variations for example.

The alternative is to use the **multiplicative model** whereby **each actual figure is expected as a proportion of the trend**. Sometimes this method is called the **proportional mode**l. Multiplicative model: Series = Trend X Seasonal X Random

$$Y = T \times S \times 1$$

MULTIPLICATIVE MODEL

The additive model example above (in Paragraph 3.3) can be reworked on this alternative basis. The trend is calculated in exactly the same way as before but we need a different approach for the seasonal variations.

The multiplicative model is $Y = T \times S \times I$ and, just as we calculated $S = Y - T$ for the additive model we can calculate $S = $ **Y/T for the multiplicative model**.

		Actual (Y)	Trend (T)	Seasonal variation (Y/T)
Week 1	Monday	80		
	Tuesday	104		
	Wednesday	94	92.0	1.022
	Thursday	120	92.4	1.299
	Friday	62	93.6	0.662
Week 2	Monday	82	94.2	0.870
	Tuesday	110	95.6	1.155
	Wednesday	97	95.0	1.015
	Thursday	125	96.0	1.302
	Friday	64	97.2	0.658
Week 3	Monday	84	97.8	0.859
	Tuesday	116	98.8	1.174
	Wednesday	100		
	Thursday	130		
	Friday	66		

SUMMING TO AN AVERAGE OF 1

The summary of the seasonal variations expressed in **proportional terms** is as follows.

	Monday	Tuesday	Wednesday	Thursday	Friday	Total
Week 1			1.022	1.299	0.662	
Week 2	0.870	1.155	1.015	1.302	0.658	
Week 3	0.859	1.174	1.008			
Total	1.729	2.329	3.045	2.601	1.320	5.0045
Average	0.8645	1.1645	1.0150	1.3005	0.6600	5.0000
						1.0045

Instead of summing to zero, as with the absolute approach, these should sum (in this case) to 5 (an average of 1).

They actually sum to 5.0045 so 0.0009 has to be deducted from each one. This is too small to make a difference to the figures above, so we should deduct 0.002 and 0.0025 to each of two seasonal variations. We could arbitrary decrease Monday's variation to 0.8625 and Tuesday's to 1.162.

WHEN TO USE THE MULTIPLICATIVE MODEL

The multiplicative model is better than the additive model for forecasting when the trend is increasing or decreasing over time. In such circumstances, seasonal variations are likely to be increasing or decreasing too. The additive model simply adds absolute and unchanging seasonal variations to the figures whereas the multiplicative model, by multiplying increasing or decreasing trend values by a constant seasonal variation factor, takes account of changing seasonal variations.

SUMMARY

We can summaries the steps to be carried out when calculating the seasonal variations as follows.

Step 1	Calculate the moving total for an appropriate period
Step 2	Calculate the moving average (the trend) for the period. (Calculate the mid-point of two moving averages if there are an even number of periods.
Step 3	Calculate the seasonal variations. For an additive model, this is $Y - T$. For a multiplicative model, this is Y/T.
Step 4	Calculate an average of the seasonal variations.
Step 5	Adjust the average seasonal variations so that they add up to **zero** for **an additive model**. When using the **multiplicative model**, the average seasonal variations should add up to an **average of 1**.

Example 8

Find the average seasonal variations for the sales data in the previous question (entitled: Four quarter moving average trend) using the multiplicative model.

Solution

	Spring	Summer	Autumn	Winter	Total
20X7			0.83*	1.42	
20X8	1.11	0.71	0.71	1.56	
20X9	<u>1.03</u>	<u>0.59</u>			
	<u>2.14</u>	1.30	<u>1.54</u>	<u>2.98</u>	

	Spring	Summer	Autumn	Winter	Total
Average variations	1.070	0.650	0.770	1.490	3.980
Adjustments to sum to 4	+<u>0.005</u>	+<u>0.005</u>	+<u>0.005</u>	+<u>0.005</u>	+<u>0.005</u>
Adjusted average variations	<u>1.075</u>	0.655	<u>0.775</u>	<u>1.490</u>	<u>4.000</u>

*Seasonal variation $Y/T = \dfrac{160}{192.5} = 0.83$

SEASONALLY-ADJUSTED DATA

Seasonally-adjusted data (depersonalized) are data which have had any seasonal various taken out. So leaving a figure which might indicate the trend seasonally adjusted data should indicate whether the overall trend is rising, falling or stationary.

Example 9

Actual sales figures for four quarters, together with appropriate seasonal adjustment factors derived from previous data, are as follows.

Quarter	Actual sales K'000	Actual model K'000	Seasonal adjustments Multiplicative model
1	150	+3	1.02
2	160	+4	1.05
3	164	‾2	0.98
4	170	‾5	0.95

FORECASTING AND TIME SERIES ANALYSIS

Forecasts can be made by extrapolating the trend and adjusting for seasonal variations. Remember, however, that all forecasts are subject to error.

MAKING A FORECAST

Time series analysis data can be used to make forecasts as follows:

Step 1   plot a trend line: use the line of best fit method or the moving averages method.

ASSUMPTIONS

1.   Conditions remain stable
2.   Extra factors will not arise

Step 2   **Extrapolate the trend line**. This means extending the trend line outside the range of known data and forecasting future results from historical data.

Step 3   **Adjust forecast trends** by the applicable average seasonal variation to obtain the actual forecast.

    (a) **Additive model** – add positive variations to and subtract negative variations from the forecast trends.

    (b) **Multiplicative model** – multiply the forecast trends by the seasonal variation.

Example 10

Use the trend values and the estimates of seasonal variations calculated in paragraphs3.3. to forecast sales in week 4.

Solution

We begin by plotting values on a graph and extrapolating the trend line.

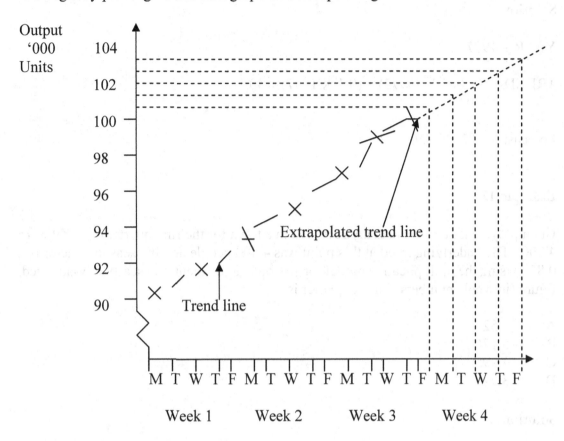

From the extrapolated trend line we can take the following readings and adjust them by the seasonal variations.

Week 4	Trend line readings	Seasonal Variations	Forecast
Monday	100.5	-13	87.5
Tuesday	101.5	+16	117.1
Wednesday	101.7	+1	102.7
Thursday	102.2	+28	130.2
Friday	102.8	-32	70.8

If we had been using the multiplicative model the forecast for Tuesday, for example, would be 10.1 X1.1645 =117.7 (from Paragraph 3.6).

Example 11

In a time series analysis, the trend equation for product Z is given by

$$TREND = 0.0002*YEAR^2 + 0.1*YEAR + 40.1$$

Due to the cyclical factor, it is estimated that the forecast sales for 1997 is estimated at 1.92 times trend. Calculate the forecast sales for 1997.

Solution

YEAR = 1997

TREND = (0.0002 X 19972) + (0.1 X 1997) + 40.1
$\qquad$ = 1,037

Forecast = 1,037 X 1.92
$\qquad$ = 1,992

Example 12

Unemployment numbers actually recorded in a town for the first quarter of 20X9 were 4,700. The underlying trend at this point was 4,400 people and the seasonal factor is 0.85. Using the multiplicative model for seasonal adjustment, the seasonally-adjusted figure (in whole numbers) for the quarter is

A   5,529
B   5,176
C   3,995
D   3,740

Solution

The correct answer is A

If you remember ed the ruling that you need to divide by the seasonal variation factor to obtain seasonally-adjusted figures (using the multiplicative model), then you should have been able to eliminate options C and D. This might have been what you did if you weren't sure whether you divided the actual results or the trend by the seasonal variation factor.

$$\text{Seasonally adjusted data} = \frac{\text{Actual results}}{\text{Seasonal factor}} = \frac{4,700}{0.85} = 5,529$$

RESIDUALS

A residual is the difference between the results which would have been predicted (for a past period for which we already have data) by the trend line adjusted for the average seasonal variation and the actual results.

The residual is therefore the difference which is not explained by the trend line and the average seasonal variation. The residual gives some indication of how much actual result were affected by other factors. Large residuals suggest that any forecast is likely to be unreliable.

In the example in Paragraph 3.3, the 'prediction' for Wednesday of week 2 would have been 95.6 + 1 = 96.6. As the actual value was 97, the residual was only 97 – 96.6 = 0.4.

THE RELIABILITY OF TIME SERIES ANALYSIS FORECASTS

All forecasts are subject to error, but the likely errors vary from case to case.

(a)   The further into the future the forecast is for, the more unreliable it is likely to be.

(b)   The less data available on which to base the forecast, the less reliable the forecast

(c)   The pattern of trend and seasonal variations cannot be guaranteed to continue in the future.

(d)   There is always the danger of random variations upsetting the pattern of trend and seasonal variation.

(e)   The extrapolation of the trend line is done by judgment and can introduce error.

Example 13

In a time series analysis, the multiplicative model is used to forecast sales and the following seasonal variations apply.

Quarter	1	2	3	4
Seasonal variation	0.8	1.9	0.75	?

The actual sales value for the last two quarters of 20X! were:

Quarter: K250, 000
Quarter 4:   K260, 000

(a)   The seasonal variation for the fourth quarter is:
      A   0.55
      B   ‾3.45
      C   1.00
      D   1.45

(b)   The trend line for sales:

A   remained constant between quarter 3 and quarter 4
B   increased between quarter 3 and quarter 4
C   decreased between quarter 3 and quarter 4
D   Cannot be determine from the information given

Solution

(a) The correct answer is A.

As this is multiple locative models, the seasonal variations should sum (in this case) to 4 (an average of 1) as there are four quarters.

Let x = seasonal variation in quarter 4

$0.8 + 1.9 + 0.75 + x = 4$

$.: 3.45 + x = 4$

$x = 4 - 3.45$

$x = 4 - 3.45$

$x = 055$

(b) The correct answer is B.

$S = Y/T$
$.: T = Y/S$

	Quarter	
Seasonal component (S)	0.75	0.55
Actual series (Y)	K250, 000	K260, 000
Trend (T) (=Y/S)	(K333, 333	K472, 727

The trend line for sales has therefore increased between quarter 3 and quarter 4.

PROGRESS CLINIC THIRTEEN

1. You are given the following information about demand for an item:

Month:	1	2	3	4	5	6	7	8	9	10	11
Demand:	220	228	217	219	258	241	239	244	256	260	265

Calculate forecasted values using:

    a. 3 – monthly moving averages
    b. 5 – monthly moving averages

2. (a) for the following data, develop a 3-month moving average forecast

   Month: Jan Feb Mar Apr May Jun Jul Aug Sep Oct Nov Dec
   Auto sales: 20   21   15   14   13   16 17   18   20   20   21   23

   (b) Comment on the sales trend over the 12 month period.

3. the number of job applications received by the bank's HR department during the year 2007 is given below:

   Month: Jan   Feb   Mar   Apr   May Jun Jul Aug Sep Oct Nov Dec
   No. of applications: 10   12   13   16   19   23 26   30   28   18   16   14

   Determine the three-month moving average.

4. (a) Assume a four-year cycle and calculate the trend by the method of moving averages from the following data relating to production of sugar at a sugar estate.

Year	Production (kg)	Year	Production (kg)
1991	464	1996	540
1992	515	1997	557
1993	518	1998	571
1994	467	1999	586
1995	502	2000	612

   (b) From the trend values obtained in part (a) above, what would you say is the main advantage of obtaining a time series trend using the method of moving averages?

   (c) Time series is an alternative forecasting technique to regression analysis.

   (i) State the components of a time series
      (ii) State three circumstances under which time series would be inappropriate.

Chapter Fourteen

INDEX NUMBERS ANALYSIS

Indexing is a technique for comparing, over time, changes in some property of a group of items (price, quantity consumed, etc) by expressing the property each year as a percentage of some earlier years, a base year.

Examples of index numbers are frequently seen in everyday life. The best-known is probably the Consumer Price Index (CPI), which measures changes in the prices of goods and services supplied to retail customers. This index is often thought of as a 'cost of living' index. Index numbers may also measure quantity changes (e.g. volumes of production or trade) or changes in values (e.g. retail sales, value of exports).

In this chapter you will learn about simple indices, weighted indices, chain base indices, Laspeyre indices and Paasche indices.

THE PURPOSE OF INDEX NUMBERS

INFLATION

Inflation is the process whereby the price of commodities steadily rises over time.

Inflation often makes information difficult to interpret. If data simply shows, for example the cost of raw materials used, it may be difficult to assess changes in quantities used when the prices of the raw materials are subject to inflation. If management wishes to interpret changes in quantities of materials used they must first adjust the expenditure figures for price changes.

INDEX NUMBERS

An index number shows the rate of change of a variable from one specified time to another.

Most accountants acknowledge that the accounts of businesses are distorted when no allowance is made for the effects of inflation. The use of index numbers is often required for the preparation of inflation-adjusted accounts. This chapter considers the range of possible methods by which such index numbers might be calculated.

TYPES OF INDEX NUMBER

The following types of index will be considered.

- Simple indices
- Weighted indices
- Chain base indices
- Laspeyre indices

- Paasche indic

SIMPLE INDICES

PRICE AND QUANTITY PERCENTAGE RELATIVES

Price and quantity percentage relatives (also called percentage relatives) are based on single item. There are two types: price relatives and quantity relatives.

A **price relative** shows changes in the price of an item over time

A **quantity relative** shows changes in quantities over time.

The formulae for calculating these relatives are as follows:

Simple price index = $\dfrac{P_1}{p_0} \times 100$

Simple quantity index = $\dfrac{q_1}{q_0} \times 100$

Where:

p_0 is the price at time 0
p_1 is the price at time 1
q_0 is the quantity at time 0
q_1 is the quantity at time 1

The concept of time 0, time 1 and so on is simply a scale counting from any given point in time. Thus, for example, if the scale started on 1 January 20X0 it would be as follows:

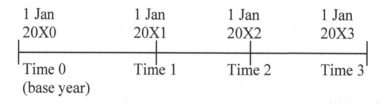

1 Jan 20X0	1 Jan 20X1	1 Jan 20X2	1 Jan 20X3
Time 0 (base year)	Time 1	Time 2	Time 3

The starting point is chosen to be most convenient for the problem under consideration.

Example 1

If a commodity costs K2.60 in 20X4 and K3.68 in 20X5, calculate the simple price index for 20X5, using 20X4 as the base year (i.e. time 0).

Solution

Simple price index $= \dfrac{P_1}{P_0} \times 100 = \dfrac{3.68}{2.60} \times 100 = 141.5$

This means that the price has increased by 41.5% of its base year value, i.e. its 20X4 value.

Example 2

6,500 items were sold in 20X8 compared with 6,000 in 20X7. Calculate the simple quantity index for 20X8 using 20X7 as base year.

Solution

Simple quantity index $\dfrac{q_1}{q_0} \times 100 = \dfrac{6,500}{6,000} \times 100 = 108.3$

This means that the quantity sold has increased by 8.3% of its 20X7 figure.

A product which cost K12.50 in 20X0, cost K13.65 in 20X1. Calculate the simple price index for 20X1 based 20X0.

MULTI-ITEM INDICES

Usually, an index number is required to show the variation in a number of items at once rather than just one as in the example above. The RPI is such an index and consists of a list of items as diverse as the price of bread, the cost of watch repairs, car repairs and cinema tickets.

By using appropriate weights, price relatives can be combined to give a multi-item price index.

WEIGHTED INDICES

WEIGHTED AVERAGE OF PRICE RELATIVES

An index number based on price relatives the price of each item in one year with the price of each item in the base year, expressing each as a percentage relative, and then finds the weighted average of the percentage relatives.

- 323 -

Example 3

From the following information, construct an index of the weighted average of price relatives, with 20X5 as the base year.

Price (pence)

Item	20X5	20X6	Weights
A	10	20	100
B	25	26	182
C	35	33	132
D	12	13	13
			427

Solution

Index of the weighted average of price relatives

$$= \frac{\sum W \left(\frac{p_1}{p_0} \times 100 \right)}{\sum W} = \frac{52,783.5}{427} = 123.6$$

Where W = weighted p_1 = prices in 20X6, P_0 = prices in 20X5

Therefore, using quantity weights only, the index is as follows:

$$\frac{\sum W_A \left(\frac{p_1}{p_0} \times 100 \right)}{\sum W_A} = \frac{833.5}{7} = 219.1$$

(This would imply an average increase in prices of 19.1%

(a) (ii) Using value weights, the index is:

$$\frac{\sum W_B \left(\frac{p_1}{p_0} \times 100 \right)}{\sum W_B} = \frac{8,602.5}{79} = 108.9$$

The fact that the value weighted average of price relatives is more realistic can be shown by considering total expenditure.

Item	Expenditure 20X5			Expenditure:		% Increase
Peas	2 X 2	4p		2 X3	6p	50%
Bread	5 X 15	75p		5 X 16	80P	6.7%
		79p			86p	8.86%

Thus, an equal money price rise for two items will cause a higher percentage price rise for the lower-priced item which is compensated for when the weights used are the value or expenditure on each item, since this reduces the importance of the lower priced item.

Algebraically, as $W = q \times p_0$ then the weighted average of price relatives, which is:

$$\frac{\sum W \left[\frac{p_1}{p_0} \times 100 \right]}{\sum W}, \text{ becomes } \frac{\sum q p_0 \times \frac{p_1}{p_0}}{\sum q p_0} \times 100 = \frac{\sum q p_1 \times 100}{\sum q p_0}$$

SIMPLE AVERAGE INDEX

If there had been no weighting then a simple average index or an aggregate index would have been formed. This method simply adds all the prices together and takes no account of volumes sold.

THE RETAIL PRICE INDEX (RPI)

The Zambian retail price index measures the percentages changes month by month in the average level of prices of goods and services purchased by most households in Zambia.

It is not, strictly speaking a cost of living index, as it includes non-essential items such as leisure and entertainment and there are a number of payments not included, such as income tax, national insurance contributions, savings, charitable subscriptions, etc. but it is the best measure of the cost of living available.

For the prices, a representative list (basket) of items and services has been selected, and prices are collected (where appropriate) by a monthly sample survey among retail outlets in some 180 urban and rural centres. The prices noted are those actually charged, where these differ from published prices.

The index is calculated as a weighted average of price relatives, the weights being the proportional parts of each K1, 000 spent by the average household on each item (i.e. value weights). These weights are updated annually and are obtained from the Family Expenditure Survey which is a continuous survey among an annual sample of about 7,000 householders, who are asked to keep a diary of all their expenditure for a period of two weeks. For the purpose of the RPI, very high and very low income families are excluded from the calculations.

The RPI is used for the following purposes:

- measuring of cost of living
- measurement of inflation, used for wage negotiations, etc.
- current cost accounting
- deflation of monetary series to obtain value in 'real terms', time series deflation.

THE INDEX OF INDUSTRIAL PRODUCTION

The index of industrial production measures changes in the general level of output of Zambian industry as a whole, so it is used as an indicator of the country's overall industrial performance.

For the purpose of the index, Zambian industry is split into 880 categories, which are classified in 20 groups to comprise the whole of the manufacturing, mining construction and energy sectors of the economy.

The index is a weighted average of quantity relatives. Each of the 20 groups is given a weight in proportion to the value of its net output, the sum of the weights of all 20 groups being 1,000. The quantities used are, as close as is possible, the actual output figures for each group.

The most common use of the index is to gauge the level of recession or economic growth occurring in the manufacturing sector of the Zambia.

DEFLATING A MONETARY SERIES

Deflating a monetary series shows the 'real term' effect.

If wages, for example, increase at exactly the same rate as inflation, the earner's purchasing power is not changed. In real terms, the wage has remained constant. The following example illustrates the method, using the RPI as the measure of inflation to deflate a set of sales values.

Example 4

Year	Actual sales (K'000)	RPI	Deflated sales (K'000)
1	275	100	$\frac{275}{100} \times 100 = 275$
2	305	112	$\frac{305}{112} \times 100 = 272$
3	336	122	$\frac{336}{122} \times 100 = 275$
4	344	127	$\frac{344}{127} \times 100 = 271$
5	363	133	$\frac{363}{133} \times 100 = 273$

It will be seen that although actual sales have increased in value by a fairly large amount, in real terms there has been a slight decrease.

Note: Deflated sales = $\frac{\text{Actual sales}}{\text{RP1}} \times 100$

CHAIN BASE INDEX NUMBERS

If a series of index numbers are required for different years, such that the rate of changes of the variable from one year to the next can be studied, the chain base method is used. This means that each index number is calculated using the previous year as base. If the rate of change is increasing then the index numbers will be rising; if it is constant, the numbers will remain the same and if it is decreasing the numbers will be falling.

Example 5

A shopkeeper received the following amounts from the sale of radios:

20 X 1	K1, 000
20 X 2	K1, 100
20 X 3	K1, 210
20 X 4	K1, 331
20 X 5	K1, 464

Is it correct to say that the annual rate of increase in revenue from sales radios is getting larger?

Solution

Year	Sales	Chain base index
20 X 1	K1, 000	
20 X 2	K1, 100	$\dfrac{1,100}{1,000} \times 100 = 110$
20 X 3	K1, 210	$\dfrac{1,210}{1,100} \times 100 = 110$
20 X 4	K1, 331	$\dfrac{1,331}{1,210} \times 100 = 110$
20 X 5	K1, 464	$\dfrac{1,464}{1,331} \times 100 = 110$

FIXED BASE INDEX

FIXED BASE METHOD

Above years in selected (index 100), and all subsequent changes are measured against this basic. Appropriate when basic nature of the commodity is unchanged over time.

2001	$\dfrac{1000}{1000} \times 100 = 100$
2002	$\dfrac{1100}{1000} \times 100 = 110$
2003	$\dfrac{1210}{1000} \times 100 = 121$
2004	$\dfrac{1331}{1000} \times 100 = 133.1$
2005	$\dfrac{1464}{1000} \times 100 = 146.4$

Although the sales revenue from radios has increased each year, the chain base index numbers have remained static at 110. Therefore, the annual rate of increase of sales revenue from radios is remaining constant rather than increasing.

The chain base is also a suitable index to calculate when the weights ascribed to the various items in the index are changing rapidly. Over a period of years, this index would have modified itself to take account of these changes whereas in a fixed-base method after a number of years the whole index would have. To be revised to allow for the changed weighting.

REVISION INDICES

It is normal to periodically revise the commodities and weights used as a basis for index calculation. In order to maintain comparability, the new index is linked to the old series so as to establish one single index series with periodic revision of the weights.

The weights used in the RPI are now revised annually. However, other indices, both in the UK and overseas, may not be subject to regular revision.

LASPEYRE AND PAASCHE INDICES

These are sometimes referred to as aggregative indices.

An aggregative price index compares the total expenditure in one year (i.e. at that year's prices) on a particular collection of goods with the total expenditure in the base year, at base year prices, on the same collection of goods.

By using the term total expenditure, this statement assumes that the weights used are the quantities purchased.

Given this assumption, a choice of weights arises between the quantity purchased in the **base year** and the quantity purchased in the **current year** for which the index is being prepared. Both choices are acceptable and both have their respective merits and demerits. The resultant indices are named after their 'inventors'.

The Laspeyre price index uses base year quantities; the Paasche uses current year quantities. The Paasche index, for instance, compares the cost of buying current year quantities at current year prices with buying them at base year prices.

FORMULAE

Laspeyre price index $= \dfrac{\sum(p_1 \times q_0)}{\sum(p_0 \times q_0)} \times 100$ (using base year quantities as weights).

Paasche price index $= \dfrac{\sum(p_1 \times q_1)}{\sum(p_0 \times q_1)} \times 100$ (using current year quantities as weights).

Example 6

The Laspeyre and Paasche price indices will be calculated for the following data, using 20X4 as base year:

Item	price (p_0)	20X4 quantity (q_0)	20X5 Price (P_1)	Quantity (q_1)
Milk	19p a pint	50,000 pints	26p a pint	70,000 pints
Bread	39p a loaf	30,000 loaves	40p a loaf	40,000 loaves
Soap	42p a pack	20,000 packs	64p a pack	25,000 packs
Sugar	60 a kilo	10,000 kilos	68p a kilo	8,000 kilos
Eggs	84 a box	3,000 boxes	72p a box	2,500 boxes

Solution

(a) **LASPEYRE INDEX**

Item	Weight (q_0)	Price (p_0)	$p_0 \times q_0$ K	price (p_1)	$p_1 \times 90$ K
Milk	50,000	19p	9,500	26p	13,000
Bread	30,000	39p	11,700	40p	12,000
Soap	20,000	42p	8,400	64p	12,800
Sugar	10,000	60p	6,000	68p	6,800
Eggs	3,000	84p	2,520	72p	2,160

$\sum p_1 q_0$ = 46,760 = last year's buying pattern at today's prices.

$\sum p_0 q_0$ = 38,120 = last year's buying pattern at last year's prices

.:
$$= \frac{\sum p_1 q_0}{\sum p_0 q_0} \times 100$$

$$= \frac{46,760}{38,120}$$

$$= 122.7$$

The cost of buying 20X4 quantities at 20X5 prices shows an increase of 22.7% over 20X4 costs.

(b) **PAASCHE INDEX**

Item	Weight (q_1)	Price (p_0)	$P_0 \times q_1$ K	price (p_1)	$P_1 \times q_1$ K
Milk	70,000	19p	13,300	26p	18,200

Bread	40,000	39p	15,600	40p	16,000
Soap	25,000	42p	10,500	64p	16,000
Sugar	8,000	60p	4,800	68p	5,440
Eggs	2,500	84p	2,100	72p	1,800
			46,300		57,440

$\sum p_0 q_1$ = 46.300 = today's buying pattern at last year's prices.

$\sum p_1 q_1$ = 57,440 = today's buying pattern at today's prices.

.: Index $= \dfrac{57,440}{46,300} \times 100$

$= 124.1$

The 20X5 index shows an increase of 24.1% over 20X4 prices when buying 20X5 quantities.

Note in calculating either type of index, a common mistake made by students is to add all the prices and all the quantities and multiply the two totals, i.e. $\sum p \times \sum q$ is calculated instead of $\sum(p \times q)$. To do so is quite wrong and will be penalized in the marking of the examination.

COMPARISON OF LASPEYRE AND PAASCHE INDICES

In a period of inflation, there is a general increase in prices. In addition, there will be relative price changes. Thus, for example, in the 1980s petrol became relatively more expensive and electric goods became relatively cheaper.

The effect of these changes is a changing pattern of consumption, with consumers switching to relatively less expensive goods, e.g. from large cars to small cars, and buying more electric goods.

This switching minimizes the effect of inflation on individual consumers. However, if a Laspeyre index is used it will fail to take account of the changing pattern of consumption. As a result, a Laspeyre index tends to overstate the real impact of inflation on individuals.

On the other hand, a Paasche index involves recalculating data for all preceding years each year. With a large number of indices to maintain, this is not practicable. Also, because a Paasche index is based on current consumption pattern it tends to understate the overall effect inflation on consumers.

RELATIVE MERITS OF TYPES OF INDICES

The relative merits and demerits of the indices are summarized below.

LASPEYRE INDEX – ADVANTAGES

1. Cheaper, as the obtaining of new quantities each year may be costly.

2. Easier to calculate where a series of years are being compared, since the denominator remains the same for all years, e.g. 20 X 7 index would be calculated

$$\frac{\sum q_7 p_0}{\sum q_0 p_0} \text{ X } 100$$

Where p_7 = prices in 20X7 and p_0 prices in 20X0.

3. Each year in a series of Laspeyre indices is directly comparable with all previous years.

LASPEYRE INDEX – DISADVANTAGES

    i. The major disadvantage of using Laspeyre indices is that an out-of-date consumption pattern may be used. In practice this is overcome by a periodic revision of the base year to keep it up-to-date, but this makes very long-term comparison almost impossible as the continuity of the series is destroyed.

    ii. As prices rise, quantities purchased tend to diminish if there are alternative goods available. This decrease is not reflected in the Laspeyre index which tends therefore, to overestimate the effect of rising prices.

PAASCHE INDEX – ADVANTAGES

    1. Since current year weights are used, it results in an index being based on the current pattern of consumption so that a less frequent revision of base year is needed.

PAASCHE INDEX – DISADVANTAGES

1. Were a series of years is involved, the amount of calculation is greater as both numerator and denominator need calculating each year, e.g. 20X7 index would be calculated:

$$\frac{\sum q_7 p_7}{\sum q_0 p_7} \text{ X } 100$$

Where: p_7 = prices in 20X7

                 q_7 = quantities in 20X7 and

                 p_0 = prices in 20X0

2. Each Paasche index in a series is only directly comparable with the base year (i.e. 20X7 does not bear comparison with 20X6; only with base year 20X0).

3. The Paasche index can only be constructed if up-to-date information is available. The RPI is a Paasche index but, although it is produced monthly, quantities are only updated annually.

4. Rising prices have the opposite effect on the weights and the Paasche index therefore tends to underestimate the effect of inflation.

QUANTITY INDEX

A quantity index measures changes in the volume of goods produced or sold.

An example is the UK Index of Industrial Production explained earlier.

Just as a price index needs to be weighted with the quantities purchased, so a quantity index must be weighted with prices. A change in the volume of gold or other precious metal would have a greater effect on the economy that the same change in the volume of sand and gravel produced, because volume for volume it is much more valuable.

A quantity index is therefore calculated in the same way a s a price index, with the role of price and quantity reversed.

Example 7

Laspeyre and Paasche quantity indices will be calculated for the data given earlier. Form the previous example:

$\sum q_1 p_0 = \sum p_0 q_1 = 46{,}300$
$\sum q_0 p_0 = \sum p_0 q_0 = 38{,}120$
$\sum q_1 p_1 = \sum p_1 q_1 = 57{,}440$
$\sum q_0 p_1 = \sum p_1 q_0 = 46{,}760$

Solution

Hence the Laspeyre index for 20X5 with 20X4 as base is $\dfrac{46{,}300}{38{,}120} \times 100 = 121.5$

And the Paasche index for 20X5 with 20X4 as base is $\dfrac{57{,}440}{46{,}760} \times 100 = 122.8$

Value index for year 1 $= \dfrac{\sum p_1 q_1}{\sum p_0 q_0} \times 100$

$\sum p_1q_1$ = value of all goods in year 1

$\sum p_0 q_0$ = value of all goods in the base year

Using the data given earlier:

Value index for 20X5 with 20X4 as base $\frac{57,440}{38,120} \times 100 = 150.7$

Hence the value of all goods purchased increased by 50.7% from 20X4 to 20X5.

PROGRESS CLINIC FOURTEEN

1.The following table gives the index numbers for different groups together with their respective weights for the year 2000 (base year 1995).

Group	Food	Clothing	Electricity and charcoal	Rent	Miscellaneous
Group index no. (1)	130	280	190	300	200
Group weight (w)	60	5	7	9	19

      (a) What is the overall cost of living index number for the year 2000?

      (b) Suppose a person was earning K1,500, 000 per month in 1995 what should be his salary in 2000, if his standard of living in that year was the same as in 1995?

2.The profits for the five products at respective prices for an electronic firm are expected to be as follows:

	Total profit K	Selling price K
Product A	48858	12.7
Product B	19231	25.1
Product C	24644	19.8
Product D	47712	\52.0
Product E	36919	67.4

Calculate the weighted average selling price per unit for the five products to the nearest Kwacha using profit as a weight.

3.A company uses three raw materials (R, S and T) in its production process. The following is the information about the prices (K per tonne) of the raw materials in 2007 and 2008 and the average weekly quantities (q) used during 2008.

Raw materials	2007 prices	2008 prices	Q
R	5800	6000	100
S	4200	4000	40
T	500	750	1000

Calculate using 2007 as the base year:
  (a) Simple price index
  (b)Weighted mean of price relatives
  (c)Distinguish between a simple index and a weighted index

4.The following table shows the total expenditure on three commodities in April 2007 and 2008 based on a representative sample of 500 households.

April 2007	Quantities purchased Kilogram	Total Expenditure Kwacha
Bread	4 500	5 000 000
Sweet potatoes	10 000	6 000 000
Oranges	3 000	150 000
	17 500	11 150 000
April 2008		
Bread	4 500	5 500 000
Sweet potatoes	9 500	7 500 000
Oranges	3 500	200 000
2. 00		13 200 000

(a) Calculate the Laspeyre's price index
(b) Explain briefly the major weakness of the Laspeyre index in this case and suggest an alternative
(c) Calculate the Paasche price index
(d) What is the major weakness of the Paasche index and suggest an alternative

Chapter Fifteen

STATISTICAL DECISION THEORY

One of the most important developments of recent years has been the increasing role played by mathematics in decision making on the managerial level. Most consequential managerial decisions must be made under conditions of certainty, because managers seldom have complete information about what the future will bring. In this chapter, we shall learn methods that are useful when we must decide among alternatives despite uncertain conditions. We shall also investigate how to determine the worth of additional information. As a student, you make complex decisions about which questions are apt to appear on examinations and what study times will be required to earn certain grades in a course. When you do this, you demonstrate initiative use of some of the techniques we shall introduce here.

DIFFERENCES BETWEEN HYPOTHESIS TESTING AND STATISTICAL DECISION THEORY

When we did hypothesis testing, we had to decide whether to accept or reject the null hypothesis. In decision theory, we must decide among alternatives by taking into account the monetary repercussions of our actions. A manager who must select from among a number of available investments should consider the profit or loss that might result from each alternative. Applying decision theory involves selecting an alternative and having a reasonable idea of the economic consequences of choosing that action. (Note: statistical decision theory is also called Bayesian decision theory named after Reverend Thomas Bayes).

THE DECISION ENVIRONMENT

Decision theory can be applied to problems whether they involve financial management or a plant assembly line, and whether they are in the public or private sector. Regardless of the environment, most of these problems have common characteristics. As a result, decision makers approach their solutions in fairly consistent ways. The elements common to most decision theory problems are as follows:

1. **An objective the decision maker is trying to reach** – If the objective is to minimize time spent by customers in banking halls, the manager may try to find the optimal of tellers on hand for quick service. Success can be measured by monitoring the reduction in customer time.

2. **Several courses of action** - The decision should involve a choice among alternatives called **actions**. In our example, the various actions open to the decision maker include increasing the number of counters and tellers within banking halls or purchasing and installing Automated Teller Machines (ATMs) located outside banking halls.

3. **A calculable measure of the benefit or worth of various alternatives**. In general, these cost can be negative or positive and are called Pay offs.

4. **Events beyond the control of the decision maker**. These uncontrollable occurrences are often called out comes or states of nature, and their existence creates difficulties as well as interest in decision making under uncertainty. Such events could be the general performance of the economy, whether slump or boom, and so on.

5. **Uncertainty concerning which outcome or state of nature will actually happen**. For example, the decision maker is uncertain as to whether there will be a slump or a boom in the economy. Probabilities can be assigned to the general states of nature that might take place.

DECISION THEORY STEPS

The following are the pertinent steps:

1. Clearly define the problem at hand. To formulate a problem situation, all above five (5) elements must be present namely objective, several courses of action, monetary worth of various outcomes, beyond control of decision maker (state of nature) and uncertainty.

2. List the possible alternatives.

3. Identify the possible outcomes

4. List the pay off (or profit) of the combination of alternatives and outcomes in a decision table.

5. Select one of the mathematical decision theory models

6. Apply the model and make your decision.

ASSUMPTIONS UNDERLYING DECISION THEORY

Two assumptions underlying decision theory are:

1. There is either a gain or a loss associated with each possible action.

2. The decision maker selects the solution which maximizes the expected gain or minimizes an expected loss.

CLASSIFICATION OF DECISION PROBLEMS

Decision problems are normally classified into three main categories namely:

1. **Decisions under conditions of uncertainty.** A decision maker is said to be conditions of uncertainty under in situations where the outcome of each action will differ depending on the event that prevails. It cannot be predicted with certainty which event will prevail, because the conditions, and the probability of occurrence, are beyond the control of the decision maker. However, the decision maker may assign subjective probabilities to the event, and these are based upon the best information that can be found.

2. **Decisions under conditions of certainty.** The decision maker knows, with certainty, the influencing factors (events) that will occur. Naturally, the alternative that results in the highest expected monetary value will be chosen. The common method used is the method of linear programming, which is not covered in this book.

3. **Decisions under conditions of risk.** Risk is a condition where the occurrence of the possible events can be assigned probabilities, or described with some probability.

CONSTRUCTING A PAY OFF TABLE

To construct a pay off table the following points must be borne in mind:

1. List all courses of action you might consider in order to solve the problem. At least 3 alternatives must be available so that a choice exists

2. List all the states of nature (events) that can occur for each alternative course of action.

3. The states of nature each indicate a separate column, and the actions each indicate a separate row of the pay off table.

4. A probability value, based on either historical information or managerial judgement, can be included for each event.

5. A pay off value is entered in each of the cells of the table. If probabilities are assigned to the events, an expected value can be calculated by multiplying each pay off with the respective probability of the event.

6. Due to the events in the payoff table being mutually exclusive as well as exhaustive, the sum of the probabilities for all possible events must equal to 1.

CONSTRUCTING AN OPPORTUNITY – LOSS TABLE

From a pay off table we can construct an opportunity loss table, which shows the opportunity loss for every action-event combination. Opportunity loss is simply the difference between the pay off actually realized for a selected action and the pay off which could have been obtained had the best or optimal action been selected.

The following are the usual considerations:

- Find the highest pay off in each column of the pay off table
- Subtract each pay off from the highest pay off in that column
- The best action for each event will have a zero entry
- Entries in the opportunity loss table will always be positive
- Entries represent losses, therefore, the smaller the value the better.

DETERMINING THE BEST ACTION

There are several methods that can be used to help in making a decision about the best action. Here we distinguish between methods without probabilities and methods with probabilities.

1. **Decision making without probabilities**. A prime consideration in choosing a method for determining the best action, when probabilities about the events are unknown, is the decision maker's general attitude towards possible losses and gains. The non- probabilistic decision making criteria include:

(a) **Maximax criterion**. Here, the decision maker is concerned only with the best that can happen with respect to each action and will tend to choose the action that could generate the highest possible pay off. It will be the typical choice of a risk – seeker (optimist).

- For each possible action, identify the maximum possible pay off i.e. the highest value in each row.

- Comparing these pay offs, select that action with the highest maximum pay off, thus maximizing the maximum pay offs.

- If the pay offs are quantities such as losses or costs, which are to be minimized, select the lowest possible cost associated with each action, and choose the action that minimizes the minimum pay off.

(b) **Maximin criterion** – This procedure guarantees that the decision maker can do no worse than to achieve the best of the poorest outcomes possible, and will be the typical choice of a risk – averter (pessimist).

- Determine the lowest pay off associated with each action, i.e. the smallest value of each row.

- Comparing these minimum pay offs, choose that action (row) with the largest pay of, thus, maximizing the minimum pay offs.

- If the pay offs are quantities such as losses or costs, which are to be minimized, select the highest value for each action (row) and choose the action that minimizes the maximum pay off.

(c) **The minimax regret criterion** – This method is applied using an opportunity – loss table.

- Find the highest (maximum) possible regret value associated with each possible action (row).

- Identify the lowest (minimum) value amongst these maxima.

- Choose that for which the maximum regret is the smallest, thus, minimizing the maximum regret.

(d) **Laplace criteria** – This procedure guarantees that the decision maker will tend to choose the action that could generate the highest possible average pay off.

- Calculate the average pay off in each row

- Comparing these average pay offs, select the action with the highest average.

EXPECTATIONS AND DECISIONS

One of the most important developments of recent years has been increasing role played by mathematics in decision making on the management level.

Generally, when faced with choice between several alternatives, it is "rational" to select the one with the "most promising" mathematical expectation: the one which maximizes expected profits, minimizes expected costs, maximizes expected tax disadvantages, minimizes expected loses, etc.

Example 1

Consider the problem faced by a manager of a summer resort, who must decide to expand the facilities now or wait at least another year. His advisors tell him that if he expands the facilities right away and the upcoming summer season is a good one, the resort will show a profit K246 000; if he expands the facilities right away and the upcoming summer season is a poor one, the resort will show a deficit of K60 000: if he delays the expansion of the facilities for at least a year and the upcoming summer season is a good one, the resort will show a profit of K120 000: and if he delays the expansion of the facilities for at least a year and the upcoming summer season is a poor one, the resort will show a profit of K12 000. Schematically, all this into. Can be presented in the following table.

	Good season	Poor season
Expand facility right away	K246 000	˙K60 000
Delay expansion of facilities	K120 000	K12 000

The way in which the above problem is referred to as a *Bayesian analysis*. In this kind of analysis the probabilities are assigned to the probabilities about which uncertainties exist, the *States of Nature*, which in our example are a good summer season and a poor.

If he is a confirmed optimists to look at the situation positively with a probability of ⅓ and decides to expand right away, the expected profit is:

$$(246\ 000 \times ⅓)\ +\ (12\ 000 \times ⅔) = K42\ 000$$

If he is a confirmed pessimist to look at the situation negatively with a probability of ⅓, and decides to delay the expansion of facilities, the expected profit is;

$$(120\ 000 \times ⅓)\ +\ (12\ 000 \times ⅔) = K48\ 000$$

Since an expected profit of K48 000 is obviously preferred to an expected profit K42 000. It stands to reason that the manager of the resort should decide to delay expansion of the facilities.

NOTE:
A confirmed optimist will want to maximize the resorts maximum profit and if he is a confirmed pessimist he will want to minimize the resort's maximum losses. This is called a **minimax** criterion, the resort's greatest possible loss is the least.

Example 2

You plan to print T-shirts to sell during a soccer game at independence stadium. A decision must be made whether to print 10 000, 15 000 or 20 000. The demand for the T-shirts will depend on attendance, which may be high, medium or low. The following pay off table shows the expected profits in K'000 for different attendance levels together with each quantity of T-shirts you may produce.

Pay off table

Actions	Attendance levels (events)		
(No. of T-shirts)	High	Medium	low
10 000	12	10	9.6
15 000	20	18	6
20 000	30	16	4

Determine the best action without probabilities using:

(a) Maximax criterion
(b) Maximin criterion
(c) Minimum regret criterion (savage criteria)
(d) Laplace criteria.

Solution

(a) Maximax criterion

Action	Highest pay off per action
10 000	12
15 000	20
20 000	30

- The action with highest maximum pay off is to produce 20 000 T-shirts.

(b) Maximin criteria

Actions	Lowest pay off per action
10 000	9.6
15 000	6
20 000	4

- The action with the highest minimum pay off is to produce 10 000 T-Shirts.

(c) Minimum regret criteria (savage criteria). Here, we need to construct the opportunity-loss or regret table first as follows:

Actions	Attendance levels (events)		
No. of T-shirts	High	Medium	Low
10 000	30 – 12 = 18	18 – 10 = 8	9.6 – 9.6 = 0
15 000	30 – 20 = 10	18 – 18 = 0	9.6 – 6 = 3.6
20 000	30 – 30 = 0	18 – 16 = 2	9.6 – 4 = 5.6

Note: We find the highest pay off in each column of the pay off table and subtract each pay off from the highest pay in that column.

- Minimum regret criterion

Actions	Maximum regret from opportunity-loss table
10 000	18
15 000	10
20 000	5.6

- The action with the smallest maximum regret is to produce 20 000 T-Shirts.

(d) Laplace criteria

- 10 000 T-Shirts: $\frac{12 + 30 + 9.6}{3} = \frac{31.6}{3} = \mathbf{10.5}$

- 15 000 T-Shirts: $\frac{20 + 18 + 6}{3} = \frac{44}{3} = \mathbf{14.7}$

- 20 000 T-Shirts: $\frac{30 + 16 + 4}{3} = \frac{50}{3} = \mathbf{16.7}$

- The action with the highest average (mean) is to produce 20 000 T-Shirts.

Example 3

Small scale maize farmers in Zambia have been enjoying government subsidy since 2002 in the form of fertilizer support programme (FSP) to promote increased production since maize is a staple food. There are rumours that the government will reduce the subsidy for the next crop. The maize farmers have to decide whether to increase or reduce the number of hectares they farm, or keep them the same. The pay offs in K'000 for these strategies under the same subsidy regime and under reduced subsidies are:

Action	State of nature	
Increased	80 000	⁻40 000
The same	40 000	15 000
Decreased	20 000	17 000

Suggest what the farmers should do using:

     (a) the Maximax decision rule
     (b) the Maximin decision rule
     (c) the Savage decision rule
     (d) the Hurwicz rule with $\alpha = 0.4$

Solution

  (a) Maximax criterion

Action	Maximum
Increased	80 000
The same	40 000
Decreased	20 000

- Maize farmers should increase hectares.

  (b) Maximin criterion

Action	Minimum
Increased	⁻40 000
The same	15 000
Decreased	17 000

- Maize farmers should decreased hectares.

(c) Savage criteria

Opportunity-loss table

Action	State of nature		
	Same subsidy	Reduced subsidy	Maximum
Increased	0	57 000	57 000
The same	40 000	2 000	40 000
Decreased	60 000	0	60 000

• The action with the smallest maximum regrets is to maintain the same hectare.

(d) $\alpha = 0.4$, $1 - \alpha = 1 - 0.4 = 0.6$

• For increased hectare: 80 000 (0.4) – 40 000 (0.6)

$$32\ 000 - 24\ 000 = 8000$$

• For the same hectare: 40 000 (0.4) + 15 000 (0.6)

$$16\ 000 + 9000 = 25\ 000$$

• For decreased hectare: 20 000 (0.4) + 17 000 (0.6)

$$8000 + 10\ 200 = 18\ 200$$

The action that should be selected is to increase hectare

2. **Decision making with probabilities**: If the decision problem falls within the risk uncertainty category, probabilities can be used to measure the likelihood of the occurrences of the various events.

• If the possible number of alternatives is limited, pay of tables can be used to solve problems, and discrete probability distributions will be applicable.

• If the number of possibilities becomes too large, it is more realistic to analyze a decision in terms of continuous probability distributions, such as the normal distribution.

Decision making with probabilities covers among others the following:

(a) Expected monetary value criterion (EMV)

This method is applied to select that action which has the highest expected pay off or monetary value.

- Specify the possible courses of action. Specify the possible events as well.

- Set up a pay off table

- Assume probabilities which represent the likelihood of the occurrence of the events, and include them in the pay off table.

- Compute the expected pay off for each event by multiplying the pay off in each cell of the pay off table by the probability of the event for that column.

- The resulting expected pay offs are then summarized for each action to determine the EMV for the action.

- Make a decision by choosing the highest expected pay off (EMV).

(b) Minimum expected opportunity – loss (EOL) criterion

The minimum expected opportunity-loss method measures the expected cost of uncertainty, due to our uncertain knowledge about which event which yields the minimum expected opportunity loss (EOL). An opportunity loss is defined as the difference between the pay off of the best action that could have been selected for an event and the pay off of any other action for the same event i.e. it is the profit foregone due to failure to take the best action. The EOL criterion will always lead to the same decision as the EMV criterion, and the EOL for each action is calculated in the same way as the EMV.

(c) The expected value of perfect information (EVPI)

Before actually selecting a decision criterion, the decision maker must decide whether to stop the analysis after using only prior information or to postpone the decision until additional sample information about the events can be obtained in order to reduce uncertainty. By eliminating uncertainty, the decision-maker will know which event is going to occur and can make a decision that is best for that event. To help in this decision, the decision maker should be concerned about the cost of additional information and its potential value.

- A measure to calculate this cost is the EVPI, which indicates the maximum expected gain in profit if additional information does provide certainty about the events. The maximum amount spent to be certain of the event that will occur should not exceed this maximum expected gain.

- To calculate the EPVI, the opportunity-loss table and the EOL can be used. The EOL of an action is the difference between the expected profit when perfect information is available and the expected profit under uncertain conditions. The minimum EOL is thus like the EVPI.

- If additional information is not available at a cost equal to or less than the EPVI, the decision-maker cannot improve profit by obtaining additional information.

(d) Hurwicz criterion

Under this criterion, the decision maker uses α (alpha) (Recall from hypothesis testing that α is defined as the probability of committing a type I error). An alpha is determined before the experiment and shows the decision maker's tolerance level.
- Calculate the expected pay off for each action by multiplying the first pay off by α and the second pay off by $1 - \alpha$ and then summing the two.
- If you have more than two pay offs multiply the highest pay off by α and the lowest pay off by $1 - \alpha$ and then sum the two.

- Make a decision by choosing the minimum of the expected pay offs for each action.

Example 4

You plan to print T-Shirts to sell during a soccer game at independence stadium. A decision must be made whether to print 10 0000, 15 000 or 20 000. The demand for the T-Shirts will depend on attendance, which may be high, medium or low. The following pay off table shows the expected profits in K'000 for different attendance levels together with each quality of T-Shirts you may produce.

Pay off table

Action	Attendance levels (events)		
No. of T-Shirts	High	Medium	Low
10 000	12	10	9.6
15 000	20	18	6
20 000	30	16	4

With the demand for T-Shirts of high, medium and low having respective probabilities of 0.4, 0.35 and 0.25. How many T-Shirts should you print? Use (a) EMV, (b) EOL, (c) EVPI

Solution

(a) To calculate the EMV, we have to construct an expected pay off table as follows:

Actions	Attendance levels (events)			
No. of T-Shirts	High	Medium	Low	Total
	0.4	0.35	0.25	1.00
10 000	4.8	3.5	2.4	10.7
15 000	8.0	6.3	1.5	15.8
20 000	12.0	5.6	1.0	18.6

- The maximum expected value (EMV) is 18.6, and the decision will be to produce 20 000 T-Shirts. Alternatively, EMV for each action can be calculated as follows:

- For 10 000 T-shirts: EMV = 12 (0.4) + 10 (0.35) + 9.6 (0.25) = 10.7

- For 15 000 T-shirts: EMV = 20 (0.4) + 18 (0.35) + 6 (0.25) 15.8

- For 20 000 T-shirts: EMV = 30 (0.4) + 16 (0.35) + 4 (0.25) = 18.6

(b) To calculate EOL, we need to construct an expected opportunity loss table as follows:

Action	Attendance levels (events)			
No. of T-shirts	High	Medium	Low	Total
	0.4	0.35	0.25	1.00
10 000	7.2	2.8	0.0	10.0
15 000	4.0	0.0	0.9	4.9
20 000	0.0	0.7	1.4	2.1

- Since we are dealing with losses, select the action that minimizes the expected opportunity loss, namely to produce 20 000 T-shirts.

Note: Expected opportunity loss for each action is calculated as follows:

- For 10 000 T-shirts, EOL = 18 (0.4) + 8 (0.35) + 0 (0.25) = 10.0

- For 15 000 T-shirts, EOL = 10 (0.4) + 0 (0.35) + 3.6 (0.25) = 4.9

- For 20 000 T-shirts, EOL = 0.(04) + 2 (0.35) + 5.6 (0.25) = 2.1

(c)   EVPI.   It can be mathematically proved that the EVPI = EOL; therefore, the maximum amount you would be willing to pay for additional sample information is K2,100, because that is the maximum expected gain in profits that could result if more accurate information is available.

Example 5

Mr. Investment Crazy has a dilemma of how to invest K10 000 000. The available options and the state of the economy are summarized in the following pay off table.

		State of the economy		
		Stagnant (0.25)	Slow growth (0.45)	Rapid growth (0.30)
Investment	Stocks	ˉK500 000	K700 000	K2200 000
Decision	Bonds	ˉK100 000	K600 000	K 900 000
Alternative	CDs	K300 000	K500 000	K 750 000
	Mixture	ˉK200 000	K650 000	K1300 000

Given that there is a 0.25 probability of having a stagnant economy, a 0.45 probability of having a slow-growth economy and a 0.30 probability of having a rapid-growth economy, and the investment is K10 000 000 for the four possibilities (stock, bonds, CDs, and mixtures). Compute the expected monetary value (EMV) for the K10 000 000 investment.

Solution

We calculate the expected monetary value for each of the investment decision alternatives for K10 000 000.

- For stock, EMV = ˉK500 000 (0.25) + K700 000 (0.45) + K2200 000 (0.30)

    = K850 000

- For bonds, EMV = ˉK100 000 (0.25) + K600 000 (0.45) + K2200 000 (0.30)

    = K515 000

- For CDs, EMV = K300 000 (0.25) + K500 000 (0.45) + K750 000 (0.30)

  = K525 000

- For mixture, EMV = -K200 000 (0.25) + K650 000 + (0.45) + K1300 000 (0.30)

  = K632 500

Mr. Investment Crazy using expected monetary value strategy will choose the maximum of the expected monetary values computed for each decision alternative.

Action	EMV
Stock	K850 000
Bonds	K515 000
CDs	K525 000
Mixture	K632 500

Mr. Investment Crazy should invest in stocks.

Example 6

Mr. Landlord Crazy has beautiful office accommodation along Cairo Road in Lusaka for which private individuals, as tenants are required to pay monthly rentals. Of late there has been a problem of failure by these tenants to pay as scheduled. Mr. Landlord is thinking of the best way to deal with this problem. According to his assessments, the decision alternatives are to put the offices on long lease or sell them. The investors may reject a sell or they may lease the offices for one or two years. Mr. Landlord can lease or sell the offices for K100 billion and his profits are summarized in the following profit pay off tale with the amounts in billions of Kwacha.

Action	State of nature		
	Reject	1 year	2 year
Lease	-100	50	150
Sell	100	100	100

(a) If the probability estimates for the state of nature are P (reject) = 0.3, P (1 year) = 0.5 and P (2 years) = 0.2.

What should Mr. Landlord do?

(b)   What is the optimal decision strategy if perfect information were available?

(c)   What is the expected value of perfect information?

Solution

(a)   We need to calculate the expected monetary value for each of the two decision alternatives.

- EMV (lease) = $^-100\ (0.3) + 50\ (0.5) + 150\ (0.2)$

  $= ^-30 + 25 + 30 = 25$ i.e. K25 billion

- EMV (sell) = $100\ (0.3 + 100\ (0.5) + 100\ (0.2)$

  $= 30 + 50 + 30 = 100$ i.e. <u>K100 billion</u>

- The action to be taken is one which gives the highest EMV: Mr. Landlord should therefore sell the office accommodation.

(b)   EMVPI = $100\ (0.3) + 100\ (0.5) + 150\ (0.2)$

  $= 30 + 50 + 30 = 110$ i.e. <u>K110 billion</u>

Note: We pick the maximum for each state of nature and multiply by the respective probabilities because with perfect information, certainty may be achieved.

(c)   EVPI = EMVPI – EMV

  $= 110 - 100 = 10$ i.e. <u>K10 billion</u>

Example 7

Consider the cost minimization problem represented by the following where entries represent cost. The prior of $S_2 = 0.3$

Decision Alternatives	S_1	S_2
a_1	k100 million	k540 million
a_2	k150 million	-k50 million
a_3	k350 million	k320 million

(a) Find EMV and recommend the course of action
(b) Find EMV under certainty
(c) Use the EVC to find the EVPI

(d) Determine the opportunity loss table

(e) Find the course of action that minimizes EOL

(f) Compare the minimum EOL with the EVPI. Comment.

Solution

(a) EMV(a_1) = 0.7(100) + 0.3(540) = k232 million
EMV(a_2) = 0.7(150) +0.3(-50)   k90 million
EMV(a_3) = 0.7(350) + 0.3(320) = k341 million

Decision: Action a_3 with the highest EMV

(b) Select the maximum for each state of nature
EVC = 0.7(350) + 0.3(5400 = k407 million

(c) EVPI = EVC – EMV
407 – 341 = k66 million

(d) Opportunity loss table

Action	S_1	S_2
a_1	250	0
a_2	200	590
a_3	0	220

(e) EOL(a_1) = 0.7(250) + 0.3(0) = k175 million
EOL(a_2) = 0.7(200) + 0.3(590) = k317 million
EOL(a_3) = 0.7(0) + 0.3(220)   = k66 million
Decision: Select a_3 ith the lowest EOL

(f) EOL = EVPI = k66 million.

DECISION-TREE ANALYSIS

A decision tree is a graphic model of a decision process. With it, we can introduce probabilities into the analysis of complex decisions involving (a) many alternatives and (b) future conditions that are not known but can be specified in terms of a set of discrete probabilities or a continuous probability distribution. Decision tree analysis is a useful tool in making decisions concerning investments, the acquisitions or disposal of physical property, project management, personnel and new product strategies.

The term decision tree is derived from the physical appearance of the usual graphic representation of this technique. A decision tree is like probability tree but it contains not only probabilities of outcomes but also the expected monetary (utility) values attached to those outcomes. Because of this we can use these trees to indicate the expected values of different actions that we can take.

DECISION-TREE SYMBOLS

Decision-trees have standard symbols:

1. ☐ Squares symbolize **decision points**, where the decision-maker must choose among several possible actions. From the decision **nodes** we draw one branch for each of the possible actions.
2. O Circles represent **chance events**, where the state of nature is realized. From these chance **nodes**, we draw one branch for each possible outcome.

Note that time flows from left to right in the tree; that is, nodes at the left represent actions or chance events which occur before nodes which fall further to the right. It is very important to maintain the proper time sequence when constructing decision trees.

GENERAL FORM OF A DECISION TREE

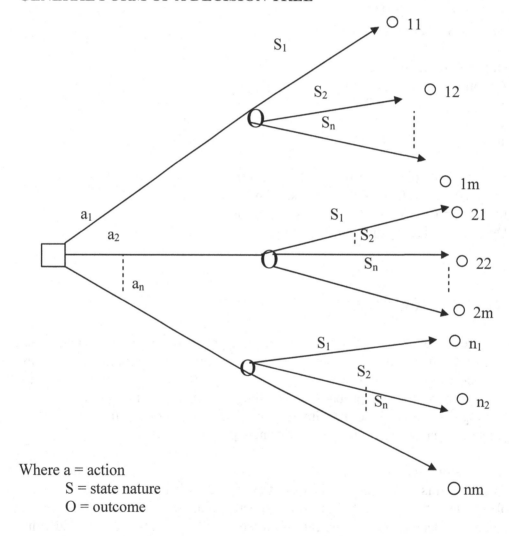

Where a = action
S = state nature
O = outcome

RULES FOR AN ANALYZING A DECISION TREE

The process starts from the right (at the top of the tree) and works back to the left (to the root of the tree). In this rollback process, by working from right to left, we make the future decisions first and then roll them back to become part of earlier decisions. There are two rules directing this process:

1.   If we are analyzing a chance node (circle), we calculate the expected value at that node by multiplying the probability on each branch emanating from the node by the profit at the end of that branch and then summing the products for all of the branches emanating from the node.

2.   If we are analyzing a decision node (square), we let the expected value at that node to be the maximum of the expected values for all of the branches emanating from the node. In this way, we choose the action with the largest expected value and we prune the branches corresponding to the less profitable actions. We mark those branches with a double slash to indicate that they have been pruned.

USING DECISION-TREE ANALYSIS

Generally, decision tree analysis requires the decision-maker to proceed through the following six steps.

1. Define the problem in structured terms. First determine which factors are relevant to the solution. Then estimate the probability distributions that are appropriate to describe the future behaviour of those factors. Collect financial data concerning conditional outcomes.

2. Model the decision process: That is, construct a decision tree that illustrates all the alternatives involved in the problem. This step structures the process to be presented schematically and in an organized, step-by-step fashion. In this step the decision-maker chooses the number of periods into which the future can be divided.

3. Apply the appropriate probability values and financial data to each of the branches and sub branches of the decision tree. This will enable you to distinguish the probability value and conditional monetary value associated with each outcome.

4. "Solve" the decision tree. Using the methodology (rules) highlighted above, proceed to locate that particular branch of the tree that has the largest excepted value or that maximizes the decision criterion, whatever it is.

5. Perform sensitivity analysis: That is, determine how the solution reacts to changes in the inputs. Changing probability values and conditional financial values allows the decision-maker to test both the magnitude and the direction of the reactions. This step allows the experiment without real commitment or real mistakes and without disrupting operations.

6. List the underlying assumptions. Explain the estimating techniques used to arrive at the probability distributions. What kinds of accounting and cost-finding assumptions underlie the conditional financial values used to arrive at a solution?

Why has the future been divided into a certain number of periods? By making these assumptions explicit, you enable others to know what risks they are taking when they use the results of your decision tree analysis. Use this step to specify limits under which the results obtained will be valid, and especially the conditions under which the decision will not be valid.

ADVANTAGES OF THE DECISION TREE APPROACH

Decision-tree analysis is a technique managers use to structure and display alternatives and decision processes. It is popular because it:

1. Structures the decision-making process, guiding managers to approach decision-making in an orderly, sequential fashion

2. Requires the decision maker to examine all possible outcomes, desirable and undesirable.

3. Communicates the decision making process to others, illustrating each assumption about the future.

4. Allows a group to discuss alternatives by focusing on each financial figure, probability value, and underlying assumption – one at a time: thus, a group can move in orderly steps toward a consensus decision, instead of debating a decision in its entirety.

5. Can be used with a computer, so that many different sets of assumptions can be simulated and their effects on the final outcome observed.

Example 8

Mr. Snowman, the owner and general manager of the Snow Fun Ski Resort in Greenland has to decide how the hotel should be run in the coming season. Snowman's profits for this year's skiing season will depend on how much snowfall occurs during the winter months. On the basis of previous experience, he believes the probability distribution of snowfall and the resulting profit are summarized in the table below".

Amount of snow	Profit	Probability of occurrence
More than 40 inches	$120 000	0.4
20 to 40 inches	40 000	0.2
Less than 20 inches	ˉ40 000	0.4

Snowman has recently received an offer from a large hotel chain to operate the resort for the winter, guaranteeing him $45 000 profit for the season. He has been considering leasing snowmaking equipment for the season. If the equipment is leased, the resort will be able to operate full time, regardless of the amount of natural snowfall. If he decides to use man –made snow to supplement the natural snowfall his profit for the season will be $120 000 minus the cost of leasing and operating the snow equipment. The leasing cost will be about $12 000 per season, regardless of how much it is used. The operating cost will be $10 000 if the natural snowfall is more than 40 inches, $50 000 if it is between 20 and 40 inches and $90 000 if it is less than 20 inches.

Construct Mr. Snowman's decision tree and advice him on the optimal course of action.

Solution

The three branches emanating from the decision node represent his three possible ways to operate his resort this winter: hiring the hotel chain, running it himself without snow-making equipment, and running it himself with the snow makers. Each of the last branches terminates in a chance node representing the amount of snow that will fall during the season. Each of these nodes has three branches emanating from it, one for each possible value of snowfall and the associated probabilities.

The decision tree is as follows:

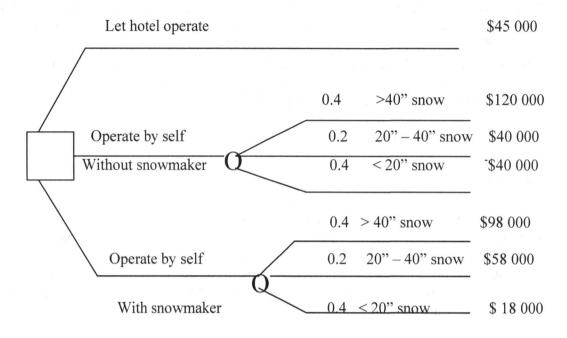

- The analyzed decision tree for Mr. Snowman is as follows

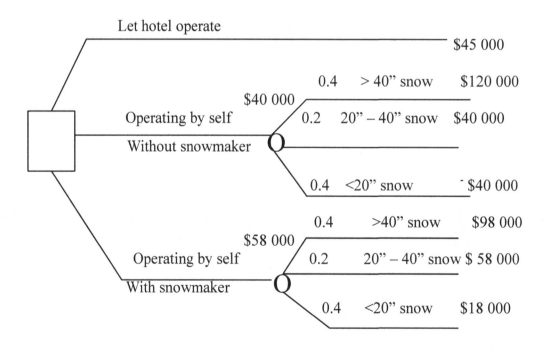

- The expected monetary value of hiring the hotel chain to manage the resort is $45 000

- Expected value of operating by self without Snowmaker is $120 000 (0.4)

+ $40 000 (0.2) - $40 000 (0.4) = $40 000

- Expected value of operating by self with snow maker is: $98 000 (0.4) + $58 000 (0.2) + $18 000(0.4) = $58 000.

- Thus, his optimal decision is to operate Snow Fun himself with snowmaking equipment.

Note: On calculation of net profit for each branch "at Snowman will earn if a node is followed from the root of the tree (at the decision node) to the top of the tree. For example, if he operates the resort himself with the snowmaker and the snowfall is between 20 and 40 inches, his profit will be $120 000 - $12000 - $50 000 = $58 000 i.e. $120 000 less $12 000 to the snowmaker and $50 000 to operate it. The other net profits are calculated similarly.

Example 9

Mr. Daka has just retired from Foreign Service and has received K100 000 000 which he wishes to invest for a year. He approaches his friend, the bank manager for advice. The bank manager informs him that he can invest in either the share market or the capital market. By investing in the capital market, he can earn a fixed rate of 12%. If the shares market reacts favorably, he will be able to make a profit of K50 000 000 on his capital, without taking dividends into account. If the share market is unfavourable, however, he will lose K20 000 000 of his capital. The probability of a favourable share market, that is rising share prices is 0.6 while the probability of an unfavourable share market is 0.4. Represent the above using a tree diagram and advice Mr. Data accordingly.

Solution

The problem can be represented diagrammatically as follows:

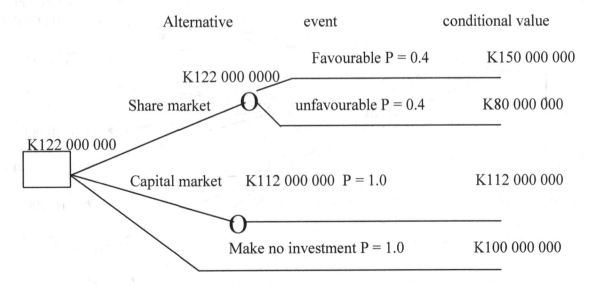

Calculation of the expected value is as follows:

- Investment on the share market = K150 000 000 (0.6) + K80 000 000 (0.4)

$$= K90\ 000\ 000 + K32\ 000\ 000$$

$$= K122\ 000\ 000$$

- Investment on the capital market = K112 000 000 (1.0)

$$= K112\ 000\ 000$$

Note: Investment on the capital market is shown as a single outcome with the probability of 1.0 because it is certain that interest of K12 000 000 will be earned. The alternative choice, namely to make no investment, should also be shown. From the example, it is clear that an amount of more than K100 000 000 will indeed be recovered at the end of the period. In most problems it is not so clear or certain that the investment amount will be recovered and as a result this alternative, namely to do nothing so as to ensure that no loss is made, must always be borne in mind. Using the expected value, Mr. Daka should invest on the share market. Further, it should be noted that the above problem could have been presented using a pay off table!

Example 10

Consider the decision tree shown here.

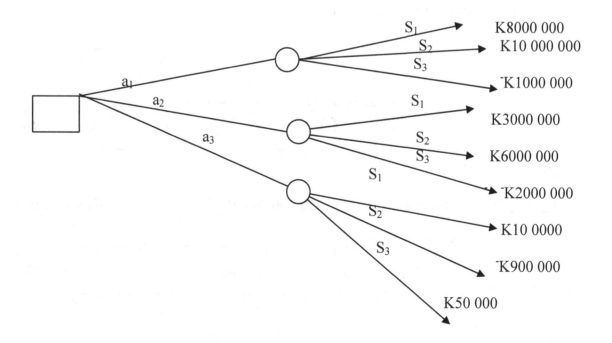

(a) Find the action that would be prescribed by the maximax criterion.
(b) Find the action that would be prescribed by the maximin criterion
(c) Explain why the action prescribed by the maximin criterion in part (b) is potentially unreasonable from a practical viewpoint.

Solution

(a) Maximax criterion

Action	Maximum
a_1	K10 000 000
a_2	K6 000 000
a_3	K50 000

- The action with the highest maximum pay off is a_1.

(b) Maximin criterion

Action	Minimum
a_1	K1000 000
a_2	K2000 000
a_3	K900 000

- The action with the maximum of the minimum pay offs is a_3.

(c) Because there are other better alternatives than the maximum of the minimum pay offs.

THE EXPECTED UTILITY CRITERION

The expected pay off or opportunity loss criterion sometimes fails to provide decisions that are consistent with the decision makers' attitude towards risk. For example, suppose you were required to choose one of these two actions:

a_1: Deposit your K1000 000 in the bank for 1 year at 7% interest.
a_2: Invest your K1000 000 for 1 year with a 0.5 probability of having a total of K2 500 000 at the end of the year and a 0.5 probability of losing all your K1000 000.

Which would you choose? Why? Most of us would probability choose a_1, basing our decision on a "safety first" strategy. The usual argument goes, "why pass up a chance for a sure K1070 000 at the end of the year for a 50 – 50 chance to end up with nothing". Notice that if you choose a_1, your decision is not in accord with the action prescribed by the expected pay off criterion because:

- Ev (a1) = K1070 000 (1) = K1070 000
- Ev (a2) = K2500 000 (0.5) + 0(0.5) = K1250, 000.

Thus, if we use the expected pay off criterion, we would select action a_2. The expected pay off criterion can be adapted to reflect our attitude toward risk if we express the outcomes of the decision problem in terms of an objective variable that better reflects the true relative values of outcomes. An objective variable that reflects the decision maker's attitude towards risk is called a **utility function**, and the values assigned to the outcomes are referred to as utility values or utilities or utiles.

A utility function is a rule that assigns numerical values to the potential outcomes of a decision problem in such a way that the values rank the outcomes in accordance with the decision maker's preferences and the function itself describes the decision maker's attitude toward risk.

ASSIGNING UTILITY VALUES TO MONETARY OUTCOMES

1. Identify the maximum and minimum pay offs in the decision table. Call them O_m and O_L respectively.

2. Set U (O_m) = 1 and U (O_L) = 0, where U (0) represents the utility value of outcome 0.

3. To determine the utility value for any other outcome O_{ij} in the pay off table, determine the value of P that makes you have no preference between the following:

    - Receiving O_{ij} with certainty
    - Partnercipating in a gamble in which you can win O_m with probability P or O_L with probability (1 – P).
      Then, U (O_{ij}) = P

EXPECTED UTILITY CRITERION

To make a decision based on expected utility criterion, we choose the action that has the greatest expected utility, where the expected utility of action a_1 is given by:

$$EU(a_1) = \sum_{\substack{\text{All states} \\ \text{of nature}}} (\text{utility of the action } a_{1/} \text{ state of nature combination})(\text{ probability of the state of nature})$$

The pay off table for our illustrative example is shown below:

		State of nature outcome of investment	
		S_1: Failure	S_2: Success
Action	a_1: Deposit K1000 000 in bank	K1070 000	K1070 000
	a_2: Invest K1000 000	0	K2 500 000

As noted earlier, many of us would be reluctant to gamble on the outcome of the investment if the chance of success were only 0.5, even though the expected pay off is higher for action a_2 (K1250 000) than for action a_1 (K1070 000). The key to assigning utility values to the action/state of nature combination is to answer the following question: what would be the probability of success for the investments have to be for you to value a_1 and a_2 equally?

The answer to this question is a_1 probability, P_1 such that if the probability of the investment's success exceeds P_1 you would prefer to invest the money (a_2), but if the success probability is less than P_1 you would prefer to deposit the money in the bank and take the safe return. The probability P is called the utility of the outcome K1070 000, and we write U (1070 000) = P. The minimum payoff (K0) and the maximum payoff (K2500 000) are assigned utility values O and 1, respectively, so that U (O) = 0 and U (2500 000) = 1.

Now if you decided that the probability of the investment's success would have to be 0.7 before the two actions are equally appealing. Then the utility value assigned to K1070 000 is 0.7, and the pay off table with the utility values as outcomes is shown below.

| | State of nature (probabilities in parentheses) outcome of investment | |
	S₁: Failure (0.5)	S₂: success (0.5)
a₁: Deposit K1000 000 Action	0.7	0.7
a₂: Invest K100 000	0	1

- The expected utilities can now be calculated as follows :
- $EU(a_1) = (0.7)\,0.5) + (0.7)\,(0.5) = 0.7$
- $EU(a_2) = 0(0.5) + 1\,(0.5) = 0.5$

We choose the action with the higher expected utility, which is action a1. You can see that this decision differs from that yielded by the expected pay off criterion and that it more accurately reflects a safety-first attitude towards risk.

Example 11

The following payoff table shows the bank branch size decision problem followed by the associated utility value associated with the monetary pay offs.

Pay off table

| Branch size | State of nature market share during fifth year of operation | | |
	S₁: 0% < 5%	S₂: 5% < 10%	S₃: 10% < 15%
a₁: Small	K3000 000	K3500 000	K4500 000
Action:a₂: medium	K2500 000	K7000 000	K8000 000
a₃: large	K2000 000	K6000 000	K10 000 000

Utility values table

| Branch size | State of nature (probabilities in parentheses) Market share during fifth year of operation | | |
	S₁: 0% <5%	S₂: 5% < 10%	S₃: 10% < 15%
a₁: Small	0.35	0.50	0.65
Action a₂: medium	0.20	0.90	0.95
a₃: large	0	0.85	1.00

(a) Interpret the utility value assigned to the K7000 000 pay off, U (7000 000) = 0.9
(b) Determine which action should be taken according to the expected utility criterion.

Solution

(a) Referring to the assignment of utility values, we see that the utility value of 0.9 represents the probability that makes us have no preference between receiving K7000 000 with certainty and participating in a gamble in which we can gain K10 000 000 (the maximum pay off) with the probability 0.9 or K2000 000 (the minimum pay off) with probability (1 – 0.9) = 0.1. You see again that we have adopted a conservative strategy, because the expected payoff for the gamble is K10 000 000 (0.9) + K2000 000 (0.1) = K9200 000 which exceeds the fixed pay off of K7000 000.In other words, the assignment of U(7000 000) = 0.9 reflects our desire to receive the fixed pay off unless the odds are very high that we will win the gamble.

(b) The expected utilities are calculated as follows:

- EU (a_1) = 0.35 (0.4) + 0.50 (0.5) + 0.65 (0.1) = 0.455
- EU (a_2) = 0.20 (0.4) + 0.90 (0.5) + 0.95 (0.1) = 0.625
- EU (a_3) = 0(0.4) + 0.85(0.5) + 1.0 (0.1) = 0.525

- Thus, according to the assigned utility values to monetary outcomes, expected utility criterion indicates that we should select action a_2 and build a medium-sized branch.

CLASSIFYING DECISION MAKERS BY THEIR UTILITY FUNCTIONS

The attitude of a decision-maker toward risk may be characterized by the type of utility function he or she uses. The three types of utility functions and risk attitudes they characterize are summarized below:

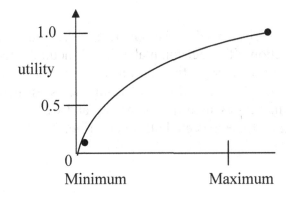

Monetary outcome

1. The concave utility function indicates that the decision maker is a risk - avoider.

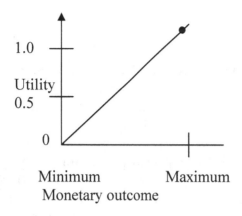

2. The straight-line utility function indicates that the decision maker is risk-neutral.

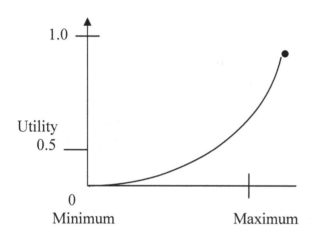

Monetary outcome

3. The convex utility function indicates that he decision maker is a risk-taker.

Thus, a decision maker can be classified as a risk avoider, risk-taker, or risk-neutral by examining the shape of his or her utility function. If a decision maker is risk-neutral, then both the expected utility criterion and the expected pay off criterion prescribe the same action. The expected pay off criterion has the advantage of not requiring the assessment of a utility function. Thus, many decision makers assume risk-neutrality and we use the expected pay off criterion as an approximation to the expected utility criterion.

PROGRESS CLINIC FIFTEEN

1. A bank is trying to decide whether to make a 1-year commercial loan of K75, 000, 000 to an automobile repair shop. Past experience has shown that one of the three outcomes will result if the loan is made:

(a) Outcome 1: The customer will repay the loan plus the 10% interest with no complications.

(b) Outcome 2: the customer will have difficulty repaying the loan with the 10% interest, but a K1000 000 collection cost will have been incurred by the bank.

(c) Outcome 3: The customer will declare bankruptcy, and the bank will recover only 60% of the amount loaned.

If the bank decides not to make the loan, the money will earn 8% for the year.

(a) Construct the payoff table for this decision problem.
(b) Convert the payoff table to an opportunity loss table
(c) Draw a decision tree for this problem.

2. Refer to question 1 above. Suppose past records yield the frequency distribution for commercial loans shown in the table.

Outcome	Frequency
1. Repaid	1104
2. Repaid with difficulty	120
3. Defaulted	56

i. Use this information to assess the probabilities of the outcomes.

ii. Using the assessed probabilities and the expected payoff criterion, decide whether the bank should make the loan.

3. Refer to question 2. Suppose no probability estimates for the outcomes are available.

(a) Use the maximax criterion to decide whether to make the loan.
(b) Use the maximin criterion to make the decision
(c) Criterion these two non probabilistic criteria for making this decision.

4. A common problem with management information systems (MIS) is that managers fail to use them, even when they are installed and are technically sound. Suppose a large computer firm is considering an MIS that will cost K1000 000 000 to build and operate over a 5-year period. If the company's managers use the system, a saving of K750 000 000 per year will be realized.

(a) Construct the payoff table for this decision problem
(b) Convert the payoff table to an opportunity loss table
(c) Suppose the probability that the MIS will be used is assessed to be only 0.5. Use the expected opportunity loss criterion to decided whether to install the M IS.

5. The credit manager of your bank is involved in a K1 billion money laundering suit. He can either settle out of court for K250 000 000 or go to court. If he goes to court and losses, he must pay K925 000 000 plus K75 000 000 in court costs. If he wins in court, the plaintiffs pay the court costs.

(a) Construct a payoff table for this decision problem

(b) Draw a decision tree for this problem

(c) The credit manager's lawyer estimates the probability of winning to be 0.2 use the expected payoff criterion to decide whether the manager should settle or go to court. Enter the lawyer's assessed probabilities and the expected payoffs associated with each action on your decision tree.

6. A financial advisor has recommended two possible mutual funds for investment: Fund A and Fund B. The return for each type of fund depends on the state of the economy and is illustrated in the following payoff table.

Investment	Good economy	Fair economy	Poor economy
Fund A	K10 000 000	K2000 000	⁻K5000 000
Fund B	K6000 000	K4000 000	0

The respective probabilities of the economy being good, fair or poor are 0.2, 0.3 and 0.5 respectively.

(a) Draw the decision tree to represent this situation.

(b) Perform the necessary calculations to determine which of the two funds is better. Which one would you choose to maximize the expected value?

(c)Suppose there is a question about the return of fund A in a good economy. It could be higher or lower than K10 000 000. What value for this would cause a person to be indifferent between Fund A and Fund B, (i.e. have the same EMVs).

7. Consider the accompanying payoff table (probabilities are in parentheses).

		STATE OF NATURE		
		S_1 (0.20)	S_2 (0.30)	S_3 (0.50)
Action	a_1	50	105	175
	a_2	⁻20	0	300

(a) Use the expected payoff criterion to select the better action.
(b) Convert the payoff table to an opportunity loss table and use the expected opportunity loss criterion to select the better action.

8. In the decision tree shown here, state probabilities are displayed in parentheses to the right of the state symbols S_1 and S_2. The outcomes on the decision tree are expressed in terms of opportunity losses. According to the expected opportunity loss criterion, which action should be selected?

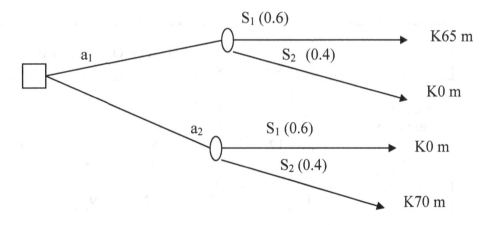

9. In the decision tree shown here, state probabilities are displayed in parentheses to the right of the state symbols, S_1 and S_2.

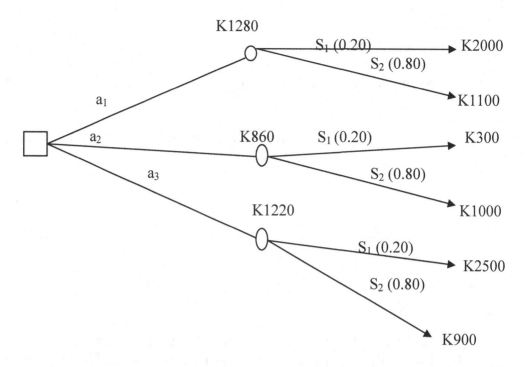

(a) The expected payoff for each action has been computed and appears to the left of the chance fork associated with each action in the decision tree. Verify that these expected payoffs are correct.

(b) Identify the action that is prescribed by the expected payoff criterion.

(c) Identify any inadmissible actions, and explain why they are inadmissible

10. Consider the following payoff table.

		STATE OF NATURE					
		S_1	S_2	S_3	S_4	S_5	S_6
Decision	d_1	7	6	9	11	10	12
Alternative	d_2	8	7	12	7	6	10
	d_3	12	10	6	8	9	12
	d_4	7	14	11	6	7	11
	d_5	5	6	8	10	11	13
	d_6	9	12	12	9	8	8

(a) if the decision maker is facing conditions of uncertainty, what decision would be made using:

(i) Laplace criteria
(ii) Maximin criteria
(iii) Maximax criteria

(iv) Savage criteria

(b) Assume the following probability estimates for the states of nature in (a) were obtained:

$P(S_1) = 0.2$, $P(S_2) = 0.1$, $P(S_3) = 0.05$, $P(S_4) = 0.25$, $P(S_5) = 0.2$ and $P(S_6) = 0.2$

(i) What decision would be made using expected monetary value as the criteria?

(ii) What is the $EVPI_6$?

11. CTV productions is considering producing a pilot for comedy series for a major television network. The network may reject the pilot and the series or it may purchase the program for one or two years. CTV may decide to produce the pilot or transfer the rights for the series to a competitor for K400 million. CTV profits are summarized in the following profit payoff table. The amounts are in millions of Kwacha.

		STATE OF NATRE		
		Reject	1 year	2 year
Action	Produce pilot	ˉ400	200	600
Alternative	Sell to competitor	400	400	400

ii. if the probability estimates for the state of nature are P (reject) = 0.3, P (1 year) = 0.5 and P (2 years) = 0.2. What should the company do?

iii. What is the optimal decision strategy if perfect information is available?

iv. What is the expected value of perfect information?

12. A bank must make a pricing decision regarding its new line of products. Two economists have been hired to develop the forecasting equations that relate the quality demanded to the price of the product. The forecasting equations the economists derive are:

Economist 1: $q = 10 - 2_p$
Economist 2 : $q = 16 - 4_p$

Where q is the quantity demanded in units of 100 000 and p is the price are being considered: K0.99, K1.98, K2.75 and K3.50. Assume that one of the economists forecasting equations will be correct, but you do not know which one.

(a) Construct the payoff table for this problem
(b) Construct the opportunity loss table for this problem.
(c) If the company believes the forecasting equations have an equal probability of being correct, which price should be charged according to the expected monetary value criterion.

13. An investor is trying to decide whether to invest in a wildcat oil well in Kaoma district. If the well is drilled and it is dry, she will lose K500 000 000. On the other hand, if the well is a gusher, she will earn K1500 000 000. it is also possible for the well to yield a lesser amount of oil than a gusher, in which case she will make K600 000 000.

(a) A decision analyst asks her the following question.

- At what value of p would you be indifferent between the two situations receive K600 000 000 with certainty, and receive K1 500 000 000 with probability $(1 - p)$? She replies, at $p = 0.90$. What is the investor's utility value for K600 000 000.

- At what value of p would you be indifferent between receiving K0 with certainty, and receiving K1 500 000 000 with probability $(1 - P)$? She replies at $P = 0.8$. Find her utility value for K0.

!4. Consider the following payoff table.

		STATE OF NATURE		
		S_1	S_2	S_3
Action	a_1	75	105	60
	a_2	70	80	60
	a_3	ˉ30	40	120
	a_4	105	90	200

(a) Eliminate any inadmissible actions.
(b) Find the action that would be prescribed by the maximax decision criterion.
(c) Find the action that would be prescribed by the maximin decision criterion.
(d) Find the action that would be prescribed by the opportunity loss decision criterion.

15. Consider the decision tree below:

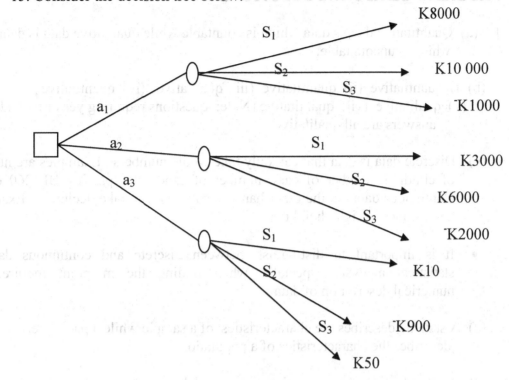

(a) Find the action that would be prescribed by the maximax criteria.

(b) Find the action that would be prescribed by the maximin criterion

(c) Explain why the action prescribed by the maximin criterion in (b) is potentially unreasonable from a practical viewpoint.

PROGRESS CLINIC ONE SOLUTIONS

1 . (a) Quantitative data is data which is countable while qualitative data is data which is uncountable.

    (b) i) quantitative (ii) quantitative (iii) qualitative (iv) quantitative
       (v) qualitative (vii) quantitative (Note: questions requiring yes or no and answers are all qualitative).

    (c) Discrete data is data that can only take whole numbers. Examples are number of children, number of cars, number of candidates passing BF 260 exam. Continuous data, on the other hand, is data that can take decimals. Examples are distance, weight, height.

- It is important to distinguish between discrete and continuous data in statistical analysis especially when finding the midpoint required for numerical description of data.

2. (a) A statistic describes the characteristics of a sample while a parameter describes the characteristics of a population.

    (b) Cost reduction, time reduction and saves labour.

    (c) Inadequate of sampling frame-state aim of survey.

- Items of selected sample not available- Return to the sampling frame and using the method.
- Interviewer or observer bias –Careful choice and training of the team coupled with close supervision when the survey is taking place.

    3. (a) Simple random sampling, systematic sampling, stratified sampling, multi-stage sampling, cluster sampling and quota sampling.

    (b) i)   Stratified. Select people who actually use ATMs
      (ii)   Simple random sampling of motorists
      (iii)   Stratified sampling select women only
      (iv)   Simple random sampling

    4. (a) Primary data is data collected by the researcher for a specific purpose. The possible source is field research. Secondary data, on the other hand, is data which has been collected by someone else for general purpose but could still be used by the researcher. Possible source is "published" data.

(b) Interviews, questionnaires and personal observations.
(c) (i) questionnaires
(ii)personal interviews
(iii)personal observation
(iv)personal observation

PROGRESS CLINIC TWO SOLUTIONS

1. (a).

Stem	Leaf							
14	5							
15	1	4	7	8				
16	0	2	2	4	5	6	8	9
17	1	1	3	5	5	7	9	
18	0	2	3	6	8			

(b)

Class	f	Relative frequency	Cumulative Relative frequency
140 but less than 150	1	0.04	0.04
150 but less than 160	4	0.16	0.20
160 but less than 170	8	0.32	0.52
170 but less than 180	7	0.28	0.80
180 but less than 190	5	0.20	1.00
	25	1.00	

(c)

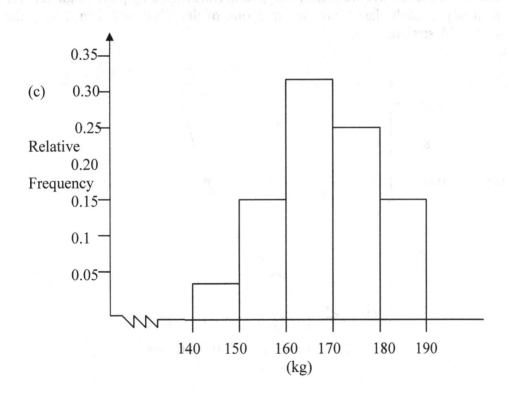

(d)

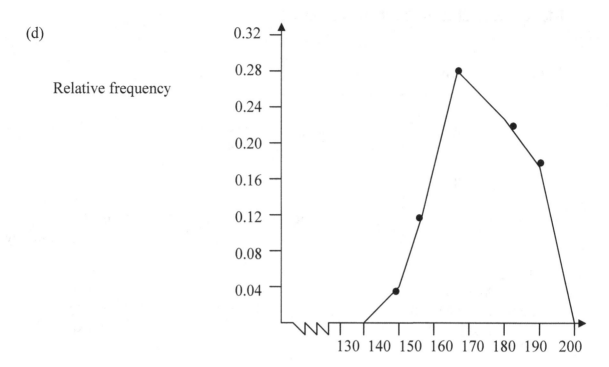

Relative frequency

Note: The relative frequency histogram is constructed by erecting over each class interval a rectangle, the height of which equals the relative frequency of that class while the relative frequency polygon is constructed by plotting the relative frequency of each class above the midpoint of that class and then joining the points with straight lines.

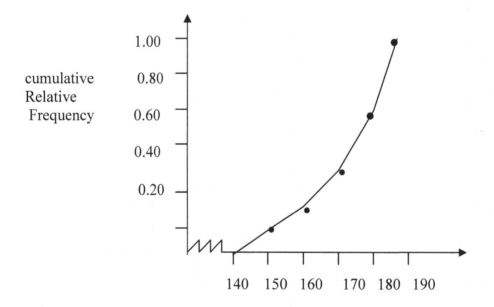

cumulative
Relative
Frequency

Note: To construct the ogive (less than), the cumulative relative frequency of each class is plotted above the upper limit of that class, and the points representing the cumulative frequencies are then joined by straight-line. The ogive is closed at the lower end by extending a straight-line to the lower limit of the first class.

2. (a) Lusaka $\dfrac{10000}{17000}$ $= 58.8\% = 212^0$

Livingstone $\dfrac{2000}{17000}$ $= 11.8\% = 42^0$

Ndola $\dfrac{3000}{17000}$ $= 17.6\% = 64^0$

Kitwe $\dfrac{2000}{17000}$ $= 11.8\% = 42^0$

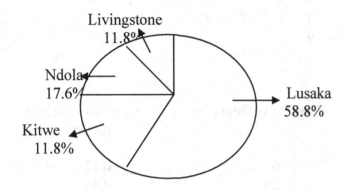

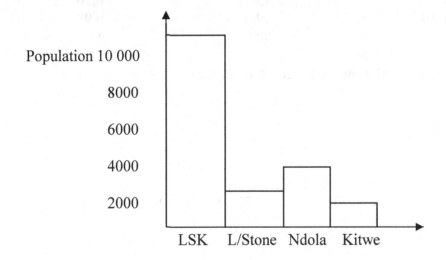

- Draw two straight lines emanating from different corners of the highest bar. Where they intersect drop a straight line to estimate the mode on the x-axis.

- Compound bar chart- analyzing trend over time e.g. sales per quarter for five years.

Pie chart – analyzing data with few figures e.g. to show gross revenues sources for a firm that only has four sources of revenue.

Pictogram – analysing distances and direction e.g. the location of the bank's 10 branches in Zambia.

Note: for suitability check the advantages and disadvantages of each.

3. (a)

Stem	Leaf
3	2 3 4 4 5 7
4	0 1 2 3 3 4 5 5 6 6 6 8 9
5	0 2 2 3 3 3 4 5 6 6 7 7 9
6	0 0 1 2 3 4 6 8 9
7	0 0 2 3 4 9
8	4

(b)

Class	Frequency	Cumulative frequency	Cumulative relative Frequency
30 but under 40	6	6	0.12
40 but under 50	14	20	0.40
50 but under 60	14	34	0.68
60 but under 70	9	43	0.86
70 but under 80	6	49	0.98
80 but under 90	1	50	1.00
	50		

(c) It is normally distributed as majority scores are in the range 40 and 69.

4.

Stem	leaf
0	8
1	1 6 9
2	0 4 5 6 6 7 8 9 9
3	3 4 5 9
4	1 5
5	0

5. Total 2.35 + 0.59 + 0.16 = K3.1 billion

(a) K' billion

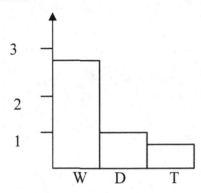

W	D	T	

Withdrawal: $\dfrac{2.35}{3.1}$ = 76% = 273^{0}

Deposit: $\dfrac{0.59}{3.1}$ = 19% = 69^{0}

Transfer: $\dfrac{0.16}{3.1}$ ≈ 5% = 19^{0}

Transfer 5%

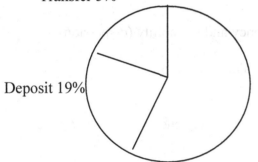

Withdrawal 76%

Deposit 19%

6. a) Gross revenue for the bank by source in 2007

(b) 0.167

(c) 192 X 0.547 = K105.024 billion

(d)   (%)

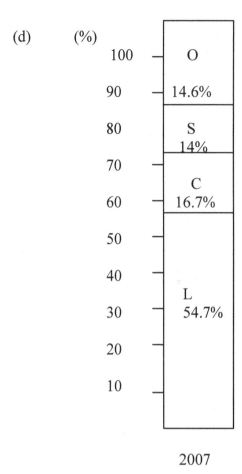

2007

7.By calculating measures of central tendency and variability (dispersion).

8.(a)distance traveled (in Km): ratio scaled: continuous.

(b)

Distance	Absolute frequency	Relative frequency	Ogive
10 but less than 15	3	10	10
15 but less than 20	11	36.7	46.7
20 but less than 25	8	26.7	73.4
25 but less than 30	5	16.7	90.0
30 but less than 35	3	10	100.0
	30		

(c) (i)

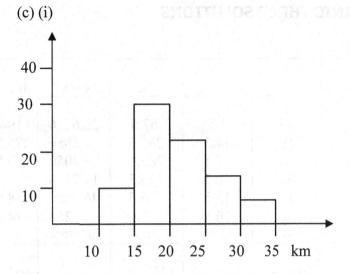

(ii) Relative frequency

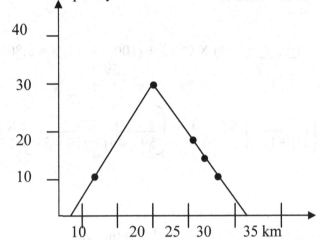

(d)(i)   approximately: $\dfrac{5}{30}$ X 10 = 17%

(ii)   approximately: $\dfrac{3 + 11 + 8}{30}$ X 100 = 73%

(iii)   approximately: $\dfrac{13}{30}$ X 100 = 43%

(iv)   under 21km

(v)   above 27km

PROGRESS CLINIC THREE SOLUTIONS

1.

Class	f	x	fx	$(x-\bar{x})^2$	$f(x-\bar{x})^2$	cf
Under 3	45	1.5	67.5	26.6256	1198.152	45
3 and under 6	59	4.5	265.5	4.6656	275.2704	104
6 and under 9	38	7.5	285.0	0.7056	26.8128	142
9 and under 12	31	10.5	325.5	14.7456	457.1136	173
12 and under 15	19	13.5	256.5	46.7856	888.9264	192
15 and under 18	8	16.5	132.0	96.8256	774.6048	200
18 and above	0	19.5	0.0	164.8656	0	200
	200		1332		3620.88	

(a) $\quad \bar{x} = \dfrac{\sum fx}{\sum f} = \dfrac{1332}{200} = 6.66$ minutes

(b) Median $= L + \dfrac{(n/2 - fm - 1)}{f} \times C = 3 + \dfrac{(100 - 45)}{59} \times 3 = 5.80$ minutes

(c) Mode $= L + \left(\dfrac{D_1}{D_1 + D_2}\right) \times C = 3 + \left(\dfrac{59 - 45}{(59 - 45) + (59 - 38)}\right) \times 3 = 4.20$ minutes

(d) $S = \sqrt{\dfrac{\sum f(x-\bar{x})^2}{\sum f}} = \sqrt{\dfrac{3620.88}{200}} = 4.25$ minutes

(e) $CV = \dfrac{S}{\bar{x}} \times 100 = \dfrac{4.25}{6.66} \times 100 = 63.8\%$

(f) The duration of the calls made are in the range 4.20 to 6.66 minutes.

2. (a).

Class	Frequency	Cumulative frequency
20 and under 25	3	3
25 and under 30	6	9
30 and under 35	11	20
35 and under 40	8	28
40 and under 45	2	30
	30	

(b)

Class	f	cf	x	fx	$(x-\bar{x})^2$	$f(x-\bar{x})^2$
20 – 25	3	3	22.5	67.5	100	300
25 – 30	6	9	27.5	165.0	25	150
30 – 35	11	20	32.5	357.5	0	0
35 – 40	8	28	37.5	300.0	25	200
40 – 45	2	30	42.5	85.0	100	200
	30			975		850

(I) Mean $= \dfrac{\sum fx}{\sum f} = \dfrac{975}{30} = 32.5$

$$\text{Median} = L + \left[\frac{n/2 - fm - 1}{f}\right] \times C = 30 + \left(\frac{15 - 9}{11}\right) \times 5 = 30.73$$

$$\text{Mode} = L + \left(\frac{D_1}{D_1 + D_2}\right) \times C = 30 + \left(\frac{11 - 6}{(11-6) + (11-8)}\right) \times 5 = 33.13$$

(ii)

$$Q_1 = L + \left(\frac{n/4 - fm - 1}{f}\right) \times C = 25 + \left(\frac{7.5 - 3}{6}\right) \times 5 = 28.75$$

$$Q_3 = L + \left[\dfrac{\dfrac{3n}{4} - fm - 1}{f}\right] \times C = 35 + \left(\dfrac{22.5 - 20}{8}\right) \times 5 = 36.56$$

Interquartile Range $= Q_3 - Q_1 = 36.56 - 28.75 = 7.81$

(iii)$S = \sqrt{\dfrac{\sum f (x - \bar{x})^2}{\sum f}} = \sqrt{\dfrac{850}{30}} = 5.32$

(iv) $CV = \dfrac{S}{\bar{x}} \times 100 = \dfrac{5.32}{32.5} \times 100 = 16.37\%$

(v)$CS = \dfrac{3\ (mean - median)}{Standard\ deviation} = \dfrac{3\ (32.5 - 3073)}{5.32} = 0.998$

3. a)

Stem	Leaf								
0	8								
1	1	6	9						
2	0	4	5	6	6	7	8	9	9
3	3	4	5	9					
4	1	5							
5	0								

(b). Mode = 26 and 29 (bimodal)

. Median $= \dfrac{27 + 28}{2} = \dfrac{55}{2} = 27.5$

. Mean $\dfrac{\sum x}{n} = \dfrac{565}{20} = 28.25$

(c) None

(d) $\dfrac{13}{20} \times 100 = 65\%$

4. (a) i) Mode = 3 (most frequent)

ii) 2, 3, 5, 6, 8.

$$\text{Median} = \frac{3+5}{2} = 4$$

iii) $\sum\limits_{i=2}^{5} xi\ 3 = 3^3 + 5^3 + 3^3 + 6^3$

$$= 27 + 125 + 27 + 216 = 395$$

vi) $\sum\limits_{i=2}^{5}\ \dfrac{\bar{x}}{xi} = \bar{x} \sum\limits_{i=2}^{5}\ \dfrac{1}{xi}$

$$\bar{x} = \frac{3+5+3+6}{4} = \frac{17}{4}$$

$$\sum\limits_{i=2}^{5}\ \frac{1}{xc} = \frac{1}{3} + \frac{1}{3} + \frac{1}{5} + \frac{1}{3} + \frac{1}{6} = \frac{10+6+10+5}{30} = \frac{31}{30}$$

$$\sum\limits_{i=2}^{5}\ \frac{\bar{x}}{xi} = \frac{17}{4} \div \frac{31}{30} = \frac{17}{4} \times \frac{30}{31} = \frac{510}{124} = 4.11$$

v) $\sum\limits_{i=2}^{5} 2\ \dfrac{1}{xi} = 2 \sum\limits_{i=2}^{5} \dfrac{1}{xi}$

$$= 2 \left(\frac{31}{30} \right) = \frac{62}{30} = 2.07$$

(b)

Measure (x)	Frequency (f)	Cumulative frequency (f)
1	3	3
2	4	7
3	5	12
4	5	17
5	$\underline{6}$	23
	23	

Or 1, 1, 1, 2, 2, 2, 2, 3, 3, 3, 3, 3, 4, 4, 4, 4, 4, 5, 5, 5, 5, 5.

i. . Mode = 5

. Median = $\dfrac{23}{2}$ = 11.5th, which is 3

. Mean = $\sum \dfrac{x}{n}$ = $\dfrac{1\,(3) + 2\,(4) + 3\,(5) + 4\,(5) + 5\,(6)}{23}$ = $\dfrac{76}{23}$ = 3.3

. Total observation = 23

ii. Check table above. Median = 3 i.e $\dfrac{23t1}{2}$ = 12th measure

5. (a) Median (b) Mode (c) Mean (d) Mean (e) Check text notes.

6. (a) $\sum\limits_{i=1}^{n} xi = 5 + 9 + 6 + 3 + 7 = 30$

(b) $\sum\limits_{i=1}^{n} xi = (5)^2 + (9)^2 + (6)^2 + (3)^2 + (7)^2$

$= 25 + 81 + 36 + 9 + 49 = 200$

(c) $\left(\sum\limits_{i=1}^{n} xi \right)^2 = (30)^2 = 900$

(d) $\sum\limits_{i=2}^{4} \overline{xi} = \dfrac{9 + 6 + 3 + 7}{4} = \dfrac{25}{4} = 6.25$

(e) $\sum\limits_{i=2}^{4} \overline{xi} = \dfrac{9 + 19 + 3 + 7}{4} = \dfrac{38}{4} = 9.5$

(f) $\overline{x} = \dfrac{5 + 9 + 6 + 3 + 7}{5} = 6$

x	x̄	x - x̄
5	6	⁻1
9	6	3
6	6	0
3	6	⁻3
7	6	1
		0

7. (a) Mean = $\dfrac{76 + 38 + 48 + 59 + 82 + 60 + 72 + 50 + 42 + 42}{10} = \dfrac{569}{10} = 56.9\%$

(b) Median: 38, 42, 42, 48, 50, 59, 60, 72, 76, 82

Median = $\dfrac{50 + 59}{2} = 54.5\%$

(c) Mode = 42%

(d) Range = 82% - 38% = 44%

PROGRESS CLINIC FOUR SOLUTIONS

1. a) Age   Frequency

Age	Frequency
160 but under 165	7
165 but under 170	11
170 but under 175	17
175 but under 180	20
180 but under 185	16
185 but under 190	9
	80

Age	f	fc	x	fx	x^2	fx^2
160 – 175	7	7	162.5	1137.5	26406.25	184843.75
165 – 170	11	18	167.5	1842.5	28056.25	308618.75
170 – 175	17	35	172.5	2932.5	29756.25	505856.25
175 – 180	20	55	177.5	3550.0	31506.25	630125.00
180 – 185	16	71	182.5	2920.0	33306.25	532900.00
185 – 190	9	80	187.5	1687.5	35156.25	316406.25
	80			14070		247850.00

(b) i) $x = \dfrac{\sum fx}{\sum f} = \dfrac{14070}{80} = 175.875$ years

ii) Median $= L + \left(\dfrac{\dfrac{n}{2} - fm - 1}{20}\right)$ X C $= 175 + \left(\dfrac{\dfrac{80}{2} - 35}{20}\right)$ X 5 $= 176.25$ years

iii) Mode $= L + \left(\dfrac{D_1}{D_1 + D_2}\right)$ X C $= 175 + \left(\dfrac{20 - 17}{(20 - 17) + (20 - 16)} \text{ X 5}\right) = 177.14$ years

iv) $S = \sqrt{\dfrac{1}{n}\left(\sum fx^2 - \dfrac{(\sum fx)^2}{n}\right)} = \sqrt{\dfrac{1}{80}\left(2478750 - \dfrac{(14070)^2}{80}\right)}$

$= \underline{7.24 \text{ years}}$

v) $S^2 = 7.24)^2 = 52.43$ years.

vi) $CV = \dfrac{S}{\overline{x}} \times 100 = \dfrac{7.24 \times 100}{175.875} = 4\%$

vii) $CS = \dfrac{3\,(\text{mean} - \text{median})}{\text{Standard deviation}} = \dfrac{3\,(175.875 - 176.25)}{7.24} = 0.16$

viii) $Q_1 = 170 + \left(\dfrac{\dfrac{80}{4} - 18}{17}\right) \times 5 = 170.588$

$Q_3 = 180 + \left(\dfrac{\dfrac{3\,(80)}{4} - 55}{16}\right) = 181.5625$

Interquartile Range $= 181.5625 - 170.588 = 10.9745$

ix) Quartile deviation $= \dfrac{Q_3 - Q_1}{2} = \dfrac{10.9745}{2} = 5.48725$

x) Range $= 190 - 160 = \underline{30}$

2.

Wages (k)	f	cf	x	fx
5000 – 5500	4	4	5250	21000
5500 – 6000	26	30	5750	149500
6000 – 6500	133	163	6250	831250
6500 – 7000	35	198	6750	236250
7000 – 7500	2	200	7250	14500
	200			1,252500

(a) $\overline{x} = \dfrac{\sum fx}{\sum f} = \dfrac{1252500}{200} = K6,262.50$

. Median $= L + \left(\dfrac{\dfrac{n}{2} - fm-1}{f}\right) \times c = 6000 + \left(\dfrac{\dfrac{200}{2} - 30}{133}\right) \times 500 = K6263.16$

$$. \text{ Mode} = L + \left(\dfrac{D_1}{D_1 + D_2}\right) X\ C = 6000 + \left(\dfrac{133 - 26}{(133 - 26) + 133 - 35}\right) X\ 500 = K6260.98$$

b) $Q_1 = 1 + \left(\dfrac{\dfrac{n}{4} - fm - 1}{f}\right) X\ C = 6000 + \left(\dfrac{\dfrac{200}{4} - 30}{133}\right) X\ 500 = K6075.19$

$$Q_3 = L + \left(\dfrac{\dfrac{3n}{4} - fm - 1}{f}\right) X\ C = 6000 + \left(\dfrac{\dfrac{3(200)}{4} - 30}{133}\right) X\ 500 = K6451.13$$

$$Q_D = \dfrac{Q_3 - Q_1}{2} = \dfrac{6451.13 - 6075.19}{2} = K187.97$$

(c) Range $= 7500 - 5000 = \underline{2500}$

3.

Class	f	x	fx	$|x - \bar{x}|$	$f|x - \bar{x}|$	c f
0 – 10	3	5	15	32	96	3
10 – 20	6	15	90	22	132	9
20 – 30	11	25	275	12	132	20
30 – 40	15	35	525	2	30	35
40 – 50	12	45	540	8	96	47
50 – 60	7	55	385	18	126	54
60 – 70	6	65	390	28	168	60
	$\underline{60}$				$\underline{780}$	

(a). $x = \dfrac{\sum fx}{\sum f} = \dfrac{2220}{60} = 37$ hours

$. \ Md = \dfrac{780}{60} = 13$ hours

(v) The 50th percentile is the 50% of the data set. The other name for a 50th percentile is the median.

$$\text{Median} = L + \left[\frac{\frac{n}{2} - fm - 1}{f}\right] \times C$$

$$= 30 + \left[\frac{\frac{60}{2} - 20}{15}\right] \times 5 = 33 \text{ hours}$$

4. (a) $\sum x = 15 + 15 + 2 + 6 + 1250$

$\sum x^2 = (15)^2 + (15)^2 + (6)^2 + (12)^2 = 634.$

$n = 5, \bar{x} = 10$

.$\sum x = 100 + 0 + 0 + 2 = 102$

$\sum x^2 = (100)^2 + (0)^2 + (0)^2 + (2)^2 = 10004$

$n = 4, \bar{x} = 25.5$

i) $S = \sqrt{\dfrac{x^2 - (x)^2}{n}}{n-1}$ $= \sqrt{\dfrac{634 - \dfrac{(50)^2}{5}}{5-1}} = \underline{7.79}$

$S = \sqrt{\dfrac{1004 - \dfrac{(102)^2}{4}}{4-1}}$

$= \underline{49.68}$

ii) $S^2 = (7.79)^2 = 60.68$

$S^2 = 2468.10$

iii) Rearranging 2, 6, 12, 15, 15

$Q_1 = \dfrac{2 + 6}{2} = 4$

$Q_3 = \dfrac{12 + 15}{2} = 13.5$

IR = 13.5 – 4 = 9.5

0, 0, 2, 100

$Q_1 = 0$

$Q_3 = 2$

1Q = 2 – 0 = 2

iv) CV = $\dfrac{S}{\bar{x}} \times 100 = \dfrac{7.79}{10} \times 100 = \underline{77.9\%}$

CV = $\dfrac{49.68}{25.5} \times 100$

$= \underline{194.8\%}$

(b) i) $S = \sqrt{\dfrac{246 - \dfrac{(63)^2}{22}}{22 - 1}} = 1.77$

ii) $S = \sqrt{\dfrac{666 - \dfrac{(106)^2}{25}}{25 - 1}} = 3.00$

iii) $S = \sqrt{\dfrac{76 - \dfrac{(11)^2}{7}}{7 - 1}} = 3.13$

(iv) $S = \sqrt{\dfrac{fx^2 - \dfrac{(fx)^2}{n}}{n - 1}} = \sqrt{\dfrac{630 - \dfrac{(10)^2}{22}}{22 - 1}} = 5.46$

5. (a) For June

$\sum x = 8 + 3 + 0 + 0 + 10\ 4 + 9 = 34$

$\sum x^2 = (8)^2 + (3)^2 + (0)^2 + (0)^2 + (10)^2 + (4)^2 + (9)^2 = 270$

$n = 10$

$\sum x = 0 + 3 + 4 + 11 + 3 + 3 + 2 = 26$

$\sum x^2 = (0)^2 + (3)^2 + (4)^2 + (11)^2 + (3)^2 + (3)^2 + (2)^2 = 168$

$n = 10$

Range for August = 11 – 0 = 11
Range for June = 10 – 0 = 10

Thus, August shows more variability as measured by range.

$S^2 = \dfrac{x^2 - \dfrac{(x)^2}{n}}{n - 1} = \dfrac{270 - \dfrac{(34)^2}{10}}{10 - 1} = 17.16$ for June

$$S^2 = \dfrac{168 - \dfrac{(26)^2}{10}}{10 - 1} = 11.16 \text{ for August}$$

Thus, June shows more variability as measured by the standard deviation

(b) $S^2 = 17.16$ No effect.

(c) $S^2 = 154.4$: is multiplied by the square of the constant.

6. (a) Statement 1: $\bar{x} = \dfrac{2 + 2 + 3 + 4 + 2 + 3 + 2 + 1 + 3 + 3 + 2 + 4}{12} = \dfrac{31}{12} = 2.6$

Statement 2: $\bar{x} = \dfrac{3 + 3 + 2 + 4 + 3 + 3 + 2 + 4 + 4 + 5 + 3 + 4}{12} = \dfrac{40}{12} = 3.3$
    i.

(b) Statement 1: $\sum x = 31, \ \sum x^2 = 89$

$$S = \sqrt{\dfrac{89 - \dfrac{(31)^2}{10}}{10 - 1}}$$

$= 0.888$

Statement 2: $\sum x = 40, \ \sum x^2 = 142$

$$S = \sqrt{\dfrac{142 - \dfrac{(40)^2}{10}}{10 - 1}}$$

$= 1.414$

(c) Statement 1: $\bar{x} \pm 2\sigma = 2.6 \pm 2\,(0.888) = 2.6 \pm 1.776$

Statement 2: $\bar{x} \pm 2\sigma = 3.3 + 2\,(1.414) = 3.3 \pm 2.828$

(d) $CV = \dfrac{S \times 100}{\bar{x}}$

Statement 1: $CV = \dfrac{0.888 \times 100}{2.6} = 34\%$

Statement 2: $CV = \dfrac{1.414}{3.3} \times 100 = 43\%$

Thus, there is low consensus on statement 2.

PROGRESS CLINIC FIVE SOLUTIONS

1. This is a combination with n = 20 and r = 5

$$\dfrac{n!}{(n-r)!r!} = \dfrac{20!}{(20-5)!5!} = 15504$$

2. (a) loan under 1000, 1000 – 3999, 4000 – 5999 and 6000 or more

   (b) $\dfrac{76}{500} = 0.152$

   (c) $\dfrac{27}{500} + \dfrac{99}{500} = 0.252$

3. (a) Length of loan i.e. 12, 24, 36, 42 and 48

   (b) Yes, $\dfrac{76}{500} = 0.152$

   (c) 0.004

   (d) $\dfrac{36}{162} + \dfrac{48}{162} = 0.518$

   (e) 0.392

4. (a) $\dfrac{83}{41}$ (b) $\dfrac{68}{152}$ (c) $\dfrac{41}{\,}$ (d) $\dfrac{6}{151}$ (e) $\dfrac{6}{151}$ 151

   5. This is a combination with n = 10 and r = 5

$$\dfrac{n!}{(n-r)!r!} = \dfrac{10!}{(10-5)!5!} = 252$$

6. Assume that the total production on all the three machines is 100

Machine A		Machine B		Machine C	
10%		40%		50%	
10		40		50	
Blue 4	Pink 6	Blue 12	Pink 28	Blue 10	Pink 40

(a) Proportion of blue elephants to the total is:

$$P(\text{Blue}) = \frac{4 + 12 + 10}{100} = \frac{26}{100} = 0.26$$

(b) Probability that a randomly selected elephant is made by machine B is:

$$P(\text{Blue made by B}) = \frac{28}{74} = 0.38$$

7. (a) There are n = 25, and r = 6 possible combinations.

$$\frac{n!}{(n-r)!\,r!} = \frac{25!}{(25-6)!\,6!} = 177100$$

Since there are 25 – 15 = 10 non defective bulbs, there

$$\frac{10!}{(10-0)!\,0!} = 1 \text{ way to choose 0 defective and}$$

$$\frac{15!}{(15-6)!\,6!} = 5005 \text{ way non defective bulbs}$$

Thus, the probability of at least one defective is: 1 – P (non defective)

$$1 - \frac{\left(\frac{10!}{(10-0)!\,0!}\right)\left(\frac{15!}{(15-6)!\,6!}\right)}{\frac{25!}{(25-6)!\,6!}} = 1 - \frac{5005}{177100} = 0.9717$$

(b) Probability of none is defective from (a) is $\frac{5005}{177100} = 0.028$

(c) The number of ways of choosing one defective bulb is $\frac{15!}{(15-1)!\,1!}$ and the number of ways of choosing non defective $\dfrac{10!}{(10-5)\,!5!}$

Probability = $\dfrac{\dfrac{15!}{(15-1)!1!}\quad \dfrac{10!}{(10-5)!5!}}{\dfrac{25!}{(25-6)\,!6!}}$ $= \dfrac{15\,(252)}{177100}$ $= \underline{0.0213}$

8.   Let μ: The employee is male

   c: The employee selected has a college education

   $\bar{\mu}$: the employee is female

   $P(\bar{\mu})$: 0.6, $P(c/\mu) = 0.7$ $P(c/\bar{\mu}) = 0.5$

9. $P(A \text{ or } B) = P(A) + P(B) - P(A \text{ and } B)$. This can be illustrated by finding the probability of picking an ace of hearts from a pack of 52 cards. Check the notes!

10.   (a) (0001,0002),(0001,0003), (0001,0004), (0001,0005), (0002,0003), (0002, 0004), (0002, 0005), (0003,0004), (0003,0005), (0004, 0005)

   (b) 1/10
   (c) 1/10; 3/10

PROGRESS CLINIC SIX SOLUTIONS

1. This depicts a poisson distribution with $\lambda = 4$, $x > 3$

. $P(x) = \dfrac{\lambda^x \cdot e^{-\lambda}}{x!}$ where e = 2.71828.............

. $P(x > 3) = 1 - P(x = 0, 1, 2 \text{ or } 3)$

. $P(x = 0) = \dfrac{4^0 \cdot (2.718)^{-4}}{0!} = 0.018323236$

. $P(x - 1) = \dfrac{4^1 \cdot (2.718)^{-4}}{2!} = 0.07329246$

. $P(x = 3) = \dfrac{4^3 \cdot (2.718)^{-4}}{3!} = 0.195447885$

Thus, $P(x > 3) = 1 - p(0) + p(1) + p(2) + p(3)$

$= 1 - (0.018323236 + 0.07329246 + 0.146585893 + 0.19544785)$

$= 1 - 0.433649925$

$= 0.56635007$

. The expected number is $4800 \times 0.56635007 = 2718$

. Average cost $2718 \times K10 \times 4 = \underline{K108720}$

2. This depicts a binomial distribution with $p = \dfrac{20}{100} = 0.2$,

$q = 1 - 0.2 = 0.8$, $n = 5$

$P(r) = \dfrac{n!}{(n-r)!\,1!}\ p^r - q^{n-r}$

(a) $r = 5$

$P(5) = \dfrac{5!}{(5-5)!\,5!}\ (0.2)^5 (0.8)^{5-5} = 0.00032$

(b) $P(x = 2, 3, 4 \text{ or } 5) = 1 - P(x = 0 \text{ or } 1)$

. $P(0) = \dfrac{5!}{(5-0)!\,0!}\ (0.2)^0 (0.8)^{5-0} = 0.32768$

$$. P(1) = \frac{5!}{(5-1)! \, 1!} (0.2)^1 (0.8)^{5-1} = 0.4096$$

Thus, p (at least 2) = 1 – P (0) + P (1)

$$= 1 - (0.32768 + 0.4096)$$

$$= 1 - 0.73728$$

$$= 0.26272$$

(c) P (x = 0,1, 3 or 4) = 1 – p (5)

$$= 1 - 0.00032$$

$$= \underline{0.99968}$$

3. This depicts a normal distribution with $\bar{x}$ = 450 ^{0}F, S = 250 ^{0}F and x = 475 ^{0}F,

$$Z = \frac{x - \bar{x}}{S}$$

$$. P(x \geq 450\ ^0F) = \frac{457\ ^0F - 450\ ^0F}{250\ ^0F} = 1.00$$

. From table 1.00 gives area of 0.3143

. P (defective) = 0.5 – 0.3143 = 0.1587

. P (450 0F < X < 470 ^{0}F)

$$Z = \frac{470\ ^0F - 450\ ^0F}{250\ ^0F} = 0.80 \text{ which gives } 0.2881$$

$$Z = \frac{460\ ^0F - 450\ ^0F}{250\ ^0F} = 0.40 \text{ which gives } 0.1554$$

Required probability = 0.2881 – 0.1554 = 1327

4. This is a binomial distribution question with n = 10, p = 0.02, q = 1 – 0.02 = 0.98

The shipment is accepted if fewer than three of the components are defective:

$P(x \le 3) = \dfrac{n!}{(n-r)!\,r!}\; p^r q^{n-r}$ where x is the number of defectives

$. P(0) = \dfrac{10!}{(10-0)!\,0!}\;(0.02)^0\,(0.98)^{10-0} = 0.81707$

$. P(1) = \dfrac{10!}{(10-1)!\,1!}\;(0.02)^1\,(0.98)^{10-1} = 0.1667$

$. p(2) = \dfrac{10!}{(10-2)!\,2!}\;(0.02)^2\,(0.98)^{10-2} = 0.0153$

$. P(3) = \dfrac{10!}{(10-3)!\,1!}\;(0.02)^3\,(0.98)^{10-3} = 0.0008$

$= 0.81707 + 0.1667 + 0.0153 + 0.0008$

$= 0.9999$

5. The question describes a binominal distribution with $p = 90\% = 0.9$, $q = 1 - 0.9 = 0.1$

$n = 8$

$P(x \ge 2) = 1 - (p(0) + p(1) + P(2))$

$. P(0) = \dfrac{8!}{(8-0)!\,0!}\;(0.9)^0\,(0.1)^{8-0} = 0.0000001$

$. P(1) = \dfrac{8!}{(8-1)!\,1!}\;(0.9)^1\,(0.1)^{8-1} = 0.00000072$

$. P(2) = \dfrac{8!}{(8-2)!\,2!}\;(0.9)^2\,(0.1)^{8-2} = 0.00002268$

. Thus, $p(x \ge 2) = 1 - (0.0000001 + 0.00000072 + 0.00002268)$

$= 1 - 0.00002341$

$= 0.99997659$

6. This depicts a poisson distribution with $\lambda = 1$, $x = 0, 1, 2$.

$P(x \ge 2) = 1 - P(0) + p(1) + p(2)$

$$. \ P\,(0) = \frac{\lambda^x \cdot e^{-\lambda}}{x!} = \frac{1^0\,(2.718)^{-1}}{0!} = 0.3679$$

$$. \ P\,(1) = \frac{1^1\,(2.718)^{-1}}{1!} = 0.3679$$

$$. \ P\,(2) = \frac{1^2\,(2.718)^{-2}}{2!} = 0.0677$$

$$. \ P\,(x \geq 2) = 1 - (0.3679 + 0.3679 + 0.0677)$$

$$= 1 - 0.8075$$

$$= 0.1965$$

7. (a) $P(30 \leq z \leq 60)$

$$Z = \frac{30 - 42}{24} = {}^-0.5 \text{ which gives } 0.1915 \text{ from the table}$$

$$Z = \frac{60 - 42}{24} = 0.75 \text{ which gives } 0.2734 \text{ from the table}$$

Required probability is $0.1915 + 0.2734 = 0.4649$

Number of candidates is $1000 \times 0.4649 = 465$

(b) Here 10% = 0.1 as a decimal. Since each half of the normal distribution has an area of 0.5, we have to subtract 0.1 from 0.5 to have 0.4000 and then check the closest area from the mass of the figures in the table to find 0.3997 which corresponds with a Z score of 1.28 and 0.4015 which corresponds to a Z score of 1.29. Having found the z score we can now work out the value of x as follows.

$$1.28 = \frac{x - 42}{24} \qquad\qquad \text{or } 1.29 = \frac{x - 42}{24}$$

$$x = 73 \qquad\qquad\qquad\qquad x = 73$$

8. (a)   f(x)

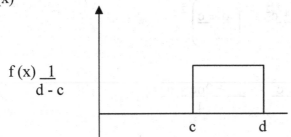

$$f(x) \frac{1}{d-c}$$

or f(x = $\begin{cases} \dfrac{1}{d-c} & \text{for } c \le X \le d \\ \\ 0 \text{ otherwise} \end{cases}$

(b) $E(x) = \int_c^d xf(x)\,dx$

$$= \int_c^d \frac{x}{d-c}\,dx = \frac{x^2}{2(d-c)}\Big|_c^d$$

$$= \frac{d^2 - c^2}{2(d-c)} = \frac{(d-c)\,d+c)}{2(d-c)}$$

$$= \frac{d+c}{2}$$

(c) $Var(x) = E(x^2) - E^2(x)$

We need $E(x^2) = \int_c^d x^2 f(x)\,dx$

$$= \int_c^d x^2 \frac{1}{d-c}\,dx$$

$$= \frac{x^3}{3(d-c)}\Big|_c^d$$

$$= \frac{d^3 - c^3}{3(d-c)} = \frac{(d-c)(d^2 + cd + c^2)}{3(d-c)}$$

$$= \frac{d^2 + cd + c^2}{3}$$

Therefore Var $(x) = \dfrac{d^2 + cd + c^2}{3} - \left(\dfrac{d+c}{2}\right)^2$

$$= \dfrac{d^2 + cd + c^2}{3} - \dfrac{d^2 + 2dc + c^2}{4}$$

$$= \dfrac{4d^2 + 4cd - 4c^2 - 3d^2 - 6dc - 3c^2}{12}$$

$$= \dfrac{d^2 - 2cd + c^2}{12} = \dfrac{(d-c)^2}{12}$$

8. (a) f (x)

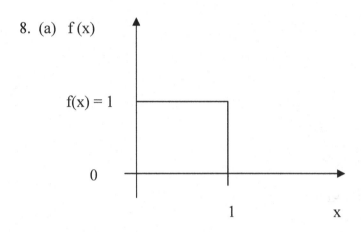

(b) P $(0.25 \leq X \leq 0.75)$

$= 0.75 - 0.25 = 0.50$

(c) P $(x \leq 0.30) = 0.30 - 0 = 0.30$

(d) P $(x \geq 0.60) = 1 - 0.6 = 0.40$

PROGRESS CLINIC SEVEN SOLUTIONS

1.   (a) Expected credit score (EV) = $\sum xp(x)$

For bank, EV = 210 (0.109) + 200 (0.117) + 190 (0.109) + 180 (0.113)

           + 170 (219) + 160 (0.102) + 150 (0.102) + 140 (0.074) + 130

           (0.035) + 120 (0.020)

        = $\underline{173.5}$

For macro finance companies:

EV = 210 (0.000) + 200 (0.023) + 190 (0.034) + 180 (0.034) + 170 (0.184) +

    160 (0.069) + 150 (0.161) + 140 (0.17) + 130 (0.105) +20 (0.218)

    = $\underline{147.54}$

Bank borrowers have a high credit score compared to micro finance borrowers hence bank borrowers are less prone to credit risk i.e. they are credit worth.

(b) For bank borrowers:

$$S^2 = \sum (x - \mu) P(x)$$

$$= (210 - 173.5)^2\, 0.109 + (200 - 173.5)^2\, 0.117 + (190 - 173.5)^2\, 0.109 +$$

$$(180 - 173.5)^2\, 0.102 + (170 - 173.5)^2\, 0.219 + (160 - 173.5)^2\, 0.102$$

$$+ (150 - 173.5)^2\, 0.102 + (140 - 173.5)^2\, 0.074 + (130 - 173.5)^2$$

$$0.035 + (120 - 173.5)^2\, 0.020 = 546.1569$$

$$S = \sqrt{546.1569} \quad = \quad \underline{23.37}$$

Micro finance companies

$$S^2 = (210 - 147.54)^2\, 0.000 + (200 - 147.54)^2\, 0.023 + (190 - 147.54)^2\, 0.034$$

$$+ (180 - 147.54)^2\, 0.034 + (170 - 147.54)^2\, 0.184 + (160 - 147.54)^2$$

$$0.069 + (150 - 147.54)^2 \, 0.161 + (140 - 147.54)^2 \, 0.172 +$$

$$(130 - 147.54)^2 \, 0.105 + (120 - 147.54)^2 \, 0.218$$

$$= \underline{472.1929}$$

$$S = \sqrt{472.1929} \quad = 21.73$$

c) The micro finance companies borrowers have a lower standard deviation when compared to bank borrowers. However, bank borrowers are less credit risk than microfinance companies' borrowers.

2. E.V = (-5000 000 (0.2) + 10 000 000 (0.5) + 30 000 0000 (0.3) = K13 000 000. Thus, the expected profit for the next six months is over K10 000 000 hence the bank must market the new line.

3. K1000 000 000 (0.001) = K1000 000

4. (a) EV $= \sum xp\,(x)$

$$= 20\,000\,000\,(0.6) - 12\,000\,000\,(0.4)$$

$$= \text{K7 200 000}$$

(b) EV $= 20\,000\,000\,(0.6) - 1000\,000 = \text{K11 000 000}$

(c) Too little

5. (a) Firm A, EV $= 0(0.01) + 500\,(0.01) + 1000\,(0.01) + 1500\,(0.02) + 2000$

$$.(0.35) + 2700\,(0.30) + 3200\,(0.15) + 37000\,(0.02) + 42000$$

$$(0.02) + 4700\,(0.01)$$

$$= \underline{2450}$$

Firm B, EV $= 0(0.00) + 200\,(0.01) + 700\,(0.02) + 1200\,(0.02) + 1700\,(0.15) +$

$$2200\,(0.30) + 2700\,(0.30) + 3200\,(0.15) + 37000\,(0.02) + 4200$$

$$(0.02) + 4700\,(0.01) = \underline{2450}$$

Thus, expected total loss is K2450 for both firms

(b) Firm A: $S^2 = (0 - 2450)^2 \, 0.01 + (500 - 2450)^2 \, 0.01 + (1000 - 2450)^2 \, 0.01 +$

$$(1500 - 2450)^2 \, 0.02 + (2000 - 2450)^2 \, 0.35 + (2500 - 2450)^2 \, 0.30 +$$

$$(3000 - 2450)^2 + (3500 - 2450)^2 \, 0.20 + (4000 - 2450)^2 \, 0.01 +$$

$$(4500 - 2450)^2 \, 0.01 + (5000 - 2450)^2 \, 0.01$$

$$= 21\,9950$$

$$S = 468.99$$

Firm B, $S^2 = (0 - 2450)^2 \, 0.00 + (200 - 2450)^2 \, 0.01 + (700 - 2450)^2 \, 0.02 + (1700 -$

$$2450)^2 \, 0.15 + (2200 - 2450)^2 \, 0.30 + (2700 - 2450)^2 \, 0.30 +$$

$$(3200 - 2450)^2 \, 0.15 + (3700 - 2450)^2 \, 0.02 + (4200 - 2450)^2 \, 0.02 +$$

$$(4700 - 2450)^2 \, 0.01$$

$$= 0$$

$$S = 0$$

Firm B faces the greater risk of physical damage to its fleet next year.

(c) Pure risk. No chance of gain.

6. (a) K2 $(0.6) - 2(0.2) = $ K0.80.

(b) No. Expected value is K0.80 while the change is K2.

7. (a) E $(x) = 10\,(0.10) + 20\,(0.25) + 30\,(0.30) + 40\,(0.20) + 50\,(0.10) + 60\,(0.05)$

$$= 31$$

(b) $S^2 = (10 - 31)^2 \, 0.10 + (20 - 31)^2 \, 0.25 + (30 - 35)^2 \, 0.30 + (40 - 31)^2 \, 0.20$

$$+ (50 - 31)^2 \, 0.10 + (60 - 31)^2 \, 0.05 = 169$$

(c) $S = \sqrt{169} = 13$

(d) $31 \pm 2(13)$

31 ± 26

$\underline{5 \text{ to } 57}$

8. (a) An estimator is said to be unbiased if its expected value is equal to that of the population parameter i.e.

$E(\bar{x}) = \mu$ in the case of the sample mean $(\bar{x})$

$\hat{\mu}_1 = \dfrac{3 x_1 + x_2 + 5 x^3}{9}$

$= E(\hat{\mu}_1) = \dfrac{E(3x_1 + x_2 + 5x_3)}{9}$

$= \dfrac{1}{9} \left(3E(x_1) + E(x_2) + 5E(x_3) \right)$

$= \dfrac{3\mu + \mu + 5\mu}{9} = \mu$

$\hat{\mu}_2 = \dfrac{x_1 + 7x_2 + x_3}{9}$

$E(\hat{\mu}) = E \dfrac{x_1 + 7x_2 + x_3}{9}$

$= \dfrac{1}{9} E x_1 + 7x_2 + x_3$

$E(\hat{\mu}_2) = E \dfrac{x_1 + 7x_2 + x_3}{9}$

$= \dfrac{1}{9} E(x_1 + 7E(x_2 + x_3))$

$$= \frac{1}{9} [E(x_1) + 7E(x_2) + E(x_3)]$$

$$= \frac{1}{9} [\mu + 7\mu + \mu] = \mu$$

Therefore both estimators are unbiased. (Take note of the use of expectation rules).

(b) An estimator is more efficient if it has the smallest variance.

$$Var(\hat{\mu_1}) = \frac{1}{81} [var(x_1) + Var(x_2) + 25 Var(x_3)]$$

$$= \frac{1}{81} (9\sigma^2 + \sigma^2 + 25\sigma^2)$$

$$= \frac{15\sigma^2}{81}$$

$$Var(\hat{\mu}) = \frac{1}{81} [Var(x_1) + 49 Var(x_2) + Var(x_3)]$$

$$= \frac{1}{81} [\sigma^2 + 49\sigma^2 + \sigma^2]$$

$$= \frac{51\sigma^2}{81}$$

Since $Var(\hat{\mu_1}) < Var(\hat{\mu_2})$, then $\hat{\mu_1}$ is a more efficient estimator than $\hat{\mu_2}$.

(c) Relative efficiency $= \dfrac{Var(\hat{\mu_1})}{Var(\hat{\mu_2})} = \dfrac{15}{81} . \dfrac{81}{51} = \dfrac{15}{51} = 29.4\%$

Alternatively, relative efficiency $= \dfrac{Var(\hat{\mu_1})}{Var(\hat{\mu_2})} = \dfrac{81}{15} = 540\%$

(d) Since we have observations, this is:

$$\hat{\mu} = \frac{x_1 + x_2 + x_3}{3} = \bar{x}$$

9. Sufficiency, efficiency, unbiasedness and consistency.

10. (a) Standard error is the standard deviation of the sampling distribution

(b) $Se = \dfrac{S}{\sqrt{n}} = \dfrac{12}{\sqrt{25}} = 2.4$

11. Central limit theorem is a concept which assures us that as the sample size increases, the distribution approaches normal regardless of the shape of the distribution from which the sample has been drawn. It allows us to use the normal distribution table in statistical analysis

12. (a) Point estimate is above a population parameter e.g. mean = 25

(b) Interval estimate is an estimate where the statistician is confident of including the parameter e.g. 2 + 1.96Se

PROGRESS CLINIC EIGHT SOLUTIONS

1. This is a proportion

$$P = \frac{40}{100} = 0.4, q = 1 - 0.4 = 0.6, n = 200$$

Ho: $\hat{P} = 0.4$

Ha: $\hat{P} < 0.4$

$\alpha = 0.05$

Critical Z value = 1.64

Rejection if Zc < ‾1.64

$$Zc = \frac{p - \hat{p}}{\sqrt{\dfrac{Pq}{n}}} = \frac{0.35 - 0.4}{\sqrt{\dfrac{(0.4)(0.6)}{200}}} = ‾1.44$$

Conclusion: Accept Ho at $\alpha = 0.05$ since Zc of -1.44 is greater than critical Z of ‾1.64.

Note: $p = \frac{70}{200} = 0.35$

2. $n = 500, x = \frac{20}{500}, \hat{P} = 20 = \frac{2}{50}, q = \frac{48}{50}$

$$\hat{P} + Z\alpha/2 \sqrt{\frac{\hat{p}\hat{q}}{n}}$$

$$0.04 \pm 1.96 \sqrt{(0.02)(0.96)}$$

$$0.04 \pm 1.96 (0.00876)$$

0.04 ± 0.017

0.023 to 0.057

3. $\hat{P} = 2 = 0.08$, $q = 1 - 0.08 = 0.02$, $n = 500$ 95% confidence level is:

$$P \pm Z_{\alpha/2} \sqrt{\frac{pq}{n}}$$

$$= 0.08 \pm 1.96 \sqrt{\frac{0.08\,(0.02)}{500}}$$

$$= 0.08 \pm 0.02432$$

$$= 0.0558 \text{ to } 0.1042$$

4. $\bar{x} = 12.2$, $S = 10$, $n = 100$

       (a) The 90% confidence interval is given by:

$$\bar{X} = + Z_{\alpha/2} \left(\frac{S}{\sqrt{n}} \right)$$

$$12.2 \pm 1.645 \left(\frac{10}{\sqrt{100}} \right)$$

$$12.2 \pm 1.645$$

$$10.555 \text{ to } 13.845$$

       (b) For a 99% confidence interval we have $Z_{\alpha/2} = 2.575$

Using $Z_{\alpha/2}\left(\dfrac{\sigma}{\sqrt{n}}\right) = B$

$$2.575\left(\dfrac{10}{\sqrt{n}}\right) = 2$$

$$\sqrt{n} = \dfrac{2.575\ (10)}{2} = 12.875$$

$$n = (12.875)^2 = 165.8$$

Thus, 166 files must would be needed.

(c) Ho: $\mu = 10.9$
  Ha: $\mu => 10.9$
  $\alpha = 0.05$
  Critical Z value = 1.645
  Reject Ho if Zc > 1.645

$$Zc = \dfrac{\overline{x} - \mu}{s/\sqrt{n}} = \dfrac{12.2 - 10.9}{10/\sqrt{1000}} = \dfrac{1.3}{1} = 1.3$$

Conclusion: The Zc falls in the acceptance region hence we accept Ho.

Decision: No. Data evidence shows that the mean number of sick days taken by employees is 10.9 days.

P – value = (Z > 1.3) = 0.5 – 0.4032 = 0.0968

(d) $\overline{x} = \dfrac{11 + 15 + 4 + 0 + 22 + 12}{6} = \dfrac{64}{6} = 10.7$

$\Sigma x = 64$

$\Sigma x^2 = (11)^2 + (15)^2 + (4)^2 + (0)^2 + (22)^2 + (12)^2 = 990$

$$S = \sqrt{\dfrac{\Sigma x^2 - (\Sigma x)^2/n}{n-1}} = \sqrt{\dfrac{990 - (64)^2/6}{6-1}} = 7.8$$

. Ho: $\mu = \mu_0$

. Ha: $\mu \neq \mu_0$

. $\alpha = \dfrac{t0.05}{2} = 0.025$

.df $= n - 1 = 6 - 1 = 5$

Critical t value = 2.571

Reject Ho if tc < -2.571 or tc > 2.571

$Tc = \dfrac{x - \mu_0}{s/\sqrt{n}} = \dfrac{12.2 - 10.7}{7.8/\sqrt{6}} = 0.47$

Conclusion: The tc falls within the acceptance region hence we accept Ho at
$\alpha = 0.05$

5. $\bar{x} = 2.001,$ $\mu = 2.0,$ n = 50,   S = 0.003

. Ho: $\mu = 2.0$
. Ha: $\mu > 2.0$ (indication of "more than")
. $\alpha = 0.05$
. Critical Z value = 1.64
. Reject if Zc > 1.64

. $Zc = \dfrac{\bar{x} - \mu}{S/\sqrt{n}} = \dfrac{2.001 - 2.0}{0.003/\sqrt{50}} = 2.36$

Conclusion : Since 2.36 > 1.64, we reject Ho at $\alpha = 0.05$
Decision: Sample evidence does suggest that the machine is set too high.

6. $\bar{x} = 57.1$kg, and $\mu = 60$kg, n= 50, S = 10

Ho: $\mu = 60$
Ha: $\mu \neq 60$
$\alpha = 0.05$
Critical Zc < -196 or Zc > 1.96

$Zc = \dfrac{\bar{x} - \mu}{} = \dfrac{57.1 - 60}{} = \text{-}2.05$

$$\frac{S/\sqrt{n}} \qquad \frac{10/\sqrt{50}}$$

P- value = 2p (Z > ̄2.05) = 2 (0.5 – 0.4798) = 0.0404.

Conclusion: We reject Ho and conclude that there is enough statistical evidence to indicate that the belief that μ is = 60 is wrong.

7. $\bar{x} = 71$, $\mu = 65$, $n = 30$, $S = 12.5$

Ho: $\mu = 65$
Ha: $\mu \neq 65$
$\alpha = 0.01$
Critical Z value = 2.58
Reject if Zc < -2.58 or Zc > 2.58

$$Zc = \frac{x - \mu}{S/\sqrt{n}} = \frac{71 - 65}{12.5/\sqrt{30}} = 2.63$$

Conclusion: Since Zc of 2.63 > 2.58, we reject Ho at α = 0.01.

Decision: Yes it appears that the PCBF candidates did perform differently from other candidates.

8. $\bar{x} = 15.56$, $\mu = 18$, $n = 9$, $S = 2.51$

Ho: $\mu = 18$
Ha: $\mu = 18$
$\alpha = 0.05$

df = (n – 1) = (q – 1) = 8
Critical t value = 1.860
Reject if tc < -1.860 or tc > 1.860

$$Tc = \frac{x - \mu}{S/\sqrt{n}} = \frac{15.56 - 18}{2.51/\sqrt{9}} = 2.92$$

Conclusion: since tc of 2.92 > 1.860, we reject Ho at α = 0.05
Decision: Customers' complaints are justified

9. This is a proportion with $\hat{p} = 0.6$, $q = 0.4$, $n = 500$

Ho: $p = 60$
Ha: $p \neq 60$
$\alpha = 0.01$
Critical Z value = 2.58
Reject if Zc < ⁻2.58 or Zc > 2.58

$$Zc = \frac{P - P}{\sqrt{\frac{[p_0(1 - p_0)]}{n}}} = \frac{0.55 - 0.6}{\sqrt{\frac{(0.6)(0.4)}{500}}} = ⁻2.282$$

Conclusion: Accept Ho at $\alpha = 0.01$ since the Zc of ⁻2.282 > ⁻2.58.

Decision: The mobile phone provider's claim is justified.

10. $\bar{x} = 6.2$, $\mu = 6.4$, $S = 1.1$, $n = 8$

Ho: $\mu = 6.4$
Ha: $\mu > 6.4$
$\alpha = 0.05$
$df = n - 1 = 8 - 1 = 7$
Critical t value = 1.895
Reject if tc > 1.895

$$t = \frac{x - \mu}{S/\sqrt{n}} = \frac{6.2 - 6.4}{1.1/\sqrt{8}} = \frac{⁻0.2}{0.39} = 0.51$$

Conclusion: The tc falls in the acceptance region hence we accept Ho at $\alpha = 0.05$

Decision: New process reduced the average training time.

PROGRESS CLINIC NINE SOLUTIONS

1.   (a) This is a large sample inference about the difference between two population means involving independent sampling.

Ho: $\mu_1 = \mu_2$
Ha: $\mu_1 < \mu_2$
$\alpha = 0.05$
Critical Z value = 1.645

Reject if Zc < -1.645

$$Zc = \frac{\bar{x}_1 - \bar{x}_2}{\sqrt{\dfrac{\sigma^2_1}{n_1} + \dfrac{\sigma^2_2}{n_2}}} = \frac{25.4 - 27.3}{\sqrt{\dfrac{(3.1)^2}{50} + \dfrac{(3.7)^2}{50}}} = \frac{^-1.9}{0.6826} = {}^-2.78$$

Conclusion: Zc = ⁻8.28 falls in the rejection region hence we reject Ho at α = 0.05.

Decision: Data provide sufficient evidence to indicate that the mean unloading time for the new machine is less than the mean unloading time for the method currently in use.

(b) P – value = 0.0027 i.e. 0.5 – 0.4973 (Note: 2.78 corresponds to 0.4973)

(c) A 90% confidence interval is:

$$(\bar{x}_1 - \bar{x}_2) \pm Z\frac{\alpha}{2} \sqrt{\frac{\sigma^2_1}{n_1} + \frac{\sigma^2_2}{n_2}}$$

(25.4 - 27.3) $\pm$ 1.645 (0.6826)

⁻1.9 $\pm$ 1.122877

⁻3.02 to ⁻078

2.   Ho: $\mu_1 = \mu_2$
Ha: $\mu_1 < \mu_2$
α = 0.05
Critical Z value = 1.645
Reject if Zc < ⁻1.645

$$Zc = \frac{(\bar{x}_1 - \bar{x}_2)}{\sqrt{\dfrac{\sigma^2_1}{n_1} \quad \dfrac{\sigma^2_2}{n_2}}} = \frac{7.295 - 14.666}{\sqrt{\dfrac{(7.374)^2}{44} + \dfrac{(16.089)^2}{44}}} = \frac{^-7.371}{2.696} = {}^-2.73$$

Conclusion: the Zc = ‾2.73 falls in the rejection region hence we reject Ho at α = 0.05.

Decision: Yes Data provides evidence that the earnings per share ratios for "merged" firms is generally smaller.

(b)   P – value= $0.5 – (Z = 2.73)$ $0.5 – 0.4968 = 0.0032$

(c) Two samples were randomly selected in an independent manner from the two populations.

(d) No. For normal distribution, the mean is always greater than the standard deviation. For data given this is not the case.

3. (a) Ho: $\mu_1 = \mu_2$
     Ha: $\mu_1 \neq \mu_2$
     $\alpha = \dfrac{0.05}{2}$

   $df = n_1 + n_2 = 27 + 23 – 2 = 48$
   Critical t value = $t.025,48 = 0$ (t- table cannot give the value).
   Reject if $t_c <$

$$t_c = \frac{\overline{x}_1 - \overline{x}_2}{\sqrt{\dfrac{(n_1 – 1)\, S^2_1 + (n_2 – 1)\, S^2_2}{n_1 + n_2 \ - 2}} \ \sqrt{\dfrac{1}{n_1} + \dfrac{1}{n_2}}}$$

$$= \frac{‾04091 - ‾(0.037)}{\sqrt{\dfrac{(27 – 1)\,(0.009800) \ + \ (23 – 1)\ \ (0.002465)}{27 + 23 – 2}} \ \sqrt{\dfrac{1}{27} + \dfrac{1}{23}}} = -13.47$$

Conclusion: Since ...... falls in the .... region, we ....
                       Ho at α = 0.05
Decision:

(b) $(\overline{x}_1 - \overline{x}_2) + t\dfrac{\alpha}{2} \sqrt{S^2_p \left(\dfrac{1}{n_1} + \dfrac{1}{n_2} \right)}$

4. The unbiased estimator of σ2 is the pooled variance given by:

$$S2p = \frac{(n_1 – 1)\, S^2_1 + (n_2 – 1)\, S^2_2 + (n_3 – 1)\, S_3^2 + (n_4 – 1)\, S^2_4}{n_1 + n_2 + n_3 + n_4 \ \text{-} \ 4}$$

$$= \frac{(15-1)(0.02)^2 + (20-1)(0.05)^2 + (35-1)(0.15)^2 + (40-1)(0.12)^2}{15+20+35+40-2}$$

$$= \frac{0.0056 + 0.0475 + 0.765 + 0.5616}{106}$$

$$= \frac{1.3797}{106}$$

$$= \underline{0.013}$$

5. Ho: $\mu_1 = \mu_2$
   Ha: $\mu_1 \neq \mu_2$
   $\alpha = 0.025$ i.e. $t_{\alpha/2} = t_{0.05/2} = 0.025$

   $df = n_1 + n_2 - 2 = 6 + 8 - 2 = 12$
   Critical t value $= 2.179$
   Reject if $t_c < 2179$ or $tc > 2.179$

$$t_c = \frac{\bar{X}_1 - \bar{X}_2}{\sqrt{\frac{(n_1-1)S^2_1 + (n_2-1)S_2^2}{n1+n_2-2}} \sqrt{\frac{1}{n_1} + \frac{1}{n_2}}}$$

$$= \frac{35-27}{\sqrt{\frac{(6-1)(6)^2 + (8-1)(7)^2}{6+8-2}} \sqrt{\frac{1}{6} + \frac{1}{8}}} = 2.24$$

Conclusion: Since 2.24 falls in the rejection region, we reject Ho at $\alpha = 0.05$

Decision: The sample evidence suggests that there is significant difference in the performance of the two training methods.

6. This is a paired difference experiment

Person	Before x_1	After x_2	Difference d1	d^2
1	83	92	⁻9	81
2	60	71	⁻11	121
3	55	56	⁻1	1
4	99	104	⁻5	25
5	77	89	⁻12	144
			⁻38	372

$$. \sum_{J=1}^{n} x_{Di} = {}^{-}38$$

$$. \sum_{J=1}^{n} x^2_{Di} = 372$$

(a) $\bar{x}_D = \dfrac{\sum x_{Di}}{n_D} = \dfrac{{}^{-}38}{5} = {}^{-}7.6$

$$S_D = \sqrt{\dfrac{\sum x_{Di} - (\sum x_D)^2/n_D}{n_D - 1}} = \sqrt{\dfrac{372 - ({}^{-}38)^2/5}{5 - 1}} = 4.56$$

(b) Proof that $\bar{x}_D = \bar{x}_1 - \bar{x}_2$

$. \bar{x}_1 = \sum_{J=1}^{5} \dfrac{xi}{5} = \dfrac{83 + 60 + 55 + 99 + 77}{5} = \dfrac{374}{5} = 74.8$

$. \bar{x}_2 = \sum_{J=1}^{5} \dfrac{xi}{5} = \dfrac{92 + 71 + 56 + 104 + 89}{5} = \dfrac{412}{5} = 82.4$

$\bar{x}_1 - x_2 = 74.8 - 82.4 = {}^{-}7.6$

(c) . Population is normally distributed
. population is randomly selected
. Persons are similar in many respects.

(d) Ho: $\mu_1 = \mu_2$
Ha: $\mu_1 \neq \mu_2$
$\alpha = \dfrac{t.05}{2} = 0.025$, df $= (n_D - 1) = 5 - 1 = 4$

Critical t value $= 2.776$
Reject if tc < -2.776 or tc > 2.776

$$ t = \dfrac{x_D}{S_D \sqrt{n_D}} = \dfrac{^-7.6}{4.56\sqrt{5}} = \dfrac{^-7.6}{2.04} = ^-3.73 $$

Conclusion: The tc falls in the rejection region hence we reject Ho at $\alpha = 0.05$

Decision: We conclude that $\mu_1 \neq \mu_2$

(e) The 95% confidence interval for μ_D is:

$$ \overline{x}_D \pm t\,\alpha/2 \left(\dfrac{S_D}{\sqrt{n_D}} \right) $$

$$ ^-7.6 \pm 2.776 \left(\dfrac{4.56}{\sqrt{5}} \right) $$

$^-7.6 \pm 5.66$

$^-13.26$ to $^-1.93$

7. This is a paired difference experiment

Day	Store 1	Store 2	x_D	x_D^2
Monday	140	100	40	1600
Tuesday	95	60	356	1225
Wednesday	75	65	10	100
Thursday	65	41	24	576
Friday	85	64	21	441
Saturday	155	114	41	1681
Sunday	132	111	21	441
			192	6064

$$. \bar{x}_D = \frac{\sum x_D}{n_D} = \frac{192}{7} = 27.43$$

$$.SD = \sqrt{\frac{\sum x_D^2 - (\sum x_D)^2/n}{n_D - 1}} = \sqrt{\frac{6064 - (192)2/7}{7-1}} = 11.53$$

The 95% confidence interval for $\mu_1 - \mu_2$ is:

$$\bar{x}_D + t\alpha/2 \left(\frac{S_D}{\sqrt{n_D}} \right)$$

$$27.43 + 2.447 \left(\frac{11.53}{\sqrt{7}} \right)$$

$$27.43 + 10.66$$

16.77 to 38.09

a)

Pair	x_1	x_2	x_D	x_{D2}
1	55	44	11	121
2	68	55	13	169
3	40	25	15	225
4	55	56	-1	1
5	75	62	13	169
6	52	38	14	196
7	49	31	18	324
			83	1205

$$\bar{x}_D = \frac{83}{7} = 11.86 \qquad x_D^2 = 1205$$

$$S^2_D = \frac{\sum x^2_{Di} - (\sum x_{Di})^2/n}{n_D - 1} = \frac{1205 - (83)^2/7}{7 - 1} = 36.81$$

$$S_D = \sqrt{36.81} = 6.067$$

Ho: $\mu_D = 10$

Ha: $\mu_D \neq 10$

$\alpha = 0.05 = 0.025$

df $= (n_D - 1) = (7 - 1) = 6$

Critical t value = 2.447

Reject Ho if tc $< ^-2.447$ or tc > 2.447

$$tc = \frac{\bar{x}_D}{S_D\sqrt{n}} = \frac{11.86}{6.067\sqrt{7}} = \frac{11.86}{2.29} = 5.18$$

Conclusion: The tc falls in the rejection region hence we reject Ho at $\alpha = 0.05$

Decision: $\mu_D \neq 10$

(b) P – value = 2p (<5.18) = 2 2 (0.5 – 0.0005) = 0.999.

Note: From t table, the figure closest to 5.18 is 5.4079 which occurs under 0.0005.

9. (a) Ho: $\mu_1 = \mu_2$
    Ha: $\mu_1 \neq \mu_2$

$\alpha = \dfrac{t0.05}{2} = 0.025$

$df = (n_D - 1) = 6 - 1 = 5$
Critical t value = 2.571
Reject Ho tc $> {}^-2.571$ or tc > 2.571

Car number	Manufacturer's shock	competitor's shock	d	d^2
1	8.8	8.4	0.4	0.16
2	10.5	10.1	0.4	0.16
3	12.5	12.0	0.5	0.25
4	9.7	9.3	0.4	0.16
5	9.6	9.0	0.6	0.36
6	13.2	13.0	0.2	0.04

1.13

$$\sum_{j=1}^{6} \bar{x}_D = \frac{2.5}{6} = 0.42$$

$$. \ S_D = \sqrt{\frac{\sum x^2_D - (\sum x_D)^2 / n_D}{n_D - 1}} = \sqrt{\frac{1.13 - (2.5)^2/6}{6 - 1}} = 0.13$$

$$tc = \frac{\bar{x}_D}{S_D / \sqrt{n_D}} = \frac{0.42}{0.13 / \sqrt{6}} = 7.82$$

Conclusion: The tc falls in the rejection region hence we reject Ho at $\alpha = 0.05$.

Decision : There is a difference in the durability of the two shocks.

(b) P – value < 0.01

(c) . independent samples
     . similarity of samples
     . normally distributed samples

(d) $x_D \pm t\alpha/2 \left(\dfrac{S_D}{\sqrt{n_D}} \right)$

$0.42 \pm 2.517 \left(\dfrac{0.13}{\sqrt{6}} \right)$

$0.42 \pm 2.571 \,(0.053)$

0.42 ± 0.136263

0.28 to 0.56

(e) i) Ho: $\mu_1 = \mu_2$
  Ha: $\mu_1 \neq \mu_2$
  $\alpha = \dfrac{t0.05}{2} = 0.025$

  df $= n_1 + n_2 - 2 = 6 + 6 - 2 = 10$
  Critical t value $= 2.228$
  Reject Ho if tc < -2.228

$tc = \dfrac{\overline{x}_1 - \overline{x}_2}{\sqrt{\dfrac{(n_1-1)\,S^2_1 + (n_2-1)\,S^2_2}{n_1 - n_2 - 2}}} = \dfrac{10.72 - 10.3 = 0.42 = 0.22}{\sqrt{\dfrac{(6-1)\,(1.92)^2 + (6-1)\,(1.82)^2}{6 + 6 - 2}}}$

$= \dfrac{0.42}{1.87} = 0.22$

$\overline{x}_1 = \dfrac{64.3}{6} = 10.72$ $\qquad$ $\overline{x}_2 = \dfrac{618}{6} = 10.3$

$\sum x_1 = 64.3$ $\qquad\qquad$ $\sum x_2 = 61.8$

$\sum x_1^2 = 704.43$ $\qquad\qquad$ $\sum x_2^2 = 653.06$

$$S_1 \sqrt{\frac{704.43 - (64.3)^2/6}{6-1}} \qquad S_2 = \sqrt{\frac{653.06 - (61.8)^2/6}{6-1}}$$

$$= 1.92 \qquad\qquad = 1.82$$

Conclusion: The calculated t value falls in the acceptance region hence we accept Ho at $\alpha = 0.05$.

Decision: Data not provide sufficient evidence to indicate a difference between the mean strengths for the two types of shocks.

ii) The 95% confidence interval for $(\mu_1 - \mu_2$ is:

$$(\overline{x}_1 - \overline{x}_2) \pm t\alpha\Big/_2 \sqrt{S_p^2 \; \frac{1}{n_1} + \frac{1}{n_2}}$$

$$(10.72 - 10.3) \pm 2.228 \sqrt{1.87 \; \frac{1}{6} + \frac{1}{6}}$$

$$0.42 \pm 1.759$$

$$^-1.339 \text{ to } 2.179$$

iii) The one obtained on (d). Pairing. Paired difference experiment interval because of blocking.

iv) Yes. However, more meaning could be obtained by pairing them.

10. (a) Ho: $\mu_1 = \mu_2$
   Ha: $\mu_1 > \mu_2$ (key word is 'greater')
   $\alpha = 0.10$
   critical Z value = 1.28
   Reject if Zc > 1.28

$$Zc = \frac{\overline{x}_1 - \overline{x}_2}{\sqrt{\frac{\sigma_1^2}{n_1} \; \frac{\sigma_2^2}{n_2}}} = \frac{2.2 - 1.8}{\sqrt{\frac{(1.15)^2}{40} + \frac{(1.10)^2}{50}}} = \frac{0.4}{0.24} = 1.67$$

Conclusion: The calculate Z falls in the rejection region hence we reject Ho at α = 0.10

Decision: The average number of services used by bank 1's customers is significantly greater than the average number of services by bank 2's customers.

(b) A 99% confidence interval for $(\mu_1 - \mu_2)$ is

$$\bar{x}_1 - \bar{x}_2 \pm Z\alpha/2 \sqrt{\frac{\sigma_1^2}{n_1} + \frac{\sigma_2^2}{n_2}}$$

$$(2 - 2 - 1.8) + 2.58 \sqrt{\frac{(1.15)^2}{40} + \frac{(1.10)^2}{50}} = 0.4 + 0.616$$

Yes. The mean difference in the average number of services fall in the interval ⁻0.216 to 1.016

11. This is a paired difference experiment.

Ho: $\mu_D = 0$
Ha: $\mu_D < 0$
α = 0.10
df = $n_D - 1 = 10 - 1 = 9$
Critical t value = 1.383
Reject if tc < ⁻1.383

Before training	After training	Difference (x_D)	x_D^2
63	78	-15	225
93	92	1	1
84	91	-7	49
72	80	-8	64
65	69	-4	16
72	85	-13	169
91	99	-8	64
84	82	-2	4
71	81	-10	100
80	87	-7	49
		-69	741

$$\sum_{i=1}^{10}\overline{x}_{Di} = 6.9, \qquad \sum_{i=1}^{10} x_{Di} = \bar{}69$$

$$S2D = \frac{\sum x^2_D - (\sum x_{Di})^2/n_D}{n_D - 1} = \frac{741 - (\bar{}69)2/10}{10 - 1} = 29.43$$

$$S_D = \sqrt{29.43} = 5.43$$

$$t = \frac{\overline{x}_D}{S_D/\sqrt{n_D}} = \frac{\bar{}69}{5.43/\sqrt{10}} = \bar{}4.02$$

(b) P – value < 0.005

. Conclusion: Reject Ho at $\alpha = 0.10$

. Decision: Yes: Data provide evidence that the training programme is effective in increasing supervisory skills, as measured by the examination scores.

12. Ho: $P_A = P_B$
 Ha: $P_A \neq P_B$
 $\alpha = 0.10$
 critical Z value < $\bar{}1.64$ or Zc > 1.64

$$Zc = \frac{P_A - P_B}{\sqrt{(Pq)\left(\frac{1}{n_A} + \frac{1}{n_B}\right)}} = \frac{0.5 - 0.6}{\sqrt{0.52\,(0.48)\left(\frac{1}{400} + \frac{1}{100}\right)}} = \bar{}1.79$$

Note: $P = \frac{n_A P_A + n_B P_B}{n_A + n_B} = \frac{400\,(0.5) + 100\,(0.6)}{400 + 100} = 0.52$

Conclusion: Since the Zc is less than the critical Z, we reject Ho at $\alpha = 0.10$

Decision: The two groups differ.

13. (a) $n_A = 400$, $x_A = 50$, $n_B = 400$, $x_B = 73$

$$\hat{P}_A = \frac{x_A}{n_A} = \frac{50}{400} = 0.125 \qquad \hat{P}_B = \frac{x_B}{n_B} = \frac{73}{400} = 0.1825$$

Ho: $P_A = P_B$

Ha: $P_A \neq P_B$

$$\hat{P} = \frac{50 + 73}{400 + 400} = \frac{123}{800} = 0.15375$$

$$\hat{q} = 0.84652$$

$$Z = \frac{P_A - P_B}{\sqrt{\dfrac{\overline{Pq}}{n_1 + n_2}}} = \frac{0.125 - 0.1825}{\sqrt{\dfrac{(0.115375)(0.84625)}{400 + 400}}} = \frac{^-0.0575}{0.01275} = {}^-4.51$$

$\alpha = 0.01$

Critical Z value = 2.58

Reject if Zc < $^-$2.85 or Zc > 2.58

Conclusion: Since Zc = $^-$4.51 is less than $^-$2.58, we reject Ho.

(b) P (Zc < $^-$4.51) = 0. Since p – value = 0 < at α = 0.01, we reject Ho and conclude that there are significant differences between the error rate for two auditors at α = 0.01.

PROGRESS CLINIC TEN SOLUTIONS

1. Ho: Cellular phone ownership is independent of age.

Ha: Cellular phone ownership is dependent on age.

α = 0.05

df = (r – 1) (k – 1) = (2 – 1) (4 – 1) = 3

Critical x^2 = 7.815

fo	fe	$(fo - fe)^2$	x^2
50	62.5	156.25	2.5
80	62.5	306.25	4.9
70	62.5	56.25	0.9

fo	fe		x^2
50	62.5	156.25	2.5
200	62.5	156.25	0.8
170	187.5	306.25	1.6
180	187.5	56.25	0.3
200	187.5	156.25	0.8
1000	1000		$x^2 = 14.3$

Conclusion: The calculated x^2 value falls in the rejection region hence we reject Ho at $\alpha = 0.05$

Decision: Cellular phone ownership is dependent on age

2. Ho: $P_1 = P_2 = P_3 = \dfrac{1}{6}$

   Ha: One of them is different

   $\alpha = 0.05$
   $df = (r - 1)(k - 1) = (2 - 1)(6 - 1) = 5$
   Critical $x^2 = 11.0705$
   Reject if $x^2_c > 11.0705$

fo	fe	$(fo - fe)$	x^2
10	16	36	2.25
16	16	0	0
21	16	25	1.5625
15	16	1	0.0625
18	16	4	0.25
16	16	0	0
96	96		$x^2 = 4.125$

Conclusion: The calculated x^2 value is less than the critical value i.e. falls in the acceptance region hence we accept Ho at $\alpha = 0.05$

Decision: We conclude that the die is unbiased.

3. Ho: there is no relationship between career progression and character i.e. The variables are independent.

   Ha: There is a relationship between career progression and characters i.e. the variables are dependent.

$\alpha = 0.05$
$df = (r-1)(k-1) = (3-1)(4-1) = 6$
Critical $x^2 = 12.5916$

Reject Ho if $x^2_c > 12.5916$

fo	fe	x^2
48	34.19	5.58
22	34.77	4.69
15	16.03	0.07
51	46.26	0.49
42	47.05	0.55
22	21.69	0.1
43	54.31	2.36
59	55.23	0.26
33	25.47	2.26
35	42.24	1.24
57	42.95	4.60
13	19.81	2.34
440	440	$x^2 = 24.45$

Conclusion: Because the test statistic ($x^2_c = 24.45$) exceeds the critical x^2 value (12.5916), the relationship between career progression and character is significant at the 5% level i.e. we reject Ho.

Decision: There is a relationship between career progression and character.

4. Ho: There is no preference in rejection of method.

   Ha: There is a preference in respect of methods

   $\alpha = 0.10$
   $df = (r-1)(k-1) = (2-1)(4-1) = 3$
   Reject if $x^2_c > 6.251$

fo	fe	$(fo - fe)^2$	$x^2 = \dfrac{(fo - fe)^2}{f}$
68	66.43	2.46	0.0370
75	79.72	22.28	0.2795
57	59.79	7.78	0.1301
79	73.07	35.16	0.4812
32	33.57	2.46	0.0733
45	40.28	22.28	0.5531
33	30.21	7.78	0.2575
31	36.93	35.16	0.9521
			$x^2 = 2.7638$

Conclusion: Reject Ho since the x^2_c is greater than the critical x^2 value.

Decision: There is a preference in respect of method of job performance reviews.

5. Ho: Length of stay and type of insurance are independent

Ha: Length of stay and type of insurance are dependent

$\alpha = 0.01$
$df = (r - 1)(k - 1) = (3 - 1) = 4$
Critical $x^2 = 13.277$

fo	fe	$fo - fe$	$x^2 = \dfrac{(fo - fe)^2}{fe}$
40	30	100	3.333
75	60	225	3.750
65	90	625	6.944
30	25	25	1.000
45	50	25	0.5000
75	75	0	0.000
40	55	225	4.091
100	110	100	0.909
190	165	625	3.788
660	660		$x^2 = 24.315$

Conclusion: The calculated x^2 value is greater that the critical x^2 value hence we reject Ho at $\alpha = 0.01$.

Decision: The length of stay and type of insurance are dependent on each other and the economist is right.

PROGRESS CLINIC ELEVEN SOLUTIONS

Note: Since the printouts have all the required figures to answer the questions, no calculations are performed here i.e. abbreviated solutions are given.

1. (a)

Source	df	SS	MS	F
Treatments	6	16.9	2.817	3.48
Error	35	28.3	0.809	
Total	42	45.2		

    (b) 7   (c) F = 3.48: yes   (d) P – value < 0.01

    (e) t = $^-$0.83, No   (f) $^-$0.4 $\pm$ 0.79   (g) 3.7 $\pm$ 0.56

2. (a) 4: 38   (b) F = 14.80: Reject Ho

   (c) Independent – samples randomly selected. Equal variances.

   (d) i) 260.1 $\pm$ 20.31   ii) $^-$87.7 $\pm$ 33.38

3. (a)

Source	df	SS	MS	F
Treatments	3	6.816	2.272	8.03
Error	105	29.710	0.283	
Total	108	36.526		

    (b) F = 8.03, yes

4. (a) F = 203, P – value = 0,   Reject Ho.

(b) . Independent samples and randomly selected.
   . Probability distributions are normal
   . Equal variances

5. (a) Worker job satisfaction: work scheduling: type of work scheduling: flextime,

   staggered and fixed: group of workers.

   (b) 571.967   (c) 7719.83

(d)

Source	df	SS	MS	F
Treatment	2	571.97	285.985	3.96
Error	107	7719.83	72.148	
Total	109	8291.80		

   (e) F = 3.96: yes

   (f) μ_1: 35.22 $\pm$ 4.18, μ_2: 30.05 $\pm$ 2.83, μ_3: 28.71 $\pm$ 4.44

6.

Source	df	SS	MS	F
Brands	3	2709.20	903.07	35.81
Error	36	907.86	25.22	
Total	39	3617.06		

   (a) 4
   (b) 40
   (c) F.10 for 3 and 36 df = 2.25. Thus, Fc > 2.25, Reject Ho.

PROGRESS CLINIC TWELVE SOLUTIONS

1. The 2000 to be year 1, 2001 to be year 2, etc.

x	y	xy	x^2
1	74	74	1
2	79	158	4
3	80	240	9
4	90	360	16
5	105	525	25
6	142	852	36
7	122	854	49
28	692	3063	140

$$b = \frac{n\sum xy - \sum x \sum y}{n\sum x^2 - (\sum x)^2} \qquad a = \frac{\sum y}{n} - b\frac{\sum x}{n}$$

$$= \frac{7(3063) - (28)(692)}{7(140) - (28)^2} \qquad = \frac{692}{7} - 10.54\left(\frac{28}{4}\right)$$

$$= \underline{10.54} \qquad = \underline{56.70}$$

(a)   Thus, y = 56.70 + 10.54 x as the required straight-line

(b)   Taking 2007 to be year 8,

Y = 56.70 + 10.54 (8)

= <u>141</u> drafts

2.

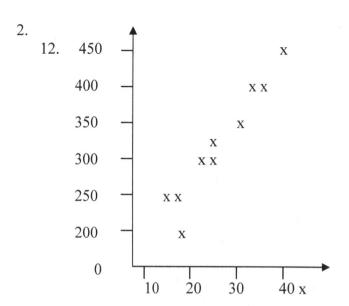

12. 450 ─
400 ─
350 ─
300 ─
250 ─
200 ─
0
10   20   30   40 x

•   There is a positive relationship

x	y	xy	x^2	y^2
15	260	3900	225	67600
18	240	4320	324	57600
21	260	4680	324	67600
23	300	6090	441	84100
23	320	6900	529	90000
26	380	7360	529	102400
28	370	9880	676	144400
32	400	10360	784	136900
37	470	12800	1024	160000
		17390	1369	160000
				220900
241	3290	83680	6225	113500

b) $b = \dfrac{n\sum xy - \sum x \sum y}{n\sum x^2 - (\sum x)^2}$ $a = \dfrac{\sum y}{n} - b\dfrac{\sum x}{n}$

$= \dfrac{10(83680) - 241(3290)}{10(6225) - (241)^2}$ $= \dfrac{3290}{10} - 10.53\left(\dfrac{241}{10}\right)$

$= \underline{10.53}$ $= \underline{75.23}$

$y = \underline{75.23 + 10.53x}$

(c) $r = \dfrac{n \sum xy - \sum x \sum y}{\sqrt{\{n \sum x^2 - (ax)^2\}\ \{n \sum y^2 - (\sum y)^2\}}}$

$= 10$

$= \underline{0.98}$

$r^2 = (0.98)^2 = 0.96\%$

About 96% of change direct labour cost is attributed to change in batch size while about 4% is attributed to other factors.

(d) $t = \dfrac{r}{\sqrt{(1 - r^2)/\,n - 2}} = \dfrac{0.98}{\sqrt{0.04\,/\,8}} = \underline{14}$

(e) $y = 75.23 + 10.53\,(25)$

$= \underline{338.48}$

3. (a) inflation (x)

x	y	xy	x^2	y^2
40	62	2480	1600	3844
38	51	1938	1444	2601
35	49	1715	1225	2401
37	55	2035	1369	3025
29	41	1189	841	1681
24	36	864	576	1296
21	36	756	441	1296
18	32	576	324	1024
13	25	325	169	625
10	20	200	100	400
265	407	12078	8089	18193

(b) $b = \dfrac{n\sum xy - \sum x \sum y}{n\sum x^2 - (\sum x)^2}$ $\qquad\qquad a = \dfrac{\sum y}{n} - b\dfrac{\sum x}{n}$

$$= \frac{10\,(12078) - (265)\,(407)}{10\,(8089) - (265)^2} \qquad\qquad = \frac{407}{10} - 1.21 \left(\frac{265}{10}\right)$$

$$= \frac{12925}{0665} \qquad\qquad\qquad\qquad = 8.64$$

$$= 1.21$$

$$y = 8.64 + 1.21x$$

(c) $y = 8.64 + 1.21\,(8)$

$$= 18.32\%$$

(d) $$r = \frac{n\sum xy - \sum x \sum y}{\sqrt{\left[\, n\sum x^2 - (\sum x)^2 \,\right]\left[\, n\sum y^2 - (\sum y)^2 \,\right]}}$$

$$= \frac{12925}{\sqrt{10665\,(16281)}}$$

$$= 0.980865\,781 = 0.98$$

(e) $r^2 = 96\%$. About 96% of the changes in interest rates are explained by changes in inflation rate while only about 4% is attributed to other factors.

(f)   The range of values used to construct the regression line is 40% to 10%. The 8% is outside this range hence extrapolation has been used which may not hold.

4.

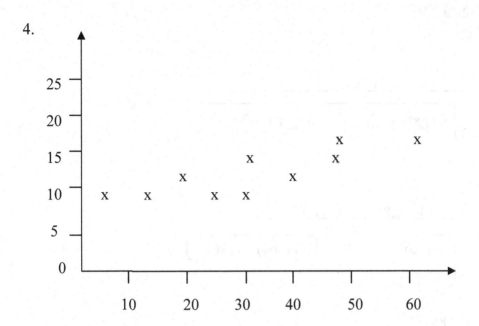

. There is a slightly positive relationship

x	y	xy	x^2	y^2
30	10	300	900	100
20	11	220	400	121
10	6	60	100	36
60	18	1080	3600	324
40	13	520	1600	169
25	10	250	625	100
13	10	130	169	100
50	20	1000	2500	400
44	17	748	1936	289
28	15	420	784	225
320	130	4728	12614	1864

(b) $b = \dfrac{n \sum xy - \sum x \sum y}{n \sum x^2 - (\sum x)^2}$ $a = \dfrac{\sum y}{n} - b \dfrac{\sum x}{n}$

$= \dfrac{10(4728) - (320)(130)}{10(12614) - (320)^2}$ $= \dfrac{130}{10} - 0.24 \left(\dfrac{320}{10} \right)$

$= \underline{0.24}$ $= \underline{5.34}$

$$y = \underline{5.34 + 0.24}$$

(c) $r^2 = \dfrac{n\sum xy - (\sum x)(\sum y)}{\sqrt{n(\sum x^2) - (\sum x)^2 \qquad n(\sum x^2) - (\sum y)^2}}$

$= \dfrac{10(4728) - (320)(130)}{\sqrt{10(12614) - (320)^2 \left[10(1864) - (130)^2\right]}}$

$= 0.88$

$r^2 = (0.88)^2 = 77\%$. About 77% of the change in electricity expenditure is explained by changes in production while about 23% is attributed to other factors.

(d) . Ho: $B_1 = 0.24$
. Ha: $B_1 \neq 0.24$
. $\alpha = 0.05/2 = 0/025$
. df $= (n - n) = 10 - 2 = 8$
. Critical t value $= 2.306$
. Reject if t calculated is < -2.306 or > 2.306

. $t = \dfrac{B_1}{S\sqrt{SS_{xx}}}$ $\qquad\qquad SS_{xx} = \sum xi^2 - \dfrac{(\sum x)^2}{n}$

$= \dfrac{0.24}{2.17\sqrt{2374}}$ $\qquad\qquad = 12614 - \dfrac{(320)^2}{10}$

$\qquad\qquad\qquad\qquad\qquad\qquad\qquad = \underline{2374}$

$= \underline{2.270}$

$$S^2 = \frac{SSE}{n-2} = \frac{37.68}{8} = \underline{4.71}$$

$$SSE = SS_{yy} - B_1 \, SS_{xy}$$

$$SS_{yy} = \sum y^2 - \frac{(\sum y)^2}{n}$$

$$= 1864 - \frac{(130)^2}{10}$$

$$= \underline{174}$$

$$SSE = SS_{yy} - B_1 \, SS_{xy}$$

$$SS_{yy} = \sum xy - \frac{(\sum y)(\sum y)}{n}$$

$$= 4728 - \frac{(320)(130)}{10}$$

$$= \underline{568}$$

$$SSE = 174 - 0.24\,(568) = 37.68$$

Thus, $S = \sqrt{4.71} = \underline{2.17}$

Conclusion: Accept Ho: at 5% level of significance

(f) $B_1 \pm t\,\alpha / 2 \; (S/\sqrt{SS_{xx}})$

$$= 0.24 \pm \frac{2.306\,(2.17)}{\sqrt{2374}}$$

$$= 0.24 \pm 0.10$$

$$= 0.14 \text{ to } 0.34. \text{ The time slope lies between 0.14 and 0.34}$$

5. (a) In linear regression $y = a + bx$

y = maintenance cost in K'000 (dependent variable)

x = production units in 1000 (independent variable)

n = 8

$\sum y = (256) + 302 + 222 + 240 + 362 + 295 + 401 + 400) = 2490$.

$\sum x = (20 + 24 + 16 + 18 + 16 + 22 + 32 + 30)\ 188$

$b = \dfrac{n\sum xy - \sum x\sum y}{n\sum x^2 - (\sum x)^2}$

$= \dfrac{(612250) - 188\,(2490)}{8(4640) - (188)^2}$

$= 12.32$

$a = \dfrac{\sum y}{n} - b\,\dfrac{\sum x}{n}$

$= \dfrac{2490}{8} - 12.32\left(\dfrac{188}{8}\right)$

$= 21.73$

Linear equation is $y = 21.73 + 12.32x$.

. Interpretation: Fixed maintenance cost per quarter is K21730 and the variable cost per unit of production is K12.32.

b) Predicted maintenance cost for the next quarter (44 000 units) is:

$y = 21.730 + (12.320 \times 44) = 563.81$ or K563810.

Major reservation about this prediction is that 44 000 units of production is well outside the range of data used to establish the linear regression equation. The data related to a range 16 000 to 32 000 units per quarter. The behaviour of costs outside this range may be quite different. For example, there may be a step in the fixed costs.

(c) The relationship between maintenance costs and production units is possible as indicated by the positive slope.

(d) Ho: $B_1 = 0$
Ha: $B_1 \neq 0$
$\alpha = 0.05/2 = 0.025$
$df = (n - 2) = 15 - 2 = 13$
Critical value t = 2.160
Reject if tc <-2.160 or tc > 2.160

$$t = \frac{\hat{B}_1}{S/\sqrt{SS_{xx}}}$$

. $SSE = \sum (y_i - \hat{y})^2 = SS_{yy} - \hat{B}_1 SS_{xy}$

$$911.51334 - (4.919331)(171.114) = 69.750929$$

. To estimate σ^2, we divide SSE by degrees of freedom available for error, $n - 2$:

$$S^2 = \frac{SSE}{n-2} = \frac{69.750929}{15-2} = 5.3655$$

$$S = \sqrt{5.3655} = 2.32$$

Thus, $t = \dfrac{\hat{B}_1}{S/\sqrt{SS_{xx}}} = \dfrac{4.919}{\sqrt{2.32/\ 34.784}} = \dfrac{4.919}{0.393} = 12.5$

This large t value leaves little doubt that the distance between the five and the fire station contributes information for the prediction of fire damage. Particularly, it appears (as we might suspect) that fire damage increases as the distance increases.

(c) A 95% confidence interval is:

$$\hat{B}_1 \pm t0.025 \ (S/\sqrt{SS_{xx}})$$

$$\pm (2.160)(0.393)$$

$$4.919 \pm 0.849$$

$$\underline{4.070 \text{ to } 5.768}$$

(d) $r = \dfrac{SS_{xy}}{\sqrt{SS_{xx}\, SS_{xy}}} = \dfrac{171.114}{\sqrt{(34.784)\,(911.517)}} = \dfrac{171.114}{178.062} = 0.96$

This high correlation provides further support for our conclusion that B_1 differs from 0: it appears that fire damage and distance from the fire station are highly correlated.

$r^2 = (0.96)^2 = 0.92$ which implies that 92% of the sum of squares of deviations of the y values about $\bar{y}$ is explained by the distance, x, between the fire and the fire station. All signs point to a strong linear relationship between y and x.

(e) A 95% prediction interval when the distance is 3.5 kilometers from the nearest fire station.

$$\hat{y} \pm t\,0.025 \quad S\sqrt{1 + \dfrac{1}{n} + \dfrac{(xp - \bar{x})}{SS_{xx}}}$$

$$27.5 \pm (2.16)\,(2.32)\sqrt{1 + \dfrac{1}{15} + \dfrac{(3.5 - 3.28)^2}{34.784}}$$

$$27.5 \pm (2.16)\,(2.32)\sqrt{1.0681}$$

$$27.5 \pm 5.2$$

$\underline{22.3 \text{ to } 32.7}$

The model yields a 95% prediction interval for fire damage in a major residential fire 3.5 kilometers from the nearest station of K22300 to K32700.

6. (a) $\hat{y} = 80.0 + 50.0x$

   b) 30

   (b) $F = \dfrac{MST}{MSE} = \dfrac{6828.6}{82.1} = 83.17$

   Ho: $B_1 = 0$

Ha: $B_1 \neq 0$

$\alpha = 0.05$

Critical F0.05, 1, 28 = 3.34

Reject if Fc > 3.384

Conclusion: Reject Ho and conclude that the relationship is significant.

(c) When x = 12

$y = 80.0 + 50.0 (12)$

$= \underline{680}$

(d) Yes: Ho accepted implying that the relationship is significant between x and y and hence a good fit.

(e) 95% confidence interval for $\hat{B_1}$:

$$\hat{B_1} \pm t\alpha\big/_2 \quad S\big/\sqrt{(SSxx)}$$

$50 \pm 2.048 (5.482)$

50 ± 11.23

$\underline{38.77 \text{ to } 61.23}$

7.

success index

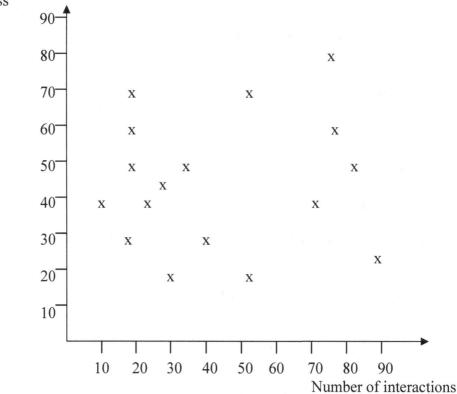

Comment: Data sets are scattered all over.

b) $\hat{B_1} = \dfrac{SS_{xy}}{SS_{xx}} = \dfrac{2561.2632}{10824.5263} = 0.2366$

$\hat{B_0} = \bar{y} - \hat{B_1}\bar{x} = 54.5789 - 0.2366\,(44.1579) = 44.13$

$\hat{y} = 44.13 + 0.2366x$

c) . $SSE = SS_{yy} - \hat{B_1}\,SS_{xy} = 7006.6316 - 0.2366\,(2561.2632)$

$\qquad = 6400.6$

. $S^2 = \dfrac{SSE}{n-2} = \dfrac{6400.6}{19-2} = 376.5$

$r^s = \qquad 376.5 \qquad = \qquad 1940$

d) Ho: $\hat{B}_1 = 0$

Ha: $\hat{B}_1 \neq 0$

$\alpha = t\alpha \Big/ 2 = 0.05 = 0.025$

df $= (n - 2) = 19 - 2 = 17$

Critical t is 2.110

Reject Ho if tc $< ^-2.110$ or tc > 2.110.

$$t = \frac{\hat{B}_1}{S/\sqrt{SS_{xx}}} = \frac{0.2366}{19.40/\sqrt{10824.5263}} = \underline{1.27}$$

Conclusion: The calculated t falls in the acceptance region hence we accept Ho at $\alpha = 0.05$

e) 95% confidence interval

$$\hat{B1} \pm t\,\alpha \quad (S/\sqrt{SSxx})$$

$$0.2366 \pm \frac{19.40}{\sqrt{108224.5263}}$$

02366 ± 0.3934

$^-0.1568$ to 0.63 the line slope lies in the range $= 0.1568$ to 0.63. The time slope lies in the range $- 0.1568$ to 0.63.

f) i. y = 44.130454 + 0.236617. It is exactly the same as that calculated in (a) when rounded off approximately.

 ii. $S^2 = \dfrac{SSE}{17} = \dfrac{6400.59407}{17} = 376.5055335$

S $= \sqrt{376.5055335} = 19.4037505$ this could have been read off from the printout directly.

iii. $r^2 = 0.0865$ from the printout

iv. t 1.27 from the printout

p – value = 0.2216 from the printout

conclusion: do not reject Ho.

(a) . $SS_{xx} = \sum xi^2 - \dfrac{(\sum xi)^2}{n} = 12150 - \dfrac{(230)^2}{5} = 1570$

. $SS_{yy} = \sum yi^2 - \dfrac{(\sum yi)^2}{n} = 12781 - \dfrac{(215)^2}{5} = 3536$

. $SS_{xy} = \sum xiyi - \dfrac{(\sum xi)(\sum yi)}{n} = 9850 - \dfrac{(230)(215)}{5} = {}^-40$

. $B_1 = \dfrac{SS_{xy}}{SS_{xx}} = \dfrac{{}^-40}{1570} = -0.025$

. $\hat{Bo} = \bar{y} - \hat{B_o} \bar{x} = \dfrac{215}{5} - (-0.025)\left(\dfrac{230}{5}\right) = 44.15$

. $y = 44.15 - 0.025x$

(d) Ho: $B_1 = 0$
Ha: $B_1 \neq 0$
α = t 0.05/2 = 0.025
df = (n – 2) = (5 – 2) = 3
Critical t value = 3.182
Reject if tc < -3.182 or tc > 3.182

$t = \dfrac{\hat{B_1}}{S/\sqrt{SS_{xx}}}$

$SSE = SS_{yy} - \hat{B_1} SS_{xy}$

$= {}^-0.025$

$= 3536 - (-0.025)({}^-40) = \underline{3535}$

$$34.33/\overline{\sqrt{1570}}$$

$$S^2 = \frac{SSE}{n-2} = \frac{3535}{3} = 1178.3$$

$$= {}^-0.03$$

$$S = \underline{34.33}$$

Conclusion: Do not reject Ho.

(c) No. It means that there is a relationship between tire price and sales volume. It means the slope provides information for the prediction of sales.

(d) $r = \dfrac{SS_{xy}}{\sqrt{SS_{xx}\,SS_{xy}}} = \dfrac{{}^-40}{\sqrt{(1570)(3536)}} = {}^-0.01697629$

$$r^2 = \underline{0.0003}$$

PROGRESS CLINIC THIRTEEN SOLUTIONS

1. You are given the following information about demand for an item:

Month	Actual	3 months moving total	3 months moving average	5 months moving total	5 months moving average
1	220	-	-	-	-
2	228	665	222	-	-
3	217	664	221	1142	228
4	219	694	231	1163	233
5	258	718	239	1174	235
6	241	738	246	1201	240
7	239	724	241	1238	248
8	244	739	246	1240	248
9	256	760	253	1264	253
10	260	781	260	-	-
11	265	-	-	-	-

2.

Month	Actual sales	3 months moving total	3 months moving average
Jan	20	-	-
Feb	21	56	19
Mar	15	50	17
April	14	42	14
May	13	43	14
Jun	16	46	15
Jul	17	51	17
Aug	18	55	18
Sep	20	58	19
Oct	20	61	20
Nov	21	64	21
Dec	23	-	-

(b) Sales were generally rising.

3.

Month	Actual applications	3 month moving total	3 month moving average
Jan	10	-	-
Feb	12	10 + 12+ 13 = 35	35 ÷ 3 = 11.67
Mar	13	12 + 13 + 16 = 41	41 ÷ 3 = 13.67
Apr	16	13 + 16 + 19 = 48	48 ÷ 3 = 16.00
May	19	19 + 23 + 26 = 58	58 ÷ 3 = 19.33
Jun	23	23 + 26 + 26 = 68	68 ÷ 3 = 22.67
Jul	26	23 + 26 + 30 = 79	79 ÷ 3 = 26.33
Aug	30	26 + 30 + 28 = 84	84 ÷ 3 = 28.00
Sep	28	30 + 28 + 18 = 76	76 ÷ 3 = 25.33
Oct	18	28 + 18 + 16 =62	62 ÷ 3 = 20.67
Nov	16	18 + 16 + 14 = 48	48 ÷ 3 = 16.00
Dec	14	-	-

4.

Year	Actual production	4 year moving total	4 year moving averages	Central averages	trend
1991	464	-	-	-	-
1992	515	1964	-	-	-
1993	518	2002	491	495.75	495.75
1994	467	2027	500.05	503.62	503.62
1995	502	2066	506.75	511.62	511.62
1996	540	2170	516.5	529.5	529.5
1997	557	2254	542.5	553.0	553.0
1998	571	2326	563.5	572.5	572.5
1999	586	-	581.5	-	-
2000	612	-	-	-	-

(b) There are no trend values corresponding to the beginning and end time points of a series in this case 1991, 1992 and 1999, 2000.

(c) (i) Trend, cyclical variations, seasonal variations and random variations.
   (ii) There is insufficient data (time series is to small)

   • There are structural breaks/anticipated futures

   • Time series assumes that historical relationships will continue in future.

PROGRESS CLINIC FOURTEEN SOLUTIONS

1. (a) Cost of living index $= \dfrac{\sum I w}{\sum w}$

$$= \frac{\{130\,(60) + 280(5) + 190\,(7) + 300\,(9) + 200\,(19)\}}{60 + 5 + 7 + 9 + 19}$$

$$= \frac{17030}{100} = \underline{170.3}$$

Thus, the cost of living index for the year 200 is 170.3

(b) 1995 = 100, the cost of living in 2000 is 170.3 Therefore=, the salary of a person in 2000 to maintain the same standard of living as in 1995 is :

$$\frac{(1,500 \times 170.3)}{100} = \underline{K2,\,554,500}$$

2.

Product	Price (p)	Profit (w)	Weighted price (wp)
A	12.7	48858	620 496.6
B	25.1	19231	482 698.0
C	19.8	24644	487 951.2
D	52.0	47712	2,481, 024.0
E	67.4	36919	2,488. 340.5
		177364	6,560,510.5

Weighted average price $= \dfrac{6\,560\,510.5}{177\,364} = K37$

3.

Material	P_0 K	P_1 K	$\dfrac{P_1}{P_0} \times 100$	w Tonnes	$\dfrac{P_1}{P_0} \times 100 \times w$
R	5800	6000	103.448	100	10344.8
S	4200	4000	95.238	40	3809.52
T	500	750	150	1000	150 000.0
	10500	10750	-	1140	164 154.32

(d) Simple price index = $\sum P_1 \times 100 = \dfrac{10750}{10500} \times 100 = \underline{102.38}$

(e) Weighted mean of price relative = $\dfrac{\sum P_1/p_0 \times 100 \times w}{\sum w}$

$$= \dfrac{164\ 154.32}{1140} = 144.00$$

(f) Simple price index takes no account of the relative importance of each item included in the construction of the index.

. Weighted price index does attempt to take relative importance into account. Prices are weighted by the quantities of the items in aggregate price indexes.

4. (a)

| | 2007 | | 2008 | |
	q_0	$p_0\ q_0$	q_1	$p_1\ q_0$
Bread	4500	5000 000	4500	5,499,999.999
Sweet potatoes	10 000	6000 000	9500	7,894,736.842
Oranges	3 000	150 000	3500	171,428.5714
	17500	11 150 000	12500	13,566,165.41

Laspeyre index = $\dfrac{13,566,165.41}{11\ 150\ 000} \times 100 = \underline{121.7}$

Note: We first needed to determine the current price (P_1). This done by dividing current total expenditure by the current quantity e.g. $\dfrac{7500\ 000}{9500} = 789.4736842$

Then $p_1q_0 = 789.4736842 \times 10\ 000 = K7, 894, 736.842$

(b) The major weakness of a Laspeyre index is that it uses a consumption pattern that may well have changed over the year! This is because when the price of a particular commodity uses considerably, there is usually some slackening in demand (providing not totally inelastic). Thus, as Laspeyre index, still using the original quantities as weight, may place too much importance on this item, and it tends to overstate the general level of price increases. An alternative is to use Paasche. However, it has its own weakness.

(c) Paasche price index = $\dfrac{\sum p_1q_1}{\sum p_0q_1} \times 100$

	2007		2008
	q_1	p_1q_0	$P_1 \, q_1$
Bread	4500	5,499,999.99	5500 000
Sweet potatoes	9500	7.894,736.842	7 500 000
Oranges	3500	171,428.5714	200 000
	12500	13,566,165.41	13,200,000

Thus, PPI = $\dfrac{13\ 200\ 000}{13566\ 165.41} \times 100 = 97.3\%$

(g) it tends to underestimate the effect of inflation and it requires up-to-date information to construct it. The alternative is to use the Fisher Index which is the square root of the product of Laspeyre and Paasche indexes.

Fisher Index = $\sqrt{\text{(Laspeyre's index) X (Paasche's index)}}$

PROGRESS CLINIC FIFTEEN SOLUTIONS

1. (a) Payoff table

	S_1	S_2	S_3
Loan	75 000 000	65 000 000	⁻30 000 000
Don't loan	60 000 000	60 000 000	60 000 000

   (b) Opportunity loss table

	S_1	S_2	S_3
Loan	0	0	36 000 000
Don't loan	15 000 000	5 000 000	0

   (c)

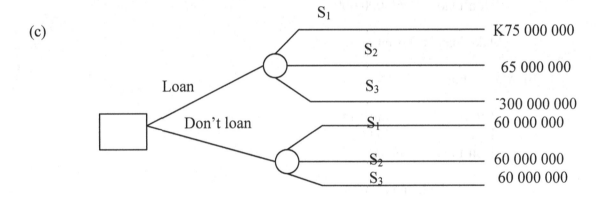

2. (a) $P(S_1) = \dfrac{1104}{1280} = 0.8625$

   $P(S_2) = \dfrac{120}{1280} = 0.09375$

   $P(S_3) = \dfrac{56}{1280} = 0.04375$

- 453 -

(b) EMV (loan) = 75 000 000 (0.8625) + 65 000 000 (0.09375) – 300 000 000

(0.04375)

= 64687500 + 6093750 – 13125000

= K57 656 250

EMV (Don't loan) = 60 000 0000 (0.08625) + 60 000 000 (0.09375)

+ 60 000 000 (0.04375)

= 51 750 000 + 562 5000 + 2625 0000

= K60 000 000

Don't make a laon deciosn is made.

3. (a) Maximax   criterion

Action	Maximum
Loan	75 000 000
Don't laon	60 000 000

Make loan is chosen.

(b) Maximum   Criterion

Action	Minimum
Loan	⁻300 000 000
Don't loan	60 000 000

Don't make loan is chosen.

(c) They concentrate on extremes leaving equally plausible alternatives like K65 000 000 unattended to.

4. (a) Payoff table

| | STATE OF NATURE | |
Action	Don't use	Use
Install	2750 000	-1
Don't install	0	0

(b) Opportunity loss table

Action	Use	Don't use
Install	0	1
Don't install	2750 000	0

(c) EOL (install) = 0 (0.5) + 1 (0.5) = 0.5

EOL (don't install) = 2750 000 (0.5) + 0 (0.5) = 1375 000

Decision: Don't install.

5. (a) payoff table

Action	Win	lose
Settle	⁻250 000 000	⁻250 000 000
Court	0	⁻1000 000 000

(b)

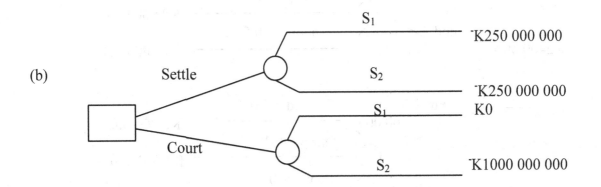

(c) Since the probability of winning = 0.2, then the probability of losing = 0.8 [i.e. 1 – 0.2]

EMV (Settle) = ¯250 000 000 (0.2) – 250 000 000 (0.8)

= ¯50 000 000 – 200 000 000

= ¯K250 000 000

EMV (court) = 0 (0.2) – 1000 000 000 (0.8) .
= 0 – 800 000 000

= ¯K800 000 000

Settle outside court will be chosen.

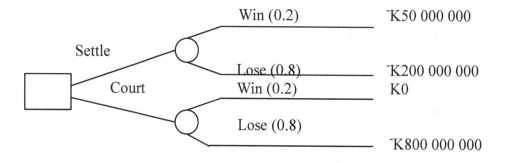

		Win (0.2)	¯K50 000 000
Settle			
	Court	Lose (0.8)	¯K200 000 000
		Win (0.2)	K0
		Lose (0.8)	
			¯K800 000 000

6. (a) The decision tree is as follows:

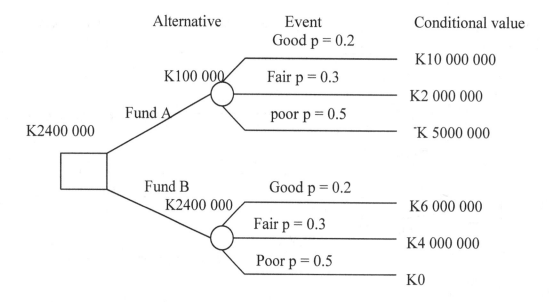

Alternative	Event	Conditional value
	Good p = 0.2	
K100 000		K10 000 000
	Fair p = 0.3	
Fund A		K2 000 000
	poor p = 0.5	
K2400 000		¯K 5000 000
Fund B	Good p = 0.2	
K2400 000		K6 000 000
	Fair p = 0.3	
		K4 000 000
	Poor p = 0.5	
		K0

(b) The expected value = conditional value X probability

For Fund A: EV = 10 000 000 (0.2) + 2000 000 (0.3) − 5000 000 (0.5)

$\qquad$ = 2 000 000 + 600 000 2500 000

$\qquad$ = K100 000

For Fund B: EV = 6 000 000 (0.2) + 4 000 000 (0.3) + 0 (0.5)

$\qquad$ = 1200 000 + 1200 000 + 0

$\qquad$ = K2400 000

The investor should choose Fund B to maximize the expected value.

(c) The expected value of Fund B is K2400 000 and if the return of Fund A is x, we can calculate the return of Fund A in a good economy as follows:

x (0.2) + 2000 000 (0.3) − 5000 000 (0.5) = 2400 000

$0.2x$ + 600 000 − 2500 000 = 2400 000

$0.2x$ − 1900 000 = 2400 000

x = K21 500 000

Thus, if the return of Fund A in a good economy is K21 500 000, the investor would be indifferent between Fund A and Fund B.

7. (a) a_1: EV = 50 (0.20) + 105 (0.30) + 175 (0.50)

$\qquad$ = 10 + 31.5 + 87.5

$\qquad$ = 129

a_2: EV = ⁻20 (0.20) + 0(0.30) + 300 (0.50)

$\qquad$ = ⁻4 + 0 + 150

$\qquad$ = 146

- 457 -

Select action a_2 as it has the highest EV

Action	S_1	S_2	S_3
a_1	$50 - 50 = 0$	$105 - 105 = 0$	$300 - 175 = 125$
a_2	$50 - (^-20) = 70$	$105 - 0 = 105$	$300 - 300 = 0$

. The action with the smallest maximum regret is a_2 i.e. 105.

8. a_1: EOL = 56 (0.6) + 0(0.4) = K33.6'million

   a_2: EOL = 0(0.6) + 70 (0.4) = K28'million

   Action a_2 should be selected as it has the lower expected opportunity loss of the two.

9. a) a_1: EV = 2000 (0.20) + 1100 (0.80)

   = 400 + 880 = K1280

   a_2: EV = 300 (0.2) + 1000(0.8)

   = 60 + 800 = K860

   a_3: EV = 2500 (0.20) + 900 (0.8)

   = 500 + 720 = K1220

   (b) Action a1 for it has the highest expected payoff.

   (c) a_2. Because it has the lowest expected payoff and the highest expected opportunity loss. (Note: expected opportunity loss could be confirmed by calculation.

10. (a) i) Laplace criteria

.

$$\overline{d_1} = \frac{7 + 6 + 9 + 11 + 10 + 12}{6} = \frac{55}{6} = 9.17$$

$$\overline{d_2} = \frac{8 + 7 + 12 + 7 + 6 + 10}{6} = \frac{50}{6} = 8.33$$

$$\bar{d}_3 = \frac{12 + 10 + 6 + 8 + 12 + 12}{6} = \frac{57}{6} = 9.50$$

$$\bar{d}_4 = \frac{7 + 14 + 11 + 6 + 7 + 11}{6} = \frac{56}{6} = 9.33$$

$$\bar{d}_5 = \frac{5 + 6 + 8 + 10 + 11 + 13}{6} = \frac{53}{6} = 8.83$$

$$\bar{d}_6 = \frac{9 + 12 + 12 + 9 + 8 + 8}{6} = \frac{58}{6} = 9.67$$

. Decision 6 is chosen

(ii) Maximin criteria

Decision	Maximin
d_1	6
d_2	6
d_3	6
d_4	6
d_5	5
d_6	8

Decision 6 is chosen

(iii) Maxmax criteria

Decision	Maxmax
d_1	12
d_2	12
d_3	12
d_4	14
d_5	13
d_6	12

. Decision 4 is chosen

iv) Savage criteria: opportunity loss table

Decision	State of nature						Maximum
	S_1	S_2	S_3	S_4	S_5	S_6	
d_1	$12 - 7 = 5$	8	3	0	1	1	8
d_2	$12 - 8 = 4$	7	0	4	5	3	7
d_3	$12 - 12 = 0$	4	6	3	2	1	6
d_4	$12 - 7 = 5$	0	1	5	4	2	5
d_5	$12 - 5 = 7$	8	4	1	0	0	8
d_6	$12 - 9 = 3$	2	0	2	3	5	5

. Either decision 4 or decision 6 would be chosen.

(b) i) $EV = xp(x)$

       S1   S2   S3   S4   S5   S6

$EV_1 = 7(0.2) + 6(0.1) + 9(0.05) + 11(10(0.2) + 12(0.2) = 10.2$

$EV_2 = 8(0.2) + 7(0.1) + 12(0.5) + 7(0.25) + 6(0.2) + 10(0.2) = 7.85$

$EV_3 = 12(0.2) + 10(0.1) + 6(0.05) + 8(0.25) + 9(0.20 + 12(0.2) = 9.9$

$EV_4 = 7(0.2) + (14(0.1) + 11(0.05) + 6(0.25) + 7(0.2) + 11(0.2) = 8.45$

$EV_5 = 5(0.2) + 6(0.1) + 8(0.05)- + 10(0.25) + 11(0.2) + 13\,90.2) = 9.3$

$EV_6 = 9(0.2) + 12(0.1) + 12(0.05) + 9(0.25) + 8(0.2) + 8(0.2) = 9.05$

Decision is chosen

(ii) EVPI = Expected Smallest Value of Opportunity Loss

    $EOL_6 = 3(0.2) + 2(0.1) + (0.05) + 2(0.25) + 3(0.2) + 5(0.2) = 2.9$

           11. a) EMV (produce pilot) = $^-400(0.3) + 200(0.5) + 600(0.2)$

                       $= {}^-120 + 100 + 120$

                       $= 100$

        EMV (sell to competitor) = $400(0.3) + 400(0.5) + 400(0.2)$

                       $= 120 + 200 + 80$

                       $= 400$

 . Since EMV (sell to competitor > EMV (produce pilot), the company should sell to the competitor

    a) EMVPI = $400(0.3) + 400(0.5) + 600(0.2)$

               $= 120 + 200 + 120$

               $= 640.$i.e. K640 million

b) EVPI = 640 – 400 = 40 i.e. K40 million

12. (a) Pay off table. We substitute P for each of the possible prices to determine
quantity for each economist.

Action	Economist $_1$	Economist $_2$
K0.99	4.44	4.08
K1.98	0.42	0
K2.75	0	2.25
K3.50	1.88	9.00

(b) Opportunity loss table is:

Action	Economist $_1$	Economist $_2$
K0.99	4.44	4.08
K1.98	0.42	0
K2.75	0	2.25
K3.50	1.88	9.00

(c) The price that should be charged is K1.98 using the expected monetary value criterion.

. EMV (Ko.99) = 7.94 (0.5) + 11.92 (0.5) = 9.93

. EMV (K1.98) = 11.96 (0.5) + 16 (0.5) = 13.98

. EMV (K2.75) = 12.38 (0.5) + 13.75 (0.5) = 13.07

. EMV (K3.50) = 10.50 (0.5) + 7 (0.5) = 8.75

Hence K1.98 is chosen.

13. (a) U (600 000 000) = 0.9

(b) U (0) = 0.8

13. (a) Actions a_1 and a_3 are inadmissible.

(b) Maximax criterion

Action	Maximum
a_1	105
a_2	80
a_3	120
a_4	200

Decision: a_4 is chosen

(c) Maximin criterion

Action	Minimum
a_1	60
a_2	60
a_3	⁻30
a_4	90

Decision: a_4 is chosen

(d) Opportunity loss table is

Action	S_1	S_2	S_3
a_1	30	0	140
a_2	35	25	140
a_3	135	65	80
a_4	0	15	0

Action	Maximum
a_1	140
a_2	140
a_3	135
a_4	15

Decision: a_4 is chosen

13. (a) Maximax criterion

Action	Maximum
a_1	10 000
a_2	6 000
a_3	50

Decision: a_1 is chosen

(b) Maximin criterion

Action	Minimum
a_1	$^-1000$
a_2	$^-2000$
a_3	$^-900$

Decision: a_3 is chosen

(c) There are other better option to be undertaken than what is prescribed by maximin criterion.

APPENDIX A

THE STANDARD NORMAL DISTRIBUTION

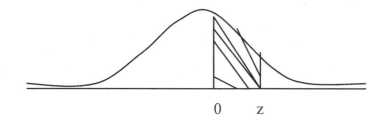

Z	0.00	0.01	0.02	0.03	0.04	0.05	0.06	0.07	0.08	0.09
0.0	0.0000	0.0040	0.0080	0.0120	0.0160	0.0199	0.0239	0.0279	0.0319	0.0359
0.1	0.0398	0.0438	0.0478	0.0517	0.0557	0.0596	0.0636	0.0675	0.0714	0.0753
0.2	0.0793	0.0832	0.0871	0.0910	0.0948	0.0987	0.1026	0.1064	0.1103	0.1141
0.3	0.1179	0.1217	0.1255	0.1293	0.1331	0.1368	0.1406	0.1443	0.1480	0.1517
0.4	0.1554	0.1591	0.1628	0.1664	0.1700	0.1736	0.1772	0.1808	0.1844	0.1879
0.5	0.1915	0.1950	0.1985	0.2019	0.2054	0.2088	0.2123	0.2157	0.2190	0.2224
0.6	0.2257	0.2291	0.2324	0.2357	0.2389	0.2422	0.2454	0.2486	0.2517	0.2549
0.7	0.2580	0.2611	0.2642	0.2673	0.2704	0.2734	0.2764	0.2486	0.2823	0.2852
0.8	0.2881	0.2910	0.2939	0.2967	0.2995	0.3023	0.3051	0.3078	0.3106	0.3133
0.9	0.3159	0.3186	0.3212	0.3238	0.3264	0.3289	0.3315	0.3340	0.3365	0.3389
1.0	0.3413	0.3438	0.3461	0.3485	0.3508	0.3531	0.3554	0.3577	0.3599	0.3621
1.1	0.3643	0.3665	0.3686	0.3708	0.3729	0.3749	0.3770	0.3790	0.3810	0.3830
1.2	0.3849	0.3869	0.3888	0.3907	0.3925	0.3944	0.3962	0.3980	0.3997	0.4015
13	0.4032	0.4049	0.4066	0.4082	0.4099	0.4115	0.4131	0.4147	0.4162	0.4177
1.4	0.4192	0.4207	0.4222	0.4236	0.4251	0.4265	0.4279	0.4292	0.4306	0.4319
1.5	0.4332	0.4345	0.4357	0.4370	0.4382	0.4394	0.4406	0.4418	0.4429	0.4441
1.6	0.4452	0.4463	0.4474	0.4484	0.4495	0.4505	0.4515	0.4525	0.535	0.4545
1.7	0.4554	0.4564	0.4573	0.4582	0.4591	0.4599	0.4608	0.4616	0.4625	0.4633
1.8	0.4641	0.4649	0.4656	0.4664	0.4671	0.4678	0.4686	0.4693	0.4699	0.4706
1.9	0.4713	0.4719	0.4726	0.4732	0.4738	0.4744	0.4750	0.4756	0.4761	0.4767
2.0	0.4772	0.4778	0.4783	0.4788	0.4793	0.4798	0.4803	0.4808	0.4812	0.4817
2.1	0.4821	0.4826	0.4830	0.4834	0.4838	0.4842	0.4846	0.4884	0.4854	0.4857
2.2	0.4861	0.4864	0.4868	0.4871	0.4875	0.4878	0.4881	0.4850	0.4887	0.4890
2.3	0.4893	0.4896	0.4898	0.4901	0.4904	0.4906	0.4909	0.4911	0.4913	0.4916
2.4	0.4918	0.4920	0.4922	0.4925	0.4927	0.4929	0.4931	0.4932	0.4934	0.4936
2.5	0.4938	0.4940	0.4941	0.4943	0.4945	0.4946	0.4948	0.4949	0.4951	0.4952
2.6	0.4953	0.4955	0.4956	0.4957	0.4959	0.4960	0.4961	0.4962	0.4963	0.4964
2.7	0.4965	0.4966	0.4967	0.4968	0.4969	0.4970	0.4971	0.4972	0.4973	0.4974
2.8	0.4974	0.4975	0.4976	0.4977	0.4977	0.4978	0.4979	0.4979	0.4980	0.4981
2.9	0.4981	0.4982	0.4982	0.4983	0.4984	0.4984	0.4985	0.4985	0.4986	0.4986
3.0	0.4987	0.4987	0.4987	0.4988	0.4988	0.4989	0.4989	0.4989	0.4990	0.4990

APPENDIX B

THE t-DISTRIBUTION

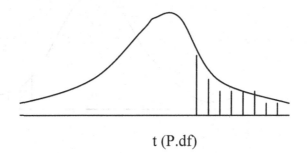

t (P.df)

df/p	0.40	0.25	0.10	0.05	0.025	0.01	0.005	0.0005
1	0.324920	1.000000	3.077684	6.313752	12.70620	31.82052	63.65674	636.6192
2	0.288675	0.816497	1.885618	2.919986	4.30265	6.96456	9.92484	31.5991
3	0.276671	0.764892	1.637744	2.353363	3.18245	4.54070	5.84091	12.9240
4	0.270722	0.740697	1.533206	2.131847	2.77645	3.74695	4.60409	8.6103
5	0.267181	0.726687	1.475884	2.015048	2.57058	3.36493	4.03214	6.8688
6	0.264835	0.717558	1.439756	1.943180	2.44691	3.14267	3.70743	5.9588
7	0.263167	0.711142	1.414924	1.894579	2.36462	2.99795	3.49948	5.4079
8	0.261921	0.706387	1.396815	1.859548	2.30600	2.89646	3.35539	5.0413
9	0.260955	0.702722	1.383029	1.833113	2.26216	2.82144	3.24984	4.7809
10	0.260185	0.699812	1.372184	1.812461	2.22814	2.76377	3.16927	4.5869
11	0.259556	0.697445	1.363430	1.795885	2.20099	2.71808	3.10581	4.4370
12	0.259033	0.695483	1.356217	1.782288	2.17881	2.68100	3.05454	4.3178
13	0.258591	0.693829	1.350171	1.770933	2.16037	2.65031	3.01228	4.2208
14	0.258213	0.692417	1.345030	1.761310	2.14479	2.62449	2.97684	4.1405
15	0.257885	0.691197	1.340606	1.753050	2.13145	2.60248	2.94671	4.0728
16	0.257599	0.690132	1.336757	1.745884	2.11991	2.58349	2.92078	4.0150
17	0.257347	0.689195	1.333379	1.739607	2.10982	256693	2.89823	3.9651
18	0.257123	0.688364	1.330391	1.734064	2.10092	2.55238	2.87844	3.9216
19	0.256923	0.687621	1.327728	1.729133	2.09302	2.53948	2.86093	3.8834
20	0.256743	0.686954	1.325341	1.724718	2.08596	2.52798	2.84534	3.8495
21	0.256580	0.686352	1.323188	1.720743	2.07961	2.51765	2.83136	3.8193
22	0.256432	0.685805	1.321237	1.717144	2.07387	2.50832	2.81876	3.7921
23	0.256297	0.685306	1.319460	1.713872	2.06866	2.49987	2.80734	3.7676
24	0.256173	0.684850	1.317836	1.710882	2.06390	2.49216	2.79694	3.7454
25	0.256060	0.684430	1.316345	1.708141	2.05954	2.48511	2.78744	3.7251
26	0.255955	0.684043	1.314972	1.705618	2.05553	2.47863	2.77871	3.7066
27	0.255858	0.683685	1.313703	1.703288	2.05183	2.47266	2.77068	3.6896
28	0.255768	0.683353	1.312527	1.701131	2.04841	2.46714	2.76326	3.6739
29	0.255684	0.683044	1.311434	1.699127	2.04523	2.46202	2.75639	3.6594
30	0.255605	0.682756	1.310415	1.697261	2.04227	2.45726	2.75000	3.6460
inf	0.253347	0.674490	1.281552	1.644854	1.95996	2.32635	2.57583	3.2905

APPENDIX C

THE CHI-SQUARE DISTRIBUTION

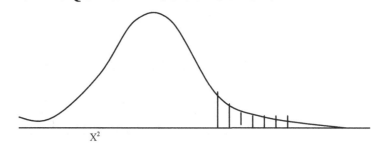

X^2

df/p	.995	.990	.975	.950	.900	.750	.500	.250	.100	.050	.025	.010	.005
1	0.00004	0.00016	0.00098	0.00393	0.01579	0.10153	0.45494	1.32330	2.70554	3.84146	5.02389	6.63490	7.87944
2	0.01003	0.02010	0.05064	0.10259	0.21072	0.57536	1.38629	2.77259	4.60517	5.99146	7.37776	9.21034	10.59663
3	0.07172	0.11483	0.21580	0.35185	0.58437	1.21253	2.36597	4.10834	6.25139	7.81473	9.34840	11.34487	12.83816
4	0.20699	0.29711	0.48442	0.71072	1.06362	1.92256	3.335669	5.38527	7.77944	9.48773	11.14329	13.27670	14.86026
5	0.41174	0.55430	0.83121	1.14548	1.61031	2.67460	4.35146	6.62568	923636	11.07050	12.83250	15.08627	16.74960
6	0.67573	0.87209	1.23734	1.63538	2.20413	3.45460	5.34812	7.84080	10.64464	12.59159	14.44938	16.81189	18.54758
7	0.98926	1.23904	1.68987	2.16735	2.83311	4.25485	6.34581	9.093715	12.01704	14.06714	16.01276	18.47531	20.27774
8	1.34441	1.64650	2.17973	2.73264	3.48954	5.07064	7.34412	10.21885	13.36157	15.50731	17.53455	20.09024	21.95495
9	1.73493	2.08790	2.70039	3.32511	4.16816	5.89883	8.34283	11.38875	14.68366	16.91898	19.02277	21.66599	23.58935
10	2.15586	2.55821	3.24697	3.94030	4.86518	6.73720	9.34182	12.54886	15.98718	18.30704	20.48318	23.20925	25.18818
11	2.60322	3.05348	3.81575	4.57481	5.57778	7.58414	10.34100	13.70069	17.27501	19.67514	21.92005	24.72497	26.75685
12	3.07382	3.57057	4.40379	5.22603	6.30380	8.43842	11.34032	14.84540	18.54935	21.02607	23.33666	26.21697	28.29952
13	3.56503	4.10692	5.00875	5.89186	7.04150	9.29907	12.33976	15.98391	19.81193	22.36203	24.73560	27.68825	29.81947
14	4.07467	4.66043	5.62873	6.57063	7.78953	10.16531	13.33927	17.11693	21.06414	23.68479	26.11895	29.14124	31.31935
15	4.60092	5.22935	6.26214	7.26094	8.54676	11.03654	14.33886	18.24509	22.30713	24.99579	27.48839	30.57791	32.80132
16	5.14221	5.81221	6.90766	7.96165	9.31224	11.91222	15.33850	19.36886	23.54183	26.29623	28.84535	31.99993	34.26719
17	5.69722	6.40776	7.56419	8.67176	10.08519	12.79193	16.33818	20.48868	24.76904	27.58711	30.19101	33.40866	35.71847
18	6.26480	7.01491	8.23075	9.39046	10.86494	13.67529	17.33790	21.60489	25.98942	28.86930	31.52638	34.80531	37.15645
19	6.84397	7.63273	8.90652	10.11701	11.65091	14.56200	18.33765	22.71781	27.20357	30.14353	32.85233	36.19087	38.8226
20	7.43384	8.26040	9.59078	10.85081	13.23960	15.45177	19.33743	23.82769	28.41198	31.41043	34.16961	37.56623	39.99685
21	8.03365	8.89720	10.28290	11.59131	14.04149	16.34438	20.33723	24.93478	29.61509	32.67057	35.47888	38.93217	41.40106
22	8.64272	9.54249	10.98232	12.33801	14.84796	17.23962	21.33704	26.03927	30.81328	33.92444	36.78071	40.28936	42.79565
23	9.26042	10.19572	11.68855	13.09051	15.65868	18.13730	22.33688	27.14134	32.00690	3517246	38.07563	41.63840	44.18128
24	9.88623	10.85636	12.40115	13.84843	15.37916	19.03725	23.336733	28.24115	33.19624	36.41503	39.36408	42.97982	45.55851
25	10.51965	11.52398	13.11972	14.61141	16.47341	19.93934	24.33659	29.33885	34.38159	37.65248	40.64647	44.31410	46.92789
26	11.16024	12.87850	13.84390	15.37916	17.29188	20.84343	25.33646	30.43457	35.56317	38.88514	41.92317	45.64168	48.28988
27	11.80759	12.19815	14.57338	16.15140	18.11390	21.74940	26.33634	31.52841	36.7122	40.11327	43.19451	46.96294	49.64492
28	12.46134	13.56471	15.30786	16.92788	18.93924	22.65716	27.33623	32.62049	37.91592	41.33714	44.46079	4827824	50.99338
29	13.12115	14.25645	16.04707	17.70837	19.76774	23.56659	28.33613	33.71091	39.08747	42.55697	45.72229	49.58788	52.33562
30	13.78672	14.95346	16.79077	18.49266	20.59923	24.47761	29.33603	34.79974	40.25602	43.77297	46.97924	50.89218	53.67196

Appendix Table 6 Values of F distributions with .05 of the area in the right tail*

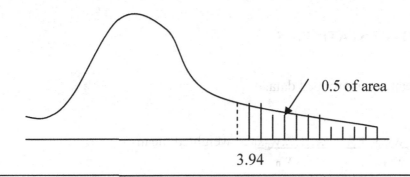

3.94

Example: for a test at a significance level of .05 where we have 15 degrees of freedom for the numerator and 6 degrees of freedom for the denominator, the appropriate F value is found by looking under the 15 degrees of freedom column and proceeding down to the 6 degrees of freedom row; there we find the appropriate F value to be 3.94.

Degrees of freedom for numerator

	1	2	3	4	5	6	7	8	9	10	12	15	20	24	30	40	60	120	∞
1	161	200	216	225	230	234	237	239	241	242	244	246	248	249	250	251	252	253	254
2	18.5	19.0	19.2	19.2	19.3	19.3	19.4	19.4	19.4	19.4	19.4	19.4	19.4	19.5	19.5	19.5	19.5	19.5	19.5
3	10.1	9.55	9.28	9.12	9.01	8.94	8.89	8.85	8.81	8.79	8.74	8.70	8.66	8.64	8.62	8.59	8.75	8.55	8.53
4	7.71	6.94	6.59	6.39	6.26	6.16	6.09	6.04	6.00	5.96	5.91	5.86	5.80	5.77	5.75	5.72	5.69	5.66	5.63
5	6.61	5.79	5.41	5.19	5.05	4.95	4.95	4.82	4.77	4.74	4.68	4.62	4.56	4.53	4.50	4.46	4.43	4.40	4.37
6	5.99	5.14	4.76	4.53	4.39	4.28	4.21	4.15	4.10	4.06	4.00	3.94	3.87	3.84	3.81	3.77	3.74	3.70	3.67
7	5.59	4.74	4.35	4.12	3.97	3.87	3.79	3.73	3.68	3.64	3.57	3.51	3.44	3.41	3.38	3.34	3.30	3.27	3.23
8	5.32	4.46	4.07	3.84	3.69	3.58	3.50	3.44	3.39	3.35	3.28	3.22	3.15	3.12	3.08	3.04	3.01	2.97	2.93
9	5.12	4.26	3.86	3.63	3.48	3.37	3.29	3.23	3.18	3.14	3.07	3.01	2.94	2.90	2.86	2.83	2.79	2.75	2.71
10	4.96	4.10	3.71	3.48	3.33	3.22	3.14	3.07	3.02	2.98	2.91	2.85	2.77	2.74	2.70	2.66	2.62	2.58	2.54
11	4.84	3.98	3.59	3.36	3.20	3.09	3.01	2.95	2.90	2.85	2.79	2.72	2.65	2.61	2.57	2.53	2.49	2.45	2.40
12	8.75	3.89	3.49	3.26	3.11	3.00	2.91	2.85	2.80	2.75	2.69	2.62	2.54	2.51	2.47	2.43	2.38	2.34	2.30
13	4.67	3.81	3.41	3.18	3.03	2.92	2.83	2.77	2.71	2.67	2.60	2.53	2.46	2.42	2.38	2.34	2.30	2.25	2.21
14	4.60	3.74	3.34	3.11	2.96	2.85	2.76	2.70	2.65	2.60	2.53	2.46	2.39	2.35	2.31	2.27	2.22	2.18	2.13
15	4.54	3.68	3.29	3.06	2.90	2.79	2.71	2.64	2.59	2.54	2.48	2.40	2.33	2.29	2.25	2.20	2.16	2.11	2.07
16	4.49	3.63	3.24	3.01	2.85	2.74	2.66	2.59	2.54	2.49	2.42	2.35	2.28	2.24	2.19	2.15	2.11	2.06	2.01
17	4.45	3.59	3.20	2.96	2.81	2.70	2.61	2.55	2.49	2.45	2.38	2.31	2.23	2.19	2.15	2.10	2.06	2.01	1.96
18	4.41	3.55	3.16	2.93	2.77	2.66	2.58	2.52	2.46	2.41	2.34	2.27	2.19	2.15	2.11	2.06	2.02	1.97	1.92
19	4.38	3.52	3.13	2.90	2.74	2.63	2.54	2.48	2.42	2.38	2.31	2.23	2.16	2.11	2.07	2.03	1.98	1.93	1.88
20	4.35	3.49	3.10	2.87	2.71	2.60	2.51	2.45	2.39	2.35	2.28	2.20	2.12	2.08	2.04	1.99	1.95	1.90	1.84
21	4.32	3.47	3.07	2.84	2.68	2.57	2.49	2.42	2.37	2.32	2.25	2.18	2.10	2.05	2.01	1.96	1.92	1.87	1.81
22	4.30	3.44	3.05	2.82	2.66	2.55	2.46	2.40	2.34	2.30	2.23	2.15	2.07	2.03	1.98	1.94	1.89	1.84	1.78
23	4.28	3.42	3.03	2.80	2.64	2.53	2.44	2.37	2.32	2.27	2.20	2.13	2.05	2.01	1.96	1.91	1.86	1.81	1.76
24	4.26	3.40	3.01	2.78	2.62	2.51	2.42	2.36	2.30	2.25	2.18	2.11	2.03	1.98	1.94	1.89	1.84	1.79	1.73
25	4.24	3.39	2.99	2.76	2.60	2.49	2.40	2.34	2.28	2.24	2.16	2.09	2.01	1.96	1.92	1.87	1.82	1.77	1.71
30	4.17	3.32	2.92	2.69	2.53	2.42	2.33	2.27	2.21	2.16	2.09	2.01	1.93	1.89	1.84	1.79	1.74	1.68	1.62
40	4.08	3.23	2.84	2.61	2.5	2.34	2.25	2.18	2.12	2.08	2.00	1.92	1.84	1.79	1.74	1.69	1.64	1.58	1.51
60	4.00	3.15	2.76	2.53	2.37	2.25	2.17	2.10	2.04	1.99	1.92	1.84	1.75	1.70	1.65	1.59	1.53	1.47	1.39
120	3.92	3.07	2.68	2.45	2.29	2.18	2.09	2.02	1.96	1.91	1.83	1.75	1.66	1.61	1.55	1.50	1.43	1.35	1.25
∞	3.84	3.00	2.60	2.37	2.21	2.10	2.01	1.94	1.88	1.83	1.75	1.67	1.57	1.52	1.46	1.39	1.32	1.22	1.00

* Source: M. Merrigton and C. M. Thompson, Biometrika, vol. 33 (1943).

APPENDIX E: ANNOTATED FORMULAE

A. DESCRIPTIVE STATISTICS

i) $\bar{x} = \sum x$, mean for ungrouped data.

ii) $\bar{x}w = \dfrac{w_1 x_1 + w_2 x_2 + \ldots\ldots\ldots w_n x_n}{w_1 + w_2 + w \ldots\ldots\ldots\ldots w_n}$, weighted mean

iii) $\bar{x} = \dfrac{\sum fx}{\sum f}$ or $\dfrac{\sum fx}{n}$, mean for grouped data

iv) Median $= L + \left(\dfrac{\frac{n}{2} - f_{m-1}}{f} \right) \times$ C, median grouped data

v) Mode $= L + \left(\dfrac{D_1}{D_1 + D_2} \right) \times$ C, mode grouped data.

vi) $S^2 = \dfrac{\sum (x - \bar{x})^2}{n-1}$, sample variance, ungrouped data

vii) $S^2 = \dfrac{\sum x^2 - \dfrac{(\sum x)^2}{n}}{n-1}$, sample variance, raw data computation form

viii) $S^2 = \dfrac{\sum f(x - \bar{x})^2}{n-1}$ or $\dfrac{\sum fx^2 - \dfrac{(fx)^2}{n}}{n-1}$, sample variance grouped data.

ix) $S = \sqrt{\dfrac{\sum x^2 - (\sum x)^2}{n-1}}$, sample standard deviation raw data

x) $S = \sqrt{\dfrac{\sum fx^2 - \dfrac{(\sum fx)^2}{n}}{n-1}}$, sample standard deviation grouped data

xi) $MD = \dfrac{\sum |x - \bar{x}|}{n}$, mean deviation, ungrouped data

xii) $MD = \dfrac{\sum f|x - \bar{x}|}{\sum f}$, mean deviation, grouped data.

xiii) $CV = \dfrac{S}{\bar{x}} \times 100$, coefficient of variation

1. $CS = \dfrac{3(\text{mean} - \text{median})}{\text{Standard deviation}}$, coefficient of skewness

2. $Lp = (n + 1)\dfrac{P}{100}$, location of percentile

3. Range = Highest value – Lowest value, Range ungrouped data.

4. Range = Maximum value in the Highest class – minimum value in the lowest class.

5. Position $Qj = \dfrac{jn}{4}$, quartile position

6. Value $Qj = L + \left(\dfrac{\dfrac{jn}{4} - f_{m-1}}{fqj} \right) \times C$, Quartile value.

7. Position $Pj = \dfrac{jn}{100}$, percentile position

8. Value $Pj = L + \left(\dfrac{\dfrac{jn}{100} - f_{m-1}}{fpj} \right) \times C$, percentile value

B. PROBABILITY DISTRIBUTIONS

i) Binomial probability Distributions

$$P(r) = {}^{n}C_{r} \, P^{r} \, q^{n-r} \quad \text{or} \quad \frac{n!}{(n-r)!r!} \, P^{r} \, q^{n-r} \quad \text{where } r = 0, 1, 2, \ldots\ldots n.$$

$$E(x) = np, \quad Var(r) = npq$$

ii) Poisson Probability Distribution:

$$P(x) = \frac{\lambda^{x} \, e^{-\lambda}}{x!}, \quad \text{where } x = 0, 1, 2, \ldots\ldots\ldots$$

$$E(x) = np, \quad Var(x) = npq$$

iii) Exponential Probability Distribution:

$$f(x) = \lambda e -\lambda x, \quad x \geq 0$$

$$P(x \geq a) = e^{-\lambda a}, \quad E(x) = \frac{1}{\lambda}, \quad Var(xc) = \frac{1}{\lambda}$$

iv) Uniform Probability Distribution:

$$E(x) = \frac{a+b}{2} \quad Var(x) = \frac{(b-a)^{2}}{12}$$

14. Conditional Probability:

$$P(A/B) = \frac{P(A \cap B)}{P(B)}$$

C. ESTIMATION AND STATISTICAL INFLUENCE

i) Confidence Intervals

- $(1 - \alpha)$ % C1 for μ: $\bar{x} \pm Z_{\alpha/2} \left(\dfrac{S}{\sqrt{n}} \right)$, for single mean large sample

- $(1 - \alpha)$ % C1 for μ: $\bar{x} \pm t_{\alpha/2} \left(\dfrac{S}{\sqrt{n}} \right)$, for single mean small sample

- $(1 - \alpha)$ % C! for p: $\hat{p} \pm z_{\alpha/2} \left(\sqrt{\dfrac{\hat{P}\hat{q}}{n}} \right)$, for population proportion

- $(1 - \alpha)$ % C1 For $\bar{d}$: $\bar{d} \pm t_{\alpha/2}, n-1 \left(\dfrac{S_D}{\sqrt{n_D}} \right)$, for paired difference

- $(1 - \alpha)$ % C1 for $\mu_1 - \mu_2$: $(\bar{x}_1 - \bar{x}_2) \pm Z_{\alpha/2} \sqrt{\sigma_1^2 + \sigma_2^2}$, for difference between means large sample

- $(1 - \alpha)$ % C1 for $\mu_1 - \mu_2$: $(\bar{x}_1 - \bar{x}_2) + t_{\alpha/2}, n-1 \sqrt{\dfrac{S_1^2}{n_1} + \dfrac{S_2^2}{n_2}}$

    Where $\sigma_1^2 = \sigma_2^2$ hence $S_p^2 = \dfrac{S_1^2 (n-1) + S_2^2 (n_2 - 1)}{n_1 + n_2 - 2}$

    and df $= n_1 + n_2 - 2$

- $n = \left(\dfrac{z_{\alpha/2}}{B} \right)^2 \sigma^2$ or $n = 4 \left(\dfrac{z_{\alpha/2}}{W} \right)^2 \sigma^2$, sample size for $(1 - \alpha)$ % confidence interval for μ

- $n = \left(\dfrac{z_{\alpha/2}}{B} \right)^2 (pq)$ or $n = 4 \dfrac{\left(z_{\alpha/2} \right)^2}{W^2} \sigma^2$, sample size for $(1 - \alpha)$ % confidence interval for p

- $n_1 = n_2 = \left[\dfrac{z\alpha/2}{B^2}\right]^2 \sigma^2$ $(\sigma_1 + \sigma_2) = \left[\dfrac{z\alpha/2}{W^2}\right]^2 (\sigma_1^2 + \sigma_2^2)$, sample size for comparing two means for independent random samples.

- $n_D = \dfrac{\left[z\alpha/2\right]^2 \sigma_D^2}{B^2} = 4\,\dfrac{\left[z\alpha/2\right]^2 \sigma_D^2}{W^2}$, sample size for paired difference experiment

- $n_1 = n_2 = \dfrac{\left[z\alpha/2\right]^2 (p_1 q_1) - p_2 q_2)}{B^2} = 4\,\dfrac{\left[z\alpha/2\right]^2 (p_1 q_1 + p_2 q_2)}{W^2}$, sample size for comparing two proportions.

ii) Hypothesis Testing

- $Z = \dfrac{x - \mu}{S}$, standard normal distribution

- $Zc = \dfrac{\bar{x} - \mu}{S/\sqrt{n}}$, , test statistic for large sample one mean

- $tc = \dfrac{\bar{x} - \mu}{s/\sqrt{n}}$, test statistic for small sample one mean

- $Zc = \sqrt{\dfrac{p - \hat{p}}{\dfrac{Pq}{n}}}$, test statistic for population proportion

- $Zc = \dfrac{\bar{x}_1 - \bar{x}_2}{\sqrt{\dfrac{S_1^2}{n_1} + \dfrac{S_2^2}{n_2}}}$, test statistic for difference between means for large sample , Test statistic for difference between means for large sample

- $Zc = \dfrac{PA - PB}{}$, test statistic for difference between two population proportions.

$$\sqrt{(pq)\left(\frac{1}{nA} + \frac{1}{nB}\right)}$$

where $p = \dfrac{nApA + nB\,pB}{nA + nB}$, $q = 1 - p$

- $tc = \dfrac{\overline{x_1} - \overline{x_2}}{\sqrt{S_P^2\left(\frac{1}{n_1} + \frac{1}{n_2}\right)}}$, test statistic for difference between ,means for small sample

C. FORECASTING

1) Regression and correlation

ii. $b = \dfrac{n\sum xy - \sum x\sum y}{\sum x^2 - (\sum x)^2}$, slope of the regression line.

iii. $a = \dfrac{\sum y}{n} - \dfrac{b\sum x}{n}$, the intercept

iv. $\hat{y} = a + bx$, least squares regression line

v. $r = \dfrac{n\sum xy - \sum x\sum y}{\sqrt{(n\sum x^2 - (\sum x)^2)(n\sum y^2 - (\sum y)^2)}}$, product moment correlation coefficient.

vi. $r = 1 - \dfrac{6\sum d^2}{n(n^2 - 1)}$, Spearman's rank correlation coefficient

vii. $(1 - \alpha)\% \; C1: \hat{y} \pm t_{\alpha/2}\, n - 2 \; Sxy/\sqrt{\dfrac{1}{n} + \dfrac{(xp - x)^2}{SSxx}}$, confidence interval for the mean value of y for x = xp

viii. $(1 - \alpha)\% \; P1: \hat{y} + t_{\alpha/2}\, n - 2, \; S\sqrt{1 + \dfrac{1}{n} + \dfrac{(xp - x)^2}{SSxx}}$, prediction interval for an individual y for x = xp.

ix. $tc = \dfrac{\hat{B_1}}{\sqrt{S/\;SSxx}}$

x. $(1 - \alpha)$ % CI: $\hat{B}_1 + t_{\alpha/2}, n-2 \dfrac{S}{\sqrt{SSxx}}$, confidence interval for slope $\hat{B}_1$

j) $r = \dfrac{SSxy}{\sqrt{SSxx \; SSyy}}$ Pearson's product moment coefficient of correlation

k) $r^2 = \dfrac{SSyy - SSE}{\sqrt{SSyy}} = 1 - \dfrac{SSE}{SSyy}$, coefficient of determination

Where $SSxx = \sum x^2 - \dfrac{(\sum x)^2}{n}$

$SSxy = \sum xy - \dfrac{(\sum x)(\sum y)}{n}$

$SSE = \sum(y - \hat{y})^2 = SSyy - \hat{B}_1 \, SSxy$

$SSyy = \sum(y - y)^2 = \sum y^2 - \dfrac{(\sum y)^2}{n}$

$S^2 = \dfrac{SSE}{n-2}$

i. $\hat{B}_1 = \dfrac{SSxy}{SSxx}$, for the slope

ii. $t = \dfrac{r}{\sqrt{(1 - r^2)/(n - 2)}}$, correlation test statistic

ii) Index Numbers

a) $\dfrac{\sum P_1 q_0}{\sum p_0 q_0}$ X 100, Laspeyre price index.

b) $\dfrac{\sum p_1 q_1}{\sum p_0 q_1}$ X 100, Paasche price index

c) $\dfrac{p_1}{p_0}$ X 100, simple price index

iii) Time Series Analysis

a.   Forecasted value = old forecasted value + α (Actual Observation – old forecasted value).

E. **CHI-SQUARED**

$$X_c^2 = \sum \dfrac{(f_0 - f_e)^2}{f_e}, \text{ where } f_e = \dfrac{\text{row total X column total}}{\text{Grand total}}$$

F. **ANOVA**

i) One way

a) $SST \text{ or } SS_{trt} = \sum\limits_{j=1}^{p} n_i \, (\overline{x_i} - \overline{x})^2$

where x = grand mean

b) $SSE = \sum\limits_{j=1}^{n_1}(x_{ii} - \overline{x_i})^2 \; + \sum\limits_{j=1}^{n_2}(x^2 j - \overline{x^2}) + \ldots\ldots.+ \sum\limits_{j=1}^{np}(x_{pj} - x_p)^2$

(c) $MST = \dfrac{SST}{P - 1}$

(d) $MSE = \dfrac{SSE}{n - p}$

(e) $F = \dfrac{MST}{MSE}$

ii) Two way

$$SSB = \frac{\sum B_i^2}{ni} - \frac{(\sum y)^2}{N}$$

$$SS_{total} = SSE + SST + SSB$$

G. DECISION THEORY

a) $EMV = \sum x \, p(x)$, Expected Monetary Value